THE MIDDLE AGES IN FRENCH LITERATURE 1851-1900

by

Janine R. Dakyns

OXFORD UNIVERSITY PRESS
1973

Oxford University Press, Ely House, London W.1

GLASGOW   NEW YORK   TORONTO   MELBOURNE   WELLINGTON
CAPE TOWN   IBADAN   NAIROBI   DAR ES SALAAM   LUSAKA   ADDIS ABABA
DELHI   BOMBAY   CALCUTTA   MADRAS   KARACHI   LAHORE   DACCA
KUALA LUMPUR   SINGAPORE   HONG KONG   TOKYO

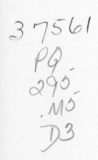
Text set in 10/12 pt. IBM Press Roman printed by photolithography,
and bound in Great Britain at The Pitman Press, Bath

PREFACE

This book was originally a doctoral thesis submitted at the University of Oxford. It is a pleasure to be able to thank those who have helped me in my research and publication. My particular gratitude is due to Professor Jean Seznec, without whose invaluable guidance and encouragement this work would never have been written. My thanks are also due to my examiners, Dr. A. W. Raitt and Mr. A. D. Crow, and to the Monographs Committee of the Faculty Board of Medieval and Modern Languages at Oxford, for their many helpful comments and suggestions. I am also greatly indebted to the Curators of the Taylor Institution, who generously awarded me a Zaharoff Scholarship to pursue my research, and to the officials of the Clarendon Press for their assistance in the final stages of my work.

University of East Anglia
1972

J.R.D.

TABLE OF CONTENTS

ABBREVIATIONS

FS	*French Studies*
HF	Michelet, *Histoire de France*
HLA	Taine, *Histoire de la littérature anglaise*
MF	*Mercure de France*
RDM	*Revue des deux mondes*
RHLF	*Revue d'histoire littéraire de la France*
RLC	*Revue de littérature comparée*

INTRODUCTION

'On voudrait connaître la destinée littéraire du Moyen-Âge à travers le dix-neuvième siècle', said Pierre Moreau in 1935.[1] This story remains untold; although 'la présence du Moyen Âge dans les temps modernes' is a question which has lately been receiving an increasing amount of critical attention,[2] no study exists as yet of the Middle Ages in French Romantic writing, even[3] − let alone of their fate in post-Romantic times, a subject of equal if not still greater interest.[4] This study is an attempt to trace the Middle Ages' fortunes from the beginning of the Second Empire to the end of the Symbolist period, which coincides with the end of the century.

French writers were as passionately preoccupied with the Middle Ages after the decline of Romanticism as before it. The Second Empire witnessed (and partly provoked, in our opinion) their depreciation; patriotic revaluation in the 1870s was followed by the remarkable return to favour which they enjoyed, among Symbolists and others, in the 1880s and 90s.

During these fifty years the Middle Ages inspired a series of major works: much of Hugo's *Légende des siècles,* many of Leconte de Lisle's poems, Michelet's *Sorcière,* Flaubert's *Légende de Saint Julien l'hospitalier,* some of Verlaine's best poetry. Huysmans's *Là-Bas* and *La Cathédrale,* and a large proportion of the Symbolist poets' verse and drama. Of interest also − on historical rather than aesthetic grounds − are works immensely popular in their day, such as Quinet's *Merlin l'Enchanteur,* Banville's *Gringoire,* Bornier's *Fille de Roland,* and

---

[1] P. Moreau, *L'Histoire en France au XIXe siècle,* 1935, p. 75.
[2] A recent congress of the Société Française de Littérature Comparée was partly devoted to it. See *Actes du Septième Congrès National de la Société Française de Littérature Comparée* (Poitiers, 1965) 1967, and in particular Jean Frappier's Avant-Propos, p. xiv.
[3] The pre-Romantic *genre troubadour* has, however, been treated fully by H. Jacoubet, *Le Comte de Tressan et les origines du genre troubadour,* 1923. See also his *Le Genre troubadour et les origines françaises du romantisme,* 1929; F. Baldensperger, 'Le Genre troubadour', in *Études d'histoire littéraire,* première série, 1907; and René Lanson, *Le Goût du moyen âge en France au XVIIIe siècle,* 1926.
[4] Paul Zumthor for instance points out that the Middle Ages of Hugo's early period (1823-32) is of minor interest compared with his post-1840 − and, more particularly, post-1851 − Middle Ages (V. Hugo, *Oeuvres complètes,* ed. J. Massin. Club Français du Livre, iv (1967), xxv-xxviii).

Rostand's *Princesse Lointaine.* Most writers cherished a private vision
of the Middle Ages, and many, including Michelet, Veuillot,
Montalembert, Mérimée, Barbey d'Aurevilly, Littré, Fustel de
Coulanges, Anatole France, Verlaine, Huysmans, and Bloy, were
convinced that to see them in their true light — so variously interpreted — was of the utmost importance to modern France.

Some questions explored here — to which little or no attention has
hitherto been given — are Michelet's shift in attitude towards the
Middle Ages, the politically-inspired views on medieval architecture and
society which he bequeathed to Renan and Taine, Théophile Gautier's
recoil from the Romantic Middle Ages, the entirely opposed position of
Baudelaire, and the nature and inspiration of the Symbolist Middle Ages.
It is hoped that, by providing a fresh context within which to examine,
in relation to each other, all those greater and lesser works inspired by
the Middle Ages in the second half of the nineteenth century, new light
may be shed on the former and some interest extracted even from the
latter. It is also hoped to shed some light on the changing relationship
to the past of Romantics, Parnassians and their contemporaries, and
Symbolists, who each in turn, and with very different intentions,
attempted an imaginative recreation of the Middle Ages.

Our study follows a chronological sequence, as writers' views on the
Middle Ages were determined in the first instance by political factors.
Each successive political upheaval brought about a reorientation in
attitudes which were coloured by fluctuating hopes and fears: the
medieval past was seen in the image of a longed-for future or a detested
present. In the period with which we are concerned the shock of 1870
produced a total revaluation of the Middle Ages, and so our survey falls
into two parts: the Second Empire, marked by fierce controversy over
the Middle Ages, and, on the part of most writers, a reaction against
Romantic idealization of them; and the post-1870 years, which saw first
a patriotic, then a Symbolist, return to them.

Most of the difficulties presented by this subject arise from the vast
amount of material which confronts the researcher into it: it involves
most of the major authors of the period, as well as a considerable number
of minor figures, such as Eugène Pelletan, Léon Gautier, or, in the
second part, Joséphin Péladan, whose vociferous — and, in its day, sen-
sational — condemnation or glorification of the Middle Ages it would
be a pity to suppress. To be seen in their true perspective, works of
literature inspired by the Middle Ages cannot be considered in isolation
from the climate of opinion which produced them; controversies among

historians and medieval scholars must be taken into account, and we
have therefore made a preliminary survey of this background for each
phase of literary exploitation of medieval themes — the Second Empire,
the immediate aftermath of 1870, and the Symbolist eighties and
nineties. The subject grows ever more complex as the nineteenth century
advances, for in each collective image of the Middle Ages — themselves
many-sided, taking colour from the variegated individual and political
complexions of the writers who had a share in forging them — traces of
former images subsisted. None was ever discarded out of hand: the
troubadour Middle Ages lingers on in the Romantic; aspects of the
Romantic survive in the fifties and sixties; and vestiges of the fifties-
and-sixties image, shattered in 1870, may be discerned in the Symbolist
Middle Ages. Also, those authors upon whose imagination the Middle
Ages exerted the most powerful influence, such as Hugo, Gautier, and
Michelet, underwent significant shifts in attitude towards them in the
course of a long literary career, and these mutations — one of the most
interesting aspects of our subject — must be carefully charted. Foreign
influences — changing, of course, with each new generation — are another
factor which must be taken into consideration: the Romantic Middle
Ages drew some of its inspiration from Scott and the Gothic novel; and
the Symbolist, from Tennyson and the Pre-Raphaelites. So the sources
of inspiration are many: besides having recourse to medieval legend,
literature, and architecture, writers borrowed from ready-made versions
of the Middle Ages supplied by a foreign, or earlier French, imagination.
And this study is a necessarily incomplete attempt to explore the uses
to which a multiplicity of medieval themes were put by a multiplicity
of writers over the space of fifty years.

Our first task — before we inquire into its fate under the Second
Empire — will be to make a survey of the Romantic Middle Ages.

CHAPTER 1

THE ROMANTIC MIDDLE AGES

'Le brillant moyen âge et la chevalerie' (T. Gautier)

A. *Before Romanticism: the 'genre troubadour'*

The first nostalgic sighs for a vanished age of chivalric virtue and ceremony were voiced early in French literature — before the Middle Ages had run their course, in fact. 'Car meilleur temps fut le temps ancien' was the refrain of one of Eustache Deschamps's *ballades*.[1] This sentiment remained alive in the centuries that followed, but literary exploitation of an imaginary Middle Ages did not begin in earnest until the second half of the eighteenth century, which saw the birth of the *genre troubadour,* and the publication of such landmarks as La Curne de Sainte-Palaye's *Mémoires sur l'ancienne chevalerie* (1753),[2] Millot's *Histoire littéraire des troubadours* (1774), and Tressan's *remaniements* of medieval romances in Paulmy's *Bibliothèque universelle des romans* (1775-89).

While *philosophes* heaped abuse upon the Middle Ages, regarded by them as 'un long intervalle d'ignorance',[3] the *genre troubadour* presented the image of an ideal 'bon vieux temps', in which knights divided their time between heroic deeds of valour and faithful service to the object of their love:

> . . . un siècle, où l'épée, où la foi,
> Où la galanterie étaient la seule loi.[4]

This never-failing *galanterie* was what the eighteenth century prized the most in its imagined Middle Ages. Sainte-Palaye's rendering of *Aucassin et Nicolette* (1752) was subtitled 'Les amours au bon vieux temps. On n'aime plus comme on aimait jadis.' Pathetic portrayal of Héloïse's unshakable fidelity to her lover accounted for the immense

---

[1] Quoted by Sainte-Palaye, *Mémoires sur l'ancienne chevalerie,* ed. Nodier, 1826, i. 377.

[2] Presented to the Académie des Inscriptions et Belles-Lettres in 1746, published in its *Mémoires de littérature,* xx (1753), and in book form, 2 vols., 1759.

[3] D'Alembert, *Discours préliminaire de l'Encyclopédie,* Édns. Gonthier, 1965, p. 76.

[4] From poem by Cérutti, 'Les Jardins de Betz', 1792, quoted by René Lanson, op. cit. (Intro., above), p. 41.

popularity of Colardeau's *Lettre d'Héloïse à Abailard* (1758). A footnote
to the famous *romance*, 'L'avez-vous vu, mon bien Aimé?', in Favart's
opera *La Fée Urgèle* (1765) reminded the reader that 'En ce tems-là les
Chevaliers Français tenaient leur parole en amour.'[5] The *romance* −
sentimental or dramatic − was the favourite vehicle for *troubadour*
sentiment. It sang of the wife or fiancée awaiting her loved one's return
from the wars, the damsel in the dark tower awaiting her rescuer, the
châtelaine with her devoted page, the troubadour with his lute at the
castle gate. They all poured forth their love with the naïveté which the
genre troubadour strove to achieve by omission of articles and pronouns,
and liberal use of archaisms such as 'las!' and 'souventesfois'.

B. *The Middle Ages' appeal for the Romantics: personal and political*

Factitious and superficial, the *genre troubadour* has been called a
mere 'jeu d'esprit' by one of its critics.[6] Its successor, the Romantic
Middle Ages, was in many respects equally frivolous and insubstantial:
'Moyen âge de fonte . . . et de carton-pierre . . . de pain d'épices et de
pendules', it was called by a mid-century medievalist.[7] Little distinction
was made between its component centuries, in which the sixteenth was
often included for good measure: 'Pauvre moyen âge!' exclaimed the
seventeen-year-old Flaubert, 'es-tu heureux d'être aimé, moyen âge du
XVIe siècle, des toques à plumes . . . des bahuts et des costumes à la
Louis XIII!'[8]
Romantic feeling for the past was, however, immeasurably more
profound than its *troubadour* equivalent.[9] Motives far more serious
prompted this return to a Middle Ages into which the fall of the
ancien régime had infused new poetry and pathos. Medieval monuments
now commanded, in the words of Nodier, 'un genre de respect plus
touchant, plus profond . . . que l'admiration, cette pitié . . . qu'on
pourroit appeler la religion du malheur'.[10] Michelet, as a boy, received
from Lenoir's Musée des Monuments français (founded in 1796), in

[5] Favart, *La Fée Urgèle*, 1765, p. 52..
[6] Baldensperger, op. cit. p. 145.
[7] Didron aîné, in *Annales archéologiques*, xv (1855), p. 112.
[8] Flaubert, *Oeuvres complètes*, 1964, i. 124.
[9] See L. Gossman's comparison between the pre- and post-Revolutionary view
of the Middle Ages, in *Medievalism and the Ideologies of the Enlightenment:
The World and Work of La Curne de Sainte-Palaye*, 1968, pp. 170-1, 332-3.
[10] Nodier, Taylor, and Cailleux, *Voyages pittoresques et romantiques dans
l'ancienne France*, Gide, i (1820), 22.

common with many others of his generation, 'l'étincelle historique, l'intérêt des grands souvenirs, le vague désir de remonter les âges'.[11]

Writers began to feel and proclaim that the appeal of the Middle Ages was more immediate and personal than that of classical antiquity. Medieval men were 'nos pères'; their ruined edifices threatened by the *bande noire,* were the 'Églises où priaient nos mères', the 'tours où combattaient nos aïeux.'[12]

The substitution of the medieval past for classical antiquity as a source of literary inspiration was energetically campaigned for in the dawn of the Romantic era by the *groupe de Coppet* – Mme de Staël, the Schlegels and Sismondi. 1813 saw the publication of A. W. Schlegel's *Cours de littérature dramatique,* Sismondi's *Littérature du midi de l'Europe,* and the second edition of Mme de Staël's *De l'Allemagne.* All these works spoke of the irresistible appeal of chivalric tradition:

> Nos habitudes, notre éducation [declared Sismondi], les morceaux touchans de notre histoire, peut-être même faudrait-il dire, les contes de nos nourrices, nous ramènent toujours aux temps et aux moeurs de la chevalerie; tout ce qui s'y rapporte agit sur notre sensibilité; tout ce qui tient aux temps mythologiques et à l'antiquité n'agit au contraire que sur la mémoire.[13]

Mme de Staël urged the French to follow the example of the Germans by giving preference to 'la littérature fondée sur les souvenirs de la chevalerie, sur le merveilleux du moyen âge' – in other words, 'La littérature romantique' – over 'celle dont la mythologie des Grecs est la base'. She declared it the only literature 'susceptible encore d'être perfectionnée, parce qu'ayant ses racines dans notre propre sol, elle est la seule qui puisse croître et se vivifier de nouveau; elle exprime notre religion; elle rappelle notre histoire.'[14]

These writers claimed that the Middle Ages had greatly enriched men's sensibilities. Emotions unknown to antiquity had come into being: melancholy, reverie, and *le vague à l'âme;*[15] poetic awe of nature;[16] respect for women, courtly love, and the *point d'honneur.*[17] If the broken tradition of *trouvères* and troubadours could only be

---

[11] Michelet, *Histoire de la Révolution Française,* ii (1962), 538.
[12] Hugo, 'La Bande noire' (1823), *Oeuvres poétiques,* i (1964), 341.
[13] Simonde de Sismondi, *De la littérature du midi de l'Europe,* 1813, ii. 158.
[14] *De l'Allemagne,* 4th edn., 1818, ii. 17.
[15] See Mme de Staël, *De la littérature,* 1812 edn., i. 250-1.
[16] Ibid. p. 261.
[17] Simonde de Sismondi, op. cit. iii. 344.

restored, all these sentiments would find expression at last, and literature would be regenerated.[18]

So the Romantic return to the Middle Ages was, as Baldensperger puts it, far more than 'une simple défroque': it was 'une révolution mythologique':[19] 'Le "merveilleux" différent auquel la littérature était invitée à demander son renouvellement, au lieu d'être une curiosité, devait former le fonds de la pensée et de l'imagination poétique.'[20]

In the early 1820s, moreover, when Romantic and royalist allegiances went hand in hand, it formed part of a political programme. Even the *genre troubadour* had been to a certain extent politically inspired. After 1750, remarks René Lanson, 'la gloire de Bayard et des anciens chevaliers consola des défaites de Rosbach, de Québec et de Pondichéry.'[21] Sainte-Palaye's golden age of chivalry corresponds with that of the monarchy: his knights are all 'fidèles soutiens du trône'.[22] During the revolutionary period the *genre troubadour* suffered an eclipse. It was 'suspect', says Jacoubet, because it represented 'le goût des ci-devant'[23] — and when it revived, under the Directoire, the troubadour's image had undergone a change. Once secure in his castle, 'le digne patron des nobles qui s'adonnaient à la poésie', he was now more often a wandering minstrel, the brother of the émigrés for whom 'leurs talents ont été, un temps, leur seul gagne-pain'.[24] They took into exile the song which became their *profession de foi*: Blondel's air from Grétry's *Richard Coeur-de-Lion* (1784):

> Ô Richard! ô mon roi!
> L'univers t'abandonne,
> Sur la terre il n'est donc que moi
> Qui s'intéresse à ta personne![25]

Under the Restoration, the image of an ideal Middle Ages shone forth with ever-increasing splendour. 'La gloire de l'ANCIENNE FRANCE est le

---

[18] See *De l'Allemagne*, i. 43.

[19] F. Baldensperger, *La Littérature*, 1913, p. 132.

[20] F. Baldensperger, *Études d'histoire littéraire*, première série, 1907, p. 145.

[21] R. Lanson, op. cit. p. 10.

[22] Sainte-Palaye, op. cit. i. 177. For the extent to which Sainte-Palaye's view of chivalry 'reflects a political outlook and a political commitment' see Gossman, op. cit. pp. 277-9, 283-5.

[23] H. Jacoubet, *Le Comte de Tressan . . .*, 1923, p. 376.

[24] Ibid. p. 386.

[25] Dumersan and Ségur, *Chansons nationales et populaires de France*, Garnier, 1866, i. 75.

patrimoine des Preux de tous les âges', proclaimed the authors of the
Voyages pittoresques. 'Elle rejaillit du fond du passé sur les hommes qui
honorent le présent.'[26] It became the earnest desire of young Romantic
writers to recreate, relive, and even to re-establish in the modern world,
this exemplary past of absolute devotion to altar and throne: the Société
royale des Bonnes-Lettres, to which Hugo, Vigny, and Nodier belonged,
adopted in 1822 'cette devise de nos pères, cette devise vraiment
française: Dieu, le Roi et les Dames'.[27] Hugo's ode 'Le Sacre de Charles X'
(1825) proclaimed that this event heralded a new age of chivalry: the
monarch was 'le chef des Douze Pairs', sending his 'preux' into battle
with the cry 'Montjoie et Saint-Denis!'[28] Nodier declared about the same
time, of 'le charme de ces souvenirs nationaux': 'Ce n'est pas la vogue
passagère d'une mode locale, c'est l'instinct universel d'une nécessité
morale et littéraire.'[29]

So a world in which hosts of 'chevaliers au coeur loyal' listened with
bowed head to 'l'édit royal' before entering the lists,[30] and in which the
poet exclaimed:

> Que j'aime à voir, près de l'austère
>   Monastère,
> Au seuil du baron feudataire,
> La croix blanche et le bénitier![31]

was conjured into being. (Twenty years later Flaubert, at the beginning
of his career, was to refer to this aspect of Romanticism as 'la sempiter-
nelle poésie des tourelles, des damoiselles, du palefroi, des fleurs de lis de
l'oriflamme de saint Louis, du panache blanc, du droit divin et d'un tas
d'autres sottises aussi innocentes'.[32])

C. *Sources of inspiration: ruins*

The Romantics, then, inherited from their *troubadour* predecessors
an insipid 'bon vieux temps' which, fired by new aesthetic and political
enthusiasm, they proceeded to transform. 'Le rôle du romantisme', says
Jacoubet, 'sera de dévêtir ce Moyen Age de son costume troubadour

---

[26] Nodier, Taylor, and Cailleux, op. cit. p. i (Dédicace).
[27] R. Bray, *Chronologie du romantisme*, Nizet, 1963, p. 60.
[28] V. Hugo, op. cit. pp. 382-3.
[29] Quoted by J. Larat, *La Tradition et l'exotisme dans l'oeuvre de Charles Nodier*, 1923, p. 162.
[30] V. Hugo, 'Le Chant du Tournoi' (1824), op. cit. p. 435.
[31] Musset, 'Stances' (1828), *Poésies complètes*, 1962, p. 82.
[32] Flaubert, *Os. cs.*, Édns. du Seuil, 1964, ii, 476 (*Par les champs et par les grèves*, 1847).

et de lui rendre ses atours archéologiques.'[33] Foreign influences contributed to this: as early as 1815 the influence of German *lieder* and the
Gothic novel began to infuse a new element of terror into the *romance*
(Goethe's 'Fiancée de Corinthe' and Lewis's ballad of Alonzo and the
fair Imogine engendered numerous sombre versions of the Crusader's
return theme);[34] and that of Scott,[35] which began in 1820, had an
equally important part in the invigoration of the *troubadour* Middle Ages.

Charles Nodier was the best-informed and the most energetic
devotee of the Middle Ages at this time. From 1817 he campaigned
for them in the *Journal des débats,* tirelessly directing the attention of
his fellow-Romantics towards medieval literature, legend, and architecture, and modern visions of the Middle Ages in German ballads, Walter
Scott, and the Gothic novel. There followed his share in the *Voyages
pittoresques et romantiques dans l'ancienne France,* which began
publication in 1820, his edition of Sainte-Palaye's *Mémoires sur l'ancienne
chevalerie* in 1826, and − most important of all − the initiatory
influence he exerted over Victor Hugo, in the medieval sphere, during
the mid twenties.[36]

We have seen that the Middle Ages, recreated in the imagination of
modern English and German writers, provided the French Romantics
with an important source of inspiration. Any direct influence they
received from the period itself was architectural rather than literary.
The medievalist Paulin Paris's first work was an *Apologie de l'école
Romantique* (1824), in which, as a disciple of Mme de Staël, he
expressed equal enthusiasm for the medieval storytellers' 'chefs-
d'oeuvre de grâce, de naïveté et de délicatesse',[37] and modern Romantic
literature, a product of the same tradition. Young Romantic
writers liked to picture themselves engrossed on winter evenings in the
works of 'le bon Alain Chartier, Rutebeuf le conteur,/ Sire Gasse-
Brulez . . .',[38] and they liked to imagine, as the poets of the *genre
troubadour* had done before them,[39] that they had rediscovered the

---

[33] H. Jacoubet, 'Moyen Âge et romantisme', *Annales de l'Université de Grenoble,*
xvi (1939), p. 93.
[34] See A. M. Killen, *Le Roman terrifiant ou roman noir et son influence sur la
littérature française jusqu'en 1840,* 1923, pp. 147 ff.
[35] See L. Maigron, *Le Roman historique à l'époque romantique,* 1898.
[36] See E. M. Schenck, *La Part de Ch. Nodier dans la formation des idées romantiques de Victor Hugo,* 1914.
[37] P. Paris, *Apologie de l'école romantique,* 1824, p. 28.
[38] Gautier, 'A mon ami Eugène de N***' (1830), *Poésies complètes,* ed. Jasinski,
2nd edn., 1970, i. 66.
[39] The *romance* was a conscious imitation of medieval poetry. Cf. Moncrif's

secrets of medieval literary composition – 'L'auteur, en les composant,' said Hugo of his *Ballades*, 'a essayé de donner quelque idée de ce que pouvaient être les poèmes des premiers troubadours du moyen-âge'[40] –, but they were in fact (with the exception of Nodier) ignorant of and indifferent to medieval literature.[41]

Gothic architecture, on the other hand, aroused the strongest emotion in them, especially when it had reached a state of dereliction sufficient to provoke angry remembrance of Revolutionary vandalism, and anxious concern for its fate in the present age of the *bande noire*. Chateaubriand laid the foundations of the *culte des ruines* in the *Génie du Christianisme* (1802). Having spoken of the part played by church spires in the 'moralization' of landscape after the demise of paganism, he went on to say that ruins produced the same effect: 'Tous les hommes ont un secret attrait pour les ruines . . . les ruines jettent une grande moralité au milieu des scènes de la nature.'[42] The pious rapture with which he regarded 'ces basiliques, toutes moussues, toutes remplies des générations des décédés et des âmes de [nos] pères . . . [ces] voûtes toutes noires de siècles,'[43] was matched by Hugo in 'La Bande Noire':

> Ô débris! ruines de France,
> Que notre amour en vain défend . . .
> Arceaux tombés, voûtes brisées!
> Vestiges des races passées!
> Lit sacré d'un fleuve tari! . . .;[44]

as was the ecstasy with which he listened to the melodious sighing of the wind through Gothic ruins – 'leurs innombrables jours deviennent autant de tuyaux d'où s'échappent des plaintes',[45] he remarked, while the poet proclaimed:

> Je vous aime, ô débris! et surtout quand l'automne
> Prolonge en vos échos sa plainte monotone.[46]

Imitation des chansons du comte de Champagne (in his *Oeuvres*, 1751) – also Tressan's famous and ludicrous 'reconstitution' of the *Chanson de Roland* (1777).

[40] Hugo, op. cit. p. 279.
[41] See the (not altogether reliable) study by D. Doolittle, *The Relations between Literature and Medieval Studies in France from 1820 to 1860*, 1933.
[42] *Génie du Christianisme*, Part 3, Bk. 5, Ch. 3.
[43] Ibid. Part 3, Bk. 1, Ch. 8.
[44] Hugo, op. cit. pp. 341-2.
[45] *Génie du Christianisme*, Part 3, Bk. 5, Ch. 5.
[46] Hugo, op. cit. p. 474 ('Aux ruines de Montfort-l'Amaury', 1825).

Wandering in the shadow of these ruins, or through landscapes once the scene of some glorious event, often served as the initial inspiration for Romantic visions of the Middle Ages. The first stirrings of Romantic feeling for the past — an elegiac sense of loss, a sense of awe and bound-less respect for 'nos pères', a vanished race of giants whose like will not be seen again — were experienced as early as 1794 by Fontanes, in his poem 'Le Vieux Château'. Fleeing from the Terror, the poet finds peace and consolation in Les Andelys, where he meditates upon his feudal ancestors, 'plus vrais que nous, plus tendres et plus graves', among the ruins:

> Ces murs, tout pleins encor de la fierté gothique,
> Dans leur muet langage entretiennent mes yeux
> Des hauts faits, des grands noms, des moeurs de nos aïeux,
> Que ne puis-je revoir ces coutumes brillantes . . .
> Ce serment d'aimer Dieu, la beauté, la patrie.

'Âge simple! âge heureux!' he cries; and conjures up a vision of ideal domestic felicity, culminating in the arrival of the castle's most eagerly-awaited visitor:

> Un troubadour paraît: ô transports enchanteurs!
> On l'entoure, à sa harpe il suspend tous les coeurs.[47]

Chateaubriand was visited by delectable visions as soon as he entered a Gothic cathedral: in that mysterious twilight, 'l'ancienne France semblait revivre: on croyait voir ces costumes singuliers, ce peuple si différent de ce qu'il est aujourd'hui.'[48] Hugo contemplates the ruins of Montfort-l'Amaury, a brooding presence in the landscape:

> Vieilles tours, que le temps l'une vers l'autre incline,
> Et qui semblez de loin, sur la haute colline,
> Deux noirs géants prêts à lutter . . .,

and declares that only the poet, with his Muse, should be allowed to venture upon this sacred ground and commune with the shades who linger there:

> Lui qui donne au moins une larme au vieux fort,
> Et, si l'air froid des nuits sous vos arceaux murmure,
> Croit qu'une ombre a froissé la gigantesque armure
> D'Amaury, comte de Montfort![49]

[47] Fontanes, *Oeuvres*, 1839, i. 50-2.
[48] *Génie du Christianisme*, Part 3, Bk. 1, Ch. 8.
[49] Hugo, op. cit. pp. 474-5.

Vigny hears a huntsman's horn at dead of night in the Pyrenees and sees in vision the tragedy of Roncevaux re-enacted:

Âmes des Chevaliers, revenez-vous encor?
Est-ce vous qui parlez avec la voix du Cor?
Roncevaux! Roncevaux! dans ta sombre vallée
L'ombre du grand Roland n'est donc pas consolée![50] ('Le Cor', 1825)

Aloysius Bertrand's Gaspard de la Nuit explores the city of Dijon, and as his familiarity with each stone of its crumbling bastions deepens, the turbulent past comes alive, invading the empty peace of the present with a riot of sound and colour: 'J'avais galvanisé un cadavre et ce cadavre s'était levé. Dijon se lève; il se lève, il marche, il court! — trente *dindelles* carillonnent dans un ciel bleu d'outremer ... Et comment douter de cette résurrection? Voici flotter aux vents l'étendard de soie, moitié vert, moitié jaune, broché des armoiries de la ville.'[51]

D. *Character of the Romantic Middle Ages:*
(i) *'Énormité' and 'délicatesse'*

We must now ask ourselves what sort of Middle Ages the Romantics saw in vision as they wandered in the haunts of their forefathers. Wherein lay its universal appeal? René Lanson remarks on the fact that Sainte-Palaye's *Mémoires sur l'ancienne chevalerie* and Voltaire's *Essai sur les moeurs* appeared simultaneously, presenting the reader of the 1750s with two contrasting visions of the Middle Ages: 'Tandis que Voltaire décrivait un moyen âge fanatique et sanguinaire, La Curne en modela un autre chevaleresque et sentimental dont l'image doucereuse ne quitta plus le souvenir des hommes.'[52] From the moment of their rediscovery as a source of aesthetic enjoyment they were that 'Moyen Âge énorme et délicat'[53] in which Verlaine was to delight, exploited for the extremes of horror and perfection they offered to the artist. The appeal of Gothic now lay in that very disproportion (Paulin Paris extolled '[les] masses énormes de pierres ... paraissant avoir la délicatesse et l'inconsistance du jonc'),[54] which pre- and post-Romantic critics deplored, finding it

[50] A. de Vigny, *Os. cs.* 1948, p. 136.
[51] A. Bertrand, *Gaspard de la nuit,* ed. B. Guégan, 1925, p. 12.
[52] R. Lanson, op. cit. p. 15 .
[53] Verlaine, 'Non. Il fut gallican . . .' (from *Sagesse,* 1881), *Oeuvres poétiques complètes,* 1962, p. 249.
[54] P. Paris, op. cit. p. 41 .

monstrous in bulk, trivial and finicking in detail.[55] And the appeal of the Middle Ages themselves lay in the fact of their being immoderately sinister or sentimental. 'Moeurs à la fois grossières et respectables', exclaimed Bougainville in his Introduction to Sainte-Palaye's *Mémoires*.[56] 'Vous y voyez à la fois de grands vices et de grandes vertus, une grossière ignorance et des coups de lumière', said Chateaubriand of medieval history.[57] Mme de Staël perceived in chivalry 'la rudesse du Nord qui s'alliait avec une sensibilité sublime';[58] Nodier marvelled at 'la grandiosité ingénue des moeurs chevaleresques'.[59]

The potent charm of this half *troubadour*, half Voltairian, Middle Ages was described in 1800 by Edmond Géraud, a *troubadour* poet whose predilection for it was so strong as to be already Romantic in character:

Ce qu'on est convenu d'appeler le bon vieux temps a toujours eu pour moi un attrait inexprimable. Les moeurs du quinzième siècle, ce mélange de galanterie, d'héroïsme et de superstition; le sombre que jettent sur la scène ces cloîtres, ces châteaux, ateliers de crimes et de fanatisme . . . voilà ce que j'aimai toujours de prédilection dans notre histoire et ce que j'ambitionne de retracer.[60]

And Hugo, possessed by the same keen excitement, exclaimed in his ode 'La Bande Noire':

> Murs voilés de tant de mystères!
> Murs brillants de tant de splendeurs![61]

(ii) *The ideal Romantic Middle Ages: poetic passion and festive display*

The ideal Romantic Middle Ages appear in full splendour in the *Génie du Christianisme*. For Chateaubriand the Dark Ages — 'les seuls temps

[55] See *Encyclopédie,* articles 'Architecture' and 'Gothique' (for French 17th- and 18th-century detraction of Gothic see J. Corblet, 'L'Architecture du moyen-âge jugée par les écrivains des deux derniers siècles', *Revue de l'art chrétien,* iii (1859); and W. Herrmann, *Laugier and Eighteenth-Century French Theory,* London, Zwemmer, 1962, Ch. V and Appendix VIII). The sight of Chartres moved Hugo to extol Gothic art in 1836 as '[le] fils de la nature. Infini comme elle dans le grand et dans le petit. Microscopique et gigantesque' (*En voyage,* Imprimerie Nationale edn., 1910, ii. 43); while Taine in 1865 reverted to the earlier view, listing 'énormité' and 'délicatesse' among the qualities of Gothic, the product of a 'fantaisie maladive' striving after 'l'infini dans la grandeur et l'infini dans la petitesse' (*Philosophie de l'art,* 1865, pp. 128-9).

[56] Sainte-Palaye, *Mémoires sur l'ancienne chevalerie,* Duchesne, 1759, i. p. ix.

[57] *Génie du Christianisme,* Part 3, Bk. 3, Ch. 2.   [58] *De l'Allemagne,* ii. 47.

[59] Nodier, *Mélanges de littérature et de critique,* 1820, ii. 322.

[60] *Un Homme de lettres sous l'Empire et la Restauration (Edmond Géraud)* ed. Maurice Albert, n.d., pp. xiii-ix.

[61] Hugo, op. cit. p. 341.

poétiques de notre histoire . . . l'âge de la féerie et des enchantements'[62] –
eclipsed all other epochs. The Romantics of the 1820s and 1830s shared
this vision of a 'temps de piété, d'amour, de courtoisie', when 'l'homme
aimait, priait, combattait tour à tour.'[63] 'Ah! rendez-nous le moyen âge!'[64]
they cried in unison: it was in their eyes a time of pristine freshness, naïveté
and purity, when all the world was young –

> . . . le temps de nature
> Où l'âme était sincère et pure,
> Où le coeur seul dictait les lois,[65]

a time when every noble passion and enthusiasm burned in men's
breasts, when faith and hope, so sadly diminished in modern times,
were universally triumphant. 'Heureux, trois et quatre fois heureux,
ceux qui croient!' declared Chateaubriand.[66] For them the world
abounds in poetic consolations; and at no time was this more so than
in the Middle Ages, when monasteries were havens of enlightenment and
felicity. Marchangy's *Gaule poétique* (1813-17) also celebrated 'la paix
du gothique monastère';[67] but it was in Musset's *Rolla* (1833) that
Romantic nostalgia for the Age of Faith found its most intense
expression:

> Regrettez-vous le temps où d'un siècle barbare
> Naquit un siècle d'or, plus fertile et plus beau? . . .
> Regrettez-vous le temps où nos vieilles romances
> Ouvraient leurs ailes d'or vers leur monde enchanté?
> Où tous nos monuments et toutes nos croyances
> Portaient le manteau blanc de leur virginité?
> Où, sous la main du Christ, tout venait de renaître? . . .
> Où la Vie était jeune, – où la Mort espérait? . . .[68]
>
> Cloîtres silencieux, voûtes des monastères,
> C'est vous, sombres caveaux, vous qui savez aimer! . . .
> Oui, c'est un vaste amour qu'au fond de vos calices
> Vous buviez à plein coeur, moines mystérieux! . . .
> Vous aimiez ardemment! oh! vous étiez heureux![69]

The poetic superstitions of the Age of Faith were an important part
of the ideal Romantic Middle Ages. The Gothic world of the imagination,

---

[62] Part 4, Bk. 5, Ch. 1.
[63] J. Bard, *Les Mélancoliques,* 1832, pp. 85-6.
[64] Ibid. p. 77.
[65] Ibid. p. 29.
[66] *Génie du Christianisme,* Part 3, Bk. 5, Ch. 6.
[67] Marchangy, *La Gaule poétique,* ii (1813), 10.
[68] Musset, op. cit. pp. 273-4.
[69] Ibid. p. 285.

dismissed by the *philosophes* as a tissue of error and superstition, was rescued from disgrace.[70] Just as 'nos grossiers aïeux' had been transmuted into 'nos pères' — objects of universal respect —, so the formula 'les siècles d'ignorance' was converted by Marchangy into 'les temps de poétique ignorance'.[71] Chateaubriand had painted an idyllic picture of these times in his chapter of the *Génie* 'Harmonies morales. Dévotions populaires': 'Chaque fontaine, chaque croix dans un chemin, chaque soupir du vent de la nuit, porte avec lui un prodige. Pour l'homme de foi, la nature est une constante merveille. Souffre-t-il, il prie sa petite image, et il est soulagé.'[72] This aspect of the Middle Ages was the one that enthralled Nodier most of all: time and again he sang its praises, notably in his essay 'Du fantastique en littérature' (1830): 'Le fantastique étoit partout alors, dans les croyances les plus sévères de la vie comme dans ses erreurs les plus gracieuses. . . . Ce fut là . . . une merveilleuse poésie . . . une imagination tout à la fois grandiose et charmante, qu'on ne renouvellera plus, et qu'on regrettera toujours.'[73] The note of melancholy here is belied by Nodier's campaign to resuscitate this 'merveilleuse poésie', in the firm belief that 'le romantique' and 'le fantastique' are one and the same.[74] He inspired in Hugo an enthusiasm equal to his own for the 'mille superstitions originales' and the 'mille imaginations pittoresques' which engendered 'ces myriades d'êtres intermédiaires que nous retrouvons tout vivants dans les traditions populaires du moyen âge'[75] — benign and poetic spirits of air, water, earth, and fire abundantly present in Nodier's tales, Hugo's *Ballades,* and Bertrand's *Gaspard de la nuit.*

Poetic love flourished no less than poetic faith and superstition in the ideal Romantic Middle Ages. 'De vastes architectures gothiques, de vieilles forêts, de grands étangs solitaires' inevitably fostered, according to Chateaubriand, 'ces passions que rien ne pouvoit détruire, et qui devenoient des espèces de sort ou d'enchantement'. Very often, he remarked, 'le jeune page y commençoit, pour la fille du seigneur, une de ces durables tendresses que des miracles de vaillance devoient immortaliser.'[76]

Warfare was waged on an equally ideal plane: the 'héros chrétien', protector of the weak, 'une espèce d'ange de la guerre, que Dieu envoie

[70] See Sismondi, op. cit. ii. 141-2.
[71] Marchangy, op. cit. iv (1817), 90.
[72] Part 3, Bk. 5, Ch. 6.
[73] Ch. Nodier, *Oeuvres,* Renduel, v (1832), 82-4. Cf. also his Introduction to vol. 1 of the *Voyages pittoresques,* 1820.   [74] Ibid. p. 79.
[75] Hugo, *Préface de 'Cromwell'* (1827), ed. M. Souriau, 1897, p. 199.
[76] *Génie du Christianisme,* Part 4, Bk. 5, Ch. 4.

pour adoucir ce fléau',[77] rode 'par *monts* et par *vaux*, cherchant périls et aventures', striving his utmost to 'se rendre *sans peur et sans reproche*'.[76]

Nostalgia for the spiritual fervour of the Middle Ages was felt by liberals as well as royalists. While the latter regretted the simple faith of monk and peasant, the page's exalted devotion to his lady, and the martial zeal of knight-errant and Crusader, the former extolled the strength of will and full-blooded passion of bygone days. The fiercely republican poet Philothée O'Neddy described in *Feu et flamme* (1833) a gathering of *Jeunes-France* in Jehan Duseigneur's studio. One of them begins to recite a *Ballade* of Victor Hugo, sending the company into transports of delight:

> Il y avait dans l'air comme une odeur magique
> De moyen-âge, — arome ardent et névralgique.

Petrus Borel proclaims that the Middle Ages hold him in thrall:

> Camarades, c'était là qu'il faisait bon vivre
> Lorsqu'on avait des flots de lave dans le sang,
> Du vampirisme à l'oeil, des volontés au flanc! . . .
> Tout homme à coeur de bronze, a rêves exaltés,
> N'avait pas un seul jour à craindre l'atonie
> D'une vie encastrée avec monotonie.[78]

Henri Beyle was subject to similar pangs of nostalgia. His worship of '*l'énergie*, . . . la qualité qui manque le plus an dix-neuvième siècle',[79] prompted an occasional regretful comment: 'Le *principe énergique* était plus fort que parmi nous dans la société du dixième siècle';[80] 'Au moyen âge, la présence du danger *trempait* les coeurs.'[81]

Historians and critics in the liberal camp experienced the same sense of loss. 'Ce moment est triste', sighed Jean-Jacques Ampère in an essay on chivalry. He saw everywhere 'une grande défaillance . . . une certaine inertie dans la vie morale', and contrasted this with the days when chivalry exerted its quickening influence on men's lives. 'Quel enthousiasme nouveau', he asked, 'remplacera cette forme évanouie de l'enthousiasme de nos pères?'[82] Guizot also detected in his contemporaries 'une certaine mollesse dans les esprits et dans les caractères'. 'L'individua-lité . . . l'énergie intime et personnelle de l'homme est faible et timide',

---

[77] Ibid. Part 1, Bk. 6, Ch. 5.
[78] P. O'Neddy (Théophile Dondey), *Feu et flamme*, ed. M. Hervier, 1926, pp. 11-12.
[79] Stendhal, *Promenades dans Rome*, Édn. du Divan, 1931, i, 309.
[80] *Mémoires d'un touriste*, Divan, 1929, i 129.
[81] *De l'amour*, Divan, 1927, ii. 14.
[82] J-J. Ampère, *Mélanges d'histoire littéraire et de littérature*, 1867, i. 264-5 ('De la chevalerie', 1838).

he complained to his audience at the Collège de France, concluding:
'Messieurs, tel n'était pas le moyen âge. . . . Dans beaucoup d'hommes,
l'individualité était forte, la volonté énergique. . . . Spectacle non-
seulement dramatique, attachant, mais instructif et utile . . .'[83]

These liberals saw in the Middle Ages — 'les siècles du mérite ignoré'[84]
— one vast 'élan général'[85] towards freedom from feudal oppression. The
spirit of emergent democracy informed both chivalry, 'espèce de grande
république dont chaque chevalier était un citoyen indépendant',[86] and
the 'mouvement ascendant'[85] of Gothic spires ('clochers silencieux
montrant du doigt le ciel'[87] for Chateaubriand and his followers).

So fervent emotion and enthusiasm characterize the ideal Romantic
Middle Ages, whether of royalist or republican inspiration. This
spiritual ferment is translated into pictorial pageantry: the age of
chivalry is seen as a never-ending festival. Chateaubriand evokes the
First Crusade: 'Le soleil vient de se lever: les armées sont en présence;
les bannières se déroulent aux vents . . . les habits, les franges, les
harnois, les armes, les couleurs, l'or et le fer, étincellent aux premiers
feux du jour';[88] Hugo, a prodigious tournament:

> Déjà la lice est ouverte . . .
> La bannière blanche et verte
> Flotte au front de chaque tour;
> La foule éclate en paroles;
> Les légères banderoles
> Se mêlent en voltigeant;
> Et le héros du portique
> Sur l'or de sa dalmatique
> Suspend le griffon d'argent.[89]

Aloysius Bertrand, the city of Dijon, 'avec ses églises, sa sainte chapelle,
ses abbayes, ses monastères, qui faisaient des processions de clochers, de
flèches, d'aiguilles, déployant pour bannières leurs vitraux d'or et d'azur';[90]
and Hugo again (in *Notre-Dame de Paris*), the scene — 'bourdonnement
dans les oreilles, éblouissement dans les yeux' — as the crowd waits to see
Gringoire's *mystère* in the great hall with its ceiling 'peinte d'azur,

---

[83] Guizot, *Histoire de la civilisation en France,* iv (1830), 30-1.
[84] Sismondi, *Histoire des républiques italiennes du moyen âge,* i (1809), p. x.
[85] Ampère, op. cit. p. 167.
[86] Ibid. p. 164.
[87] Gautier, *Poésies complètes,* i. 118. ('Un vers de Wordsworth', 1832).
[88] *Génie du Christianisme,* Part 2, Bk. 2, Ch. 12.
[89] Hugo, op. cit. p. 434.
[90] *Gaspard de la nuit,* p. 11.

fleurdelysée en or', its 'vitraux de mille couleurs', and every inch of its walls 'recouvert de haut en bas d'une splendide enluminure bleu et or'.[91] These dazzling scenes come alive with sound of rejoicing as well as colour: heralds trumpet from towers; the populace cries 'Noël! Noël!' as royal personages pass by;[92] shouts of 'Honneur aux fils des Preux!'[93] or 'Los aux dames!/Au roi los!'[94] ring forth during the tournament from crowd and combatants.

What most appealed to the creators of this imaginary world was its rich diversity, its multifarious activity and picturesque disorder. Mme de Staël had expressed the opinion that 'l'intérêt pittoresque du moyen âge tient à cette diversité de scènes et de caractères, dont les romans des troubadours ont fait ressortir des effets si touchans';[95] and Marchangy had welcomed as a new source of inspiration for literature 'les pélerins, les troubadours, les chevaliers, les pages et les gabeurs, personnages poétiques . . . inconnus à l'antiquité'.[96] These caractères invade Romantic literature in full force: Bertrand's Dijon, for example, swarms with 'bourgeois, nobles, vilains, soudrilles, prêtres, moines, clercs, marchands, varlets, juifs, lombards, pèlerins, ménestrels . . . qui clament, qui sifflent, qui chantent, qui geignent, qui prient, qui maugréent'.[97] Hugo's fifteenth-century Paris, seen from the towers of Notre-Dame, is as bewilderingly and magnificently diverse: 'un éblouissement de toits, de cheminées, de rues, de ponts, de places, de flèches, de clochers'.[98]

(iii) More melancholy aspects

This, then, was the resplendent side of the Romantic Middle Ages, steeped in perpetual sunlight:

> Paré de souvenirs d'amour et de féerie,
> Le brillant moyen âge et la chevalerie.[99]

What of the other side, that lay in shadow — a shadow with gradations all the way from a veil of melancholy clouding the bright scene to a pall of sinister and impenetrable darkness? For, as we have seen, the

---

[91] Hugo, *Notre-Dame de Paris* (1831), 1959, pp. 14-15.
[92] See e.g. *Gaspard de la nuit*, p. 13.
[93] *Génie du Christianisme*, Part 4, Bk. 5, Ch. 4.
[94] Hugo, 'Le Pas d'armes du Roi Jean' (1828), *Oeuvres poétiques*, i. 531.
[95] *De l'Allemagne*, ii. 97.
[96] *La Gaule poétique*, ii (1813), 211.
[97] *Gaspard de la nuit*, p. 12.
[98] *Notre-Dame de Paris*, p. 141.
[99] T. Gautier, 'Moyen Âge' (1830), op. cit. i. 4.

Romantics took as much pleasure in the lugubrious aspect of the Middle Ages as in their ideal aspect.

Since the earliest days of their exploitation in literature the Middle Ages had been associated with a certain degree of wholly pleasurable melancholy. They themselves were 'les siècles mélancoliques' (Nodier, 1809)[100] (according to Mme de Staël, it was the peoples of the North, particularly prone to 'les souffrances de l'âme',[101] who gave them this complexion), and literary products inspired by them frequently sought to evoke a corresponding *vague à l'âme* in the reader. A contemporary description of the *romance* declared that 'le récit en est assez brillant s'il laisse dans l'âme du lecteur une impression délicieuse de tristesse et de mélancolie.'[102] Romantic literature on medieval themes was often pervaded with an elegiac sadness, a sense of mutability and mortality. Nodier said in the Introduction to his *Voyages* that 'quelque disposition mélancolique dans les pensées, ... le sentiment de je ne sais quelle communauté de décadence et d'infortune entre ces vieux édifices et la génération qui s'achève',[103] had led him to undertake the work. The poet Saint-Valry wandered in the footsteps of Hugo through the ruins of Montfort l'Amaury. He saw in them an 'image de ses jours dévastés et flétris', and savoured 'cette douce tristesse/Que le temps qui n'est plus à sa suite nous laisse.'[104] The same sadness overwhelms Hugo himself in his long elegiac lament for the vanished glories of Gothic architecture in *Notre-Dame de Paris*: 'Qu'a fait le temps, qu'ont fait les hommes de ces merveilles?'[105] But the masterpiece in this genre is of course Vigny's evocation of 'old, unhappy, far-off things, and battles long ago':

Dieu! que le son du Cor est triste au fond des bois![106]

---

[100] 'De la romance', Nodier. *Poésies diverses,* 1827, p. 49. Cf. Quinet, *Philosophie de l'histoire de l'humanité* (1825): 'Il y avait [i.e. au moyen âge] un fond de tristesse qui se répandait sur toutes les relations de la vie, qui jetait sur les coutumes, sur les traditions, sur les monuments, sur la physionomie des hommes, un caractère particulier de sérieux et de mélancolie' (Quinet, *Os. cs.* ii, Germer-Baillière, n.d., p. 373).

[101] Mme de Staël, *De la littérature . . .,* pp. 250-1.

[102] Quoted by Pauphilet in his essay 'Le Mythe du moyen âge' (*Le Legs du moyen âge,* 1950, p. 44).

[103] *Voyages pittoresques et romantiques,* i (1820), 4.

[104] A-S. Saint-Valry, *La Chapelle de Notre-Dame-du-Chêne. Les Ruines de Montfort l'Amaury,* 1826, p. 40.

[105] *Notre-Dame de Paris,* p. 17.

[106] Vigny, op. cit. p. 139.

Tales of unhappy love, 'ces passions mélancoliques, nées au sein de la féodalité',[107] were another productive source of Romantic melancholy. 'Oh! que d'adieux touchants, que de séparations déchirantes!'[108] cried the enraptured Marchangy. Such a farewell was Raoul de Coucy's in the Duc de la Vallière's *romance* 'Les Infortunées Amours de Gabrielle de Vergi et de Raoul de Coucy' (1752) – a message, sent with his heart to his loved one after he had perished in the Crusades: 'Je vous adore: adieu, je meurs.'[109] This *romance,* and Moncrif's contemporaneous 'Les Infortunes inouïes de la tant belle, honnête et renommée Comtesse de Saulx' (1751) – another tale of a brutal husband's jealous rage[110] (both as arresting as any Romantic work), – were among the first of innumerable *troubadour* and Romantic ballads of unhappy medieval love, many of them variations on the theme of the Crusader's return, such as Musset's famous 'Chanson de Barberine' and Hugo's ballad 'La Fiancée du Timbalier'.

This gentle elegiac melancholy, these pathetic lovers' misfortunes (which sometimes reach a happy conclusion, like Vigny's 'La Neige') still belong, however, to the ideal Romantic Middle Ages rather than to its sinister counterpart, which yet remains for us to explore.

(iv) *The sinister Romantic Middle Ages: Gothic terrors; Victor Hugo*

This world owes its existence in a large measure to the English Gothic novel, whose immense popularity in France began in the closing years of the eighteenth century.[111] Gothic architecture, in the novels of Anne Radcliffe, with their strongly anti-Catholic undertones, is associated with gloom and suffering. Ruined abbeys are referred to as 'le repaire de la superstition'.[112] Birds of ill omen perch upon their topmost crenellations; sinister monks with flickering tapers patrol them at dead of night. Castles which have been the theatre of nameless crimes collapse upon their owners – fiendish barons, like Arthur d'Almaroës in Flaubert's early exercise in the genre, *Rêve d'enfer* (1837), 'lui dont les dents blanches exhalaient une odeur de chair humaine . . . lui dont on voyait, pendant les nuits d'hiver, la figure sombre et lugubre planant sur le vieux donjon féodal'.[113]

[107] Marchangy, *La Gaule poétique,* iv (1815), 230.
[108] Ibid. v (1817), 201.
[109] De Lusse, *Recueil de romances historiques, tendres et burlesques,* 1767, p. 26.
[110] See ibid. pp. 27-36.
[111] See Killen, op. cit.
[112] A. Radcliffe, *La Forêt, ou l'Abbaye de Saint-Clair (The Romance of the Forest,* 1791), i (1830), 31.
[113] Flaubert, *Os. cs.* i. 90-1.

Much as they revered in principle Gothic architecture and the Middle Ages, the Romantics were tempted at moments to see them in the same sinister light as did Mrs. Radcliffe. The knight-errant, says Chateaubriand, was usually welcomed into a great hall ablaze with light and filled with festal cheer, but once in a while he came upon a very different sort of castle: 'Des varlets silencieux, aux regards farouches, l'introduisoient, par de longues galeries à peine éclairées, dans la chambre solitaire qu'on lui destinoit. . . . Vers minuit, on entendoit un bruit léger, les tapisseries s'agitoient, la lampe du paladin s'éteignoit, un cercueil s'élevoit autour de sa couche. . . .'[114] Marchangy's *Gaule poétique* embraces 'les manoirs ténébreux des félons' as well as 'les beaux pages et leurs belles marraines, les séances des Troubadours, les défis joyeux des ménestrels et des jongleurs';[115] one feature of his 'Vie poétique des anciens châteaux' is 'le bruit des eaux invisibles grondant sourdement sous des voûtes lugubres'.[116] Even the pious Saint-Valry, when he approaches the ruins of Montfort l'Amaury, in order to 'D'un oeil religieux/Interroger plus près ce débris respectable', cannot repress the eager question: 'Dans quels noirs souterrains plongent ces soupiraux?'[117]

Victor Hugo, fascinated as he was by extremes of good and evil, beauty and deformity, naturally made the Middle Ages his province from the very beginning of his career. In his *Odes et ballades,* the ideal Middle Ages of 'La Fée et la Péri' —

> Tu verras les barons, sous leurs tours féodales,
> De l'humble pèlerin détachant les sandales;
> Et les sombres créneaux d'écussons décorés;
> Et la dame tout bas priant, pour un beau page,
> Quelque mystérieuse image
> Peinte sur des vitraux dorés.[118]

— is evoked in company with the sinister: the Gothic monuments extolled in 'La Bande noire' are 'Séjours de joie ou de souffrance'. Their roofs are a meeting-ground for flocks of 'oiseaux funèbres . . . levant des voix sépulcrales'.[119] The 'Chant du Tournoi' exhorts all 'chevaliers au coeur loyal' to eschew the example of the felonious warrior, lurking in his 'infâme château', and relying for victory on

[114] *Génie du Christianisme,* Part 4, Bk. 5, Ch. 4.
[115] *La Gaule poétique,* iii (1815), 189-90.
[116] Ibid. iv (1815), 296.
[117] A. S. Saint-Valry, op. cit. p. 39.
[118] V. Hugo, op. cit. p. 551.
[119] Ibid. pp. 341-2.

'hideux nécromants' and 'impurs talismans'.[120] Ballads such as 'Le Sylphe', 'Les Deux Archers', and 'La Légende de la nonne' show that the Gothic imagination engendered creatures of darkness as well as light: the gentle, ethereal sylph, 'fils du printemps qui naît, du matin qui se lève', is put to flight by his nocturnal counterparts:

> . . . les spectres blancs et les fantômes noirs,
> Les démons, dont l'enfer même ignore le nombre,
> Les hiboux du sépulcre et l'autour des manoirs!

Night couses the 'hideux vampire'[121] to emerge from the grave; it brings forth the manifold terrors — tongues of blue flame creeping along the ground, demons cackling in the wind — that interrupt the profane revels of the archers in the cemetery; and it transfigures the evil castle from which the benighted traveller is warned to keep his distance:

> Ces murs maudits par Dieu, par Satan profanés,
> Ce magique château dont l'enfer sait l'histoire,
> Et qui, désert le jour, quand tombe la nuit noire,
> Enflamme ses vitraux dans l'ombre illuminés![122]

A few years later, in *Notre-Dame de Paris* (1831), Hugo gave the most memorable picture of all of the sinister Romantic Middle Ages. The very first page introduces the cathedral as a place of darkness. The word 'ΑΝΑΓΚΗ' — 'ce stigmate de crime ou de malheur' — has been cut deep into the wall of one of its towers by 'une main du moyen âge'.[123] The demoniacal shadow of Quasimodo — 'Souvent, la nuit, on voyait errer une forme hideuse sur la frêle balustrade découpée en dentelle qui couronne les tours' — transforms it into a monstrous, evil presence: 'toute l'église prenait quelque chose de fantastique, de surnaturel, d'horrible . . . on eût dit que le grand portail dévorait la foule et que la rosace la regardait.'[124] And on nights when the archdeacon Frollo — a Gothic novel personage who, with his glowing eye like 'un trou percé dans la paroi d'une fournaise', closely resembles Lewis's Monk — performs his alchemical experiments in one of the towers, 'une clarté rouge,

---

[120] Ibid. pp. 435-6.
[121] Ibid. pp. 501-2.
[122] Ibid. p. 522.
[123] *Notre-Dame de Paris*, p. 3.
[124] Ibid. pp. 183-4.

intermittente, bizarre' illumines the window of his cell, causing passers-by to murmur: 'Voilà l'archidiacre qui souffle, l'enfer pétille là-haut.'[125]

At nightfall, then, in *Notre-Dame de Paris,* sunlit pageantry gives way to a world of darkness aglow here and there with Satanic fires; but the soaring spires and gilded ceilings of Gothic architecture conceal a yet more sinister realm of perpetual night: 'un palais, une forteresse, une église', Hugo tells the reader, 'avaient toujours un double fond': 'Dans les cathédrales, c'était en quelque sorte une autre cathédrale souterraine, basse, obscure, mystérieuse, aveugle et muette, sous la nef supérieure qui regorgeait de lumière et retentissait d'orgues et de cloches jour et nuit; quelquefois c'était un sépulcre.' Beneath the Louvre and the Palais de Justice is a vast subterranean hive of prison cells, 'autant de zones où s'échelonnaient les nuances de l'horreur'. The deepest of all these *oubliettes* is the *in-pace,* 'un cul de basse-fosse à fond de cuve où Dante a mis Satan, où la société mettait le condamné à mort'.[126] And the whole of Paris lies in the shadow of Montfaucon, a colossal gibbet which also conceals another world, more hideous still, beneath its foundations: the charnel-house where innumerable corpses, including, at the last, those of Esmeralda and Quasimodo, moulder away together.

(v) *Polemical use of the sinister Middle Ages: Mérimée, Ampère*
Although Hugo stated that he wrote *Notre-Dame* in order to recreate – and, presumably, to condemn – 'le moyen âge sacerdotal',[127] the

---

[125] *Notre-Dame de Paris,* pp. 191-2. This infernal red glow reappears in the torture-chamber filled with 'rouges réverbérations' to which Esmeralda is taken in a later chapter: 'La herse de fer qui servait à fermer le four . . . ne laissait voir, à l'orifice du soupirail flamboyant sur le mur ténébreux, que l'extrémité inférieure de ses barreaux, comme une rangée de dents noires. . . . La sanglante lueur de la fournaise n'éclairait dans toute la chambre qu'un fouillis de choses horribles' (pp. 359-60); in the cathedral itself, where Frollo, maddened by remorse, seeks solace from the public breviary, which, however, is illumined by an ominous 'lueur rougeâtre' and open at a passage from the Book of Job spelling out his doom (p. 414); and in the tower – 'le point . . . le plus hideux de la truanderie' – where the inhabitants of the *Cour des Miracles* hold their nocturnal orgies: 'on reconnaissait toujours la joyeuse tour . . . à la lumière écarlate qui, rayonnant à la fois aux soupiraux, aux fenêtres, aux fissures des murs lézardés, s'échappait pour ainsi dire de tous ses pores' (p. 455). Reproduced by, e.g., Dumas in *La Tour de Nesle* (1832), Act 2, Scene 2, where the tower, on nights when the queen entertains her doomed lovers there, is 'cette grande masse immobile, jetant par intervalles du feu de toutes ses ouvertures comme un soupirail de l'enfer'; and by Roger de Beauvoir in *L'Écolier de Cluny* (1832), where Buridan is lured into the same tower and seduced by Jeanne de Bourgogne ('En ce moment, le lit rougeâtre de clarté lui apparut. "L'enfer!" cria-t-il. – "L'enfer à deux!" reprit-elle' (*L'Écolier de Cluny,* 1832, i, 132-3)) – it became part of the stock-in-trade of the sinister Romantic and – as we shall see – post-Romantic Middle Ages.

[126] Ibid. pp. 367-8.   [127] *Victor Hugo raconté par un témoin de sa vie,* Ch. LVI.

sinister Middle Ages which we have just examined must not be confused with dramatic recreations of the period written as political or anti-clerical propaganda. These were of rare occurrence in Romantic writing. The Gothic novel, anti-clerical though it was, aimed to arouse an aesthetic *frisson,* rather than moral indignation, in the reader. When the hero of Mrs. Radcliffe's *Romance of the Forest* ventures into the ruined abbey, that 'repaire de la superstition', he feels 'une sorte d'impression sublime, mêlée de terreur'.[128] And Hugo recognized that *Notre-Dame de Paris* was not primarily a work of historical reconstruction, but rather '[une] oeuvre d'imagination, de caprice et de fantaisie'.[129]

Moral censure of the Middle Ages was of course a tradition of long standing. Outrage at feudal tyranny had blinded the *philosophes* to the more picturesque aspects of the age. '[Ces] tournois ... c'était le peuple qui les payait', declared Voltaire.[130] Even Sainte-Palaye spoke of 'des siècles de débauche, de brigandage, de barbarie et d'horreur',[131] and mentioned the existence of 'des chevaliers souillés de crimes'.[132] We have seen that certain liberal Romantics extolled medieval men for their independent spirit and virile hardihood; but some still saw them through the *philosophes'* eyes. For these liberals, the sinister dwellings of their feudal forefathers,

> Ces forteresses crénelées
> Jetant leurs ombres dentelées
> Sur les vassaux glacés d'effroi,[133]

had no compensatory awe-inspiring quality. This view was taken by Étienne-Jean Delécluze, the 'enemy of Gothic',[134] who denounced Romantic literature as '[des] efforts pour redonner la vie intellectuelle et matérielle à un monde qui n'a plus de raison d'exister',[135] and

---

[128] A. Radcliffe, op. cit. i, 31.

[129] *Victor Hugo raconté ...,* Ch. LVI. Pierre Halbwachs exaggerates, I think, in stating that Hugo's view of the past in *Notre-Dame* was a pure and simple product of his changed political beliefs: 'Il s'agit d'un Moyen Âge vu par un moderne qui rejette le passé et le noircit d'autant plus qu'il l'a plus idéalisé ... un Moyen Âge qui s'oppose trait à trait à celui que le jeune royaliste avait conçu à la suite du vicomte de Chateaubriand' (Hugo, *Os. cs.,* ed. Massin, vii (1968), pp. xxix-xxx). There is truth in this (we shall see later how in its turn the Empire cast a dark shadow over Hugo's Middle Ages), but it is not the whole truth.

[130] *Essai sur les moeurs,* Ch. XCVII ('De la Chevalerie').

[131] Sainte-Palaye, op. cit. i. 337.

[132] Ibid. p. 346.

[133] A. Bignan, 'Les Ruines de la France', *Almanach des muses,* 1830, p. 11.

[134] See R. Baschet, *E.-J. Delécluze,* 1942, Part 4, Ch. 1, 'Un ennemi du gothique'.

[135] E.-J. Delécluze, *Souvenirs de soixante années,* 1862, p. 501.

medieval architecture as a thing monstrously mis-shapen and 'mangée aux mites'.[136] His *dimanches* — for some years a rival to Nodier's Arsenal salon — were attended by such liberal Romantics as Stendhal, Mérimée, Jean-Jacques Ampère, and Ludovic Vitet. Some of these tried their hand at fictional denigration of the Middle Ages. The results, inevitably, lack vitality when compared with the truly Romantic sinister Middle Ages. Hugo's Louis XI fulminates against his subjects ('Extermine, Tristan! extermine! et que pas un n'en réchappe que pour Montfaucon . . .')[137] with far more impressive abandon than the pre-fabricated feudal tyrants of politically inspired fiction. Mérimée's play *La Jaquerie* (1828) was a diligent attempt to 'donner une idée des moeurs atroces du XIVe siècle'[138] (later, we shall see, he repented of this youthful *parti pris*). It re-examines, for instance, the question of those steadfast passions which were so poetic in the eyes of Chateaubriand and Marchangy. Here it is not a sentimental page, but an anguished serf, who is in love with the lord's daughter — 'Je suis vilain; elle est noble!'[139] A picture is given of rapacity and bitter dissension at every level of medieval society. Jean-Jacques Ampère, despite the praise he bestowed on the Middle Ages in his essays, versified the same state of affairs in 'Le Droit de naufrage,' written in the same year, a dramatic scene inspired by the Bayeux tapestry, in which ugly strife breaks out between a group of serfs, a priest, and their overlord, all eager to lay hands on the shipwrecked Harold. Ampère's rendering of Bürger's ballad 'Der wilde Jäger' ('Le Chasseur féroce') is in the same strain:

> Meurs, vilain, meurs! que ton âme aille au diable!
> Plaisir de roi ne doit point en souffrir. . . .[140]

(vi) *Absence of mystery in the Romantic Middle Ages: picturesqueness and exuberance; exceptions: Vigny and Nerval; its decline*

We have now surveyed every province of the French Romantic Middle Ages. Whether ideal, melancholy, or sinister, it is characterized above all by a lack of mystery. These writers tended to *see* the past rather than to dream of it. Their Middle Ages conforms to Remy de Gourmont's definition of Romanticism — 'une interprétation réaliste de l'idéal'.[141]

---

[136] See Didron aîné, *Paganisme dans l'art chrétien*, 1853, p. 19.
[137] *Notre-Dame de Paris*, p. 516.
[138] Mérimée, *La Jaquerie*, ed. P. Jourda, 1931, Preface, p. 3.   [139] Ibid. p. 111.
[140] J-J. Ampère, *Littérature, voyages et poésies*, 1850, ii. 263.
[141] R. de Gourmont, *Promenades littéraires*, v (1923), 157.

We have followed them in their wanderings through Gothic ruins, as multicoloured visions crowd in upon them. What fascinated them above all else were spectacles such as Hugo's 'Paris à vol d'oiseau',[142] or the Flemish city spread out below Bertrand's mason perched on the cathedral tower: 'Il voit les fortifications qui se découpent en étoile, la citadelle qui se rengorge comme une géline dans un tourteau . . . les cloîtres des monastères où l'ombre tourne autour des piliers.'[143] Sainte-Beuve praised Bertrand's evocations for 'l'exquise curiosité pittoresque du vocabulaire'. 'Tout cela est vu et saisi à la loupe', he remarked.[144] Bertrand's chief concern was with the visible. The same could be said of Gautier's early poems on the Middle Ages. Colours and shapes – the 'fantasques dessins' of stained glass,[145] the 'fantastiques fleurs' of illuminated manuscripts,[146] Gothic architecture, with its

> Cent colonnes découpées
> Par de bizarres ciseaux,[147]

– endlessly enchant his eye.

Exuberance is a major attribute of this feast for the eyes which the Romantic Middle Ages provided. In speaking of its ideal side, we saw that teeming life and rich diversity were what attracted the Romantics to the period. This diversity never failed to captivate them, whatever form it took – beautiful, grotesque, or horrific: the myriad creatures of Gothic superstition, Nodier's 'fantastique riant'[148] – *sylphides, ondines, follets, lutins,* and the like –, or its infernal counterpart – 'les vampires, les ogres, les aulnes, les psylles, les goules, les brucolaques, les aspioles',[149] perpetuated in the countless legendary beasts of the Gothic cathedral:

> Dogues hurlant au bout des gouttières, tarasques,
> Guivres et basilics, dragons et nains fantasques.[150]

The same exuberant life swarms in the Cour des Miracles – 'un nouveau monde, inconnu, inouï, difforme, reptile, fourmillant, fantastique',[151]

---

[142] *Notre-Dame de Paris,* Bk. 3, Ch. 2.
[143] *Gaspard de la Nuit,* pp. 35-6.
[144] Ibid. p. xxv.
[145] Gautier, *Poésies complètes,* i. 4.
[146] Ibid. p. 45.
[147] Ibid. p. 32.
[148] See E.M. Schenck, op. cit. p. 67.
[149] *Préface de 'Cromwell',* pp. 204-5.
[150] Gautier, op. cit. ii. 149.
[151] *Notre-Dame de Paris,* p. 98.

and manifests itself throughout *Notre-Dame de Paris* – in Louis XI's
sinister jocularity, in the spate of picturesque oaths let forth by Captain
Phoebus: 'Sang-Dieu! ventre-Dieu! bédieu! corps de Dieu! nombril de
Belzébuth! nom d'un pape! corne et tonnerre!'[152] (The Romantics
attempted to recreate it for a brief space in their own century, in the
'Fête des Truands' held by Gautier, Nerval and their friends in 1835.)[153]
Irresistible exuberance characterizes the galloping, triumphal rhythms of
Hugo's 'Chasse du Burgrave' and 'Pas d'armes du Roi Jean', each
announcing a joyous departure:

> Çà, qu'on selle,
> Ecuyer,
> Mon fidèle
> Destrier.
> Mon coeur ploie
> Sous la joie,
> Quand je broie
> L'étrier.[154]

This impertinent gaiety of the *Ballades* is matched in *Gaspard de la nuit*
by a certain astringency of tone, a malicious, mocking note which one
catches in the 'rires moqueurs' of the salamander at the unsuccessful
alchemist,[155] and the burst of laughter, more disconcerting still, from
the gargoyle which interrupts the author in his inspection of Dijon
cathedral: 'La figure de pierre avait ri, – ri d'un rire grimaçant,
effroyable, infernal, mais – sarcastique, incisif, pittoresque.'[156]

So, despite the fact that some of the medieval era's attraction for
French Romantic writers lay in 'L'obscurité mystérieuse dont elle est
enveloppée',[157] their almost exclusive concern with the visual and the
picturesque, together with their lack of seriousness and lightness of
touch,[158] robbed of a large part of its mystery the Middle Ages

---

[152] Ibid. p. 327.
[153] See L. Maigron, *Le Romantisme et la mode*, 1911, pp. 164-6.
[154] Hugo, *Oeuvres poétiques*, i. 528-9.
[155] *Gaspard de la nuit*, p. 51.
[156] Ibid. p. 18.
[157] Nodier (1824), quoted by Larat, op. cit. p. 162.
[158] Noted by A. M. Killen at the dawn of French Romanticism, in the *troubadour*
poetry influenced by the Gothic novel (see Killen, op. cit. p. 147). Paul
Zumthor, in his essay 'Le Moyen Âge de Victor Hugo' (Hugo, *Os. cs.*, ed.
Massin, iv (1967)), makes some interesting remarks on this aspect of Hugo's
early work: *Odes et ballades* and *Notre-Dame de Paris*. He sees in them '[des]
jeux d'humour' and a ' "détachement" ironique' which disappear in Hugo's
later work inspired by the Middle Ages, with a consequent gain in epic
power (see especially pp. xi-xii, pp. xxv-xxvi).

recreated by them. The haunting, unearthly quality of German *lieder*, revealed to the French by Mme de Staël, who appreciated in them 'cette veine de superstition qui conduit si loin dans le fond du coeur',[159] appealed very strongly to them: Dumas records in his *Mémoires* the intoxicating effect which the 'terrible refrain' of Bürger's Lénore − 'Hourra! les morts vont vite!' − had upon him when he first heard it in 1820.[160] Goethe's 'Roi des aulnes' ('Qui passe donc si tard à travers la vallée?')[161] was also extremely popular at this time. Some of the mysterious atmosphere of these *lieder* passed into Hugo's *Ballades* − 'A un passant', for example:

> Voyageur, qui, la nuit, sur le pavé sonore
> De ton chien inquiet passes accompagné,
> Après le jour brûlant, pourquoi marcher encore?
> Où mènes-tu si tard ton cheval résigné?[162]

and 'La Légende de la nonne', with its magic stairways confounding the two guilty spectres condemned for eternity to seek each other in vain; but in general the French Romantics failed to understand the true nature of the German *lied*, reducing it to a Nodiéresque fanciful whimsicality, or overlaying it with picturesque *enjolivements* − as Edmond Duméril has pointed out in his work on French adaptations of the genre.[163]

One may say, then, that their Middle Ages remained for the most part at the stage of picturesque historical evocation. They produced nothing comparable with Keats' 'Belle Dame sans merci' (1820), Tennyson's 'Lady of Shalott' (1832), or Browning's 'Childe Roland to the Dark Tower came' (1852), which all made a subjective use of medieval backgrounds corresponding with the poet's mood, with a hauntingly mysterious, rather than picturesque, effect. Important exceptions to this, however, are Vigny's above-mentioned 'Le Cor' − an excellent poem in which precise description of scene and event dissolves into an *état d'âme* with endless reverberations − and the work of Gérard de Nerval.

Nerval was, according to Duméril, the first to reach in translation the spirit of German *lieder*, as, alone among his fellow-Romantics, he was an 'auditif' rather than a 'visuel'.[164] His sonnet 'El Desdichado' (1853), with its subtly medieval atmosphere −

[159] *De l'Allemagne*, ii, 63-4.
[160] A. Dumas, *Mes mémoires*, ed. Josserand, i (1954), 455.
[161] H. de Latouche's translation, *Tablettes romantiques*, 1823, pp. 55-7.
[162] Hugo, op. cit. p. 521.
[163] *Le Lied allemand et ses traductions poétiques en France*, 1933.
[164] Op. cit. p. 146.

Je suis le ténébreux, − le veuf, − l'inconsolé,
Le prince d'Aquitaine à la tour abolie . . .

− was inspired by his belief that he was descended from the three mysterious '*Labrunie* ou *Brunyer de la Brunie,* chevaliers *d'Othon* empereur d'Allemagne', possessors of 'les trois anciennes tours de Labrunie' in the Périgord,[165] by Scott's dispossessed knight in *Ivanhoe,* and by various tarot cards − the 'prince of Darkness', the 'Blasted Tower' and the 'Star'. It is both the last Romantic poem of medieval inspiration, and the first to use medieval colouring for purely subjective ends, as a symbol of the poet's personal destiny.[166] The sonnet can be compared with certain poems of Baudelaire:

Je suis comme le roi d'un pays pluvieux ('Spleen'),

and

Mon esprit est pareil à la tour qui succombe
Sous les coups du bélier infatigable et lourd
('Chant d'Automne').

But consideration of these poems takes us into the distant future of Verlaine and his Symbolist followers. We must end our survey of the purely Romantic phase of enthusiasm for the Middle Ages with a brief glance at its decline.

This had already begun in the late 1820s. A *Mercure de France* article declared in 1827: 'Châtelains et châtelaines qui étiez nos aïeux, qui viviez dans nos livres, vous avez eu votre règne. Nous disons adieu aux siècles chevaleresques. Ils sont beaux mais ils sont morts. . . . Soyons de notre temps!'[167] It was now (in the words of Michelet) 'le brillant matin de juillet',[168] and the turn of the political tide was bringing about widespread disaffection from the Middle Ages. Although the 1830s witnessed an outbreak of 'fureur gothique' among the general public − the fashion for 'robes à la châtelaine', 'manches à gigot', and 'toques à créneaux', and for 'ameublements gothiques'[169]−, writers were satiated with a theme that had been exploited to excess, especially by the innumerable imitators of

[165] See J. Richer, *Nerval, expérience et création,* 1963, p. 33.
[166] Cf. 'A Alexandre Dumas' (1844): 'Ainsi, moi . . . le prince ignoré, l'amant mystérieux, le déshérité, le banni de liesse, le beau ténébreux . . .' (*Oeuvres,* 1960, i, 151-2). See also K. Schärer, *Thématique de Nerval ou le monde recomposé,* 1968, pp. 101-2.
[167] Quoted by Jacoubet, *Le Genre troubadour et les origines françaises du romantisme,* 1929, p. 255.
[168] Michelet, *Histoire de France* (1869 Preface), i (1879), 4.
[169] See Maigron's excellent account of this vogue in *Le Romantisme et la mode,* 1911.

Notre-Dame de Paris in the two or three years following its publication. Chateaubriand exclaimed in 1833 to Didron, who had confided in him his resolve – inspired by the *Génie du Christianisme* and *Notre-Dame de Paris* – to dedicate his life to the exclusive study of the Middle Ages: 'Oh mon Dieu! . . . on l'a déjà trop étudié ce moyen âge, on a trop fait de poésie là-dessus.'[170] Two years before this Edgar Quinet had declared them 'déjà lieu commun' as a literary theme:[171] he wrote in the Preface to *Ahasvérus* (1833) that the new generation had fallen prey to 'une étrange maladie': 'Ce n'est plus, comme la tienne, René, celle des ruines; la nôtre est plus vive et plus cuisante. . . . C'est le mal de l'avenir.'[172]

By the opening years of the next decade, what Gautier's exasperated critic in the Preface of *Mademoiselle de Maupin* (1834) called 'ce moyen-âge qui n'est pas le moyen-âge'[173] was virtually defunct. It lingered on·in the spectral presence of Roger de Beauvoir, former leading light of the 'école mâchicoulis' and author of *L'Écolier de Cluny* (1832), who came to grief in 1842 at a fancy dress ball which he attended in his suit of armour. 'Pour être tout à fait "moyen âge"', records Maxime Du Camp in his memoirs, he had imprudently lowered the visor of his helmet, with the result that he fainted during a waltz, falling 'avec le fracas d'un tuyau de poêle abattu par le vent'.[174] The Romantic Middle Ages was amusingly commemorated the following year by Louis Reybaud in the second part of his satire on the follies of the recent past, *Jérôme Paturot à la recherche d'une position sociale*. Paturot falls into the clutches of an 'architecte chevelu' whom he has commissioned to build him a 'maison moyen âge'. He is plagued unmercifully by the demands of this energumen: 'En entrant dans votre maison, je veux que vous respiriez le moyen âge. . . . D'abord, salle d'attente. C'est là que vous déposez, en entrant, le hoqueton et la pertuisane. . . . Et les vitraux de couleur, ne les oublions pas. . . . Et les bahuts! Avez-vous songé aux bahuts? . . .[175] Et les clochetons? '[176] Although the architect is well satisfied with his work – 'Non, Pâques-Dieu! on n'a jamais attrapé l'ogive *rutilante* à ce degré! c'est mieux que les originaux!' – and with his enormous fee, which contributes in large measure to

---

[170] *Annales archéologiques,* xv (1855), 113.
[171] E. Quinet, *Lettres à sa mère,* ii, 178.
[172] E. Quinet, *Ahasvérus,* nouvelle édition, 1843, p. x.
[173] T. Gautier, *Préface de 'Mlle de Maupin',* ed. G. Matoré, 1946, pp. 18-19.
[174] M. Du Camp, *Souvenirs littéraires,* i (1882), 190.
[175] L. Reybaud, *Jérôme Paturot à la recherche d'une position sociale et politique,* ii (1843), 208-9.
[176] Ibid. p. 224.

Paturot's ruin, the house, when finished, is 'souverainement ridicule'.[177]

At this low point in its fortunes, it is time for us to take leave of the Romantic Middle Ages, but we have by no means seen the last of it. We shall be encountering many of its aspects again — both ideal and sinister — in the course of our inquiry into the fate of the Middle Ages as a literary theme in the second half of the nineteenth century; for, initially, it is the fate of the Romantic Middle Ages which is at stake.

[177] Ibid. iii (1843), 162. Cases recounted by Maigron (op. cit. pp. 125-36) show that there was very little exaggeration in Reybaud's satire.

SECTION ONE: 1851–1870

CHAPTER 2

LOUIS NAPOLEON AND THE MIDDLE AGES

'Nos pères furent des grands hommes;
S'ils étaient braves, nous le sommes' (Belmontet)

The Second Empire is generally thought of as a period of artistic eclecticism, indulging in a masquerade of historical styles, the product of a debased and spent Romanticism.[1] Louis Napoleon himself, it has been said, inherited the 'moyenâgeux' tastes of his mother Queen Hortense, composer in 1809 of the celebrated 'troubadour' *romance* 'Partant pour la Syrie' or 'le Beau Dunois'.[2]

Although interest in the Middle Ages was only one among various more or less frivolous historical enthusiasms of the Emperor and his court, and had to take its place with Gallo-Roman antiquities, the life of Caesar, and hunting in the forest of Compiègne attired in Louis-XV costume, it remains a fact that the Empire saw itself on occasion as an age of chivalry revived. In this, of course, it followed the example of its predecessors — the First Empire, the Restoration, and the July Monarchy — who all, in the words of Paul Léon, sought 'dans le respect du passé, dans le culte de l'ancienne France, les garanties de stabilité qui manquaient à [leurs] origines'.[3] We shall see presently that official government promotion of medieval scholarship was largely a continuation of enterprises initiated in Louis-Philippe's reign, during which

---

[1] See H. Bouchot, *Les Élégances du Second Empire*, Librairie illustrée, 1896, pp. x-xiii. In literature, as Romanticism ebbed, historical settings tended to become semi-conventional, selected half-cynically, with the public in mind. This was already happening in the 1840s (Sainte-Beuve asked in 1843: 'N'en est-il pas aujourd'hui de certaines époques historiques comme du parc de Maisons? on les découpe, on les met en lots' (*Portraits contemporains*, Didier, 1855, ii. 334-5); it reached its height during the Empire and was denounced by Laurent-Pichat, an opponent of the regime, in *Les Poètes du combat* (1862, p. 8): 'Quel est ce bazar et quelles sont ces bijouteries étalées? . . . A quoi servent . . . ces paillettes de tous les siècles qui miroitent à nos regards et font froid aux yeux?' Even Flaubert wrote in 1856 that he would soon be able to 'fournir du moderne, du moyen âge et de l'antiquité', now that he had finished *Madame Bovary* and was working on *La Légende de Saint Julien* and *La Tentation de Saint Antoine* (*Correspondance*, iv, 105).

[2] Sarcastic mention of the Emperor's 'troubadour' tastes is made by Hugo in *Napoléon le Petit* (1852), which refers, e.g., to his participation in the Eglinton Castle Tournament of 1839 (*Napoléon le Petit*, 1964, p. 45). See also Bouchot, op. cit. pp. 113-14: P. Berret, *Le Moyen Âge dans la 'Légende des siècles'*, pp. 76-7; and L. Grodecki, *Le Château de Pierrefonds*, n.d.

[3] P. Léon, *La Vie des monuments français*, 1951, p. 115.

Romantic enthusiasm for the past had been converted into practical activity.

In his attempt to give inherited institutions a fresh political complexion appropriate to the Imperial regime, and in several new projects which he set in motion, Louis Napoleon was given to hark back to the Middle Ages. Anxious to create a climate of nationalism modelled on that of the First Empire, when epic poems extolling Charlemagne were produced in scores, he encouraged reverence for 'nos antiquités nationales'. Inevitably, attempted expression of this 'new' spirit had a stale, factitious, *troubadour* flavour. Maxime Du Camp states that if Queen Hortense's air 'Partant pour la Syrie' attained the status of a national anthem during the Second Empire, it was against the will of the Emperor, who each time he heard it 'avait un fléchissement d'épaules qui était plus éloquent que toutes les paroles'.[4] However, in his speech to the expeditionary force leaving for Syria in 1860 to avenge a massacre of Maronite Christians, he proclaimed: 'Vous partez pour la Syrie . . . Sur cette terre lointaine, riche en grands souvenirs . . . vous vous montrerez les dignes enfants de ces héros qui ont porté glorieusement dans ce pays la bannière du Christ.'[5] An anonymous pamphlet reached the conclusion: 'Napoléon III n'est pas seulement l'Empereur des Français, il est le chef de la dernière croisade . . . comme à une autre époque; la France dit à son souverain: "Dieu le veut! Dieu le veut!" '[6] The earlier Crimean compaign had also taken on the nature of a crusade. The soldiers of the Second Empire, like those of the Restoration hymned by the youthful Victor Hugo, were a race of fearless 'preux' riding forth into battle. They, however, had no Hugo to sing their praises — only the Empire's official bard, Louis Belmontet, whose loyalty to the Imperial family in its hour of adversity had earned him the title of Queen Hortense's 'Blondel'. His 'Chant des braves' was composed in 1854:

> La France adore les batailles.
> Les preux nouveaux auront les tailles
> De ceux d'hier
> Au coeur si fier.
> Nos pères furent des grands hommes;
> S'ils étaient braves, nous le sommes.[7]

[4] M. Du Camp, *Souvenirs d'un demi-siècle,* 1949, i. 131.
[5] T. Delord, *Histoire du Second Empire,* iii (1873), 31.
[6] *La Question d'Orient,* Dentu, 1860, p. 48.
[7] L. Belmontet, *Poésies guerrières,* 1858, p. 73.

In the same year, Sainte-Beuve, writing about Villehardouin in the *Moniteur,* defended with great fervour the French Crusaders of the twelfth century against Daunou's Voltairian depreciation of them in Volume XVII of the *Histoire littéraire de la France* (1832)[8] In 1856 the Comité de la Langue, de l'Histoire, et des Arts de la France decided to publish a 'Recueil de documents originaux sur la domination française en Orient pendant le moyen âge'.[9] This project came to nothing. In 1859-60 Alfred Delvau published a new version of the *Bibliothèque Bleue* in monthly instalments, several of which bore on their back cover his explanation for the popularity of the series — its topicality:

> Où pourrait-on voir . . . une plus grandiose analogie qu'entre les prouesses épiques des chevaliers du Moyen-Âge, des preux du roi Artus et du roi Charlemagne, et les héroïques faits d'armes de nos soldats. . . . C'est la même fougue, la même vaillance . . . le même bonheur aussi, il faut le dire avec empressement. Là et là, ce sont des héros qui combattent et qui vainquent. Le *Moniteur* inscrit les noms des champions modernes: La *Bibliothèque Bleue* enregistre les titres des champions d'autrefois.[10]

The medievalist Mary-Lafon brought out in 1857 a translation of *Fierabras* illustrated by Doré, and ventured to suggest in his Preface:

> Pourquoi la politique ne profiterait-elle point, dans l'intérêt de la France, des découvertes de la philologie? . . . Pourquoi ne montrerait-on pas dans cette épopée chevaleresque la grande figure de Charlemagne aux Arabes d'Afrique . . . qui verraient probablement, avec leur foi fataliste . . . le doigt d'Allah dans la soumission et le baptême du plus brillant de leurs héros? . . . Dans ce fait si étrangement remarquable, du Fierabras de la légende s'agenouillant aux pieds de Charlemagne et de l'Abd-el-Kader de l'histoire s'agenouillant devant Napoléon, n'y a-t-il pas de quoi frapper des imaginations moins impressionnables que celles des Arabes?[11]

A. *Hippolyte Fortoul and medieval studies*

Louis Napoleon's first Minister of Education, Hippolyte Fortoul,[12] who held office from 1851 to 1856, was something of a medievalist, having in 1842 published a study of Holbein's 'Dance of Death' and an essay 'De la littérature antique au moyen âge'. His revision (by a Decree

---

[8] *Causeries du Lundi,* ix.
[9] *Bulletin du Comité de la Langue, de l'Histoire, et des Arts de la France,* iii (1857), p. 136.
[10] *Bibliothèque Bleue,* ed. A. Delvau, nos. 7-17. 1859.
[11] Mary-Lafon, *Fierabras,* 1857, p. xiii.
[12] For an interesting account of Fortoul's career see X. Marmier, *Journal,* ed. E. Kaye, Geneva, 1968, i. 206-8.

of April 1852) of the syllabus to be followed in lycées, including suppression of the study of philosophy, which was to be replaced by logic — 'lorsque l'intelligence n'est pas encore formée, ces recherches intempestives ne produisent que la vanité et le doute',[13] he declared —, aroused fierce opposition.[14] In a speech delivered at the Concours Général des Lycées in 1854, he went as far as to proclaim:

[Les] traditions de nos anciennes Universités . . . ont inspiré . . . les réformes que le Gouvernement de l'Empereur a apportées dans vos études . . . Les lettres et les sciences . . . ont formé une alliance nouvelle. Ne craignons pas de saluer ces bienfaitrices du monde moderne sous le nom que le moyen âge leur avait consacré: le *Trivium* et le *Quadrivium* se retrouvent, rajeunis et rapprochés, dans l'enceinte agrandie de nos colléges.[15]

Other measures taken by him to enlist the Middle Ages in the service of the modern Empire were less controversial. The first one was the publication of a 'Recueil des poésies populaires de la France', ordered by a Decree of September 1852.[16] In his 'Rapport au Prince-Président', Fortoul declared: 'Fondateur d'un Gouvernement qui aime à s'appuyer sur la fidélité des souvenirs poétiques du peuple, vous avez voulu, Monseigneur, conserver avec respect les chants qui rappellent les luttes héroïques de nos pères et les joies paisibles de leurs foyers domestiques'; and expressed the hope that 'au contact de l'expression naïve du vieil esprit français, notre littérature se surprendra peut-être à rougir des fausses délicatesses où s'égare parfois sa subtilité.'[17] He referred again to the Decree in the following year: 'Encourager les recherches qui, en reportant les esprits vers les anciennes et glorieuses traditions de la patrie, contribuent à relever le sentiment national, c'était un but digne de la sollicitude d'un prince dont le pays tout entier venait d'édifier le pouvoir par ses unanimes suffrages.'[18] But although the Comité de la Langue, de l'Histoire, et des Arts spent a large part of its sessions sifting through material which

---

[13] *Réforme de l'enseignement . . . pendant le ministère de M. H. Fortoul,* 1856, i. 36.

[14] It was restored to the syllabus by the liberal Minister of Education, Victor Duruy, in 1863.

[15] Ibid. ii. 247.

[16] This project was originally conceived during the First Empire, revived by Louis-Philippe's minister Salvandy, and interrupted by the events of 1848. See P. Bénichou, *Nerval et la chanson folklorique,* 1970, pp. 49-52.

[17] Ibid. i. 274.

[18] Ibid. i, xciii ('Rapport à l'Empereur sur la situation de l'instruction publique depuis le 2 décembre 1851').

poured in for several years from correspondents in every *département,* the 'Recueil' was never published.[19]

The next measure taken by Fortoul was the creation in January 1853 of a Chair of Medieval French Language and Literature at the Collège de France. Paulin Paris, its first incumbent, delivered a spirited inaugural lecture, concluding with the words: 'Salut donc, Messieurs, à notre moyen âge . . . salut à la vieille muse nationale.'[20] (It was not until 1882 that a similar chair was founded at the Sorbonne.)

A considerable amount of work in the field of medieval scholarship had been published in the 1830s and 40s; this activity continued throughout the Second Empire.[21] Many texts were published in the *Bibliothèque Elzévirienne* series begun by Jannet in 1853. Luzarche brought out the first edition of the *Mystère d'Adam* in 1854. 1859 saw the publication of Campaux' study of Villon's life and work, Lenient's *La Satire en France au moyen âge,* and the first volume in Célestin Hippeau's *Collection des poètes français du moyen âge* (1859-77). In 1865 Gaston Paris's *Histoire poétique de Charlemagne,* Natalis de Wailly's very successful modern version of Joinville's *Histoire de saint Louis,* and the first volume of Léon Gautier's *Les Épopées françaises* were published. The first volume of Paulin Paris's *Les Romans de la Table Ronde mis en nouveau langage* came out in 1868. Four new volumes of the *Histoire littéraire de la France* were published during the Empire. The first three were of major importance: Volumes 22 and 23 (1852 and 1856) contained some of Paulin Paris's best work on *chansons de geste* and lyric poetry, Littré on the *romans d'aventure,* and Victor Le Clerc on the *fabliaux;* Volume 24 (1862), with the Introduction to the fourteenth century, comprised Victor Le Clerc's *Discours sur l'état des lettres* and Renan's *Discours sur l'état des beaux-arts.* Another important work was the first edition, by Guessard and E. de Certain, of the *Mistère du siège d'Orléans* (in the *Collection des documents inédits relatifs à l'histoire de*

[19] Nevertheless Fortoul's Decree, and Jean-Jacques Ampère's 'Instructions' (1853) resulting from it, mark an important landmark in French folklore studies. See Bénichou, op. cit. pp. 170-3.

[20] P. Paris, *Collège de France: Cours de langue et de littérature françaises du moyen âge, discours d'ouverture, Ier mars 1853,* p. 19.

[21] For an account of medieval studies under Louis-Philippe and Louis Napoleon see L. Gautier, *Les Épopées françaises,* 2nd edn., ii (1892), Ch. XV; the *Rapport sur les progrès des études classiques et du moyen âge,* 1868; and A. Jeanroy, 'Les Études sur la littérature française du moyen âge': (1) 'Du XVIe siècle à 1914', in *La Science française* ii (1933).

France, 1862), addressed in the Preface to 'tous ceux qu'intéressent les grands souvenirs de la patrie'.[22]

When new ventures were attempted, government-sponsored work in the medieval field was of a somewhat hesitant nature. In the early 1850s the Comité de la Langue, de l'Histoire, et des Arts planned to publish a collection of Provençal epic poetry, but it was brought to their notice that much of the work had already been done, or was about to be done, and the project was abandoned, to the fury of Mary-Lafon who had been chosen as editor. In 1854 Victor Le Clerc issued some instructions to correspondents of the Comité, in which he urged the publication of as many *chansons de geste* as possible. 'De telles publications', he observed, 'intéressent . . . l'honneur de l'esprit français.'[23] Two years later, Fortoul issued a Decree ordering the publication of a *Recueil des anciens poëtes français:* 'Faire revivre notre ancienne littérature', he declared, 'est un soin digne du règne où l'on a revu les entreprises et les caractères chevaleresques dont elle fut l'expression. . . . Quelles inspirations même l'imagination ne pourrait-elle pas puiser à ces sources primitives, d'où sont émanées de si puissantes, de si généreuses conceptions!'[24]

Guessard was given charge of this project: with Léon Gautier and Michelant, he was sent to Italy and Switzerland to copy manuscripts. Fortoul in his enthusiasm envisaged the publication of all medieval French literature in verse form written before 1328, in sixty Elzévirienne volumes of sixty thousand lines each. 'Publiez tout, *tout,* TOUT!' he wrote in the margin of a report sent in by Guessard.[25] However, he died in 1856 and his successor Rouland limited the project to the Carolingian cycle, to be published in forty volumes of ten thousand lines each. In fact the *Recueil,* terminated by the outbreak of war, formed a series of ten volumes, *Les Anciens Poètes de la France* (1858-70).

Official verbiage redirecting the nation towards chivalric tradition continued to flow forth – the Comte de Persigny, in a speech given before the Société historique et archéologique du Forez, proclaimed: 'La préoccupation exclusive des intérêts matériels serait un danger pour l'esprit, un désenchantement pour l'âme, si la contemplation des temps chevaleresques et religieux ne réveillait sans cesse en nous les traditions

---

[22] *Le Mistère du siège d'Orléans,* ed. F. Guessard and E. de Certain, Imprimerie Impériale, 1862, p. i.
[23] *Réforme de l'enseignement,* op. cit. ii. 191.
[24] Ibid. p. 1168.
[25] L. Gautier, *Les Épopées françaises,* 2nd edn., ii (1892), 737.

d'honneur et de dévouement'[26]; and, towards the end of the Empire, one last measure was taken to foster medieval studies: the creation by Duruy of the École Pratique des Hautes Études, where Gaston Paris was entrusted with the teaching of Old French.

B. *Viollet-le-Duc and Gothic architecture*

The Emperor's personal interest in medieval architecture, in his patronage of Viollet-le-Duc, attracted far more public attention than his government's attempts to promote the study of medieval literature.

Here again, the Empire witnessed the continuation and completion of work set in motion in the 1830s and 40s. Hugo's *Guerre aux démolisseurs*! (1825-32), and Montalembert's articles published during the 1830s, had publicized the plight of France's ancient buildings; Arcisse de Caumont published his *Cours d'antiquités monumentales* in 1830, and founded the Société française d'Archéologie in 1834; in 1830 the government created the post of Inspecteur des Monuments Historiques for Ludovic Vitet, who was succeeded by Mérimée in 1834;[27] the Commission des Monuments Historiques was created in 1837; in 1843 the Hôtel de Cluny, with Du Sommerard's collection, was bought by the State, and a year later opened to the public; the militant Napoléon Didron founded the *Annales archéologiques* with its 'Chronique du vandalisme' in 1844, his publishing-house specializing in works defending medieval art in 1845, and his workshops producing stained glass for church restoration in 1849. The Empire saw the completion of various ambitious architectural projects begun in the 1840s. In 1840 Viollet-le-Duc, backed by Mérimée, was given his first major job by the Commission: the restoration of Vézelay, completed in 1859. In 1841 Lassus was appointed to restore the Sainte-Chapelle. In the years that followed, new angels and apostles were sculptured for it; and Lassus's spire was erected in 1853. Viollet-le-Duc and Lassus began the restoration of Notre-Dame in 1845; the central spire designed by Viollet was erected in 1859,[28] and the restoration was completed in 1864. One new enterprise carried out under the Empire was the restoration by Ballu of the Tour Saint-Jacques (1853-5), refurbished

---

[26] *Le Duc de Persigny et les doctrines de l'Empire,* Plon, 1865, pp. 312-13.
[27] For a useful account of Mérimée's career as Inspecteur des Monuments Historiques see A. W. Raitt, *Prosper Mérimée,* 1970, Ch. VIII.
[28] Hugo had lamented the disappearance of these two spires in *Notre-Dame de Paris* (Bk. 3, Ch. 1, p. 128).

with its full complement of saints, angels, and winged beasts.

In Paris, the work of restoration proceeded side by side with the demolition of many medieval buildings. The Second Empire has been called the age of 'le vandalisme urbaniste d'Haussmann et le vandalisme restaurateur de Viollet-le-Duc'.[29] Mérimée is reported to have made the comment: 'La façon dont Haussmann a traité le vieux Paris équivaut à un massacre de la France médiévale. Eh bien! c'est partout une jubilation. Un peu plus et on danserait autour des chantiers, comme les nègres autour d'un scalp.'[30] Louis Veuillot complained in *Les Odeurs de Paris* (1866): 'Les vieux monuments même qui restent debout ne disent plus rien, parce que tout a changé autour d'eux. Notre-Dame et la Tour Saint-Jacques ne sont pas plus à leur place que l'Obélisque, et semblent aussi bien avoir été apportées d'ailleurs comme de vaines curiosités.'[31]

The Emperor's patronage of Viollet-le-Duc and his work of restoration aroused as much criticism as Haussmann's work of destruction. Admirers of Gothic considered that Viollet, the enemy of ruins, who desired to see all ancient buildings restored to unblemished newness, was as guilty of disrespect for the Middle Ages as those who tore down Gothic churches to make way for modern thoroughfares. Viollet's career entered its most active phase during the Empire. His *Dictionnaire raisonné de l'architecture française* began to appear in 1854; the *Dictionnaire du mobilier* followed in 1858. He carried out restorations such as that of Carcassonne, begun in 1852, and looked upon with particular favour by the Emperor, whose interest in medieval buildings was mainly concentrated on military fortifications.[32] Viollet employed multitudes of workmen on sites throughout the country. In January 1852 he told a correspondent that his work was playing an important part in the moral regeneration of the new nation:

N'oublions pas que le manque de goût a contribué pour beaucoup à la chute de la monarchie constitutionnelle. . . . Partout où nous avons pu faire exécuter des travaux en province, nous avons fait remonter la population ouvrière à un degré supérieur . . . et, nulle part, sur nos chantiers . . . même à Paris, nous n'avons eu de désordre à réprimer, car nous n'occupions pas que des bras, tant s'en faut.[33]

[29] L. Réau, *Histoire du vandalisme,* Hachette, 1959, ii, 181.
[30] F. Bac, *Mérimée inconnu,* 1939, p. 103.
[31] L. Veuillot, *Oeuvres diverses,* xi (1926), 5.
[32] See Prince Napoléon-Louis Bonaparte, *Études sur le passé et l'avenir de l'artillerie,* ii (1851), Ch. 1.
[33] E. Viollet-le-Duc, 1814-1879 (*Catalogue de l'Exposition*), 1965, p. 88.

As a personal friend of the Imperial family, Viollet had many enemies among opponents of the regime. Their hostility found an outlet in the affair of the École des Beaux-Arts. In 1863, at the instigation of Nieuwerkerke, a Decree was issued ordering the School's reorganization. Viollet, who had published a series of articles in the previous year proposing its reform, was appointed Professor of the History of Art and Aesthetics. The Decree was seen as dictatorial government intervention, and such fury was aroused among the outraged opponents of Gothic architecture — in particular Ingres and Beulé — at the entry of a 'gothique' into the School, that Viollet, who had given his first lectures in early 1864 amid uproar, was forced to resign his post.[34]

His commissions for the Imperial circle, on the other hand, were carried out in peace and earned him great approbation. In 1853, for Louis Napoleon's marriage, he decorated the façade of Notre-Dame with equestrian statues of Charlemagne and Napoleon, and a porch with panels imitating tapestries illustrating French kings and saints.[35] In 1855-7 he designed a set of railway carriages presented to the Emperor by the Compagnie des Chemins de Fer d'Orléans, and devised wrought-iron and carved-wood ornamentation for them, using the Gothic floral motifs of which he was particularly fond. Most notable of all was his work on the castle of Pierrefonds, restored at the cost of 5,000,000 francs to provide a summer residence for the Imperial family, begun in 1858 and not finished until 1870.[36] The Imperial eagle and Louis d'Orléans' porcupine were painted on the walls of the Salle de Réception. For Louis Napoleon's bedchamber Viollet executed a frieze with painted scenes from the life of a fourteenth-century noble-man. The Empress's apartment was decorated with scenes from the Round Table. Especially remarkable was the famous 'salle des Preuses', with its nine statues in the likeness of the Empress and her ladies-in-waiting. Viollet's friend and patron Mérimée is said to have disapproved of Pierrefonds: 'C'est une oeuvre', he is reported to have cautiously remarked to the Empress, 'devant laquelle je reste comme anéanti.'[37]

[34] See Mérimée, *Correspondance générale,* deuxième série, vi (1958), 41 n.
[35] Cf. Fontaine's sham Gothic décor, superimposed on the façade of Notre-Dame for Napoleon I's Coronation in 1804.
[36] Here again, Louis-Philippe had forestalled Louis Napoleon, with his banquet in the ruins of Pierrefonds (on the occasion of his daughter's marriage in 1832), for which an Aeolian harp was installed in one of the towers. Cf. also the *salles des Croisades* (opened in 1844), with the Princess Marie d'Orléans's statue of Joan of Arc, in the museum created by Louis-Philippe at Versailles.
[37] F. Bac, op. cit. p. 86.

With Pierrefonds could be mentioned Rochet's colossal equestrian group 'Charlemagne et ses Leudes', shown at the Exposition Universelle of 1867, representing Charlemagne on horseback with Roland and Ogier le Danois holding either rein.

These fitful efforts to bestow on the Second Empire an aura of past glory and medieval pomp met with a hostile reception. Fervent Ultramontane Catholic supporters of Louis Napoleon's 1849 Expedition to Rome considered that they did not go far enough. Their applause turned to reproach in the years that followed, as they lamented the Emperor's derogation from glorious medieval tradition in his failure to succour the Pope.[38] Writers of the day in opposition to the regime considered them ludicrous and, as we shall see in the next chapter, sinister. 'L'Empereur', protested Victor de Laprade in 1862, 'donne des croix, des évêchés, de l'argent pour achever en carton-pierre les cathédrales du moyen âge!'[39] Eugène Garcin, in an article of October 1869, lamented: 'Vieux us, vieilles coutumes, vieux costumes, vieilles fêtes, vieilles cavalcades, vieilles mascarades, vieilles superstitions, vieux patois: on veut ressusciter tout cela, et l'on insulte à qui combat pour l'idée contraire. Ô bouffonne revendication du gothique!'[40]

---

[38] 'Au moment même où j'écris ces lignes', wrote Léon Gautier in conclusion to his study of the Charlemagne legend, 'on achève de détruire toute l'oeuvre du fils de Pépin. . . . La Papauté, que Charlemagne avait replacée sur le trône défend en ce moment les derniers lambeaux du grand domaine dont il lui avait confirmé le présent' (L. Gautier, *Les Épopées françaises,* ii (1867), 609. Cf. also Veuillot's lament, *infra,* p. 77).

[39] *Lettres inédites de V. de Laprade a Ch. Alexandre,* ed. Séchaud, 1934, p. 63.

[40] *Revue moderne,* liv, 10 Oct. 1869, p. 507.

CHAPTER 3

CATHOLIC AND REPUBLICAN CONTROVERSY: I. MEDIEVAL ARCHITECTURE AND SOCIETY

'L'histoire ne servira à rien si on n'y met les tristesses du présent'
(Michelet)

A. Romieu's Spectre Rouge: 'J'annonce la Jacquerie . . .'

'De 1852 à 1860', a republican novel published in 1865 began, 'un voile sombre parut s'étendre sur notre beau pays. . . . Le dix-neuvième siècle sembla vouloir s'arrêter au milieu de sa course et redescendre au moyen-âge.'[1] Liberal opponents of Louis Napoleon were not content merely to deride official attempts to give his regime an aura of chivalric glory. They took every opportunity to identify the Empire with the Dark Ages and denounce it as an infamous restoration of medieval tyranny. Hugo was the first to sound the alarm: 'Le coup d'État affirme, ce qui est douteux, que nous sommes revenus à l'époque des jacqueries; ce qui est certain, c'est qu'il nous ramène au temps des croisades. César se croise pour le pape. *Diex el volt*. L'Élysée a la foi du templier, et la soif aussi.'[2]

This referred to Auguste Romieu's remarkable pamphlet, *Le Spectre Rouge de 1852*, published a few months before the *coup d'état*. A second *Jacquerie* was imminent, warned Romieu. Inflamed by socialism, 'les pauvres . . . sont prêts à ravager, par leurs millions de bras, les châteaux, les appartements luxueux. . . . [Leur] folie sera furieuse.'[3] A sworn enemy of legislative processes, Romieu declared that the only hope of salvation lay in recourse to the methods employed against the *Jacques* in the fourteenth century: 'Les gentilshommes ne nommèrent pas de *commission*, qui eût à présenter un *rapport* . . . ils se servirent de leurs longues et solides lances, et, bardés de fer comme leurs chevaux, ils eurent promptement raison de ces paysans nus.'[4] Charlemagne, carving out his empire 'à l'aide du sabre et de la hache', marching to victory 'sous son impériale bannière de foi terrible', was also held up as an example to modern rulers: 'De son oeuvre . . . sortit le régime féodal. De tous ceux que l'Europe a essayés, c'est encore le meilleur.'[5]

[1] Louise Gagneur, *La Croisade noire*, 1865, p. 11.
[2] Hugo, *Napoléon le Petit*, 1964, pp. 88-9.
[3] A. Romieu, *Le Spectre rouge de 1852*, 1851, pp. 47-8.
[4] Ibid. p. 17.
[5] *Le Spectre rouge*, pp. 31-2.

'Oh! Foi et Force!', rhapsodized Romieu, 'leviers uniques des
mouvements humains.' Beside the dispiriting spectacle of the
Assemblée Législative, with its 'crânes chauves ou blanchis' engaged
in perpetual and futile debate, he set that of the fortress of Vincennes,
'cette haute tour, qui représente les vieux temps de force.' 'Pénétrez
dans les cours', he urged his readers, 'et voyez cette longue file de
canons, ces rangées de boulets . . . ces saluts de chacun aux chefs
qui passent, cet ORDRE enfin . . . vous conviendrez que le faux est
chez vous, et le vrai dans la forteresse.'[6]

B. *Republican abuse of the Middle Ages:*
'A vous la nuit, à nous la lumière!'

Throughout the 1850s and even after the Empire had entered its
liberal phase, there was no subject which inflamed French imaginations
more than the Middle Ages, for some a lost paradise eternally to be
regretted, and for others, alarmed by the utterances of Romieu and his
ilk, a malignant presence to be combated with every weapon available.
'Ce moyen âge trop vanté et trop calomnié'[7] became a battle-ground
for Catholics and republicans. Flaubert in *Bouvard et Pécuchet* gives a
sample of banal, mechanical debate conducted between the two parties
shortly before the *coup d'état*. At a gathering of the 'notables du pays'
the priest and others express approval of the projected invasion of
England by General Changarnier –

'Vous exprimez', dit Pécuchet, 'des sentiments du moyen âge!'
'Le moyen âge avait du bon!' reprit Marescot. 'Ainsi nos cathé-
drales! . . .'
'Cependant, monsieur, les abus!'
'Ah! la Révolution, voilà le malheur!' dit l'ecclésiastique en soupi- . . .
rant . . .[8]

– and so the debate runs its predictable course.[9]

---

[6] Ibid. pp. 88-90.
[7] E. Montégut, 'Perspectives sur le temps présent', *RDM,* 1 Mar. 1855, p. 1010.
[8] *Bouvard et Pécuchet,* 1965, pp. 211-12.
[9] Cf. Flaubert and Le Poittevin's youthful impersonation of *le Garçon,* each time
they passed by Rouen cathedral: 'L'un disait aussitôt: "C'est beau, cette
architecture gothique, ça élève l'âme." Aussitôt, celui qui faisait le *Garçon*
pressait son rire et ses gestes: "Oui, c'est beau . . . et la Saint-Barthélemy aussi!
Et l'Édit de Nantes et les Dragonnades, c'est beau aussi!" ' (*Journal des Goncourt,*
ed. Ricatte, 1956, i. 729).

A liberal Catholic, Albert de Broglie, discussing in 1852 some recent works by Ultramontane defenders of the Middle Ages, exclaimed in a sudden burst of indignation:

Pour notre part, nous avouerons sans détour que, toutes les fois que nous voyons engager dans la presse contemporaine un débat sur l'excellence ou la corruption . . . de la société du moyen-âge, sur l'horreur ou l'admiration qu'elle mérite, notre premier sentiment est celui d'un profond ennui. De telles discussions nous semblent à la fois également stériles et interminables.[10]

This protest was in vain: propaganda for and against the Middle Ages from those whom Montalembert had termed in 1844 'les fils des croisés et les fils de Voltaire'[11] took on new and enduring life, as liberal opponents of the regime started their campaign against the government's alliance with the forces of reaction. Each side provoked the other into increasingly extravagant utterances of praise or blame. Violent abuse was hurled by republicans against the Middle Ages, which, they declared, were being dragged from the tomb by the Emperor and his ministers. The long-standing tradition of denigration of feudalism was effortlessly revived. A popular compilation by Charles Fellens was entitled *La Féodalité, ou les droits du seigneur. Événements mystérieux, lugubres, scandaleux; exactions, despotisme, libertinage de la noblesse et du clergé* (1850; 2nd edn. 1852). In the first month of the Empire's existence, Eugène Pelletan, one of its most energetic opponents, affirmed in a review of a new edition of Thierry's *Lettres sur l'histoire de France* that 'le siècle féodal tant admiré de l'école du césarisme, était tout uniment le monde au pillage.'[12] He exclaimed in *Le Siècle* the following year: 'Quant à moi, je n'ose retourner la tête du côté du moyen-âge. Je sens le froid de l'ombre me gagner. A vous la nuit, à nous la lumière!'[13]

(i) *Michelet: 'Il faut faire volte-face. . . .'*

Barbey d'Aurevilly, reviewing Charles Labutte's *Histoire des ducs de Normandie* in August 1855, poured scorn upon the republican historian: 'C'est un de ces pleurards historiques qui versent, sur les malheurs de l'humanité au Moyen Âge, ces larmes de crocodile qui ont toujours le même succès sur les esprits ignorants et les âmes sensibles.'[14]Rendered

---

[10] A. de Broglie, 'Le Moyen Âge et l'Église Catholique', *RDM*, 1 Nov. 1852, p. 439.
[11] Montalembert, *Oeuvres:* (1) *Discours 1837-1844*, 1860, p. 401.
[12] *La Presse*, 23 Nov. 1851.
[13] *Le Siècle*, 16-17 Aug. 1852.
[14] Barbey d'Aurevilly, *De l'histoire*, 1905, pp. 211-12.

impatient by 'la vulgarité de ces caduques malédictions',[15] Barbey
d'Aurevilly expressed the hope that one day some enemy of the Middle
Ages endowed with superior powers of invective might at last give
utterance to 'un cri énergique, une réprobation digne de ce temps
immense, quelque chose, enfin, qui aurait eu son éloquence, son
injuste, mais réelle beauté . . .'.[15] Jules Michelet's writings published
during the 1850s and 60s should have satisfied him in this respect: if not
the Introduction to the *Renaissance* (January 1855), then surely *La
Sorcière* (1862).

The remarkable shift in Michelet's attitude towards the Middle Ages,
from the 1830s to the 1860s, reflects the whole changing tide of opinion
during this period. He had been the most eloquent of those who praised
medieval society in the 1830s. 'Merveilleux système', he called it in
1831, as he lamented its passing: 'Ainsi s'accomplit en mille ans ce long
miracle du moyen âge, cette merveilleuse légende dont la trace s'efface
chaque jour de la terre.'[16] In his *Tableau de la France* (1833), speaking
of humanity at the close of the tenth century, he reaches the impassioned conclusion:

> Dans quelles douleurs elle va s'enfanter elle-même! Il faut qu'elle sue
> la sueur et le sang pour amener au monde le moyen-âge, et qu'elle le voie
> mourir, quand elle l'a si long-temps élevé, nourri, caressé. Triste enfant,
> arraché des entrailles même du christianisme, qui naquit dans les larmes,
> qui grandit dans la prière et la rêverie, dans les angoisses du coeur, qui
> mourut sans achever rien; mais il nous a laissé de lui un si poignant
> souvenir, que toutes les joies, toutes les grandeurs des âges modernes
> ne suffiront pas à nous consoler.[17]

In 1864, in the last section of his *Bible de l'humanité*, entitled
'Défaillance du Monde. L'Écrasement du Moyen Âge,' he was to pro-
nounce his final verdict on the Middle Ages:

> Il faut faire volte-face, et vivement, franchement, tourner le dos au
> moyen âge, à ce passé morbide, qui, même quand il n'agit pas, influe
> terriblement par la contagion de la mort. Il ne faut ni combattre, ni
> critiquer, mais oublier.
> Oublions et marchons!
> Marchons aux sciences de la vie, au musée, aux écoles, au Collège de
> France. . . .[18]

It took him thirty years to reach this conclusion, and pass through
all the stages from plaintive, elegiac regret to feverish, almost hysterical

---

[16] Michelet, *Introduction à l'histoire universelle*, 1962, p. 47.   [15] Ibid. pp. 206-7.
[18] *Bible de l'humanité*, 1864, p. 483.   [17] *Histoire de France*, 2nd edn., ii (1835), 130.

condemnation. It was in the Introduction to his *Renaissance* (1855) that he formally and at some length denounced the Middle Ages and recanted his former indulgence towards them; but this was no sudden change of front. His tender regard for them had gradually evaporated during the 1840s, when, as we have seen in the previous chapter, the increased momentum of medieval studies, promoted by the government and by Catholic propagandists, provoked counter-measures from the opposing camp. Michelet's career as a militantly anti-clerical writer began with his and Quinet's campaign against the Jesuits (1843): from then on he was bound to set his face against the Middle Ages. Already in 1833, on a visit to Reims, he had remarked with distaste upon the sculptured figures (destroyed in 1918) below the Angel spire, representing human beings undergoing various torments, as 'une terrible condamnation du Moyen Âge'.[19] He seized upon the sculptures as a symbol of feudal oppression, and mentioned them in Volume II of his *Histoire de France* (1833): 'Cette figure du peuple pilorié est un stigmate pour l'église elle-même. La voix des suppliciés s'élevait avec les chants.'[20] In this chapter on Gothic architecture fervent praise is already mingled with a certain amount of blame, to be developed into total condemnation in his Introduction to the *Renaissance*. Gothic art is attacked for its structural deficiency – 'La maison menaçait, elle ne pouvait s'achever. . . . La masse énorme de l'église s'appuie sur d'innombrables contreforts, laborieusement dressée et soutenue . . .'[21] – and this is attributed to the unjust society of which it is a product: 'Cet art, attaquable dans sa forme, défaillait aussi dans son principe social. La société d'où il était sorti, était trop inégale et trop injuste.'[21] However, the predominating tone is one of Romantic, elegiac melancholy. Michelet sees the passing of the Middle Ages as inevitable and necessary, but at the same time a spectacle full of pathos. Speaking of Saint Louis and the Sainte-Chapelle, he remarks: 'Un monde de religion et de poésie, tout un Orient chrétien est en ces vitraux, fragile et précieuse peinture que l'on néglige trop et que le vent emportera quelque jour. . . .[22] Cette pureté, cette douceur d'âme, cette élévation merveilleuse où le christianisme porta son héros, qui nous la rendra?'[23]

[19] Michelet, *Journal,* ed. Viallaneix, i (1959), 111 (July 1833). Apparently Michelet was led astray by a monograph published in 1823, which misinterpreted the figures as victims of Louis XI or a bishop, punished for failing to pay their taxes. See J. Pommier's article, 'Michelet et l'architecture gothique', in *Études de lettres* (Lausanne), xxvi (Dec. 1954).

[20] *Histoire de France,* ii, 694.   [21] Ibid. p. 693.   [22] Ibid. p. 619.

[23] Ibid. p. 622.

(The last sentence, and the whole lament of which it forms a part, were cut out of the 1861 and subsequent editions.) Michelet states here that medieval society and the Christian faith which informed it had to die, to make way for a better world — 'Il faut que le vieux monde passe, que la trace du moyen-âge achève de s'effacer, que nous voyions mourir tout ce que nous aimions, ce qui nous allaita tout petit, ce qui fut notre père et notre mère . . .'[24] — and yet the thought of this brings tears into his eyes. 'Touchons ces pierres avec précaution . . .' he exclaims, as he evokes a Gothic cathedral — 'Tout cela saigne et souffre encore. Un grand mystère se passe ici. J'y vois partout la mort, et je suis tenté de pleurer.'[25] (In 1861 the second of these sentences was excised, and the fourth was emended to 'Je n'y vois plus que la mort', as regret gave way to disparagement and a hint of gloating satisfaction.) Medieval Christianity is seen as a 'chère et précieuse dépouille', and hope is expressed that it may in the fulness of time, having heroically consented to temporary extinction, rise from its tomb, miraculously purified, to begin life anew: 'Il se transformera pour vivre encore. Il apparaitra un matin aux yeux de ceux qui croient garder son tombeau, et ressuscitera le troisième jour.'[26] Thus Michelet gives expression to a certain quality of regret, kept within reasonable bounds, yet none the less real and reverential, which he was still prescribing for the historian in his Collège de France lectures of 1839: 'Il faut, tout à la fois, regretter et [ne] point regretter, garder au passé un souvenir légitime, reconnaissant et tendre, et ne pas oublier que nous devons faire autre chose.'[27] Yet this elegiac image of Christianity as a 'chère dépouille' was to transform itself into the sinister symbol of a decaying corpse spreading foul contagion, as Michelet's meditations on the theme of death, through personal experience of bereavement, accompanied by increasing anticlericalism, became progressively more sombre in tone. On a foggy February morning in 1834 he was walking to the Archives admiring Notre-Dame enshrouded in mist, when all at once he noticed that 'Les parties antérieures et voisines de moi étaient sombres et noires; elles devenaient grises et fantastiques à mesure qu'elles s'éloignaient.' The spectacle took on symbolic significance — 'C'était l'enterrement de Notre-Dame et du catholicisme' — and a line of Shakespeare came into his mind: '*Ah*! dit Juliette à Roméo, qui descend, *il me semble*

---

[24] *Histoire de France,* ii. 697.   [25] Ibid. pp. 662-3.
[26] Ibid. pp. 697-8.
[27] Michelet, 'Cours au Collège de France' (1839), ed. Haac, in *RHLF,* liv (1954), p. 77.

que je te vois dans un tombeau.[28] Nine years later, in the church of
Saint-Ouen in Rouen, he had a similar experience; but this time a far
more violent shudder went through him, as by then Christianity and
the Middle Ages were beginning to seem repellent to him, and in his
newly-assumed militant role he sternly apostrophized the church and
prophesied its defeat: 'Je regardai dans le bénitier l'église renversée et
je lui dis, comme Juliette à Roméo: *Il me semble que d'ici je te vois
dans un tombeau.*'[29] After the death of his first wife Pauline in 1839
he confided to his diary increasingly sombre meditations on the theme
of death; and the fourth volume of the *Histoire de France,* which deals
with the late fourteenth and early fifteenth centuries, a time when 'la
mort morale, qui est la vraie, était au fond de tous les coeurs',[30] was
written in these months of despair. 'Je me plongeai', he explains,
'avec un plaisir sombre dans la mort de la France au XVe siècle.'[31] A
note of revolt against death was first sounded in August 1840, when he
wrote in his diary of 'Deux manières de supporter le monde: l'accepter,
l'approuver, comme les chrétiens, le refaire, comme les artistes. L'époque
de la Renaissance, c'est celle où la résignation chrétienne manquant, les
hommes, n'acceptant plus le monde, se sont mis à le refaire.'[32] He began
to see himself as one who had left behind a tragic past ruled over by death
and the forces of darkness. 'Tout a péri pour moi,' he declared in the
following year, 'l'antiquité, le Moyen Âge; je me sens profondément
moderne, en ce moment.'[33] However, he still professed reverence and
respect for the past; he said in 1842: 'Que le présent ne tue pas son père,
mais l'inhume avec respect. Qu'il révère en lui son auteur.'[34] But a month
later, in a lecture at the Collège de France, the Gothic cathedral appeared
to him in a sinister light:

Quand nous passons au parvis devant la cathédrale et que nous voyons
sur nos têtes cette harmonie colossale . . . nous croyons entendre . . .
une immense alléluia, un majestueux noël. Et puis, si vous regardez une
à une ces figures qui sont pour la plupart des portraits, qui nous ressemblent tout à fait et qui sont presque nous-mêmes, vous n'entendrez plus
ni alléluia, ni noël sur leurs visages inquiets, abattus, vous lirez plutôt
le *dies irae.*[35]

These faces are haunted by the presence of the Devil hovering over the
church. 'Ne voyez-vous pas planer partout sur l'église', Michelet asked

---

[28] *Journal,* i, 115.   [29] Ibid. p. 516 (4 Aug. 1843).
[30] *H.F.,* iv (1840), 414.   [31] *Journal,* i, 361 (29 April 1841).
[32] Ibid. p. 353.   [33] Ibid. p. 364 (13 August 1841).
[34] Ibid. p. 392 (4 April 1842).
[35] Unpublished lecture of 12 May 1842, quoted by Pommier, op. cit. pp. 30-1.

his audience, 'cette ombre de chauve-souris?'[35] He now understands why the medieval saints' eyes are filled with tears. In 1833 he had interpreted this as the infinitely pathetic lament of a doomed world: 'C'est en vain que la vieille église gothique élève toujours au ciel ses tours suppliantes, en vain que ses vitraux pleurent, en vain que ses saints font pénitence dans leurs niches de pierre.'[39] Now he explains that they are weeping not only because medieval society was doomed to perish, but because it was a dark world full of discord, the very opposite of the ideal Romantic Middle Ages, irradiated with faith, hope, and love: 'Sans liberté, sans égalité, nul amour. Et voilà pourquoi le Moyen Âge n'avait pu aimer ni imiter l'idéal d'amour. Et voilà pourquoi ses saints pleurent toujours dans leurs niches de pierre.'[36] Michelet is here about to set his face against the Middle Ages. In a letter to Alfred Dumesnil, who had (in 1862) sent him notes taken at his 1842-3 lectures, he recalls this time: 'J'aimais le moyen âge. C'est le dernier moment où je l'ai aimé, l'hiver de 1842-1843. Le cours est doré de cette lueur, éteinte à jamais, non par la polémique, mais par la ferme vérité.'[38] In April 1843 the campaign against the Jesuits began. In August, two days after the marriage of his daughter Adèle, he pronounced a solemn farewell to the past: 'Adieu passé, adieu douces années solitaires, adieu Adèle, adieu Pauline! Tout cela fini. Mes rêves du Moyen Âge aussi. A moi donc, ô avenir! . . . C'est bien, mes amis, délivrez-nous du passé. Forcez-nous d'aller en avant. . . . Adieu Église, adieu ma mère et ma fille; *adieu douces fontaines qui me fûtes si amères!*'[39] The 'friends' whom he sardonically thanks for delivering him from the past are the clergy. They are busy restoring churches such as Saint-Ouen, once beloved by Michelet, but now profaned in his eyes, since it fell into the hands of the restorers, who obliterate the true past and set in its place a hideous travesty of the Middle Ages: 'La mort est encore une vie tant que le tombeau vit comme tombeau, par la vénération, les regrets, les larmes. Mais hélas! un joli tombeau, un tombeau coquet . . . c'est la mort de la mort même.'[39]

So the Middle Ages, once dignified in death, have now become ridiculous, and will soon be regarded as a menace and source of contagion. The years of angry polemic have begun. Michelet's friend Quinet, in his Collège de France lectures on Ultramontanism (1844),

---

[36] *H.F.* ii. 697.
[37] Lecture of 12 May 1842, quoted in *Journal,* i. 826 n.
[38] Michelet, *Lettres inédites,* ed. P. Sirven, 1924, p. 291.
[39] *Journal,* i. 516-7.

warned those followers of Montalembert who formed the ranks of the 'fils des croisés', pledged to wage war on the 'fils de Voltaire', that 'd'autres jours sont venus; les croisades du moyen âge sont finies; ceux qui reprennent ce chemin n'arrivent qu'à la mort.'[40]

Michelet begins wholeheartedly to attack the Middle Ages in a diary entry for August 1845. For the first time he adopts the tone which he is to use in all subsequent denunciations of them – caustic and malicious, with dramatic snatches of dialogue and urgent interpellations on the part of Michelet himself. He dwells on the frivolity and emptiness of medieval life: the land does not belong to those who toil on it, and the present is drained of all significance by exclusive concentration on the hereafter. Mysterious and sinister voices chime in the ears of the wretched serf: *'Sème, sème, un autre récoltera. . . . Là-haut, là-haut, ici rien.*'[41] In *Le Peuple* (written in the autumn of 1845, published in January 1846) Michelet pursues his attack ('Le moyen âge posa une formule d'amour, et il n'aboutit qu'à la haine . . .';[42] 'Le moyen âge promit l'union, et ne donna que la guerre')[43] and justifies it in the following terms: 'Le moyen âge . . . où j'ai passé ma vie, dont j'ai reproduit dans mes histoires la touchante, l'impuissante aspiration, j'ai dû lui dire: *Arrière!* aujourd'hui que des mains impures l'arrachent de sa tombe. . . .'[44] In a note he assures the reader that his present disapprobation can be reconciled with his praise of 1833. The explanation which he offers is ingenious: 'Je n'efface pas un mot de ce que j'en ai dit [i.e. du moyen-âge] au second volume de l'*Histoire de France*. Seulement, j'ai donné là son élan, son idéal; aujourd'hui, dans un livre d'intérêt pratique, je ne puis donner que le réel, les résultats.'[45] Privately, to his diary, in November of the same year (1846), he admits that his conscience is troubled: 'Mon regret, je ne dis pas mon remords, car j'étais de bonne foi, c'est d'avoir donné l'idéal de cet affreux Moyen Âge. Idéal vrai, telle fut sa poésie, son aspiration, mais combien peu en rapport avec la réalité!' . . .[46] 'Qu'ai-je fait lorsque j'ai embelli l'idéal du Moyen Âge, caché le réel? J'ai travaillé contre moi, contre le progrès du monde.'[47]

In December – January 1846-7 he prepared the Introduction to his *Histoire de la Révolution* (published in February). 'Pendant quinze jours ou trois semaines, enfermé par la grippe,' he writes in his diary, 'je

[40] E. Quinet. *Os. cs.* ii. 182.
[42] *Le Peuple,* ed. L. Refort, 1946, p. 126.
[44] Ibid. p. 271.
[46] *Journal,* i. 654-5 (20 Nov. 1846).

[41] *Journal,* i. 623 (23 Aug. 1845).
[43] Ibid. p. 229.
[45] *Le Peuple,* p. 168 n.
[47] Ibid. p. 658 (21 Nov.).

conçus le sombre aspect du Moyen Âge catholique qui est dans mon *Introduction.* [48] Again, in this Introduction, he sees the medieval world in the grip of inertia: 'L'homme se croisait les bras, s'asseyait et attendait. . . . Toute activité morale cessait en ce monde';[49] and he views with compassionate indignation the fate of the common people: 'D'abord, une vie de douleur, puis, pour consolation, l'enfer! . . . Damnés d'avance!'[50] There follows a dramatic vision of the serf's first stirrings of discontent:

Et le matin, avant jour, il allait sur son sillon. . . . Il trouvait la vallée et la plaine de labour plus basses, beaucoup plus basses, profondes, comme un sépulcre; et plus hautes, plus sombres, plus lourdes, les deux tours à l'horizon, sombre le clocher de l'église, sombre le donjon féodal. . . . Et il commençait aussi à comprendre la voix des deux cloches. L'Église sonnait: *Toujours.* Le donjon sonnait: *Jamais.* . . . Mais en même temps, une voix forte parla plus haute dans son coeur. . . . Cette voix disait: *Un jour! . . . Un jour* reviendra la Justice![51]

Arbitrary Christian Grace is seen in perpetual conflict with republican Justice. The medieval world, deprived of Justice, is in a state of total desolation. The serf reappears in Chapter 3 of the *Histoire de la Révolution,* plagued by the same sinister voice of feudal tyranny, whispering in his ear: 'Travaille, travaille, fils de serf, gagne, un autre profitera.' And all at once Michelet himself appears at his side: 'Moi-même, leur compagnon, labourant à côté d'eux dans le sillon de l'histoire, buvant à leur coupe amère, qui m'a permis de revivre le douloureux Moyen âge, et pourtant de n'en pas mourir, n'est-ce pas vous, ô beau jour, premier jour le la délivrance? . . . J'ai vécu pour vous raconter!'[52]

And so, when the Second Empire came into being, Michelet was fully equipped to lead the ranks of its republican opponents, whose mission was to discredit the Middle Ages. He had at his disposal a store of images which he was to enrich and elaborate in the years ahead.

His favourite image, of course, is that of the past as an exhumed corpse spreading pestilence through the land. In 1853, on a visit to Nantes, he deplored the all-pervading influence of the clergy there: 'La pesanteur d'une association morte d'idées, vivante d'intrigues se sent ici partout. . . . Elle tue la vie publique sans en faire une vie à elle. Et l'on sent, en même temps, la nullité de l'État qui devait être cette vie et qui, ne voulant pas

[48] *Journal,* i. 661.
[49] *Histoire de la Révolution,* i (1961), 28.
[50] Ibid. p. 32.
[51] *H. Rév.* i. 33. Repeated in *Bible de l'humanité,* 1864, pp. 479-80.
[52] Ibid. p. 203.

l'être, appelle cette mort du passé à soutenir la mort du présent.'[53]

Le Banquet, published after Michelet's death in 1879, was written in Italy in 1853-4. Here, the image is further developed: the Middle Ages are now '[le] mort que j'ai trop aimé, que j'ai ressuscité, ranimé de mon souffle et réchauffé de ma vie'.[54] There is yet another picture of a somnolent, spiritless world;[55] and sinister voices issue the command: 'Meurs à toi-même, à la nature!'[56] The bells of Nervi peal forth: 'Aux Apennins qui disent: soif, vous répondez: famine!'; and Michelet apostrophizes them: 'N'êtes-vous donc pas lasses, ô cloches, de sonner depuis mille ans? Et n'êtes-vous pas honteuses de sonner toujours en vain?'[57] – setting them in opposition to the bells of the free city of Ghent, calling the weavers forth from their underground dens to repel feudal tyranny. A dramatic scene follows:

> Ils l'entendaient . . . la cloche redoutée, les chevaliers, barons, et ils frémissaient. . . . Pâle, élancé des caves, le tisserand marchait, mais grandi de dix pieds. Unis comme un seul homme au moment du combat, ils communiaient de la patrie. . . . Quelle joie dans la ville quand la mère en prière disait 'Il a vaincu! Je n'entends plus Roelandt!'[58]

In *Le Banquet* Michelet communicates for the first time, with great excitement, his discovery (gleaned from Ludovic Vitet's *Monographie de Notre-Dame de Noyon,* 1845) that Gothic architecture was built not by 'l'église de jeûne, d'abstinence et de célibat', but by secular masons, 'de vrais hommes complets, qui vécurent de la vie d'équilibre'.[59]

Michelet has by now discovered and set down in writing almost every charge which he is to level against the Middle Ages in his famous diatribe in the Introduction to the *Renaissance* (published in February

---

[53] *Journal,* ii (1962), 214. Cf. two letters of Quinet, written in the same year, one to Michelet (*Lettres d'exil,* i (1885), 58, 62).

[54] *Le Banquet,* 1879, p. 156.

[55] Ibid. p. 81.

[56] Ibid. p. 217.

[57] Ibid. p. 239 (cf. Michelet's elegiac lament for lost faith in 1840, when he asked: 'Qui de nous, parmi les agitations du monde moderne . . . n'entend sans émotion le bruit de ces belles fêtes chrétiennes, la voix touchante des cloches et comme leur doux reproche maternel?' *H.F.* v (1841), p. 145 (Aug. 1840)).

[58] Ibid. pp. 244-5. In 1840 this same spectacle had been described by a Michelet awestruck, but at the same time appalled: 'C'était l'ouvrier mystique, le lollard illuminé, . . . échappé des caves, effaré du jour, pâle et hâve. . . . Un seul de ces frénétiques, un ouvrier moine, égorgea quatre cents hommes dans le fossé de Courtrai. . . . Confréries, peuple, bannières, tout branlait au même son, un son lugubre. . . . Cette note uniforme et sinistre de la monstrueuse cloche était: Roland! Roland! Roland!' (*H.F.* v. 354-5).

[59] Ibid. p. 81.

1855), where he repeats that in 1833 he gave 'l'idéal que se posa le moyen âge. Et ce que nous donnons ici c'est sa réalité, accusée par lui-même.'[60] The Middle Ages represent *'l'anti-nature . . . la contre-famille et la contre-éducation'.*[61] Incarnated in the clergy, they obstinately refuse to die.[62] The only nobility to be found in them is in certain isolated heroes such as Abelard, Giotto, and Joan of Arc, visitants from the future imbued with the free spirit of the Renaissance and the Revolution. (In the *Histoire de France* (1840) Joan of Arc had been presented as belonging in spirit to the early, ideal Middle Ages, and falling victim to the modern world, which was already beginning to deny medieval ideals.)[63] The monastery bell repeats hourly: 'Humiliez-vous, obéissez, dormez, enfants. . . .'[64] The movement to restore churches and cathedrals is a squalid conspiracy between architects, clergy, and government officials, all greedy for gain: 'Les Gothiques, complétement rassurés et maîtres du terrain, vont de la truelle, de la plume, vont hardiment.'[65] Gothic architecture was on the one hand built by free-masons, *laïques et mariés*',[66] who alone were capable of executing works of genius, but on the other hand — and here Michelet defies Viollet-le-Duc, whose *Dictionnaire raisonné de l'architecture française* had begun to appear in 1854 — it is structurally unsound, maintained in position by 'un pénible appareil d'étais et de contre-forts'[67] and 'des crampons de fer qu'on cachait soigneusement',[68] in need of constant repair and shoring up (this charge was first made by Quatremère de Quincy in 1788,[69] repeated by Michelet in 1833, and, as we shall see, eagerly developed by Renan and Taine in the 1860s). 'Riez donc, bons vieux temps joyeux; riez, facétieux noëls; riez, plaisants fabliaux; amusez-vous de votre honte . . .',[70] Michelet sardonically declares, as once again he addresses with personal venom a past into which momentary life has been breathed, in order that it may be attacked all the more dramatically.

There is, however, one new element in this work of 1855. In 1839 Michelet had declared: 'L'histoire ne servira à rien si on n'y met les tristesses du présent.'[71] Quinet, in a letter of 1853 to an Italian friend, set forth a despairing vision of the future as an endless prolongation of

---

[60] *La Renaissance,* 2nd edn., 1857, p. 7.
[61] Ibid. p. 164.   [62] Ibid. p. 16.
[63] *H.F.* v. 102-4.   [64] *Renaissance,* p. 38.
[65] Ibid. p. 170.   [66] Ibid. p. 168.
[67] Ibid. p. 20.   [68] Ibid. p. 95.
[69] Quatremère de Quincy, *Encyclopédie méthodique: Architecture,* i (1788), article ARCS BUTTANS.
[70] *Renaissance,* p. 35.   [71] 'Cours au Collège de France' (1839), op. cit., p. 19.

the Second Empire – 'une unité de servitude croissante . . . les foules amoureuses de despotes . . . les temps s'écoulant sans qu'on en ait conscience, et à l'horizon les cathédrales gothiques remplaçant pour ce monde mourant les pyramides d'Égypte':[72] the return of the Dark Ages in fact, with their total inertia and despair, so often described by his friend Michelet.[73] The Second Empire was declared a state of entombment.[74] Michelet had already as a child under the First Empire experienced the same debilitating, corrosive atmosphere. In her compilation *Ma Jeunesse* his widow, under the heading 'Mon Moyen Âge', reassembled several passages from various works of Michelet describing this experience:

Rien ne m'a mieux aidé à comprendre la sombre monotonie du moyen âge, l'attente sans espoir, sans désir, sinon celui de la mort, que d'avoir langui, enfant, dans les dernières années de l'Empire.[75] J'étais né dans un si profond rapport avec ces temps de malheur, que personne, j'ose dire, n'en sentira au même degré, la vérité accablante.[76] J'ai vu le temps le plus mort, le plus vide qui fut jamais, éteint pour la pensée, temps de destruction qui promena la mort sur l'Europe.[77]

Under the Second Empire Michelet again experienced the restoration of the Middle Ages, and, in 1855, it is the Empire he is describing, in the guise of the late Middle Ages:

L'âme . . . s'hébète d'ennui et se bâille. . . .[78] Un monotone brouillard décolore la création. . . . Tout est prévu; on n'espère rien de ce monde. Les choses reviendront les mêmes. L'ennui certain de demain fait bâiller dès aujourd'hui, et la perspective des jours, des années d'ennui qui suivront, pèse d'avance, dégoûte de vivre.[79]

Émile Montégut, describing contemporary France in the *Revue des deux mondes* (1858), was to echo this: 'Tout s'en va, tout se décolore et s'abâtardit, même le désespoir, même l'ennui. On dirait que l'âme

---

[72] *Lettres d'exil*, i, 83.
[73] Cf. the Second Empire transposed by Quinet, in *Merlin l'Enchanteur* (1860), to Arthur's court bound by an evil spell: 'Les corps vivaient, mais les âmes étaient mortes. . . .' 'Il y avait . . . une cloche qui sonnait jour et nuit un glas. . . . Les formes de toutes choses semblaient s'enfuir et s'évanouir dans un linceul de brume. . . . Le monde muet et glacé semblait résigné à mourir' (Quinet, *Os. cs.* xvii, *Merlin l'Enchanteur*, 4th edn., n.d., ii. pp. 241-5).
[74] Cf. again Quinet's *Merlin, infra*, p. 177.
[75] *Ma Jeunesse*, 1884, p. 76 (from *Journal*, i. 621-2 (23 Aug. 1845)).
[76] Ibid. (I have not been able to find this sentence in Michelet's published work. It may be taken from that part of the *Journal* which remains to be published.)
[77] Ibid. (from *Nos Fils*, 1870, pp. 273-4).
[78] *Renaissance*, p. 39.
[79] Ibid. p. 114.

humaine a atteint la limite de volupté, de pensée, de curiosité, qu'elle ne peut franchir sans se paralyser ou s'hébéter.'[80]

Michelet wrote to Quinet in January 1855 that the principal theme of his 'Introduction sur le moyen âge' was 'la création du peuple des sots, des bourgeois et des ennuyeux, de la petite prudence'.[81] These people are one and the same as the citizens of the Empire.

In 1856 Michelet returned to his favourite theme in a letter to Hugo: 'Quand le christianisme ne sera plus à l'état de vampire (ni mort ni vivant), mais, comme un honnête mort, paisible et couché, comme sont l'Inde, l'Égypte et Rome, alors, alors seulement, nous en défendrons tout ce qui est défendable.'[82] Quinet expressed the opinion that 'le progrès serait immense si l'on pouvait en un jour arracher les peuples au catholicisme . . . et les attirer vers une des formes les plus modernes du christianisme. Ce serait les enlever au moyen âge, où ils gisent ensevelis.'[83] And a year later he made an appeal to 'tous ceux qui veulent, non pas seulement médire du moyen âge, mais en sortir et l'abolir' to join in 'ce grand et suprême effort contre la mort qui jette déjà son ombre sur nous'.[84]

In 1861 Michelet brought out his revised edition of the *Histoire de France*. Much praise of the Middle Ages was excised; the last chapter of Volume II, greatly reduced, was removed from the main text and put as an appendix under the heading 'Éclaircissements'.

The year 1862 saw a furious onslaught delivered against the Middle Ages from all quarters, from Renan and Taine (as we shall presently see), from Quinet, who in the course of the year made the following pronouncements:

Il en est de ce moyen âge comme de la peste. On peut avoir toute sorte de systèmes à son égard. Mais il ne faut jamais oublier que la peste est la peste . . . (Mar.);[85]

Nous avons été étouffés par ce moyen âge que nous n'avons pas eu la force de vomir . . . (12 Dec.);[86]

---

[80] 'Confidences d'un hypocondriaque', *RDM,* 15 Jan. 1858, p. 476.
[81] Mme E. Quinet, *Cinquante ans d'amitié: Michelet-Quinet,* 1899, p. 225. Cf. Michelet, *Renaissance,* p. 232.
[82] J-M. Carré, *Michelet et son temps,* 1926, p. 56.
[83] E. Quinet, 'Lettre à E. Sue sur la situation religieuse et morale de l'Europe' (1856), in *Os. cs.* xxiv, *Le Livre de l'exilé,* 1882, p. 451.
[84] E. Quinet, *La Révolution religieuse au dix-neuvième siècle.* p. 535.
[85] *Lettres d'exil,* 1885, ii. 191.
[86] Ibid. p. 283.

Les masses reprennent . . . les instincts du serf, elles attendent tout
de l'*Imperator Imperatorum,* comme elles attendaient tout du roi . . .
(23 Dec.);[87]

and from Michelet, whose *La Sorcière* was published in November.
In this work the Middle Ages are presented as a hell on earth. Dramatic
scenes, interviews between pitiless overlord and trembling serf, abound.
Michelet himself delivers the message of despair to the latter, toiling
in his master's field: 'Travaille, travaille, bonhomme. Pendant que tu es
aux champs, la bande redoutée de là-haut peut s'abattre sur la maison,
enlever ce qui lui plaît "pour le service du seigneur." '[88] Terms more
dramatic than any used in Michelet's previous works are found to
describe the enslavement of the freeman, enmeshed in the diabolical
law which changes him overnight into a serf: 'La terre visqueuse
retient le pied, enracine le passant. L'air contagieux le tue, c'est-à-dire
le fait de *main morte,* un mort, un néant, une bête.'[89]

In this nightmare world, which outdoes in horrific intensity any
literary exploitation of the Dark Ages by republicans such as Leconte
de Lisle, romantic 'poncifs' reappear, strangely transmuted. The
châtelaine and her adoring page are evil tormentors of the serf and his
wife. She rides forth on her white horse to meet her lord returning from
the wars, absorbed in plans for sadistic revenge on the sorceress. Walter
Scott is taken to task for concealing 'la réalité immonde' of the Middle
Ages.[90]

It is in *La Sorcière* that Michelet's life-long meditations on Gothic
architecture are brought to a dramatic climax. In 1833 he had been
moved by the poignancy of medieval faith, trembling always on the
brink of self-doubt. Insatiable yearning had caused perpetual tears to
flow forth in the Middle Ages; and it was these tears, he declares in one
of his most eloquent passages, that had formed the cathedral: 'Larmes
précieuses, elles ont coulé en limpides légendes, en merveilleux poèmes,
et s'amoncelant vers le ciel, elles se sont cristallisées en gigantesques
cathédrales qui voulaient monter au Seigneur!'[91] In the same volume of
the *Histoire de France,* however, there is a hint of warning that tears of
a very different nature were shed in the Age of Faith — by despairing
victims of feudal oppression —, and that these tears might one day become potent to destroy what the others had built: 'Sous ces pierres, il
y avait trop de pleurs.'[92] This prophecy is fulfilled in *La Sorcière,* in

---

[87] Ibid. p. 285.　　[88] *La Sorcière,* ed. L. Refort, i (1952), 52.　　[89] Ibid. p. 38.
[90] Ibid. p. 55. Cf. Taine's attack on Scott in the same year, *infra,* pp. 71, 72.
[91] *H.F.* ii. 642.　　[92] Ibid. p. 695.

Michelet's vision of the final dissolution of the Church, astonishingly brought about: '. . . quels que soient les soutiens, contre-forts, arcs-boutants, dont le monument s'appuie, une chose le fait branler. Non les coups bruyants du dehors, mais je ne sais quoi de doux qui est dans les fondements, qui travaille ce cristal d'un insensible dégel . . .'[93] This agency is 'l'humble flot des tièdes larmes' shed by the medieval world in its long agony, 'une mer de pleurs'.[94] As in the case of the weeping saints in their 'niches de pierre' whom we have already mentioned, tears of passionate longing have been transmuted into tears of bitter suffering. It may be noted in passing how Michelet develops this theme after *La Sorcière*. In *La Bible de l'humanité* (1864) all pathos has evaporated and contemptuous mention is made of 'le pleureur Moyen âge'.[95] But in the 1869 Preface to the *Histoire de France* emotion returns to Michelet in a renewed access of outrage at the 'guirlande de suppliciés' below the spire at Reims, whose tears, 'onction redoutable de la Révolution', he imagines anointing the heads of successive kings below.[96]

Michelet's frenzied railing against the Middle Ages in *La Sorcière* reaches heights of invective which he will be unable to surpass. 'On ne peut écrire ces blasphèmes,' he cries at one point, 'sans que le coeur

---

[93] *La Sorcière*, i. 95.
[94] Ibid. pp. 95-6. Cf. this passage of *La Sorcière* with Hugo's vision (in *Napoléon le Petit*) of the Second Empire as the frozen river Néva melting in the rays of the rising sun of Liberty:

Hugo: 'Une lueur blafarde et blême se traîne sur la neige; on dirait que le soleil meurt. Non, tu ne meurs pas, liberté! un de ces jours, au moment où on s'y attendra le moins, à l'heure même où on t'aura le plus profondément oubliée, tu te lèveras! . . . Sur toute cette neige, sur toute cette glace, sur cette plaine dure et blanche, sur tout cet infâme hiver, tu lanceras ta flèche d'or . . . la lumière, la chaleur, la vie! – Et alors, écoutez! entendez-vous ce bruit sourd? entendez-vous ce craquement profond et formidable? c'est la débâcle! c'est la Néva qui s'écroule! . . . c'est l'eau vivante, joyeuse et terrible qui soulève la glace hideuse et morte et qui la brise! – C'était du granit, disiez-vous; voyez, cela se fend comme une vitre! . . . C'est la vérité qui revient; c'est le progrès qui recommence' (*Napoléon le Petit*, pp. 40-1).

Michelet: 'Âpre liberté solitaire, salut! . . . Toute la terre encore semble vêtue d'un blanc linceul, captive d'une glace pesante, d'impitoyables cristaux, uniformes, aigus, cruels. Surtout depuis 1200, le monde a été fermé comme un sépulcre transparent où l'on voit avec effroi toute chose immobile et durcie. . . . Vers 1300, l'architecture . . . rivalise avec les prismes monotones du Sptizberg. Vraie et redoutable image de la dure cité de cristal dans lequel un dogme terrible a cru enterrer la vie. Mais, quels que soient les soutiens . . . dont le monument s'appuie, une chose le fait branler. . . . Quelle? l'humble flot des tièdes larmes qu'un monde a versées, une mer de pleurs. Quelle? une haleine d'avenir, la puissante, l'invincible résurrection de la vie naturelle' (*La Sorcière*, i, 95-6).
[95] *Bible de l'humanité*, p. 192.   [96] *H.F.* i (1879), 38.

soit gonflé, que le papier ne grince, et la plume, d'indignation!'[97]
Sometimes the expression of anti-Romantic sentiment borders on the
ludicrous, as in the famous outburst: 'Nul bain pendant mille ans!
Soyez sûr que pas un de ces chevaliers, de ces belles si éthérées, les
Parceval, les Tristan, les Iseult, ne se lavaient [sic] jamais.'[98] Certain
of the remarks put into the mouths of the oppressors in the castle (e.g.
'C'est dimanche; on rirait bien si on te voyait d'en bas gambiller à mes
créneaux',[99] and 'Vilain jaloux, vilaine face de carême, on ne la prend
pas ta femme, on te la rendra ce soir, et pour comble d'honneur, grosse!'[100])
are indistinguishable from those accompanying the crudely-executed
vignettes at the head of each chapter of Fellens's above-mentioned
work, *La Féodalité, ou les droits du seigneur.* . . . But for the most part
Michelet succeeds in giving remarkably poetic force to the eighteenth-
century denunciations of the Middle Ages whose tradition he is continuing. In conclusion, he breaks into an alexandrine:

Ô temps dur! temps maudit! et gros de désespoir![101]

He has in effect here, and in the stern conclusion to his *Bible de
l'humanité,*[102] spoken his last word on the Middle Ages. His 1869
Preface repeats various themes already stated, and has little to add;
though in his last work, *Histoire du XIXe siècle* (1872), there is a final
shaft of malice directed against Gothic architecture. In 1793, he recounts
with cheerful relish, 'un 2 Septembre se fit sur les bonshommes gothiques
du portail de *Notre-Dame.* Grande pitié chez les simples, chez ceux qui
ne savaient pas que cette vieille construction sortit des sanglantes
dépouilles des Albigeois, des Templiers, de tant d'autres.'[103]

Now we shall see how Renan and Taine, inspired in some measure
by Michelet's example, continued his attack on the Middle Ages, Gothic
architecture, and, through these, the Second Empire.

(ii) *Renan: 'un désert où ne germait aucune fleur'*

Léon Gautier, a prominent Catholic champion of the Middle Ages,
called Renan in 1865 'cet ennemi du Moyen Âge'.[104] Three years earlier,
however (29 June 1862), Sainte-Beuve had remarked that Renan

[97] *La Sorcière,* i. 88.
[98] Ibid. p. 104.
[99] Ibid. p. 73.
[100] *La Sorcière,* i. 58-9.
[101] Ibid. p. 148.
[102] Cf. *supra.* p. 44.
[103] *Histoire du XIX⁰ siècle,* i (1872), 21.
[104] L. Gautier, *Études littéraires pour la défense de l'Église,* 1865, p. 126.

cherished 'une affection particulière' for the Middle Ages;[105] and certainly his writings up to 1 July 1862, when his article 'L'Art du moyen âge et les causes de sa décadence' appeared in the *Revue des deux mondes,* would seem to bear this out. 'Dans la vie des individus, comme dans celle de l'humanité,' he declares in *L'Avenir de la science,* 'il y a des moyens âges, des moments où la réflexion se voile, s'obscurcit, et où les instincts reprennent momentanément le dessus.'[106] So he, like Michelet, has experienced his own, personal 'moyen âge'; but for him this has been an enriching experience, and not a death in life. 'Ces instincts étant de la nature humaine, il ne faut pas les blâmer',[106] he goes on to say. There is, during the 1840s and 50s, a side of him that responds romantically to the poetic melancholy of the Middle Ages, and seeks in it a refuge from the vulgarity of modern life. It is his Celtic, Breton self that craves for the pagan South, but remains a captive in the Celtic Middle Ages. It was the same with Flaubert and his native Normandy; he wrote to Louise Colet in 1846: 'Tu veux faire de moi un païen . . . ô ma muse! . . . Mais j'ai beau m'y exciter par l'imagination et par le parti pris, j'ai au fond de l'âme le brouillard du Nord que j'ai respiré à ma naissance. Je porte en moi la mélancolie des races barbares . . .';[107] and later: 'J'ai toujours au fond de moi comme l'arrière-saveur des mélancolies moyen âge de mon pays';[108] and 'Je suis un catholique; j'ai au coeur quelque chose du suintement vert des cathédrales normandes. Mes tendresses d'esprit sont pour les inactifs, pour les ascètes, pour les rêveurs.'[109] Renan, in 1846, is assailed by sudden nostalgia: 'Tout à l'heure j'avais un sentiment si vif de la vieille vie féodale au fond d'un manoir, que je languissais d'y désespérer';[110] and Flaubert in the autumn of 1853 writes: 'Tout a je ne sais quel parfum triste qui m'enivre. Je pense à de grandes chasses féodales, à des vies de château. Sous de larges cheminées, on entend bramer les cerfs au bord des lacs.'[111] Ozanam's lectures in 1846, and the thought of the Crusades, move Renan to commit to paper poetic prose that foreshadows that of the Symbolist Marcel Schwob: 'M. Ozanam nous a fait aujourd'hui une incomparable

---

[105] Sainte-Beuve, *Nouveaux lundis,* 407.
[106] Renan, *Os. cs.* iii. 769.
[107] Flaubert, *Correspondance,* i. 217.
[108] Ibid. ii. 348 (1852).
[109] Ibid. iii. 398 (1853).
[110] *Os. cs.* ix. 177-8 (*Cahiers de jeunesse*).
[111] *Correspondance,* iii. 350.

leçon sur cette délicieuse littérature irlandaise, toute pure, vague,
blanche . . .'[112] '. . . quelle poésie n'y avait-il pas dans ces bandes
errantes, allant sans but, marchant *vaguement* vers la Jérusalem.'[113]
And a medieval hymn composed in an Irish monastery sends him into
a transport of admiration: 'Pièce charmante de douceur; ah! qu'ils
étaient heureux . . .',[114] which recalls Musset's *Rolla,* and anticipates
Huysmans's Symbolist celebration of monastic life. Throughout the
1850s life in medieval monasteries continues to enthral Renan as the
antithesis of all that is profane, vulgar, and frivolous in modern life.
His enthusiasm equals that of a Montalembert, or of a Barbey d'Aurevilly,
who, as we shall see, detested 'l'individualisme antichevaleresque de
ces derniers temps'.[115] Renan wrote to his sister from Monte Cassino in
1850: 'Quel homme que ce saint Benoit et quelle force dans ces
institutions qui ont traversé tant de siècles! . . . Nous voilà tous . . .
philosophes du XIXe siècle . . . incapables de faire cohabiter deux
hommes sous le même toit, de les faire coopérer à la même oeuvre!
L'individualisme nous disperse.'[116] In his essay 'La Poésie des races
celtiques' (1854) he creates an ideal world and elegiacally mourns its
passing. 'Hélas!', he laments in a rough draft of this article, 'la poésie de
notre âge est tout entière dans la réminiscence du passé. Le monde pour
nous n'est plus enchanté';[117] and in the final version he sees the Celtic
Middle Ages as an infinitely poetic, doomed world: 'Hélas! elle est aussi
condamnée à disparaître, cette émeraude des mers du couchant! Arthur
ne reviendra pas de son ile enchantée, et saint Patrice avait raison de dire
à Ossian: "Les héros que tu pleures sont morts; peuvent-ils renaitre?".'[118]
In his *Essais de morale et de critique* (1859) 'La Poésie des races
celtiques' immediately follows, in ironic juxtaposition, another essay,
'La Poésie de l'Exposition' (1855), in which he evokes the spiritual
fervour of the great pilgrimage to Rome in 1300. Now, in an age of
bourgeois materialism, 'aux jeux antiques, aux pèlerinages, aux tournois,
aux jubilés ont succédé des comices industriels.'[119] He concludes: 'J'ai
voulu montrer . . . combien les sources poétiques du monde contemporain
sont taries, comment enfin la poésie n'est plus que dans le passé.'[120]

---

[112] *Os. cs.* ix. 108.
[113] Ibid. p. 324 (*Cahiers de jeunesse*). Cf. *infra,* p. 278.
[114] Lecture notes quoted by R. Galand, *L'Âme celtique de Renan,* 1959, p. 64.
[115] Barbey d'Aurevilly, *De l'histoire,* 1905, p. 234 (Article published in 1857).
[116] Renan, *Os. cs.* ix. 1259.
[117] Quoted by R. Galand, op. cit. p.83.   [118] *Os. cs.* ii, 253.
[119] Ibid. p. 241.   [120] Ibid. pp. 250-1.

The Middle Ages which Renan delights to contemplate at this time
are generally unorthodox and non-Roman. He inclines in 'La Poésie des
races celtiques' towards Henri Martin's sympathy for bardic resistance to
Christian missionaries; the Irish and Welsh monks create their admirable
society in isolation from far-distant Rome; the Latin medieval world
looks askance on the Celts and debases their chaste legend by introducing
into it an element of 'galanterie effrontée'.[121] The multitude of Breton
and Irish saints extolled in Renan's article 'La Vie des saints' (1854)
belong also to this non-Roman Middle Ages. He declares: 'Dans les
moments d'ennui et d'abattement quand l'âme, blessée par la vulgarité
du monde moderne, cherche dans le passé la noblesse qu'elle ne trouve
plus dans le présent, rien ne vaut la *Vie des Saints.*'[122] These saints are
free from all taint of bourgeois materialism; not one has 'l'air vulgaire'.
'Quelle incomparable galerie, en effet,' he cries, 'que celle de ces 25,000
héros de la vie désintéressée! quel air de haute distinction! quelle noblesse!
quelle poésie!';[123] and he sets their 'sublimes folies' beside 'ces existences
affairées que n'a jamais traversées le rayon divin'[123] with an exaltation
approaching that of Louis Veuillot, who, as we shall see, declared in that
same summer of 1854 that in the Middle Ages 'l'âme inondée de rayons
divins voyagea de ce monde dans le ciel et dans l'éternité.'[124] In 1855
he returns to the theme of medieval monasteries as ideal refuges for the
élite, conferring added distinction on those already distinguished above
their fellows: 'La vie monastique . . . avait l'avantage de soustraire à
la vulgarité quelques âmes choisies, destinées à une mission spéciale
d'enseignement religieux ou moral.'[125] In his article on *La Farce de
Patelin* (1856) he is saddened (as Michelet had been in his *Histoire de
France*)[126] by the advent of 'cet esprit goguenard, destructeur de
toute noblesse et de tout idéal', which destroyed the early, heroic,
aristocratic Middle Ages — 'un monde de grandeur et de fierté'[127] —
and heralded the modern age of bourgeois scepticism. In the Preface
to the *Études d'histoire religieuse* (1857) he exclaims: 'Qui ne s'est
arrêté, en parcourant nos anciennes villes, devant ces gigantesques
monuments de la foi antique, qui seuls appellent le regard au milieu
du niveau de la vulgarité moderne?'[128] In 1858 he expresses regret, in
an article on Victor Cousin, that the philosopher, absorbed in classical
antiquity and the seventeenth century,'ne connaît guère le moyen âge,

---

[121] *Os. cs.* ii. 274.   [122] Ibid. vii. 228.
[123] Ibid. 224.   [124] Cf. *infra,* p. 78.
[125] *Os. cs.* vii. 242.   [126] Vol. iii (1837).
[127] *Os. cs.* ii. 212-13.   [128] Ibid. vii. 28.

cette admirable source de poésie'.[129] Four months later he addresses
the same reproach to Silvestre de Sacy, whom he considers to be 'trop
peu soucieux des origines'. For his own part, declares Renan: 'J'aime le
moyen âge, j'aime la haute antiquité.'[130]

It is then hardly surprising that Sainte-Beuve should in June 1862
have stated that Renan looked upon the Middle Ages with especial
favour. They were for him up to this time a world ideally far removed
from the uncongenial mid-nineteenth century. Yet from July 1862, when
his article 'L'Art du moyen âge et les causes de sa décadence',[131]
appeared in the *Revue des deux mondes,* Renan began to attack the
Middle Ages. As time went on, his attacks grew increasingly violent; and
he substituted for the ideal, Celtic, monastic world in which he had
previously delighted, an ideal Greece, in which, as we shall see, many
opponents of the Second Empire sought consolation for their disappointed republicanism. Renan, although he called himself in 1876
'bien plus un fils de la Révolution qu'un fils des croisés',[132] was far
from being a republican; but the governmental favour which he had
enjoyed since being sent on his archaeological mission to Phoenicia in
1860 came to an end when, in February 1862, his Collège de France
course of lectures was suspended in its first week, after the uproar caused
by his calling Jesus 'un homme incomparable'. In 1863 the *Vie de Jésus*
was published; and in June 1864 he was formally deprived of his chair
at the Collège de France. Although Renan bore the Emperor no personal
grudge, he felt bitterly about the loss of his chair, brought about by
pressure of Catholic opinion.[133] His attack on Gothic architecture and
the society which produced it, in 'L'Art du moyen âge' and the *Discours
sur les beaux-arts,* repeats much of what Michelet had said on the subject,
and seems to have been written with the same intention: oblique censure
of the Empire. Looking back on this time in 1889, Renan recalled that

Les temps, sous le second Empire, furent pour la presse d'une
difficulté extrême. . . . La politique était si peu libre que la vie passa
aux arts littéraires et moraux. . . . Sous apparence de littérature . . .
on insinua les plus hauts principes de la politique libérale.[134]

[129] *Os. cs.* ii. 78.   [130] Ibid. pp. 43-4.
[131] Reprinted (with slight revision) in Vol. XXIV of the *Histoire littéraire de la
France* (1863), as part of Renan's *Discours sur l'état des beaux-arts au XIVe
siècle;* and in his *Mélanges d'histoire et de voyages,* 1878.
[132] *Os. cs.* ii, 775.
[133] For an account of Renan's relations with the Emperor see H. Psichari, *Renan
et la Guerre de 70,* 1947, pp. 163-91.
[134] *Os. cs.* ii, 1030.

In 1850 he had expressed the opinion that

La vie antique si sereine, si gracieuse dans ses étroites proportions, manquait d'ouverture du côté de l'infini. . . .[135] Un temple ancien est incontestablement d'une beauté plus pure qu'une église gothique, et pourtant nous passons des heures dans celle-ci sans fatigue, et nous ne pouvons sans ennui rester cinq minutes dans celui-là.'[136]

Twelve years later, in 'L'Art du moyen âge at les causes de sa décadence', he was abruptly to reveal himself as an enemy of Gothic barbarism and admirer of Greek perfection in the tradition of Quatremère de Quincy. He follows Michelet in directing his attack on Gothic architecture in decline, viewed no longer elegiacally, as in Volume II of Michelet's *Histoire* (1833) or Quinet's essay on the church of Brou (1834), but censoriously. However, Gothic as a whole is inculpated, as the seeds of decline were in it from the very beginning. Poetic imagery used by its Romantic admirers is subtly converted into condemnation. Renan speaks of 'toute une broderie de pierre, qui, comme le dit Vasari, a l'air d'être faite en carton'.[137] His remark 'l'église semble l'épanouissement d'un faisceau de roseaux'[138] is made disparagingly. The 'éblouissante parure' (borrowed from Michelet) 'qui le fait ressembler à une fiancée' is also considered deplorable; for 'pendant ce temps, le mal croissait à l'intérieur, et la ruine de ces beaux rêves éclos dans un moment d'enthousiasme se préparait lentement.'[139] It is evident that he looks upon this 'ruin' with some satisfaction, as the just and inevitable outcome of culpable temerity. The tone is very different from that adopted by Michelet in his plaintive lament of 1833:

Riches croisées coiffées de triangles imposans . . . fine et transparente dentelle de pierre filée au fuseau des fées; elle alla ainsi de plus en plus ornée et triomphante, à mesure qu'au-dedans le mal augmentait. Vous avez beau faire, souffrante beauté, le bracelet flotte autour d'un bras amaigri; vous savez trop, la pensée vous brûle, vous languissez d'amour impuissant.[140]

Gothic architecture is attacked by Renan not only for its temerity (following Quatremère de Quincy, who in the article EXAGÉRATION of his *Dictionnaire historique d'architecture* devotes considerable space to the definition of 'l'*exagération* vicieuse'),[141] but also for its attempt to intimidate. Here, too, he is developing a suggestion made by Quatremère (who speaks of 'un bâtiment étayé de toutes parts, & qui menace ruine'),[142]

[135] *Os. cs.* vii. 291.   [136] Ibid. p. 293.
[137] *Os. cs.* ii. 486.   [138] Ibid. p. 480.
[139] *Os. cs.* ii. 486.   [140] *H.F.* ii. 688.
[141] Quatremère de Quincy, *Dictionnaire historique d'architecture,* i (1832), 611.
[142] Quatremère de Quincy, *Encyclopédie méthodique: Architecture,* i (1788), 88.

taken up by Jules Quicherat in 1853 ('. . . la menace que semble suspendre au-dessus de la tête du spectateur toute cette charpente de pierre'),[143] and expanded by Michelet in 1855 into a remarkable image: 'Les stalactites artificielles, pendentifs hasardés qu'on admirait dans les bijoux, dans les meubles, on les fait en pierres; elles descendent des choeurs et des nefs, énormes, lourdes à faire peur, écrasantes; le fidèle, sous cette menace, ne se hasarde qu'en tremblant.'[144] Renan goes further than this. The to him disagreeable effect of Gothic is attributed not merely to incompetence or misjudgement on the part of its builders, but to deliberate, calculated menace. 'Les vides s'augmentent', he says, 'dans une effrayante proportion', and he goes on to speak of 'ces masses branlantes'. Blame is placed on 'l'artiste, surtout avide de faire naitre un sentiment d'étonnement', who does not scruple to use 'des moyens d'illusion et de fantasmagorie'.[145] The note of moral censure is stronger than in Michelet. He repeats the latter's strictures concerning the use of exterior props to shore up the unsound edifice: Gothic architecture is characterized by 'un défaut général de solidité', while 'le style grec est la raison même. . . . L'édifice grec . . . n'a besoin d'aucune réparation'; but he speaks of 'une impression douteuse' which is left 'entre l'imagination, qui est charmée, et le jugement, qui réprouve', with a sternness all his own. 'L'architecture gothique était malade', he concludes.[146] It was 'une exagération d'un moment, non un système fécond';[147] 'né de l'enthousiasme, il ne pouvait vivre que d'enthousiasme.'[146] The force of his moral indignation is directed not only against the architecture but against the society which produced it, in the days of its discreditable decline: the pleasure-seeking court of the Valois. 'Philippe de Valois et son fils Jean apparaissaient . . . à l'imagination de leurs contemporains comme des rois de chanson de geste, passant leur vie en guerres et en fêtes. . . . Mais l'art véritable ne va pas sans une solide culture de jugement.'[148] Had it not been for 'la légèreté des Valois, le peu de sérieux de la noblesse, l'esprit étroit de la bourgeoisie', the Renaissance might have originated in France.[149]

---

[143] J. Quicherat, 'Cours d'archéologie française du moyen âge', *Journal général de l'instruction publique,* xxii, 21 May 1853, p. 322.

[144] Michelet, *Renaissance,* p. 387.

[145] Renan, *Os. cs.* ii, 480-1. The first version (*RDM,* 1 July 1862, p. 212) reads 'un sentiment d'étonnement et de terreur'. Cf. Stendhal's viewpoint, reported by Mérimée in 1855: 'Nos églises sombres et lugubres avaient été inventées, disait-il, par des moines fripons qui voulaient s'enrichir en faisant peur aux gens timides' (Mérimée, *Portraits historiques et littéraires,* ed. Jourda, 1928, p. 186).

[146] Renan, *Os. cs.* ii, 486-7.   [147] Ibid. p. 489.
[148] Ibid. p. 493.   [149] Ibid. p. 484.

In his *Discours sur l'état des beaux-arts en France au XIVe siècle* Renan declares: 'Les grandes cours, et en particulier celle de France, étaient un spectacle continuel, où l'amour du plaisir se donnait carrière, souvent aux dépens de la sévère morale et du bon goût';[150] and he shakes his head over Louis d'Orléans: 'le manque de sérieux le perdit.'[151] We shall see how Taine was to repeat these accusations. In his case it is certain that contemporary society is being attacked in the guise of fourteenth-century France, and in the case of Renan, it is highly probable. It was, of course, Louis d'Orléans' castle of Pierrefonds that Louis Napoleon had chosen for his summer residence; and the emblems of the Valois prince, linked with those of the Bonaparte family, were painted on its walls by Viollet-le-Duc.

Renan has scarcely a good word to say for the Middle Ages after 1862. There are traces of his old nostalgia for the peace of the cloister. In 1866 he holds up the example of St. Francis of Assisi to the modern world, greedy for material gain,[152] and in the Preface to his *Nouvelles Études d'histoire religieuse* (1884) he identifies himself with the saint — 'Comme le patriarche d'Assise, j'ai traversé le monde, sans attache sérieuse au monde'[153] —, as he used to identify himself with the chosen few monks in their studious retreat. In the *Souvenirs d'enfance et de jeunesse,* in particular, he recreates the old mood, seeing the Tréguier of his youth and its cathedral as 'une forte protestation contre tout ce qui est plat et banal', seeing himself as 'un homme chimérique, disciple de saint Tudwal, de saint Iltud et de saint Cadoc, dans un siècle où l'enseignement de ces saints n'a plus aucune application'.[154] Neverthe-less, although his Celtic self lives on,[155] it is the Greek world which is now increasingly held up as an example of perfection, putting to shame both the modern world and the Middle Ages. Renan was, of course, from the beginning of his career convinced of the superiority of Greek art,[156] but in 1865, when he visited Athens, its perfection was revealed to him afresh, and the temptation to abuse the Middle Ages, first felt in 1862, was revived. Quant à l'antiquité . . .,' he wrote to a correspondent, 'c'est la perfection. Le soin, la conscience, la réflexion apportées à ces ouvrages sont une éternelle leçon de goût et d'honnêteté';[157] and to another: 'Pas une ombre de charlatanisme; rien pour le décor. . . . Le

---

[150] Ibid. viii. 599.   [151] Ibid. p. 696.
[152] See Ibid. vii. 920.   [153] Ibid. p. 707.
[154] Ibid. ii. 728.   [155] See, e.g., ibid. iv. 871 (Preface to *Saint Paul,* 1869).
[156] See H. Tronchon, *E. Renan et l'étranger,* 1928, Ch. 1.
[157] *Os. cs.* x. 420.

Parthénon dépasse en vraie grandeur nos églises gothiques les plus gigantesques.'[158] To Victor Le Clerc he expressed the regret that in the *Discours sur l'état des beaux-arts* he did not use terms strong enough to indicate the immense superiority of Greek over Gothic.[159]

This revelation resulted in the *Prière sur l'Acropole* (1876): 'Le beau n'est ici que l'honnêteté absolue. . . . Les parties cachées de l'édifice sont aussi soignées que celles qui sont vues. . . . Leurs temples sont trois fois hauts comme le tien, ô Eurhythmie, et semblables à des forêts; seulement ils ne sont pas solides.'[160]

Not only did Renan pursue his attack on Gothic architecture during his visit to Athens; he prepared a more radical offensive against the Middle Ages themselves. He jotted down some rancorous notes which were also used in the *Prière sur l'Acropole*: 'Durant plus de 10 s. ce monde a été un désert. . . . Lourds badauds, laids de figure, de costume. Le monde occupé par badauds. . . .'[161] Le M.A! grotesque fierté! pédantisme niais. . . .'[162] In the manuscript version of the *Prière* this became: 'Pendant mille ans, le monde a été un désert, traversé par des sauvages . . . laids de figure, ridicules de costume',[163] and in the final version, simply: 'Pendant mille ans, le monde a été un désert où ne germait aucune fleur.'[164] The 'lourds badauds' changed into 'des lourdauds': 'Je trouvai notre moyen âge sans élégance ni tournure, entaché de fierté déplacée et de pédantisme. Charlemagne m'apparut comme un gros palefrenier allemand; nos chevaliers me semblèrent des lourdauds, dont Thémistocle et Alcibiade eussent souri.'[165]

Renan's most savage remarks on the Middle Ages were made in his obituary article on Victor Le Clerc (1868).[166] Here he has arrived at the position of Michelet, to whom, as we have seen, the Middle Ages represented 'l'ennemi',[167] 'l'étranger',[168] or 'la Fiancée de Corinthe'[169] in whose embrace lies mortal peril. Renan too warns that 'l'étude du moyen âge, quand elle est exclusive, est dangereuse.' The unwary historian may be bewitched into forgetting 'le code féroce de l'inquisi-

---

[158] Ibid. p. 422.   [159] Ibid. p. 428.   [160] Ibid. ii. 754-5.
[161] H. Psichari, *La 'Prière sur l'Acropole' et ses mystères*, 1956, p. 62.
[162] Ibid. p. 72.   [163] Ibid. p. 61.   [164] Renan, *Os. cs.* ii. 756.
[165] Ibid. p. 754. Cf. Taine's *Voyage en Italie* (1866). Some Romanesque sculptures on a church in Verona 'ressemblent à de grosses caricatures, à des lourdauds allemands en grandes capotes' (*V. en It.*, 1965, ii, 339).
[166] *RDM*, 15 March 1868, pp. 341-74. Reprinted (with slight revision) in *Histoire littéraire de la France*, xxv (1869), and in Renan's *Mélanges d'histoire et de voyages*, 1878. Text quoted from here is that of the 1869 version, in *Os. cs.* ii.
[167] *La Régence*, 1863, p. xii (Preface).   [168] *Bible de l'humanité*, 1864, p. 485.
[169] *H.F.* i (1879), 19 (1869 Preface).

tion, ces massacres, ces atrocités de la persécution religieuse . . . des scènes d'horreur comme les règnes de Dèce et de Dioclétien n'en connurent pas.'[170] He insists – doubtless in reaction to Léon Gautier's *Épopées françaises* (1865-8) – that in that dark age 'le style et le goût firent défaut presque en toute chose. Les chansons de geste ne valent pas plus Homère que les voussures sculptées d'une église gothique ne valent les frises du Parthénon. . . . De pesants heros[171] ne remplaceront jamais . . . les formes divines du monde épique de la Grèce.' 'Ajoutez', he continues, 'le manque de lumière, de délicatesse, l'énorme chaîne créée par des dogmes terribles'; and he concludes that the Middle Ages were 'une déchéance, une éclipse dans l'histoire de la civilisation', whereas 'la Renaissance fut un légitime retour à la grande tradition de l'humanité.'[172] Medieval men, certain of whom he once used to consider the antithesis of the modern bourgeois, were 'des bourgeois dans le royaume de la beauté'.[173] A passing reference is made in the Preface to Renan's *L'Antéchrist* (1873) to 'ce long deuil de la beauté qu'on appelle le moyen âge';[174] and in the Preface to his *Souvenirs d'enfance et de jeunesse* he goes into the attack again, raising his voice against State-imposed religion. The Second Empire lies behind as a warning to those whose sympathies incline them towards the setting up of 'l'état théocratique': 'Il ne faut pas oublier combien ce gouvernement fut fort lorsqu'il s'agit d'écraser l'esprit, et faible lorsqu'il s'agit de le relever';[175] and in the more distant past there is 'l'effroyable aventure du moyen âge', when 'un poids colossal de stupidité a écrasé l'esprit humain.'[176]

(iii) *Taine: 'La vérité pure, telle qu'elle est, atroce et sale . . .'*
Taine, who in his writings on medieval art and society drew inspiration from both Michelet and Renan, differed from them in the fact that he had never for one moment been swayed by the slightest feeling of affection for the Middle Ages. From his earliest years they inspired in him the utmost horror and (a feeling peculiar to him, which gives his writings on the subject their particular flavour) fear. Taine's abuse of the Middle Ages lacks Michelet's poetic force, as he is not burning what he once adored; but it has the violent and vehement quality characteristic of all his writing, and which Charles Seignobos deplores as a form of Romanticism unfitting in a historian: 'Il obtenait un tronçon monstrueux, frappant pour l'imagination. . . . En voulant frapper fort,

---

[170] Renan, *Os. cs.* ii. 664.   [171] 'Des lourdauds héroïques' in the 1868 version.
[172] Renan, *Os. cs.* ii. 664-5.   [173] *RDM*, 15 March 1868, p. 352 (deleted in 1869).
[174] *Os. cs.* iv. 1123.   [175] Ibid. ii. 718.
[176] *Os. cs.* ii. 719.

il a souvent frappé faux.'[177] Taine in 1855 had pronounced the same judgement on Michelet, calling him a Romantic visionary whose hyperbolic utterances fail to carry conviction in an age increasingly insistent on scientific impartiality. 'Railleries amères . . ., haine et colère, toutes les passions violentes s'accumulent en lui',[178] he complained: 'L'émotion trop vive l'empêche de douter quand il compose.'[179] Yet these remarks could also be applied to his own less tormented, but equally passionate, denunciations of the Middle Ages. Taine was in theory an advocate of the dispassionate scrutiny of past civilizations. The modern historian, he more than once proclaimed, abstained from passing judgement upon them in the manner of his eighteenth-century predecessors. 'La science ne proscrit ni ne pardonne,' he declares in his *Philosophie de l'art* (1865), 'elle constate et elle explique.'[180] The spirit of a past age was to be divined through impartial examination of the works of art it has left to posterity; but the Middle Ages were by Taine condemned as soon as divined; and when he proceeds to analyse the infirmity of Gothic art, the force of his moral indignation is greater even than Renan's. Like Michelet and Renan, he dwells upon the 'decadence' of Gothic architecture in the fourteenth and fifteenth centuries. Tracing the history of this decline, and subjecting medieval society to his special brand of psychological analysis, give him ample scope for the passing of moral judgements, ruled out in theory by refusal to employ absolute aesthetic standards. He first expounds his views in the *Histoire de la littérature anglaise*. Most of that section of it which concerns us appeared in the *Journal des débats* and the *Revue germanique* (December 1862 – January 1863); and in book form (Volume 1 of the *Histoire*) in January 1864. Taine proclaims Gothic architecture to be the infirm, fragile product of an ailing society, whose stagnation and overpowering 'ennui' he dwells on in the manner of Michelet, and whose frivolity he inveighs against in the manner of Renan.[181] Once again, it is the Empire which appears to be under attack.

---

[177] Petit de Julleville, *Histoire de la langue et de la littérature française*, A. Colin, viii (1899), 278.

[178] Taine, *Essais de critique et d'histoire,* 2nd edn., 1866, p. 194.

[179] Ibid. p. 203.   [180] *Philosophie de l'art*, 1865, p. 21.

[181] Renan's and Taine's criticism of Gothic disproves Paul Frankl's contention that confusion of ethics with aesthetics – the Ruskinian notion that 'good men build good buildings', which Frankl calls 'pharisaism carried over into the history of art' – was 'a completely isolated English phenomenon' (Frankl, *The Gothic: Literary Sources and Interpretations through Eight Centuries,* Princeton, N.J., 1960, pp. 561-3). Pugin and Ruskin used the idea to exalt Gothic; Renan and Taine, to confound it.

Taine had, of course, been in disfavour with the authorities in the early days of the regime. In 1852 it had been made impossible for him to continue his university career. In 1863 the patronage of the Princesse Mathilde secured him a post as examiner at Saint-Cyr, and the following year the liberal Minister of Education Victor Duruy made amends for the earlier persecutions of the reactionary Fortoul by giving him the chair at the École des Beaux-Arts left vacant by Viollet-le-Duc's enforced resignation; but Taine used this chair to denounce the Middle Ages and extol Greece and Renaissance Italy, like so many of the regime's opponents, in whose ranks he, being a political neutral, was not officially included.

In the *Histoire de la littérature anglaise,* and subsequent works,[182] Taine continued Michelet's and Renan's depreciation of Gothic. One feature of it alone aroused his whole-hearted enthusiasm: stained glass. This satisfied the craving for colour which often caused his generation to recoil from the Dark Ages. (The Goncourts, for instance, in the Musée de Cluny, were depressed by 'ces bois, ces cuirs, tout ce noir, tout ce sombre, cet enfumé', and exclaimed 'Depuis le Moyen Âge, le monde semble sortir d'une cave et se pousser au jour avec tout ce qui y rit, les tapisseries à fond blanc, les bois dorés').[183] But Taine was seized with admiration whenever he moved on from derision of a cathedral's exterior structure to examine its interior: 'Dans ce jour violet, sous cette pourpre vacillante, parmi ces flèches d'or qui percent l'ombre, l'édifice entier ressemble à la queue d'un paon mystique.'[184] 'La queue d'un paon n'est pas plus magnifique; mais l'effet est tout autre, douloureux, violent. Ces couleurs parlent; elles sont toutes excessives.'[185] One feels that 'excessives' here is a term of praise. In the *Philosophie de l'art* the fact that fear-ridden men were driven by their religion to shun the clear light of day is not entirely to be regretted, for it produced the splendour of stained glass, with its 'illuminations étranges, qui semblent des percées sur le paradis'.[186]

In all other respects, however, Taine views the cathedral with anger rather than admiration. 'Sans le placage extérieur des contre-forts', he declares, 'et l'aide artificielle des crampons de fer, l'édifice aurait croulé au premier jour; tel qu'il est, il se défait de lui-même, et il faut entretenir sur place des colonies de maçons pour combattre incessamment sa ruine

---

[182] The *Carnets de voyage* (1863-5, published posthumously in 1897); the *Philosophie de l'art* (1865), *Voyage en Italie* (1866), and *Philosophie de l'art en Grèce* (1869).
[183] *Journal des Goncourt,* ii, 139.   [184] *HLA* i. 178.
[185] *Carnets de voyage,* 1897, p. 62.   [186] *Philosophie de l'art,* p. 127.

incessante.'[187] He discovers a new term of disparagement for these
buttresses. Michelet had called the cathedral in 1855 'un faible insecte
montrant, traînant après lui un cortége de membres grêles, qui, blessés,
le feront choir'.[188] Renan in 1862 had spoken of 'un animal ayant sa
charpente osseuse autour de lui'.[189] Taine shows a still more pronounced
disrespect, when in 1863 he disdainfully describes Tours cathedral:
'Plusieurs contreforts enjambent la rue, comme une patte de crabe luxée.'[190]
With Michelet and Renan, he saw only infirmity where the Romantics had
seen grandiose beauty,[191] and converted all their eloquent praise of Gothic
into dispraise. He remarked (again of Tours), with evident disapproval:
'Rien que des dentelles de pierre; c'est du filigrane.'[192] Gothic in general,
'cette broderie de pierre travaillée à jour qui va s'amincissant jusqu'à la
flèche', he termed 'cette mensongère magnificence' − a 'parure de femme',
as in Michelet's panegyric of 1833, but the woman is 'nerveuse et
surexcitée'.[193] In his *Histoire de la littérature anglaise* he refers to this
medieval sculpture as 'ces décorations d'opéra', and declares with scorn:
'C'est le *besoin d'excitation* qui les produit.'[194] He remarks further on
of 'l'homme féodal' that 'la persécution de l'ennui avait agrandi chez
lui, outre mesure, le besoin d'excitation.'[195] This 'besoin' is mentioned
again in Taine's *Frédéric-Thomas Graindorge* (1867); but this time it is
deplored as a feature of modern Paris, noted in the restless, murmuring
crowd of the audience at the Théâtre des Italiens: 'le *besoin d'excitation;*
ce mot à Paris revient toujours aux lèvres.'[196] So the late Middle Ages and

---

[187] *HLA*, 2nd edn., 1866, i. 178. Cf. *Philosophie de l'art*, p. 130, and *Philosophie de l'art en Grèce*, 2nd edn., 1882, p. 62. These 'colonies' are the 'villages de maçons' which aroused Michelet's alarm in 1855, 'établis au pied de ces édifices, vivant, engraissant là-dessus, eux et leurs nombreux enfants' (*Renaissance*, pp. 89-90).

[188] Michelet, *Renaissance*, p. 89.

[189] Renan, *Os. cs.* ii. 480.

[190] *Carnets de voyage*, p. 62. (See also ibid. p. 230, and *Voyage en Italie*, i. 27.) Cf. Hugo's defence in 1863 of medieval taste, which 'tirant une beauté d'une infirmité', devised 'ces sublimes arcs-boutants, si stupidement critiqués, lesquels semblent les arches obliques d'un pont de la terre au ciel' (*William Shakespeare*, 1937, p. 287 ('Reliquat')).

[191] Cf. Hugo, in *Han d'Islande* (1823): 'Voici la cathédrale, dont les arcs-boutants . . . se dessinent comme les côtes de la carcasse d'un mammouth' (Édn. de l'Imprimerie Nationale, 1910, p. 87); Gautier's 'Notre-Dame' (1831): 'La nef épanouie, entre ses côtes minces,/Semble un crabe géant faisant mouvoir ses pinces' (*Poésies complètes*, ii, 148); and Hugo's famous likening of Notre-Dame to 'une sorte d'éléphant prodigieux', bearing down upon the guilty Frollo (*Notre-Dame de Paris*, p. 414).

[192] *Carnets de voyage*, p. 61.   [193] *Philosophie de l'art*, pp. 130-1.

[194] *HLA* i. 169.   [195] Ibid. pp. 328-9.

[196] *Vie et opinions de M. Frédéric-Thomas Graindorge*, 1867, p. 170.

the Second Empire are suffering from the same malady; and so too the
meretricious 'décorations d'opéra' produced in this fevered climate are
mentioned from time to time by more than one writer of the period,
sometimes in a modern, sometimes in a medieval context. Hugo
addresses Louis Napoleon in *Les Châtiments*:

> Te figures-tu donc que ceci durera?
> Prends-tu pour du granit ce décor d'opéra?[197]

Michelet in 1855 was the first to speak of Gothic cathedrals as
'd'immenses décorations qu'on ne soutient debout que par des efforts
constamment renouvelés'.[198] Renan in 1858 spoke of 'nos villes sans
cesse rebâties, où le passé semble resté debout, non par son droit, mais
par grâce et comme un décor théâtral'.[199] Taine, in 1863, a month after
he had referred to Gothic architecture as 'ces décorations d'opéra', expressed stern disapproval of the literature in vogue in the France of
Louis d'Orléans, and of the society which eagerly devoured it: 'Que
diriez-vous d'une société qui, pour toute littérature, aurait l'opéra et
ses fantasmagories?'[200] In the same year, he was captivated by the
Renaissance mansions of Toulouse: 'Comme à côté de cela toutes nos
constructions modernes, nos rues de Richelieu sont plates! Comme le
Louvre et la place de la Concorde ne semblent plus que des décorations
d'opéra!';[201] but at Carcassonne, in 1865, he deplored Viollet-le-Duc's
restoration: 'Malheureusement on répare l'enceinte; les constructions,
neuves et propres, si dépaysées aujourd'hui, semblent un décor d'opéra.'[202]
So the Middle Ages, the Second Empire, and the Empire's attempt to
restore the Middle Ages, were all condemned as the same factitious,
fragile outward show. Consideration of their fragility inevitably led to
prediction of the doom awaiting them. Victor de Laprade dismissed the
buildings of Haussmann's Paris:

> . . . toutes ces laideurs, mille autres qui naîtront,
> Portent les mots: fragile et provisoire au front;
> A ces énormités la solidité manque:
> Un souffle emportera baraque et saltimbanque.[203]

In the wake of Renan, Taine declared that Louis d'Orléans' pursuit of
pleasure brought about France's ruin: '. . . cette civilisation romanesque,
dépourvue de bon sens, livrée à la passion, tournée vers le plaisir,

---

[197] V. Hugo, *Oeuvres poétiques,* ii (1967), 87.   [198] Michelet, *Renaissance,* p. 171.
[199] Renan, *Os. cs.* ii. 31.   [200] *HLA* i. 120 (*Revue germanique,* 1 Jan. 1863).
[201] *Carnets de voyage,* p. 93.   [202] *Carnets de voyage,* p. 291.
[203] V. de Laprade, 'Aux démolisseurs' (1860), *Oeuvres poétiques,* iii: *Poèmes civiques.*
Tribuns et courtisans, Lemerre, n.d., p. 50.

immorale et brillante, et qui . . . faute de sérieux, ne put durer.'[204]
In its insatiable hunger for 'le divertissement violent et vide',[205] 'le
moyen âge sombr[a] sous ses vices.'[206] (Similarly, Taine remarked
maliciously of Walter Scott's bankruptcy in the *Histoire de la littérature
anglaise:* 'Ni dans sa conduite ni dans sa littérature ses goûts féodaux ne
lui avaient réussi, et ses splendeurs seigneuriales s'étaient trouvées aussi
fragiles que ses imaginations gothiques',[207] implying, as had the course
of events recounted by Flaubert in *Madame Bovary,* that no good can
come of Romantic medievalizing, and that it is likely to lead anyone
foolish enough to indulge in it into a particularly unpleasant reality.)
His description of the late Middle Ages combines Renan's disgust with
the frivolity of medieval courtly society — 'Insensiblement le sérieux
diminue dans les écrits comme dans les moeurs'[208] — with Michelet's
sombre portrayal of ecclesiastical tyranny:

De main en main la chimère grandit, ouvre davantage ses vastes ailes
ténébreuses.'[209] 'Le régime scolastique a érigé en reine la lettre morte et
peuplé le monde d'esprits morts.'[210] 'Âge triste et morne, amusé par des
divertissements extérieurs, opprimé par une misère plate, qui souffre et
craint sans consolation ni espérance. . . . Le Hasard, comme une noire
fumée, plane au-dessus des choses et bouche la vue du ciel.[211]

'Le Hasard' represents all that is most abhorrent to the determinist
Taine; but the Renaissance is close at hand, a radiant dawn: 'Tous les
fléaux du moyen âge reculent et s'effacent dans le passé.'[212] 'Après
l'affreuse nuit du moyen âge et les douloureuses légendes des revenants
et des damnés, c'est un charme que de revoir l'olympe rayonnant de la
Grèce.'[213] Fixing the gaze upon the promise of the Renaissance affords
the same relief to the despondent historian of the Middle Ages as stern
predictions of the dissolution of the medieval world. In his discussion
of the sorry state of English literature in the fifteenth century Taine
speaks with sermonic vehemence: '. . . au-dessous de la vaine parade
officielle il n'y a plus qu'un pêle-mêle de débris.'[214] And the same note
is sounded in his exposition of the state of society in fourteenth- and
fifteenth-century France: 'Au-dessous de ce songe chimérique, qu'y
a-t-il? Les brutales et méchantes passions humaines.'[215]

[204] Taine, *HLA* i. 116 (*Revue germanique* (Jan. 1863)).
[205] Ibid. p. 120.   [206] Ibid. p. 123.   [207] *HLA* iv. 302 (*RDM,* 15 Sept. 1862).
[208] Ibid. i. 168-9 (*Journal des débats* (Dec. 1862)).
[209] Ibid. p. 224 (– do –).   [210] Ibid. p. 230 (– do –).
[211] Ibid. p. 232 (– do –).   [212] Ibid. p. 243.
[213] Ibid. p. 258.   [214] Ibid. p. 234.   [215] Ibid. p. 121.

Here Taine has reached what he considers to be the true Middle Ages, 'la vérité pure, telle qu'elle est, atroce et sale',[216] concealed by Scott, who was not equal to the task of portraying 'la sensualité débridée, la férocité bestiale, . . . [les] brutes héroïques et [les] bêtes féroces du moyen âge'.[217] Taine is fully confident that he has discovered the ignoble reality beneath the painted surface. In his Introduction to the *Histoire de la littérature anglaise* he states that the new scientific method of scrutinizing the past enables the historian to see men from a vanished civilization 'avec nos yeux, *avec les yeux de notre tête*'.[218] 'Cette divination précise et prouvée des sentiments évanouis', he proclaims, 'a, de nos jours, renouvelé l'histoire';[219] and boldly he calls to his fellow-workers: 'Rendons-nous le passé présent.'[220] But by so doing, in his writings on the Middle Ages, he conjures up a nightmare world which at once strikes terror into its creator. This fear of his is all the more intense because, as in the case of their surface glitter, their 'décor d'opéra', the modern and medieval worlds in their 'vérité atroce et sale' are at moments one and the same. Medieval men are for Taine wild animals. The term 'brutes' is the one which most readily occurs to him when speaking of them.[221] In 1857 he declares:

Cette spoliation et ces meurtres des faibles, ce commerce de guet-apens et d'assassinats entre les forts, cette habitude d'outrager et d'égorger la loi et la justice, composent presque dans tout le moyen âge les moeurs féodales, et, après avoir pesé attentivement les bienfaits et les félicités de cet âge vanté, je trouve que j'aimerais autant vivre au fond d'un bois dans une bande de loups.[222]

In his essay on *Renaud de Montauban* (1864) he repeats that in the Middle Ages 'on tuait et on était tué sans avoir eu le temps d'y penser . . . à chaque instant l'explosion des instincts farouches venait déchirer le tissu régulier dans lequel toute société tend à s'enfermer.'[223] But these wild animals still exist in the increasingly feared proletariat, which presents a constant threat to settled bourgeois society. Taine's friend Renan had in *L'Avenir de la science* (1848-9) expressed fear that, '. . . si l'on ne se hâte d'élever le peuple, nous sommes à la veille d'une

---

[216] *HLA* iv. 300.   [217] Ibid. pp. 301-2.   [218] Ibid. i. p. v.
[219] Ibid. pp. xi-xii.   [220] Ibid. p. ix.
[221] Cf. *HLA* i. 122; *Voyage en Italie*, i. 26; ii. 237. Stendhal, whose influence on Taine was considerable, called medieval men '[des] brutes . . . [des] sauvages dégradés . . . des animaux féroces' (Introduction to *Histoire de la peinture en Italie* (1817), Édn. du Divan, 1929, i. 11).
[222] *Essais de critique et d'histoire*, pp. 8-9.
[223] *Nouveaux Essais de critique et d'histoire*, 2nd edn., 1866, p. 196.

affreuse barbarie. Car, si le peuple triomphe tel qu'il est, ce sera pis que
les Francs et les Vandales . . . Il faudra traverser un autre moyen âge.'[224]
And his friend Flaubert, in 1871, declared that with the Commune the
twelfth century had returned — 'Pauvre France, qui ne se dégagera
jamais du moyen âge!'[225] — and that he felt within himself the return
of sanguinary instincts: 'Quelle barbarie. Quelle reculade. J'en veux à
mes contemporains de m'avoir donné les sentiments d'une brute du
XIIe siècle.'[226]

Taine re-enters the Middle Ages whenever he explores the alley-ways
of an old city. He is far from sharing that sense of 'la poésie du
délabrement',[227] which Hugo communicated to his readers in *Notre-
Dame de Paris,* calling to their attention 'le profil gothique de ce vieux
Paris . . . noyez-le dans une nuit profonde, et regardez le jeu bizarre des
ténèbres et des lumières dans ce sombre labyrinthe.'[228] It is with a
shudder that he contemplates the old streets of Marseille in 1863: 'On
dirait un dessin de Doré, une horrible vision après une peste, pendant
le Moyen âge.'[229] Two years later some houses in Vannes appear equally
sinister, forming 'un pêle-mêle biscornu'. 'Voilà les restes du Moyen
âge,' he laments, 'la fantaisie et l'anti-hygiène.'[230]

So the Middle Ages are for Taine entirely non-reassuring. They are
unsound, ramshackle, not built to last. They are a state of squalor and
anarchy lurking beneath the surface of the modern world. Above all,
they are not to be viewed romantically. When he evokes the following
scene: 'Le poëte arrive, offre son manuscrit "richement enluminé, relié
en violet cramoisi, embelli de fermoirs, de bossettes d'argent, de roses
d'or"; on lui demande de quoi il traite, et il répond "d'amour"',[231] it is
not, as it would have been in the 1820s and 30s, and will be once more
in the 80s and 90s, regarded as a poetic spectacle, delighting both author
and reader; it is cited as an example of the contemptibly futile diversions
indulged in by a decadent society. The naïveté of the medieval world is
regarded as reprehensible, 'une puérilité vieillotte',[232] and sinister: 'Ce
babil enfantin des poëmes et des contes dissimule la rude voix des
furieux qui égorgeaient soixante-dix mille musulmans, femmes et enfants,

---

[224] Renan, *Os. cs.* iii. 999.   [226] Ibid. pp. 202-3.
[225] Flaubert, *Correspondance*, vi. 224.
[227] An expression used by Hugo in a letter of 1864, recalling Blois in 1825 (quoted
by P. Dufay, *V. Hugo à vingt ans,* Mercure de France, 1909, p. 151).
[228] *Notre-Dame de Paris,* p. 162.
[229] *Carnets de voyage,* p. 118.   [230] Ibid. p. 260.
[231] *HLA* i. 170. The episode referred to is Froissart's presentation of his poems to
Richard II. See *Chroniques,* ed. Kervyn de Lettenhove, xv (Brussels, 1871), 167.
[232] Ibid. p. 123.

à Jérusalem, qui empalaient et arrosaient de plomb fondu les députés des malheureux serfs normands.'[233] These last remarks are examples of the 'petits faits vrais' cherished by Taine, and marshalled by him in a considerable array in the *Histoire de la littérature anglaise,* to illustrate the appalling savagery of the medieval world. Léon Gautier, in his *Comment faut-il juger le moyen âge?* (1858) protested at the unrestrained joy with which republican enemies of the Middle Ages went about their work of destruction: 'Rien n'arrête ces fanatiques. . . . A chaque scandale, à chaque crime qu'ils trouvent dans les âges de foi, leur joie éclate; l'esclave qui a trouvé un riche diamant dans les sables du Brésil n'est pas plus heureux en le montrant à ses maîtres qu'ils ne sont heureux de montrer le crime qu'ils ont habilement déterré.'[234] Taine would seem to bear this out when on a visit in 1865 to the church of the Jacobins at Toulouse he is given 'quantité de brochures' on the Dominican Inquisition, and reads in one of them 'une histoire de femme malade, brûlée vive, qui est admirable'.[235] He was delighted by the results of the experiment carried out in 1862 by Dr. Paul Broca on skulls from various Parisian cemeteries. Measurement of these skulls, reported the doctor, showed that the capacity of twelfth-century crania was less than that of nineteenth-century ones. Taine mentions this in *De l'idéal dans l'art* (1867),[236] and again, at greater length, in 1873, in an article on Ribot's *L'Hérédité,* where he reassures himself:

Si aujourd'hui l'enfant d'un Européen naît doux et civilisé d'avance, au lieu d'être poussé par une force irrésistible à se sauver dans les bois comme le négrito des Philippines, ou à vivre, comme le gitano, en vagabond et en voleur, c'est que, par un progrès insensible, les habitudes raisonnables et sociables accumulées par les générations antérieures se sont emmagasinées dans l'organisme[237] —

[233] Taine, 'De l'esprit française importé en Angleterre: Littérature des Normands', *Revue de l'instruction publique,* xv. 28 Feb. 1856, p. 658.

[234] L. Gautier, *Comment faut-il juger le moyen âge?,* 1858, pp. 13-14.

[235] *Carnets de voyage,* p. 281.

[236] Taine, *De l'idéal dans l'art,* 1867, p. 67.

[237] Taine, *Derniers Essais de critique et d'histoire,* 1894, pp. 108-9. Broca's experiment also inspired Quinet's curious divagation on Gothic sculpture (in *L'Esprit nouveau,* 1874): 'Au moyen âge, lorsque . . . les figures humaines des statues se trouvèrent amaigries, émaciées, il ne faut pas seulement l'expliquer pas les maladresses d'un art barbare. Les crânes du douzième siècle, mesurés aujourd'hui dans les cimetières, expliquent par leur rétrécissement celui des figures des cathédrales gothiques. L'humanité, en s'interdisant de penser pendant mille ans, avait réduit pour le plus grand nombre la masse cérébrale' (*L'Esprit nouveau,* 5th edn., n.d., p. 88).

seeing once more the Middle Ages as the state of absolute savagery which
he had described in *La Philosophie de l'art*:

On en était arrivé aux moeurs des anthropophages de la Nouvelle-
Zélande, à l'abrutissement ignoble des Calédoniens et des Papous, au
plus bas-fond du cloaque humain, puisque le souvenir du passé
empirait la misère présente, et que les quelques têtes pensantes qui
lisaient encore l'ancienne langue sentaient obscurément l'immensité
de la chute et toute la profondeur de l'abîme dans lequel le genre
humain s'enfonçait depuis mille ans.[238]

C. *Catholic glorification: the Ultramontane group*
(i) *Gaume: 'une question de vie ou de mort'*

Most Catholic contemporaries of Michelet, Renan, and Taine set out
to glorify the Age of Faith and defend it against its detractors. They fall
into two main groups: Ultramontanes and liberals. The first Second
Empire polemicist in the former camp, the Abbé Gaume, and the
'Querelle des Classiques' which he initiated in 1851 with his pamphlet
Le Ver rongeur des sociétés modernes, at once illustrate how the pagan
and Renaissance worlds celebrated by the three writers whom we have
just examined became a meeting-ground for opponents of the Empire,
a paradise into which they escaped, and from which they emerged
refreshed to carry on their struggle. The Middle Ages were, as we have
seen, the Empire; Greece ('l'envers du moyen âge'[239] according to
Michelet) its antithesis; and the Renaissance, the hope that one day it
might come to an end. Measures taken by the Minister of Education
Fortoul at the beginning of the regime (suppression of the study of
philosophy, and its replacement by formal logic – mentioned in the
previous chapter; and the system of 'bifurcation', exempting pupils
specializing in science from all but elementary study of Greek and
Latin) met with angry opposition. 'M. Bonaparte', declared Hugo,
'déclare, par décret, suspectes les lettres grecques et latines, et interdit
le plus qu'il peut aux intelligences le commerce des vieux poètes et
des vieux historiens d'Athènes et de Rome, flairant dans Eschyle et
dans Tacite une vague odeur de démagogie.'[240]

---

[238] *Philosophie de l'art,* 1865, pp. 121-2. Here, or course, Taine is merely
reproducing the hyperbolic language employed by eighteenth-century enemies
of the Middle Ages. Cf. Voltaire (*Essai sur les moeurs,* Ch. XLV): 'A
n'envisager que les coutumes que je viens de rapporter, on croirait voir le
portrait des Nègres et des Hottentots'; and Dulaure (*Crimes et forfaits de la
noblesse et du clergé* (1793), on an eleventh-century famine: 'Un siècle
d'horreur devoit produire des anthropophages' (p. 18).

[239] *Bible de l'humanité,* 1864, p. 170.   [240] *Napoléon le Petit,* pp. 92-3.

The Abbé Gaume, in *Le Ver rongeur,* warned the government that
'les doctrines subversives auxquelles on a donné le nom de *socialisme*
ou de *communisme* sont le fruit de l'enseignement classique';[241] and
he recommended that pagan classics should be replaced in schools by
the Early Fathers and the Lives of the Saints. 'Ce n'est, ni plus ni moins,
qu'une question de vie ou de mort',[242] he declared. Urgent measures
were needed to counteract 'ce paganisme hideux qui déborde aujourd'hui
d'une manière si formidable sur l'Europe'.[243] A campaign against the
Renaissance, which was 'un immense pas rétrograde',[244] must be set in
motion. The Middle Ages, when 'cette société chrétienne créa une Europe
merveilleuse de grandeur, de force, de vertus héroïques',[245] were a
model of perfection — 'nos pères valaient mieux que nous'[246] — and
must be defended against their enemies: 'Étaient-ils des sauvages, fils
et frères de sauvages, ceux qui lancèrent dans les nues les flèches de nos
cathédrales?'[247] The Ultramontane Catholic Louis Veuillot, a fervent
supporter of the Emperor, immediately came out in support of Gaume
in his newspaper *L'Univers.* A bitter quarrel was started by *Le Ver
rongeur,* which was attacked by many Catholics, led by the Gallican
Dupanloup. Feelings ran high and continued to simmer for many years.
In the summer of 1852 the dispute in the newspaper columns focused
itself on the Middle Ages, and the opposing sides engaged in the first of
many skirmishes. Léon Aubineau in *L'Univers* spoke out in impassioned
defence of Gaume and the Middle Ages, recently under attack from the
Journal des débats: 'Le moyen âge n'avait rien que la charité et la foi . . .
de toutes les formes politiques et sociales, la féodalité a été celle qui a
répandu sur le plus grand nombre d'individus la plus grande masse de
bonheur.'[248] Silvestre de Sacy in the *Journal des débats* retorted that
'le cri qui sort de toutes les chroniques, de tous les monuments profanes
ou ecclésiastiques de la littérature de ce temps-là . . . est un long cri de
douleur et de désespoir.'[249] Jules Simon let forth a cry of outrage in *Le
Siècle:* 'Préférer le quinzième siècle au dix-neuvième!', and warned:
'M. l'abbé Gaume n'est qu'un soldat dans une armée. Le quinzième
siècle n'est pas mort, comme on le croyait; il existe, il est parmi nous,
nous le heurtons à chaque coin de rue, et même il est une puissance.'[250]

---

[241] J. Gaume, *Le Ver rongeur des sociétés modernes,* 1851, p. 32.
[242] *Lettre de M. Gaume à M. le Rédacteur en chef de 'L'Univers'* (Nevers, Nov.
1851). p. 4.
[243] Ibid. pp. 1-2.   [244] *Le Ver rongeur,* p. 196.   [245] Ibid. p. 25.
[246] Ibid. p. 271.   [247] Ibid. p. 273.   [248] *L'Univers,* 11 June 1852.
[249] *Journal des débats,* 26 June 1852.   [250] *Le Siècle,* 4 April 1852.

Le Charivari, as a rejoinder to *L'Univers*, issued with one of its numbers an appendix, *Un Journal au Moyen Âge*, with its 'partie Commerciale', reporting 'une stagnation dans les affaires ... depuis quelque temps les routes sont infestées de voleurs encore plus que de coutume'; 'Partie Politique' — 'la guerre va ... continuer encore. ... Depuis près de cent ans qu'elle dure, il n'y a pas de mal à en désirer la fin'; 'Nouvelles diverses' — 'La peste noire vient de se déclarer dans la Picardie. ... La peste ordinaire règne à Marseille. Au marché de Bourges, on a mis en vente de la chair humaine. ... Sept potences nouvelles viennent d'être élevées dans différens quartiers de Paris'; 'Annonces' — 'A louer plusieurs fenêtres d'une maison de la place de Grève pour assister au supplice de la sorcière Médarde'; and various other items in the same strain.[251]

(ii) *Louis Veuillot: 'Fonçons sur la chiennaille . . .'*

Strife broke out again in 1854, when Veuillot clashed with the prominent lawyer Jacques Dupin over the 'droit du seigneur'. During the 1850s Veuillot was an enthusiastic supporter of Louis Napoleon. 'Jusqu'à présent', he said of him in 1852, 'il paraît à nos yeux comme un homme suscité et assisté d'En Haut.'[252] But the Emperor's withdrawal of support from the Pope was a bitter blow to him: 'Mes rêves sont cruellement renversés: où est maintenant mon Charlemagne?' he wrote in May 1859.[253] Eight months later *L'Univers* was suppressed by the government for its Ultramontane sympathies.

Eternally bellicose, Veuillot sustained his reputation as the principal survivor from the Middle Ages during the Empire's first decade by issuing such injunctions as: 'Mon cheval hennit, mon sabre frémit dans le fourreau. Fonçons sur la chiennaille!'[254] (to a correspondent who had reproached him for harsh treatment of free-thinkers). During the *Ver rongeur* dispute, he retorted to Silvestre de Sacy, who had sneered at Saint Louis for going off to 'se faire emprisonner en Égypte, et mourir de la peste à Tunis': 'Le roi ou l'empereur français qui, pour abattre la puissance anglaise, cet islamisme de notre temps, risquera de trouver la mort en Égypte ou ailleurs, ne fera pas une folie trop nuisible à la France.'[255] In 1860, in his *Çà et là*, he hurled imprecations at 'les vilains de France', i.e. republicans attempting to replace the Crusaders' 'Dieu le veut!' with their cry 'Chacun pour soi',[256] and 'nos pères' of the Middle

---

[251] *Le Charivari*, 20 June 1852 (written by Clément Caraguel).
[252] Veuillot, *Mélanges*, v (1934), 263.
[253] Veuillot, *Correspondance*, vi (1931), 34.   [254] Ibid. iii (1931), 18-19.
[255] *Mélanges*, v. 150.   [256] Veuillot, *Oeuvres diverses*, viii (1926), 441-2.

Ages with 'nos pères' of the Revolution: 'A nous, fils de Clovis, fils de Charlemagne, fils de saint Louis, avant tout fils de saint Pierre; à nous, ces vilains, reniant notre gloire, prétendent faire accepter pour ancêtres des niais, des faquins et des brigands qu'ils appellent *leurs pères*.'[257]

When, in a session of the Académie des Sciences Morales et Politiques in April 1854, Dupin, reporting on Bouthors' *Coutumes locales du baillage d'Amiens*, challenged the 'amis posthumes de la féodalité'[258] to disprove the existence of the 'droit du seigneur', Veuillot took up the challenge with alacrity. With the help of his brother-in-law, a student at the École des Chartes, he composed in three months *Le Droit du seigneur*, which sold by the end of October 5,000 copies. In this work, the Middle Ages were presented as an earthly paradise. Where Michelet and his followers had seen only servitude, strife, inertia, and decrepitude, Veuillot saw peace, prosperity, contented endeavour, and 'l'âge d'or de la raison humaine'.[259]

Jamais [he declares] l'esprit humain n'a déployé plus de vigueur, et l'âme humaine plus d'amour. . . .[260] L'âme inondée de rayons divins voyagea de ce monde dans le ciel et dans l'éternité. . . . Partout des églises, des monastères, des écoles; partout l'hospitalité, la charité, la lumière du Christ, et nul autre travail que celui des champs, de la lumière et de l'art. Un parfum d'encens s'élevait de la terre, un feu et une fleur de jeunesse animaient les entreprises et égayaient les labeurs.[261]

A few words in support of the Empire were slipped into this panegyric. Veuillot reminded his readers that in the thirteenth century 'la France se couronna d'une gloire pure, durable, féconde. Elle terrassa l'hérésie albigeoise, qui était le socialisme d'alors',[260] and proceeded to affirm that 'la dictature même, lorsqu'elle est venue châtier la révolte, loin de consommer chez nous la servitude, a au contraire toujours relevé la liberté. Inestimable bienfait du moyen âge! il nous a légué une notion du pouvoir si intimement chrétienne, que nous sommes incapables de concevoir, de subir et même d'exercer la tyrannie.'[262]

Although Veuillot considered that he had put forward irrefragable proof that the 'droit du seigneur' was a myth, this did not deter Michelet from devoting considerable space in *La Sorcière* to a dramatic account of its exaction ('On voit d'ici la scène honteuse', etc.)[263] — in fact it almost

[257] Ibid. p. 433.
[258] *Séances et travaux de l'Académie des Sciences Morales et Politiques*, xxviii (1854), p. 131.
[259] Veuillot, *Oeuvres diverses*, vi (1925), 52.
[260] Ibid. p. 24.   [261] Ibid. p. 53.
[262] Ibid. p. 31.   [263] Michelet, *La Sorcière*, i. 56-9.

certainly inspired him to do so. It was in the tempestuous climate of 1854 (September-December) that he composed his Introduction to the *Renaissance*. In October, Jules Janin, in a review of E. Viollet-le-Duc's *Ancien Théâtre françois* in the *Journal des débats,* said that the first three volumes revealed the 'immense tristesse' of 'ce cher moyen-âge, que nous avons proclamé comme l'âge d'or: ces plaisanteries de l'heureux moyen-âge, on a le frisson rien qu'à les lire.'[264] A few days later, the aged poet Viennet read his 'Épitre à Clio' to the Académie:

> Par les nouveaux Frérons tout est glorifié:
> L'âge d'or va pâlir devant le Moyen Âge.[265]

Early in the next year Charles Renouvier applauded Michelet's *Renaissance,* calling the Middle Ages 'ce monde d'oubli et de douleurs', and proclaiming that 'le danger de cette seconde renaissance, ennemie de la première . . . paraît grand et palpable.'[266] In the same year was published and seized by the police Alexandre Erdan's *La France mystique,* with its Prologue devoted to furious abuse of 'l'école vengeresse du passé':[267] 'La résurrection du moyen-âge est maintenant achevée. La hideuse cohorte des musaraignes et des ratepenades a recommencé d'hier à grouiller en pleine civilisation. . . .'[268] Hé bien! spectre du moyen-âge, soit! En garde! Je te le dis, au nom de la seconde moitié du dix-neuvième siècle qui vient de s'ouvrir: En garde! ton gant est relevé!'[269]

(iii) *Léon Gautier*

A Catholic of the same extremist group as Veuillot, who devoted his entire career to the defence of the Middle Ages, was Léon Gautier. As we have seen, he called Renan in 1862 'cet ennemi du Moyen Âge'. He wrote of the first volume of Taine's *Histoire de la littérature anglaise:* 'Jamais le Moyen Âge n'a été à ce point traîné dans la boue',[270] and of *La Sorcière:* 'Ce livre est l'histoire de Satan, écrite sous sa dictée',[271] calling its author 'un fou furieux'.[272] In 1858, in his *Comment faut-il juger le moyen âge?,* he had stated that 'la question du moyen âge est devenue de nos jours la préoccupation la plus sérieuse des esprits éclairés.'[273] He concluded this work with a fervent invocation: 'Ô cher

---

[264] *Journal des débats,* 16 Oct. 1854.
[265] Veuillot, *Mélanges,* vi (1935), 101.   [266] *La Revue,* i (1855), pp. 37-8.
[267] A. Erdan, *La France mystique,* 2nd. edn., Amsterdam, 1858, p. 8.
[268] Ibid. pp. 6-7.   [269] Ibid. p. 11.
[270] L. Gautier, *Études littéraires pour la défense de l'Église,* 1865, p. 55.
[271] Ibid. p. 149.   [272] Ibid. p. 157.
[273] L. Gautier, *Comment faut-il juger le moyen âge?,* 1858, p. 38.

moyen âge! . . . L'étude de l'antiquité m'est devenue fade, depuis que j'ai goûté la douceur de tes saints, le miel de tes écrivains et la suavité de tes Églises.'[274] Gautier was a regular contributor to *Le Croisé*, a periodical which came into being in 1859, merged with *La Revue du monde catholique* in 1861, and reappeared from 1865 to 1869. He also wrote for the *Revue des questions historiques,* which was launched in 1866. Both these publications devoted much space to the refutation of attacks on the Middle Ages. Georges Seigneur, the editor of *Le Croisé*, insisted in 1866 that they were, in spite of Taine's denigration of them in his articles on Italy in the *Revue des deux mondes,* 'l'époque joyeuse de l'humanité'.[275]

D. *Liberal Catholics*

(i) *Montalembert: 'le vrai et le faux moyen âge'*

Liberal Catholics naturally put forward a version of the Age of Faith very different from that of Veuillot and his followers. They strove to dissociate the Middle Ages from the Empire and set them up as an antidote to it, a source of consolation comparable with the republicans' ancient Greece.

Charles de Montalembert was the most active of this group. Early in his career he had supported Hugo's campaign against the 'bande noire'. In his *Histoire de sainte Élisabeth de Hongrie* (1836) his admiration for the Middle Ages had known no bounds. They were for him a land of lost content, in which there reigned 'une immense santé morale'.[276] 'Qui pourrait calculer', he laments in his Introduction, 'combien la vie s'est appauvrie depuis lors?'[277] Constitutional government was his political ideal. From England in 1839 he wrote a eulogy of the great estates, with their contented tenants and herds of deer, seeing in them 'la féodalité idéale'.[278] In France no such ideal state of society had been achieved, because early in her history absolute monarchy had swept away the liberties that were beginning to be established in the Middle Ages. Montalembert saw in the Second Empire an odious dictatorship in the tradition of *ancien régime* absolutism. Until 1857 he spoke out against its policies in the Corps législatif. He was expelled from the Commission des Monuments Historiques in 1860, and from the Comité des Arts et

---

[274] Ibid. p. 112.   [275] *Le Croisé,* 3 Feb. 1866, p. 71.
[276] Montalembert, *Histoire de sainte Élisabeth de Hongrie,* 6th edn., 1854, p. cx.
[277] Ibid. p. cvi.   [278] E. Lacanuet, *Montalembert,* ii (1899), 93.

Monuments two years later. The increased momentum, under the Empire, of the movement to restore Gothic churches, regarded by Michelet in a sinister light ('les Gothiques, complètement rassurés et maîtres du terrain, vont de la truelle, de la plume, vont hardiment'),[279] was applauded by Montalembert, who saw in it the realization of the hopes of his youth: 'C'est une nouvelle renaissance qui s'opère sous nos yeux',[280] he declared in 1852; but the Empire itself he detested and energetically opposed. This caused a rift between him and his former friend Veuillot. Montalembert was particularly exasperated by what he considered to be *L'Univers*'s misappropriation of the Middle Ages in the service of the Imperial dictatorship. In a letter written in 1852 he declared that 'l'étude et l'amour du moyen âge catholique'[281] had implanted in him and nourished his love of liberty; and in his *Des Intérêts catholiques au dix-neuvième siècle* (1852) he explained himself fully: he and his fellow-Catholics who had arrived at a sane appreciation of the past wished not to 'ressusciter le moyen âge',[282] but to 'puiser dans cette étude du passé la force nécessaire pour tenir tête aux adversaires présents et futurs de l'Église . . . et maintenir le niveau des courages catholiques à la hauteur du coeur de nos pères.'[282] These forefathers were all lovers of liberty: 'l'étroite alliance de l'Église avec le pouvoir absolu'[283] in the Middle Ages was a myth. 'Tous les grands papes, tous les grands catholiques de ces grands siècles ont combattu pour la liberté, sous la forme qu'elle avait alors.'[284] Insisting that 'le gouvernement représentatif est né au moyen âge et du moyen âge',[285] Montalembert told Catholic supporters of the Empire, 'les courtisans de la victoire',[286] who cherished the myth of the authoritarian Age of Faith, that dictatorship was a pagan concept quite foreign to the Middle Ages. In an article published in July 1860 he returned to his attack upon 'les écrivains superficiels qui aiment à se figurer ou à dépeindre le moyen âge comme une époque de béatitude et de paix, où tout le monde obéissait docilement au pouvoir spirituel et temporel'. What Montalembert saw in the Middle Ages was 'une immense somme de libertés', preserved by 'un état de lutte universelle et permanente'.[287]

---

[279] Michelet, *Renaissance*, p. 170.
[280] Montalembert, *Des Intérêts catholiques au dix-neuvième siècle,* 3rd (revised) edn., Dec. 1852, pp. 56-7.
[281] *Correspondance de Montalembert et de l'abbé Texier,* ed. H. Texier, n.d., pp. 349-50.
[282] *Des Intérêts catholiques . . .,* p. 54.
[283] Ibid. p. 89.　　　[284] Ibid. p. 90.　　　[285] Ibid. p. 163.　　　[286] Ibid. p. 101.
[287] *Oeuvres*, vi: *Mélanges d'art et de littérature,* 1861, pp. 514-15.

'Ce repos absolu, qui est la suprême ambition des lâches,' was a characteristic of '[les] sociétés en déclin, prêtes à s'abîmer dans la honte'.[288] Here we have the equation of Louis Napoleon's Empire with the Roman Empire in decline, a theme further developed by Montalembert in the section 'Le Vrai et le Faux Moyen Âge' of the Introduction to his *Les Moines d'Occident* (1860). Hugo had said of Louis Napoleon: 'Il y a en lui du moyen âge et du bas-empire.'[289] Montalembert's work vigorously denies the first contention while upholding the second. His picture, at the beginning of *Les Moines d'Occident,* of the late Roman Empire: 'Tout y est énervé, étiolé, décrépit. Pas un grand homme, pas un grand caractère ne surnage dans cette fange'[290] closely resembles Michelet's 1855 description of the late Middle Ages, as does the corresponding picture of contemporary France (in the Introduction), in which Montalembert speaks of 'cette servitude envahissante et corruptrice . . . cette écrasante monotonie, cet immense ennui qui menace d'être le caractère distinctif de la civilisation future'.[291] Against this dismal spectacle he sets that of the Middle Ages, where Michelet had seen only 'des attributs de vieillesse, subtilité, servilité, impuissance',[292] but where Montalembert sees 'une époque de lutte, de discussion, de dignité et avant tout de liberté',[293] comparable with the ideal Middle Ages whose praises we heard sung by liberals of the Romantic era, such as Guizot and Ampère:[294] 'Jamais l'humanité ne fut plus féconde, plus virile, plus puissante.[293] . . . Tout y respire la franchise, la santé et la vie. Tout y est plein de séve, de force et de jeunesse, . . .[295] une envie dévorante d'agir et de savoir enflammait les âmes. . . . La religion dominait tout, il est vrai, mais elle n'étouffait rien.'[296] It was the monks, 'les représentants de la virilité sous sa forme la plus pure et la plus énergique',[297] who kept alive this spirit of liberty. Montalembert ascribes to them much the same role as that performed by Hugo's 'chevaliers errants' in *La Légende des siècles,* who went through the world righting wrongs and defying tyranny.[298] Montalembert's monks, however, do not have the equivocal, half-sinister aura of Hugo's paladins, but a calm radiance, 'ce pur et profond bonheur qui régnait en eux et autour d'eux',[299] making them the antithesis of the totally sinister and sanguinary monks whom we shall meet in Leconte de Lisle's poetry. They are 'des coeurs trempés

[288] Ibid. p. 515.   [289] *Napoléon le Petit,* p. 46.
[290] Montalembert, *Les Moines d'Occident,* i (1860), 23-5. [291] Ibid. pp. cclxi-cclxii.
[292] *La Sorcière,* i, 27.   [293] Montalembert, *Les Moines d'Occident,* i, p. ccxli.
[294] Cf. *supra,* pp. 13-14.   [295] *Les Moines d'Occident,* i, p. cclvii.
[296] Ibid. pp. ccxliii-ccxliv.   [297] Ibid. p. xxxi.
[298] Cf. *infra,* pp. 138-9.   [299] *Les Moines d'Occident,* i, p. lxxv.

pour la guerre contre l'injustice, d'indomptables champions du droit et
de la vérité', quite free from 'la crainte du plus fort . . . les lâches com-
plaisances envers le pouvoir',[300] virtually never 'des instruments ou des
apôtres du pouvoir absolu'.[301] Once again, in this section of his Introduction, Montalembert chides Veuillot and his friends for bringing
discredit on the Middle Ages by their misplaced praise of them: 'En
combinant l'apologie du Moyen Âge avec l'apothéose de la servitude
contemporaine, on a ranimé . . . et en apparence justifié l'horreur du
passé catholique.'[302] The duty of liberal Catholics is plain: 'Il importe
d'affranchir le vrai Moyen Âge dans sa splendeur catholique de toute
solidarité avec la théorie et la pratique de ce vieux despotisme
renouvelé du paganisme, qui lutte encore çà et là contre la liberté
moderne.'[303]

(ii) *Laprade*

Victor de Laprade was another liberal Catholic who praised the
Middle Ages at the expense of the Second Empire. In 1861 he lost his
chair at Lyon University for his satirical poem, 'Les Muses d'État',
directed against the government and its ally Sainte-Beuve. Laprade's
version of the Middle Ages is rather different from Montalembert's; but
it too is held up as an antidote to the Empire. In his article 'Le Sentiment de la nature au moyen âge'[304] Laprade contrasts the poetic awe
of nature felt in the Middle Ages with the materialism of modern
industrial society and its sordid 'sentiment de l'utile dans la nature'.[305]
He condemns those of his contemporaries who boast that the conquest
of Nature is imminent, and praises medieval man, 'mis en garde contre la
nature par sa foi religieuse',[306] regarding it as an enemy, absorbed in
the spiritual world, admirable in his heroism and self-abnegation. This
view of the Middle Ages is versified in Laprade's *La Tour d'ivoire*
(1864).[307]

E. *An independent Catholic: Barbey d'Aurevilly*

Yet another version of the Middle Ages, the most memorable of all,
is presented in the works of Barbey d'Aurevilly. The critic Armand de

[300] Ibid. p. xxxix.   [301] Ibid. p. xl.
[302] *Les Moines d'Occident*, i, p. ccxxxviii.   [303] Ibid. pp. ccxxix-ccxxx.
[304] Published in *Le Correspondant* (Sept. 1861), and forming part of Laprade's
Sentiment de la nature chez les modernes, 1868.
[305] Laprade, *Le Sentiment de la nature chez les modernes*, 1868, p. 26.
[306] Laprade, *Le Sentiment de la nature chez les modernes*, p. 20.
[307] Cf. *infra*, pp. 177-8.

Pontmartin deplored in 1863 the isolation of the individual in modern society, 'condamné à la loi rigide et triste du *chacun pour soi* par le nivellement et le déclassement démocratique', and cast a nostalgic glance towards the vanished security of the Middle Ages: 'Sous ce régime de corporations et de confréries, comme l'individu était appuyé, soutenu. . . .'
Barbey, too, was dismayed by modern democracy; but for him it provided an excess of stupefying security. What he missed, and found in the Middle Ages, 'ce temps colossal où les hommes avaient la force', was danger, fanaticism, holy wars. 'Ô chevalerie, tu n'as plus ni épée ni éperons!'[309] he cried out in a letter written in 1852. A supporter of the Imperial government, he despised the citizens of the Empire. 'Les Éclatants' of bygone days, he complained, had been replaced by 'les Effacés' and 'les Lâcheurs'.[310] He shared Renan's disgust at the 1855 Exhibition. 'Une pareille fête', he declared, 'date l'*ère de la fin* de toute pensée, de toute âme, de toute forte spiritualité.'[311] In 1857, in an article on Sémichon's *La Paix et la trêve de Dieu,* he speaks of 'le cadavre du Moyen Âge, égorgé par nos pères', marvels at 'l'énergie sublime de son esprit et la grandeur cordiale de ses institutions',[312] and declares that it was the 'point d'honneur' that ennobled and quickened life in the Middle Ages, creating 'la plus magnifique hiérarchie qu'aient vue les hommes', and 'des duels splendides . . . élargissant devant la mort la personnalité humaine, et entraînant des tourbillons d'amis dans un cercle chevaleresque de dévouements et de dangers'.[313] (His ancestors in the Romantic era were the *Jeunes-France* and Stendhal.)[314] 'La guerre pour la guerre', he declares, was a far nobler preoccupation than 'l'art pour l'art'; and he contemplates with sorrow 'la poudre de l'individualisme antichevaleresque de ces derniers temps',[312] echoing his words spoken in 1851 on 'le fléau démocratique qui ne cessera de battre que quand il aura tout pulvérisé'.[315] Republican 'larmes de crocodile' shed over the horrors of the Middle Ages aroused his wrath, as we have seen. He contemptuously dismissed Guizot's Preface to his translation of Grégoire de Tours: 'C'est toujours cette injure de tradition et de rhétorique sur le compte

---

[308] Pontmartin, *Dernières Semaines littéraires*, Lévy, 1864, p. 315.
[309] Barbey d'Aurevilly, *Lettres à Trébutien,* 1927, ii. 289.
[310] Barbey d'Aurevilly, 'Les Effacés' (1866), and 'Les Lâcheurs' (1867), in *Les Ridicules du temps,* 2nd edn., 1883, pp. 63-73, 181-90.
[311] *Lettres à Trébutien,* iii. 266-7.
[312] Barbey d'Aurevilly, *De l'histoire,* 1905, pp. 227-9.
[313] Ibid. pp. 233-4.
[314] Cf. *supra*, p. 13.
[315] Barbey d'Aurevilly, *Les Prophètes du passé,* 3rd edn., 1880, p. 104.

de ces époques ignorantes, superstitieuses et barbares, et la même
fatuité de moderne qui se préfère à ces époques, où la vie, cette chose
inférieure pour Guizot, du moins existait!'[316] He had nothing but
contempt, too, for Augustin Thierry's sentimental concern for con-
quered races; and he was exasperated by liberal historians in the
tradition of Thierry who sought in the Middle Ages the birth of all
that he most detested in modern society: democracy, pacifism, and
philanthropy. He was delighted by those very aspects of medieval life
that sent a shudder through republican sensibilities; he revelled in the
savage repression of heresy: 'Oui, l'Hérésie, la Bête aux mille langues,
répondait,' he says in *Les Prophètes du passé* (1851), 'mais on savait
la faire taire.'[317] The life of Villon, recounted by Antoine Campaux,
provoked in him reflections very different from those of his sentimental contemporaries, who were aroused either to compassion at the
cruel hardships endured by the poet, or to moralizing deprecation of
the dissolute life he led. Barbey's reaction was one of wholehearted
admiration for the rigorous measures taken by the strong hand of
fifteenth-century justice, in dealing with criminal elements: 'La
société d'alors ne badinait pas. La philanthropie n'était pas inventée.
Les moeurs étaient fortes et la législation sévère.'[318]

F. *Attempts at dispassionate appraisal; the positivist approach:*
'le moyen-âge sérieux'

We have looked at several versions of the Middle Ages identified with
or set in opposition to the Second Empire by its enemies and supporters
– horrific or Arcadian worlds revealed to modern France as a warning or
an example. There were also at this time a number of writers who condemned intemperate praise or dispraise of the Middle Ages. The time
had come, they considered, to scrutinize the past with the impartiality
appropriate to a positivist, scientific age which had left Romanticism
behind. Renan and Taine, as we have seen, were in theory advocates of
this approach. History, declared Renan in 1852, no longer concerned
itself with the passing of moral judgements: 'Il ne faut demander au
passé que le passé lui-même.'[319] The past should be sought in the works
of art which survive from it. This was the time when historical works
were beginning to be illustrated by reproductions of coins, seals,

---

[316] Barbey d'Aurevilly, *Sensations d'histoire*, 1887, p. 368.
[317] *Les Prophètes du passé*, p. 16 (Introduction).
[318] *Les Critiques*, 1885, p. 303 (*Pays*, Jan. 1862).
[319] *Os. cs.* iii (*Averroès*), p. 15.

manuscripts, stained glass, and other works of art of the period which they treated (one of the first was Charton and Bordier's *Histoire de France par les monuments,* 1859), and the era of the Romantic chromolithograph was declared to be at an end. We have seen, however, that Renan and Taine interpreted Gothic art prejudicially, seeing in medieval architecture the irresponsible frivolity of the men who built it, or — worse still — a sinister intent to cow the faithful into submission.

(i) *Viollet-le-Duc*

Viollet-le-Duc had no patience at all with this attitude: 'En quoi les édifices sont-ils les complices de ceux qui les ont fait bâtir?' he asks in his *Dictionnaire raisonné de l'architecture:* 'Une construction n'est pas *fanatique, oppressive, tyrannique.* '[320] In an article objecting to Renan's contention that cathedrals were built to inspire 'un sentiment d'étonnement et de terreur', he charged him with melodramatic Romanticism: 'Ce sont là de ces appréciations qu'il faut laisser à l'école, un peu vieillie, de Kotzebue.'[321] Viollet-le-Duc, often accused of the profanation of ruins, prided himself on his practical, unsentimental approach to the past. Neither the ideal nor the sinister Romantic Middle Ages found favour in his sight. The former he dismissed as puerile 'rêvasseries'[322] which one by one, in his *Dictionnaire,* evaporate in the cold light of geometry: the 'trèfle ogival', beloved of the Romantics, whom it reminded of the mysterious East, he defines as 'un membre d'architecture . . . obtenu au moyen de trois cercles dont les centres sont placés aux sommets des angles d'un triangle équilatéral.'[323] The latter left him equally unmoved: he refused to display any reaction to dungeons — even those of Carcassonne, where a skeleton had been found chained to a pillar — save that of admiration for their impeccably sound construction;[324] he declared that molten lead was unlikely to have been employed by defenders of castles under siege, because 'tombant de cette hauteur, [il] serait arrivé en bas en gouttes froides';[325]

---

[320] Viollet-le-Duc, *Dictionnaire raisonné de l'architecture française,* iv (1861), 9.

[321] *Revue archéologique* (Feb. 1863), p. 114. Viollet is referring to Kotzebue's description of Lenoir's Musée des Monuments Français in the convent of the Petits-Augustins: 'Tout y est sombre et triste, et il est impossible de marcher dans cette obscurité des tombeaux sans être saisi d'une terreur secrète' (*Souvenirs de Paris en 1804,* par A. Kotzebue, 1805, i. 173).

[322] *Dictionnaire raisonné de l'architecture,* ix (1868), 535.

[323] *Dictionnaire raisonné de l'architecture,* ix, 260.

[324] See ibid. iv. 9; vii. 482-3.   [325] Ibid. ix. 78n.

and he ventured the opinion that 'le sifflement du vent à travers les créneaux . . . qui fait naître dans notre esprit de sinistres pensées était peut-être pour les oreilles de nos pères une harmonie réjouissante.'[326]

'La vérité est un besoin de notre temps', proclaimed Viollet; and he shared Taine's conviction that modern science had revealed at last 'le passé tel qu'il était'.[327] But whereas in Taine's Middle Ages 'le Hasard' held sway over a world from which Reason had fled, Viollet's was a positivist paradise, in which rigour, logic, and 'le sérieux' were everywhere in evidence. Gothic, he insisted in his *Dictionnaire*, was 'un système raisonné, logique',[328] in which 'rien n'est livré au hasard[329] . . . tout est prévu, tout vient se poser à la place nécessaire et préparée.'[330] Medieval architects were 'des *rationalistes*'.[331] Set-square and rule in hand, they went about their business with calm deliberation: 'ils marchaient méthodiquement, géométriquement, sans passer leur temps à crayonner au hasard.'[332]

Time and again Viollet insisted that his viewpoint was that of a *practicien*, unswayed by ethical or aesthetical considerations: 'Il faut fouiller le passé avec soin . . . s'attacher, non pas à le faire revivre, mais à le connaître, pour s'en servir[333] . . . rechercher dans le travail de la veille ce qu'il y a d'utile pour nous aujourd'hui';[334] and yet his interest in the Middle Ages was not entirely unromantic. The very passion with which he defended medieval architects and craftsmen − 'Le jour de la justice ne viendra-t-il jamais pour eux?' he asks in his *Dictionnaire*[335] − testifies to this. Like Montalembert, he paid frequent tribute to

---

[326] Ibid. v (1861), 364.

[327] *Dictionnaire raisonné du mobilier français,* i (1858), 297.

[328] *Dictionnaire raisonné de l'architecture,* v. 509. Hugo had already declared in *Notre-Dame de Paris:* 'Tout se tient dans cet art venu de lui-même, logique et bien proportionné' (p. 126). Cf. Quatremère de Quincy's comparison of Gothic cathedrals with 'les travaux instinctifs de certains animaux' (*Dictionnaire historique d'architecture,* i (1832), 678), endorsed by Delécluze, who said in a session of the Comité Historique des Arts et Monuments that they reminded him of 'des fourmilières . . . des tumulus d'insectes' (Didron, *Paganisme dans l'art chrétien,* 1853, p. 20), and by Stendhal, who remarked in 1837: 'Nulle mesure exacte, nulle symétrie dans les édifices du moyen âge; tout se faisait de sentiment' (*Mémoires d'un touriste,* Édn. du Divan, 1929, ii. 119. Cf. ibid. i. 70, 314-17, 362).

[329] *Dictionnaire raisonné de l'architecture,* viii (1866), 495.

[330] Ibid. iv. 347.   [331] Ibid. p. 196.   [332] Ibid. vii (1864), 550.

[333] *Entretiens sur l'architecture,* i (1863), 32.

[334] *Dictionnaire raisonné de l'architecture,* iv. 8.

[335] Ibid. p. 245. See especially the *Dictionnaire* articles 'Architecture', 'Château', 'Construction', 'Goût' (in which he stresses the honesty of Gothic construction), 'Maison', 'Porte', 'Sculpture', 'Siège', and 'Tour'.

medieval man's 'énergie morale et physique'[336] — on the faces carved
in stone, where Michelet and Taine had seen despair, and Quinet,
quasi-idiocy, he perceived 'l'empreinte de l'intelligence, de la puissance
morale, sous toutes les formes';[337] but unlike him, he combined this
view of the Middle Ages with allegiance to Louis Napoleon, and
acclaimed 'ce besoin ardent d'union, d'unité nationale qui fait notre
force aujourd'hui' as a precious legacy of feudalism. 'La féodalité', he
declared, 'fut la trempe de l'esprit national en France; et cette trempe
est bonne.'[338] He confesses in the *Dictionnaire* that more than once,
in the course of his researches into Gothic, a cry rose to his lips:
'Ramenez-nous à ce moyen âge qui savait faire de tels hommes.'[339]
Another testimony to his latent Romanticism are the curious painted
and sculptured beasts of Pierrefonds. His identification of himself with
a medieval 'maître d'oeuvre' is well-known. A pupil reported of him:
'Viollet-le-Duc disait parfois en plaisantant qu'il était à peu près certain
d'avoir déjà vécu il y a cinq ou six siècles, et qu'il ne faisait que se
souvenir de ce qu'il avait vu et étudié à une autre époque.'[340]

(ii) *Gaston Paris*

A critic stated in 1858: 'Depuis que le moyen âge de fantaisie a
disparu, depuis qu'on n'entend plus parler de "bonnes lames de Tolède",
de "hanaps", de "mangonneaux", de "varlets", le moyen âge sérieux
reparaît à l'horizon.'[341] Gaston Paris, like Viollet-le-Duc, declared himself to be concerned exclusively with this 'moyen âge sérieux'. He
spoke indulgently of his father Paulin Paris's uncritical enthusiasm for
medieval literature as a thing of the past: 'Nous comprenons aujourd'hui
un peu différemment l'étude du moyen âge. Nous nous attachons moins
à l'apprécier et à le faire apprécier qu'à le connaître et à le comprendre.'[342]
In the Preface to his *Histoire poétique de Charlemagne* (1865) he
condemned 'l'enthousiasme aveugle qui s'est maintes fois répandu . . .
sur ces mêmes études', and proclaimed that 'le moyen âge . . . est digne
d'être étudié avec le plus grand sérieux et l'exactitude la plus minutieuse.'[343]
To this end he and Paul Meyer founded in 1866 the *Revue critique*,
which set a new standard of critical rigour in examination of scholarly

---

[336] Ibid. ix. 130.   [337] Ibid. viii. 142.   [338] Ibid. iii (1859), 146-7.
[339] *Dictionnaire raisonné de l'architecture*, viii. 424.
[340] C. Sauvageot, *Viollet-le-Duc et son oeuvre dessiné*, Morel, 1880.
[341] *La Correspondance littéraire*, ii, 5 Aug. 1858. p. 234. (Gustave Masson.)
[342] G. Paris, *La Poésie du moyen âge*, première série, 1885, p. 219.
[343] G. Paris, *Histoire poétique de Charlemagne*, 1865, p. viii.

works. In a speech to the Société des Anciens Textes in 1879 he repeated: 'Nous ne prétendons ni dénigrer ni réhabiliter le moyen âge . . . nous prétendons le faire connaître et le faire comprendre', and yet emotion began to creep into his voice as he spoke of his forefathers: 'Oui, de ces pages élégantes où l'imprimeur a fait passer pour toujours les lignes confiées jadis au fragile parchemin, leurs paroles, telles qu'ils les prononçaient et les écoutaient, peuvent se détacher et retentir à nos âmes comme l'écho tout vibrant des leurs.'[344] Like Viollet, he was not as coldly sober as he professed to be. Had he not even gone as far as to suggest on his inaugural lecture at the Collège de France (1866) that 'Prise dans son ensemble, et mise en regard de la nôtre, la vie au moyen âge nous apparaît comme éminemment poétique'?[345]

(iii) *Littré*

Émile Littré, throughout the 1850s and 60s, worked untiringly in the cause of dispassionate appreciation of the Middle Ages. He wrote in 1863: 'Prôner le moyen âge pour faire pièce à la liberté moderne, ou le dénigrer pour faire pièce au catholicisme, est désormais chose puérile et qui avortera toujours. Quoi qu'on fasse pour ou contre, le moyen âge, dans l'irrévocable immobilité du passé, ne se prête plus qu'à une seule opération intellectuelle, celle qui a pour but de la comprendre.'[346] 'La justice que je rends au moyen âge', he repeated in 1867, 'est une justice historique qui ne réagit aucunement sur la lutte contemporaine.'[347]

Littré, a staunch republican, abhorred the Second Empire, but he was among those who equated it with the Roman Empire in decline rather than with the Middle Ages. In 1856 he declared that feudalism was an admirably regulated system, 'mais l'empire n'en fut pas un; tout ce qu'on peut dire de lui, c'est qu'il eut le pouvoir pendant que cheminait la dés-organisation commencée avant lui.'[348] And in 1864 he called the Roman Empire 'une phase lourde, sans souffle, inhabile au dedans à ranimer la vie sociale, au dehors à écarter l'effroyable catastrophe des barbares'.[349] Three years later he warned that 'César ne fonda qu'une décadence terminée par une catastrophe.'[350]

Fortified by the positivist philosophy of his master Auguste Comte, Littré considered himself able to view the Middle Ages with equanimity. For the historian attentive to 'l'enchaînement et la filiation des choses',[351]

---

[344] *Bibliothèque de l'École des Chartes,* xl (1879), p. 640.
[345] G. Paris, *La Poésie du moyen âge,* 1885, 19.
[346] Littré, *Études sur les barbares et le moyen âge,* 1867, p. 181.
[347] Ibid. pp. iii-iv.   [348] Ibid. p. 44.   [349] Ibid. p. 383.   [350] Ibid. p. xvi.
[351] Littré, *Histoire de la langue française,* 1863, i, 255.

the past was past and presented no danger to the modern world. Former
societies each came into being at the time appointed, and none was to be
regarded as reprehensible. Yet there is in Littré's appreciation of the
Middle Ages more than cool detachment; there is positive enthusiasm,
and indeed love. Comte had been a devotee of the period – in 1841 he
called medieval Catholic society 'le chef-d'oeuvre politique de la sagesse
humaine'[352] – and Littré followed suit: for him the Middle Ages were
an admirable and consoling spectacle, demonstrating, in the superiority
over classical antiquity which he insistently claimed for them, the laws
of progress governing civilization. An essay of his, published in the *Revue
des deux mondes* in 1849, in which some of the *Iliad* was translated into
thirteenth-century French, scandalized most of those who read it; but
Littré continued to work for the recognition of 'la langue de nos aieux,
plus correcte que la nôtre, la grammaire plus régulière, l'analogie mieux
conservée',[353] in a long series of articles collected together in his
Histoire de la langue française (1863). With the same ardour that
Viollet-le-Duc put into proving the rationality of Gothic architecture,
he insisted that Old French was not 'un patois informe'.[354] Like Gaston
Paris, he was moved by the echo he heard in it of 'les voix chères qui se
sont tues', calling it 'ce français archaïque, qui est pourtant du français
et qui nous plait comme la voix lointaine de nos aïeux'.[355] In 1854 he
declared: 'Nous [sommes] fils du moyen âge, et seulement petits-fils
de la Grèce et de Rome';[356] and in 1864, in an article on Volume
XXIV of the *Histoire littéraire de la France* (containing Renan's and
Le Clerc's *Discours* on the fourteenth century), he claimed for the
Middle Ages 'une place honorable dans le développement humain',[357]
stating: 'J'avoue que je suis de ceux qui tiennent aux lointains souvenirs,
et que ce n'est pas sans un certain orgueil national que je vois l'esprit de
la vieille France se signaler par des oeuvres considérables qui plurent
partout.'[358]

(iv) *Mérimée*

So, in spite of themselves, Viollet, Paris, and Littré were moved by
something approaching Romantic reverence for 'nos pères' when they

---

[352] A. Comte, *Cours de philosophie positive*, v (1841), 326. Cf. Saint-Simon, with
whose view of the Middle Ages as a progressive stage in human history both
Comte and Littré were in accord. See D. G. Charlton, *Secular Religions in
France, 1815-1870*, Oxford, Clarendon Press, 1963, pp. 165-6.
[353] Littré, *Histoire de la langue française*, 1863, ii. 29.
[354] Ibid. i. 310.   [355] *Études sur les barbares*, p. 451.
[356] *Histoire de la langue française*, i. 290.
[357] *Études sur les barbares*, p. 378.   [358] Ibid. p. 385

attempted to turn a severely professional gaze upon the Middle Ages. They were swayed by the same 'prédilection involontaire pour les moeurs poétiques et les arts de nos aïeux' which Nodier had experienced in 1820.[359] The only truly dispassionate appraiser of the Middle Ages at this time was Prosper Mérimée, that sworn enemy of 'l'emphase', who remarked approvingly of his protégé Viollet-le-Duc in 1855: 'Son amour pour le moyen âge est toujours raisonné et raisonnable.'[360] While he saved countless medieval buildings from ruin, during his term of office as Inspecteur des Monuments Historiques, he was quite without Romantic or republican emotion.[361] (Ludovic Vitet said regretfully of him: 'Mérimée admire les beaux monuments, mais il n'a jamais senti ses yeux se mouiller à l'aspect de leurs ruines.')[362] We have seen that he privately disapproved of Viollet's excesses;[363] he also disapproved of Louis Napoleon's Syrian 'crusade', declaring: 'Je n'aime pas la politique chevaleresque';[364] and we shall presently encounter him pouring scorn upon republicans who mistook castle cellars for *oubliettes*.[365] His *Histoire de Don Pèdre 1er* (1848) was written in a spirit of severe impartiality: while working on it in 1846 (a time when, as we have seen, republican passion was beginning to run high), he told a correspondent:

Je suis convaincu que le bon et le mauvais principe travaillent de concert, si bien que la somme de bonheur et de malheur sur le globe ne change en aucune façon, quelques révolutions que subissent les choses et les hommes. Maintenant que mon ami Pierre le Cruel me fait vivre en plein moyen âge, je ne trouve pas que l'on fût alors sensiblement plus malheureux ou plus heureux qu'à présent;[366]

and, in the work itself, he anticipates the reader's reaction of outrage at his narrative of bloodshed, torture, and betrayal with repeated reminders that medieval actions must be regarded in their context and not judged by modern standards.[367]

---

[359] *Voyages pittoresque et romantiques*, i (1820), 4
[360] See *Lettres de Mérimée à Viollet-le-Duc*, ed. Trahard, 1927, p. 242.
[361] Except, as we have seen (*supra*, p. 22), in his very early work *La Jaquerie* (1828).
[362] Reported by Guizot in *RDM*, 1 Mar. 1874, p. 44.
[363] Cf. *supra*, p. 39.
[364] Mérimée, *Correspondance générale*, deuxième série, iv (1956), 218 (Cf. ibid. p.232).
[365] Cf. *infra*, p. 142n.
[366] *Correspondance générale*, première série, iv (1945), 449.
[367] Cf. Mérimée, *Histoire de Don Pèdre 1er*, ed. G. Laplane, 1961, pp. 263, 382-5. See also *Corr. gén.*, deuxième série, ii, 439.

CHAPTER 4

CATHOLIC AND REPUBLICAN CONTROVERSY:
II. MEDIEVAL LITERATURE

'Où retrouver cette vigueur perdue et nécessaire? Où prendre la sève
nouvelle?' (E. Lepelletier)

Whether or not Chateaubriand had been right to recommend the Middle
Ages, in *Le Génie du Christianisme,* as a source of inspiration for the
modern writer, was a question that by no means lost its topicality with
the decline of Romanticism. In 1830 Nerval had urged his fellow-writers
to seek inspiration from this source. As medieval French writers had in
his opinion been incapable of producing any enduring work of literature,
he considered that it was the task of their nineteenth-century descendants
to improve on their imperfection and write their literature for them: 'Il
faut cultiver, il faut perfectionner ce qui est resté inculte ou imparfait. . . .
Que de riches matériaux, auxquels il n'a manqué que d'être mis en oeuvre
par des mains habiles! que de ruines de monuments inachevés! . . . Voilà
ce qui s'offre à nous. . .!',[1] he exclaimed. (We have seen that the 'troubadour' *romance* and the Romantic *ballade* gave themselves out to be
samples of 'reconstituted' medieval verse.)[2]

Seven years later, however, Quinet proclaimed that this ghost of a
literature which might have been was, like the Middle Ages themselves,
beyond all hope of resurrection, and would communicate the chill of
the grave to anyone who touched it:

Épopée des jours passés, trouvères, chevalerie, amours enchantées,
légendes, charmes commencés, larves, images ébauchées, poésie qui
aurait pu être, qui n'a été qu'à demi, flottez, errez dans les limbes des
vides souvenirs. Vainement vous redemandez à naître. il est trop tard. . . .
Vous nous feriez mourir, et nous ne vous ferions pas vivre une heure.[3]

Shorn of its Romantic trappings, this statement is repeated by Renan in
his *Cahiers de jeunesse:*

La vraie poésie d'une époque est la sienne, celle du lieu et du temps;
et si elle n'en a pas, ou plutôt n'en a pas conservé, c'est que cette poésie

---

[1] Nerval, *Oeuvres complémentaires: (1) La Vie des lettres,* ed. J. Richer, 1959,
pp. 291-2.

[2] Cf. *supra,* pp. 6-7.

[3] Quinet, *Os cs.: (IX) La Grèce moderne: Histoire de la poésie,* 4th edn., n.d.,
pp. 421-2 (*RDM* (Jan. 1837)).

n'était pas scriptible ou conservable; et c'est déjà une missreprésentation [*sic*] de l'écrire.[4]

In *L'Avenir de la science* he further develops this theme, condemning 'ces modernes églises gothiques, bâties par un architecte en redingote', and Romantic resurrection of the past in literature:

La vraie littérature d'une époque est celle qui la peint et l'exprime.... La couleur locale a un charme incontestable quand elle est vraie; elle est insipide dans le pastiche. J'aime l'Alhambra et Brocéliande dans leur vérité; je me ris du romantique qui croit, en combinant ces mots, faire une oeuvre belle. Là est l'erreur de Chateaubriand et la raison de l'incroyable médiocrité de son école.[5]

In a rough draft of his article 'La Poésie des races celtiques' (1854), he reaffirmed that 'le véritable poète de ce temps-ci, c'est l'historien et le critique, qui sait comprendre les différentes formes de la vie poétique du passé.'[6]

Taine in 1862, explaining how the English Romantics at last came to their senses, expresses the same opinions:

On en vint à comprendre ... que la littérature archéologique est un genre faux. On sentait enfin que c'est dans les écrivains du passé qu'il faut chercher le portrait du passé ... que le roman arrangé doit faire place aux mémoires authentiques ... que la littérature historique doit s'évanouir et se transformer en critique et en histoire.[7]

So a new generation of serious scholars frowned on Romantic re-creation of the past. Historical fiction was declared to have been rendered null and void by the progress of modern science, now possessed of the instruments to determine, once and for all, the truth about the past. 'D'où vient que l'art est mort...?' asked Michelet in 1855 — 'c'est que l'histoire l'a tué.'[8] Not all creative writers of the day took this view, as we shall see in our sixth chapter, but Mérimée certainly did: he announced to a correspondent in 1856 that he had abandoned fiction altogether: 'Je n'aime plus maintenant que l'histoire.'[9]

[4] Renan, *Os. cs.* ix. 325.
[5] Ibid. iii. 881-2. Cf. Viollet-le-Duc (*Dictionnaire raisonné du mobilier français,* i (1858), 298); 'Qu'y a-t-il de plus poétique que la vérité? L'imagination des poëtes ou des romanciers a-t-elle jamais pu offrir un spectacle plus émouvant que celui de l'histoire ...?'
[6] See R. Galand, *L'Âme celtique de Renan*, p. 84. Cf. Renan, *Os. cs.* ii. 25.
[7] Taine, *Histoire de la littérature anglaise*, iv. 289-90 (*RDM*, 15 Sept. 1862).
[8] Michelet, *Renaissance*, p. 8.
[9] Mérimée, *Correspondance générale*, deuxième série, ii (1955), 183. For a full discussion of Mérimée's abandonment of fiction in favour of history see A. W. Raitt, 'History and Fiction in the Works of Mérimée', *History Today* (April 1969); and *Prosper Mérimée*, 1970, Ch. XIII.

Numerous critics sought to dissuade writers from seeking inspiration in the medieval past with arguments less subtle than those put forward by Renan and Taine. Animated by pure and simple detestation of the Middle Ages, they condemned return to them because it usually went with a desire to rehabilitate them. Most of these critics were republican – Edmond About proclaimed in 1854: 'Vos héros vêtus de ferraille ont porté malheur à tous ceux qui y ont touché. La poésie des *Chansons de geste* est-elle si poétique?'[10] Some were liberal Catholics – Albert de Broglie in 1852 issued the injunction to his fellows: 'Soyons de notre temps et parlons notre langue. . . . Il n'y a . . . suivant nous, pour les écrivains et les hommes catholiques de nos jours, rien à imiter du moyen-âge.'[11] The *Revue des deux mondes* regarded all manifestations of medievalism with stern disapproval. Its music critic P. Scudo called Berlioz' *L'Enfance du Christ* (1854) 'ce pieux mystère, qui doit faire le bonheur de M. l'abbé Gaume. . . . C'est à la fois puéril et insensé.'[12] In 1861 he was attacking those who were seeking to revive 'le plain-chant grégorien chanté par les furieux qui ont fait la guerre des Albigeois, les croisades, la Saint-Barthélemy'.[13] His colleague Gustave Planche never lost an opportunity to admonish writers of historical plays in the Romantic tradition – 'A quoi sert . . . l'archéologie dans un poème dramatique?', he asked in a review of Latour de Saint-Ybar's *Les Routiers* (1851), 'C'est un passe-temps puéril, un placage sans valeur'[14] – or to condemn the Romantic drama itself for its exclusive concern with the picturesque and refusal to judge the past in the light of modern historical science. 'L'école dramatique de la restauration', he lamented in 1856, 'se souvient et ne juge pas.'[15] About the same time Saint-René Taillandier poured scorn upon 'ce romantisme religieux qui s'est créé un moyen âge de fantaisie, un moyen âge tout rempli de séraphiques douceurs',[16] and Charles de Rémusat denounced those Catholics who squandered their energies in '[des] restaurations éphémères d'un semblant de moyen âge affecté et puéril'.[17]

If many critics undertook to dissuade writers from seeking inspiration in the Middle Ages, and to reprove those who disregarded their words of warning, there were also a few who declared that medieval literature, now increasingly accessible, provided an ideal source of refreshment for the modern writer. We have seen in Chapter 2 how

---

[10] *Revue de l'instruction publique*, xiv, 14 Sept. 1854, p. 359.
[11] Broglie, 'Le Moyen Âge et l'Église catholique', *RDM*, 1 Nov. 1852, p. 444.
[12] *RDM*, 15 Dec. 1854, p. 1251.   [13] *RDM*, 15 Aug. 1861, p.1013.
[14] *RDM*, 1 Apr. 1851, p. 175.   [15] *RDM*, 1 Sept. 1856, p. 129.
[16] *RDM*, 1 Dec. 1856, pp. 514-15.   [17] *RDM*, 15 May 1857, p. 270.

enthusiastically Fortoul spoke of this in his report to the Emperor on
the proposed 'Recueil des Anciens poëtes français' (1856).[18] Some
years before, in 1852, Louis Moland and Charles d'Héricault had
begun their campaign for the propagation of medieval literature, in
which they addressed themselves time and again to the modern writer
in need of a new source of inspiration. Moland wrote in the *Revue de
l'enseignement chrétien:*

> On commence à sentir le besoin de renouer la chaîne des traditions,
> de s'inspirer aux sources vives du moyen-âge. . . . . On commence à
> comprendre que le meilleur, le seul moyen de sortir de l'impasse où nos
> lettres acculées expirent d'épuisement ou se débattent en fiévreuses
> folies, c'est de retrouver et de reprendre la voie que s'étaient frayée nos
> instincts primitifs. . . . Nulle étude ne saurait être plus saine, plus
> féconde, plus propre à fortifier les âmes et à vivifier les intelligences.[19]

In 1856 they issued a joint declaration in the Preface to their *Nouvelles
françoises en prose du XIIIe siècle:*

> Nous pensons qu'il est temps pour ce moyen âge d'exercer une plus
> large influence sur les tendances littéraires de notre époque. . . . La
> littérature du moyen âge est vivante . . . elle nous prend par les liens
> du sang . . . l'invention de ce temps-ci a grandement besoin de cette
> observation sincère . . . regardant de haut, fouillant profondément
> parfois et concluant moralement.[20]

D'Héricault, recalling this Preface in his memoirs, says that he and
Moland were two voices crying in the wilderness;[21] but they none the
less continued their campaign.[22]

In 1860 Edgar Quinet, about to publish *Merlin l'Enchanteur* and
forgetting his words of 1837 on the futility of trying to resuscitate
medieval epic, also spoke of a possible 'rajeunissement de l'esprit dans
les sources nationales'.[23] Sainte-Beuve, in his Introduction to Crépet's
anthology *Les Poëtes français* (1861), did not go as far as to say that
poets of the 1860s should take *chansons de geste* as their model, but
he expressed regret that the Romantic poets had not had this source of
inspiration at their disposal:

> Il en sort un souffle parfois puissant, il y court une source d'âpre
> fraîcheur, et aussi elles renferment bien des traits saillants de vérité

---

[18] Cf. *supra*, p. 36.   [19] *Revue de l'enseignement chrétien*, i (Nov. 1852), pp. 581-2.
[20] Moland & D'Héricault, *Nouvelles françoises en prose du XIIIe siècle*, 1856,
pp. vii-ix.
[21] Ch. d'Héricault, *Souvenirs et portraits*, 1902, pp. 79-80.
[22] Cf. Moland, *Origines littéraires de la France*, 1862, p. 320.
[23] Quinet, *Lettres d'exil*, ii. 35.

pittoresque . . . dont un grand poète s'attachant à peindre et à
ressusciter le Moyen-Âge eût fait son profit. . . . Au lieu de se créer
un Moyen-Âge de fantaisie et presque tout d'imagination, on aurait
pu . . . sauver, ressaisir, reproduire et remettre en circulation bien des
beautés caractéristiques, sobres et mâles.[24]

(It is true that this may be no more than a preamble to his malicious
allusion to Hugo's *Légende des siècles:* 'On l'a tenté depuis, mais trop
tard.')[24]

A. *'Poésie populaire':* republican territory

Many republicans, dismayed by the 'insalubrious' nature of modern
literary works (e.g. *Les Fleurs du mal*), prescribed as a remedy not
chansons de geste but *chansons populaires,* 'ces purs effluves d'un esprit
encore vierge',[25] as Thalès Bernard, one of the chief propagandists of
the folklore movement, termed them in 1855. Writers of this period felt
a sense of oppression and loss of inspiration, due in part to the uncongenial atmosphere of the Empire, called in the *Revue des deux mondes*
in 1859 '[le] marasme intellectuel et moral qui a envahi la France',[26]
and in part to the inhibiting memory of their inspired elders, the
Romantics, and of the age of primitive epic to which philosophers and
critics were constantly calling their attention. 'Nous sommes une
génération savante,' declared Leconte de Lisle in 1852, 'la vie instinctive,
spontanée, aveuglément féconde de la jeunesse, s'est retirée de nous.'[27]
All asked, with Edmond Lepelletier, 'Où retrouver cette vigueur perdue
et nécessaire? Où prendre la sève nouvelle?[28] Bernard was quite sure
where the remedy lay: 'La poésie populaire se présente à nous comme
un baume prédestiné à nous guérir.'[29] He and his fellow-republicans,
advising poets to seek refreshment in folklore, made it clear that their
activities were not to be confused with those of reactionary Romantic
medievalists. Saint-René Taillandier, writing in the *Revue des deux
mondes* in 1851, praised those who were striving to bring 'la poésie
populaire' back into fashion, but reproved 'cette école fourvoyée qui
espérait endormir le XIXe siècle avec les légendes du moyen-âge'.[30]

[24] *Les Poëtes français,* ed. E. Crépet, i (1861), xvii-xix.
[25] T. Bernard, *Adorations,* 1855, xxix.
[26] *RDM,* 15 Nov. 1859, p. 512 (E. Forcade).
[27] Leconte de Lisle, *Articles, préfaces, discours,* ed. E. Pich, 1971, p. 110
(Preface to *Poèmes antiques*).
[28] *L'Art,* 9 Nov. 1865, p. 4.
[29] T. Bernard, *Histoire de la poésie,* 1864, p. 832.
[30] *RDM,* 15 Feb. 1851, p. 762.

Bernard wrote in his Preface to Achille Millien's *La Moisson:* 'Les jeunes gens ont raison d'abandonner la mosaïque et le plâtrage littéraires, pour se tourner vers la nature . . . ils ne veulent plus . . . des épouvantails du moyen-âge.'[31] In his *Lettre sur la poésie* (1868) he exhorted his fellow-poets: 'Écoutons la poésie provinciale nous parler, et voyons si elle n'a pas de ces accens suaves qui enchantent l'âme, bien autrement que le fouillis moyen âge de M. Théophile Gautier ne satisfait l'esprit.'[32] Émile Blémont, in his youth a minor Parnassian poet, wrote in his *Esthétique de la tradition* (1890): 'La tradition n'est pas la réaction; elle n'est pas condamnée à être fatalement cléricale et féodale. Par essence, elle est *populaire*.'[33] It was denied by this group of writers that France had produced any folk poetry worthy of attention. They had the authority of Michelet, who stated in 1855 that the medieval Church had stifled the voice of the people: 'Le clergé a gardé le peuple et s'est couché dessus . . . pas un chant vraiment populaire. . . .'[34] Nerval had already published seventeen French folk-songs in his essay 'Les vieilles ballades françaises' (1842), and ventured to suggest: 'Il serait à désirer que de bons poètes modernes missent à profit l'inspiration naïve de nos pères.'[35] Both the article 'Chants populaires' in Lacroix and Seré's *Le Moyen Âge et la Renaissance* (Vol. ii, 1849)[36] and Fortoul in his report on the Imperial Decree ordering the publication of a 'Recueil des poésies populaires de la France' (1852)[37] had declared that France's heritage in this domain was very rich indeed, but Bernard, expressing consternation at 'les oeuvres brutales qui se produisent', urged his fellow-poets to study Finnish, Hungarian, Rumanian, and Estonian folk-songs, affirming that the only part of Europe where they would not find popular ballads was 'les régions de langue française, où [cette poésie] se réduit à d'ineptes complaintes'.[38] Édouard Schuré in his *Histoire du lied* (1868) remarked on the poverty of French folk poetry: 'Je doute qu'elle soit assez riche pour nourrir un art jeune et nouveau.'[39] Work did of course proceed

---

[31] A. Millien, *La Moisson,* 1860, p. 7.   [32] Bernard, *Lettre sur la poésie,* 1868, p. 2.

[33] E. Blémont, *Esthétique de la tradition,* 1890, p. 46.

[34] Michelet, *Renaissance,* p. 84.

[35] Nerval, *Oeuvres,* 1960, i. 284. From the 1820s onwards, widely differing views were expressed concerning the existence of French folk poetry. See P. Bénichou, *Nerval et la chanson folklorique,* 1970, pp. 87ff.

[36] See Lacroix & Seré, *Le Moyen Âge et la Renaissance,* ii (1849) (F. Fertiault).

[37] See *Réforme de l'enseignement . . . pendant le ministère de M. H. Fortoul,* 1856, i. 274.

[38] Bernard, *Lettres sur la poésie,* 1857, pp. 1-2.

[39] Schuré, *Histoire du lied,* 2nd edn., 1876, p. 507.

throughout this period on the collection and publication of folk-songs from all the provinces of France. Schuré records in the Preface to the 1903 edition of the *Histoire du lied* the activities of folklorists such as Champfleury and Jean-François Bladé who disproved his statement in the first edition. The work of these men was, however, ignored by their contemporaries, the Parnassians, who, in obedience to Bernard and his fellows, would, when seeking inspiration in folklore, produce a 'Chant livonien' or 'Chant souabe' (Bernard himself in *Mélodies pastorales,* 1856), a 'Chant de guerre circassien' (Coppée in *Poèmes divers,* 1869), or a 'Chanson de route Arya' (Charles Cros in *Le Coffret de santal,* 1873). Banville made tentative use of a refrain from a French folk-song, in 'Nous n'irons plus au bois' (1845), but hastened to associate it with 'Les Amours des bassins, les Naïades en groupe'.[40] It was the Symbolist poets of the 80s and 90s who profited by the work of the earlier generation of folklorists.[41]

So republicans, while recommending folk-songs as a source of refreshment for the modern poet, denied that France had produced any worth consideration. They took a similar view of medieval French epic. Primitive epic commanded universal respect, with the exception of one branch alone: 'Le cycle chrétien tout entier est barbare', proclaimed Leconte de Lisle.[42] Michelet in his *Bible de l'humanité* extolled Greek, Indian, and Persian legend, concluding with a resounding attack on the Middle Ages. Littré had declared in 1854: 'Nous [sommes] fils du moyen âge, et seulement petits-fils de la Grèce et de Rome',[43] but the militantly republican historian and poet André Lefèvre persisted in speaking of 'nos pères de l'Himalaya . . . nos oncles de Grèce'.[44]

B. *Medieval literature: a territory in dispute; 'balbutiements' and 'bégayements'; 'esprit gaulois'; satire; Arthurian romance; Roland*

Medieval literature, however, like every aspect of the Middle Ages, was a territory in dispute between opposing parties. Republicans did not abandon it in its entirety to their Catholic opponents. They also took an interest in its rediscovery, and favoured, if not the *chanson de geste,* certain other genres which they recommended to the modern reader.

---

[40] Banville, *Les Stalactites,* Lemerre, 1873, p. 16.
[41] Cf. *infra,* p. 275.
[42] Leconte de Lisle, *Articles, préfaces, discours,* p. 114 (Preface to *Poèmes antiques,* 1852).
[43] Cf. *supra,* p. 90.
[44] A. Lefèvre, *Religions et mythologies comparées,* 1877, p. 11.

There were, of course, quite a few intransigents who condemned medieval literature out of hand. D'Héricault relates how, as late as 1874, Jules Soury, a disciple of Renan who wrote reviews for a republican newspaper, flew into a rage when he was given D'Héricault's edition of Charles d'Orléans:'J'ai une telle horreur du moyen âge, s'écria-t-il, indigné, que j'aimerais mieux ne jamais écrire que de dire un mot de Charles d'Orléans.'[45] Bernard declared in his *Histoire de la poésie:* 'Les érudits s'épuisent en vain à publier les productions littéraires du moyen-âge. . . . L'ancienne France n'a pas eu de poésie, à proprement parler.'[46] It was the custom to refer to the works of medieval writers as 'balbutiements' or 'bégayements'. Marchangy in *La Gaule poétique* had spoken of 'les vers informes, bégayés par les Troubadours dans l'enfance de notre poésie';[47] and this term recurs innumerable times in subsequent criticism. Nisard warns the reader who might be tempted into excessive admiration of Guillaume de Lorris's style: 'La grâce d'un bon nombre de traits n'est que dans le bégaiement de cette langue.'[48] Jules Simon, reviewing Géruzez's *Histoire de la littérature française* (1852) in *Le Siècle,* says: 'Nous glisserons sur toute la première partie du livre . . . où il traite du moyen âge. Nous n'avons pas la même passion que M. Géruzez pour les littératures qui bégayent. . . . Un trait naïf, un mot heureux, peut-être parfois un éclair qui brille dans cette nuit, ne sauraient compenser tant de fatras, de mauvais goût et d'absurdité.'[49] Another expression often used by critics of this period in presenting medieval literature to the public was that their labours could be termed the extraction of pearls from the dunghill. Édouard Laboulaye, speaking of the service rendered to the general reader by intermediaries such as Géruzez, said: 'Jeunes ou vieux, il en est peu d'entre nous qui aient assez de loisir ou de courage pour chercher parmi ces poëmes, qui ne finissent jamais, quelques richesses perdues dans le fumier d'Ennius.'[50] This is the attitude adopted by Sainte-Beuve, whenever he has occasion to bring to the attention of his readers some lines of a *chanson de geste,* or a scene from a *mystère,* deserving praise.[51] Any such praise should, in his

---

[45] D'Héricault, *Souvenirs et portraits,* p. 70.
[46] Bernard, *Histoire de la poésie,* p. 181.
[47] Marchangy, *La Gaule poétique,* vii (1817), 23.
[48] D. Nisard, *Histoire de la littérature française,* i (1844), 119.
[49] *Le Siècle,* 18 Aug. 1852.
[50] *Journal des débats,* 22 Aug. 1852.
[51] See, e.g., his *lundis* (1853) on Vol. XXII of the *Histoire Littéraire de la France* (*Causeries du lundi,* Vol. VIII); his Introduction to Crépet's *Poëtes français* (1861); and his *lundis* (1862) on the *mystères* (*Nouveaux lundis,* Vol. III).

opinion, be carefully qualified; in order to safeguard the canons of taste, the greatest circumspection must be displayed by the critic who ventures into this field. Fastidious precautions are taken by him when he speaks of medieval drama in 1862:

> N'oublions . . . jamais, nous tous qui l'avons vue ou entrevue, la beauté véritable; gardons-en fidèlement la haute et délicate image au dedans de nous, ne fût-ce que pour n'en pas prodiguer à tout propos et n'en jamais profaner le nom, comme je le vois faire à d'estimables travailleurs qui ont beaucoup paperassé sur le moyen âge et qui ne connaissent que cela. Qu'on me dise que c'est *curieux* tant qu'on le voudra, − oui; − mais que c'est *beau,* − non.[52]

Enemies and allies of the Middle Ages spoke with one voice to declare that medieval literature in its original form could be read only by the specialist − from Delécluze, who spoke of 'un langage vieilli, fort difficile à débrouiller, et que personne, à l'exception des érudits, n'a de véritables raisons d'étudier',[53] to Léon Gautier in the Preface to Volume II of his *Épopées françaises:* 'Nous voudrions que la lecture de nos résumés pût en quelque manière remplacer celle des textes originaux dont la lecture est familière aux seuls érudits';[54] Laprade: 'Écrits sans art, dans une langue qui bégaye encore, ces poëmes . . . ne sont plus visités que des érudits, avec le genre d'intérêt qui s'attache à des ruines';[55] and Théophile Gautier, in his *Rapport sur les progrès de la poésie* (1868): 'les poëmes du cycle carlovingien sont écrits dans une langue que seuls les érudits entendent.'[56]

Many critics, however, were convinced that medieval literature was of value and did contain a message for the modern world; but opinions differed as to which of its branches had value and wherein this message lay. Republican and anti-clerical writers of the Second Empire, from the eminent Renan, whose absorption in the unorthodox, non-Roman Middle Ages we have discussed in the previous chapter, to the eccentric Eugène Aroux (author of *Dante hérétique, révolutionnaire et socialiste,* 1854, and *Les Mystères de la chevalerie et de l'amour platonique au moyen âge,* 1858), were at pains to demonstrate how the Age of Faith celebrated

---

[52] *Nouveaux lundis,* iii. 378-9. This provoked an acrimonious exchange of letters between the critic and Paulin Paris, to whom Sainte-Beuve wrote: 'Je ne fais pas la guerre au moyen-âge, je l'étudie' (S.-B., *Correspondance générale,* ed. Bonnerot, xii (1962), 462-5).

[53] Delécluze, *Roland, ou la chevalerie,* 1845, i. xxiii.

[54] L. Gautier, *Les Épopées françaises,* ii (1867), p. ix.

[55] Laprade, *Le Sentiment de la nature chez les modernes,* 1868, p. 47.

[56] T. Gautier, *Histoire du romantisme,* Charpentier, 1905, p. 390.

by Catholics had in reality been an age of sedition and free-thought. Eager to bring to light what Henri Martin termed 'l'histoire souterraine de ces temps',[57] these writers turned their attention towards medieval mystics – such as Joachim de Flore and the Vaudois, in whom Michelet, Quinet, and Renan took a keen interest[58] – and satirists, examined at length in Charles Lenient's *La Satire en France au moyen âge* (1859), which was acclaimed by one critic as a study of 'le moyen âge officiel miné par la critique et la parodie.' 'Le faux moyen âge des néo-paladins littéraires', he said, 'a fait rechercher, retrouver, reconstruire le vrai, lequel ne répond guère à l'idéal que l'on s'en était fait.'[59] The same spirit inspired Méray's *Les Libres Prêcheurs devanciers de Luther et de Rabelais* (1860), written to disabuse 'ceux qui se sont fait en imagination un moyen âge angélique, tout confit en dévotion. . . .'[60] Eugène Aroux also claimed to be in a position to substitute for the unreal Middle Ages of Romantic convention, with its 'guerriers sans peur et sans reproche' and 'gentils troubadours . . . vivant en joie et soulas', the real Middle Ages at last unveiled to the public gaze: 'A l'imagination nous opposons la raison,' he proclaimed, 'à la fiction la réalité, la vérité au mensonge.'[61] In this Middle Ages of Aroux's a vast anti-Catholic conspiracy is at work, disseminating Albigensian doctrine. *Les Mystères de la chevalerie* purported to reveal 'sous le voile des fictions les plus diverses, un esprit d'opposition toujours le même, poursuivant son but sans trêve ni merci'.[62] Courts of love were in reality secret gatherings of Albigensian conspirators; *jongleurs* were ministers of the Albigensian Church; knights errant were Albigensian missionaries. *Aucassin et Nicolette* is 'le petit chef d'oeuvre d'un Parfait inconnu';[63] indeed all medieval literature, *chansons de geste, fabliaux* and the rest, forms 'les chroniques de l'opposition'.[64]

Since the 1830s, republicans had laid claim to Gothic architecture.[65] In the chapter of *Notre-Dame de Paris,* 'Ceci tuera cela', Hugo had declared it to be of secular inspiration, and often, in its sculptural detail, hostile to the Church: 'Saint-Jacques-de-la-Boucherie était toute

---

[57] H. Martin, *Histoire de France,* 4th edn., iii (1858), 398.
[58] See Z. Markiewicz, 'L'*Évangile éternel* de Joachim de Flore et les Romantiques', *Revue des études italiennes,* vi (1959), pp. 149-60.
[59] *Revue française,* xvi (1859), p. 529 (C.-L. Chassin).
[60] A. Méray, *Les Libres Prêcheurs devanciers de Luther et de Rabelais,* 1860, p. 189.
[61] E. Aroux, *Les Mystères de la chevalerie et de l'amour platonique au moyen âge,* 1858, p. 205.
[62] Aroux, *Les Mystères de la chevalerie,* p. xvi.   [63] Ibid. p. 59.
[64] Ibid. p. xvii.   [65] Cf. *supra,* p. 14.

une église d'opposition.'[66] In their turn Ludovic Vitet[67] and Viollet-le-Duc[68] saw in Gothic spires the spirit of democracy emancipating itself from feudalism and monasticism. 'L'art . . . devint . . . une sorte de *liberté de la presse*'[69] says Viollet in his *Dictionnaire raisonné*, borrowing an expression of Hugo's. In the fabulous beasts of thirteenth-century sculpture he discerns 'la trace effacée, mais appréciable encore, du panthéisme splendide des Aryas. Le vieil esprit gaulois perçait ainsi à travers le christianisme.'[70] The historian Henri Martin carried these speculations still further. A disciple of Jean Reynaud (who had said of the Druids in his *Terre et ciel* (1854) 'Ils sont nos pères'),[71] Martin contended that the Gallic — and, more specifically, Druidic — element was responsible for all that was best in France's history. In volume III of his *Histoire de France* (1858) he maintained that Gothic architecture was a product of the Celtic 'esprit d'amour qui est aussi esprit de liberté'.[72] Far from being 'l'art catholique', it was 'l'art gaulois et français . . . anti-monastique, extrà-sacerdotal'.[72] He drew the reader's attention to the figure of LIBERTAS among the Virtues on the north door of Chartres cathedral, reminded him that the church was built on the site of a Druid sanctuary, and remarked: 'Les restes mortels des ancêtres durent tressaillir de joie sous les *pierres levées* des Carnutes, quand cette solennelle figure de la LIBERTÉ fut inaugurée sur la face du temple chrétien.'[73]

The conflict between Franks and Gauls, aristocrats and republicans, which Augustin Thierry had seen as the dominant factor in France's history, raged fiercely in literary criticism concerned with the medieval period. Léon Gautier, angered by Martin's theories, protested in *Le Croisé* in 1860: 'Je suis Chrétien avant d'être Gaulois.'[74]

Medieval works of satire — Jean de Meung's *Roman de la Rose,* the *Roman de Renart* and the *fabliaux* — aroused republican enthusiasm as repositories of *esprit gaulois;* but Michelet, even in the later, militantly

[66] *Notre-Dame de Paris*, pp. 214-15.
[67] In his *Rapport à M. le Ministre de l'Intérieur sur les monumens . . .*, 1831, and *Monographie de l'église Notre-Dame de Noyon*, 1845.
[68] See *Dictionnaire raisonné de l'architecture française*, articles 'Architecture', 'Cathédrale', 'Sculpture', etc., and *Entretiens sur l'architecture*, i (1863), 3rd and 6th *entretiens.*
[69] *Dictionnaire raisonné de l'architecture française*, viii (1866), 142 (cf. *Notre-Dame de Paris*, p. 214).
[70] Ibid. p. 244.
[71] J. Reynaud, *Terre et ciel*, Furne, 1854, p. 195.   [72] H. Martin, op. cit. pp. 410-12.
[73] Ibid. pp. 414-15.   [74] *Le Croisé*, i (1860), p. 336.

anticlerical phase of his career, could not bring himself to admire them. In 1833 the long decline of twelfth-century heroic and chivalric poetry had filled him with grief: 'Décrépite, elle grimaça encore pendant le quatorzième siècle dans les tristes imitations du triste roman de la Rose, tandis que par-dessus s'élevait peu à peu l'aigre voix de la dérision populaire dans les contes et les fabliaux.'[75] In 1840 he again expressed detestation of the *Roman de la Rose:* 'Cet insipide ouvrage . . . semble la profession de foi du sensualisme grossier qui règne au quatorzième siècle';[76] and he still maintained these opinions in 1855: 'Des trente poëmes épiques du douzième siècle, imités de toute l'Europe, jusqu'à la platitude du *Roman de la Rose,* jusqu'aux tristes gaietés de Villon, quel pas rétrograde!'[77] Renan, on the other hand, agreed with Michelet in 1856, condemning 'l'esprit gaulois, esprit plat, positif, sans élévation . . . destructeur de toute noblesse et de tout idéal':[78] 'Quand on passe des nobles fictions créées par les belles époques du moyen âge aux oeuvres plates et roturières du XIVe et du XVe siècle, on sent tout d'abord une profonde déchéance';[79] but by 1868 he had evolved to a different position, agreeing with Victor Le Clerc that the *fabliaux,* 'ces compositions parfois charmantes', were 'chose admirable'.[80] Catholic writers, of course, expressed the strongest disapproval of these works. Moland, speaking of his and D'Héricault's plan to publish an anthology of extracts from medieval literature, said of the *fabliaux* and 'le triste Roman de la Rose': 'A tout cela, nous ne ferons que de modiques emprunts et avec une extrême réserve; car ce que nous cherchons dans le moyen-âge, contrairement à la plupart de nos devanciers, c'est ce qui est bon et ce qui est beau.'[81] Léon Gautier fulminated against 'ces ignobles fabliaux, honte du moyen âge, qu'il eût fallu laisser à tout jamais enfouis dans la juste obscurité des bibliothèques, où quelques paléographes paillards auraient eu seuls le courage d'aller les chercher.'[82] 'Surtout, il ne fallait pas traduire ces vilenies', he protested.[83] 'On est épouvanté quand on lit le *Roman de Renard*', he commented, 'c'est du Voltaire';[34] and he drew a dividing-line between what was wholesome and what was noxious in medieval literature, between 'le groupe des

---

[75] Michelet, *H. F.* ii. 652.   [76] Ibid. iii. 209.
[77] Michelet, *Renaissance*, pp. 22-3.   [78] Renan, *Os. cs.* ii. 211-12.
[79] Ibid. p. 213.   [80] Ibid. p. 675.
[81] *Revue de l'enseignement chrétien,* i (Nov. 1852), p. 587.
[82] L. Gautier, *Les Épopées françaises,* i (1865), 578. Cf. *Comment faut-il juger le moyen-âge?*, 1858, p. 37.
[83] *Les Épopées françaises,* 2nd edn., ii (1892), 676.
[84] *Les Épopées françaises,* ii (1865), 448.

gaulois, des railleurs et, s'il m'est permis de parler ainsi, des "boule-vardiers" (including the *Roman de Renart,* the *Roman de la Rose,* and the *fabliaux*), and the works produced by 'les "braves gens" . . . les génies honnêtes': the *chansons de geste,* the chronicles of Villehardouin, Joinville, and Froissart.[85] Gautier devoted his career to the popularization of the *chansons de geste,* particularly those of the Carolingian cycle. 'La France possède plus de cent épopées, dont quelques-unes sont d'inimitables chefs-d'oeuvre', he proclaimed in 1864.[86] The following year he published the first volume of *Les Épopées françaises,* with its fervent Preface: 'Il est temps de les lire et les faire lire.'[87]

Among those who spoke out in praise of medieval satirical literature, already extolled in Louis-Philippe's reign by Ampère[88] and Nisard,[89] were Victor Le Clerc, who called the *fabliaux* 'peut-être le plus riche héritage que nous ait légué le vieil esprit français',[90] and Taine, who, unlike Michelet and Renan, had no nostalgia for the early, chivalric Middle Ages, and delighted in the *esprit gaulois* of the *fabliaux* and *Roman de Renart.*[91]

The two writers who did most to popularize Arthurian legend during the Second Empire were both Catholic. One was La Villemarqué, inspired by patriotism to publicize Breton folklore in *La Légende celtique en Irlande, en Cambrie, et en Bretagne* (1859), *Les Romans de la Table Ronde et les contes des anciens Bretons* (3rd, enlarged, edition, 1860; Renan drew on the 1st edition (1842) for 'La poésie des races celtiques'), and *Myrdhinn ou l'enchanteur Merlin* (1862). The other was Paulin Paris, whose Catholic allegiances did not prevent him from having a predilection for Arthurian romance. Gaston Paris describes him in his youth, in the Bibliothèque du Roi, engrossed for weeks on end in the *romans d'aventure,* 'laissant passer les heures sans en avoir conscience'.[92] In 1868-77 Paulin Paris published his *Romans de la Table Ronde mis en nouveau langage.*

Arthurian romance, like satire, was, however, on the whole republican territory. Alfred Michiels, in his *Histoire des idées littéraires en France*

[85] *Portraits du XIXe siècle,* ii (1894), 260-1.
[86] *Études historiques pour la défense de l'Église,* 1864, p. 256.
[87] *Les Épopées françaises,* i (1865), p. viii.
[88] In his articles 'Vue générale de la littérature française au moyen-âge' (*RDM,* 1839) and 'La Poésie du moyen-âge: le *Roman de la Rose*' (*RDM,* 1843), both reprinted in *Mélanges d'histoire littéraire et de littérature,* i (1867)).
[89] In his *Histoire de la littérature française,* i (1844).
[90] *Histoire littéraire de la France,* Firmin Didot, xxiii (1856), 69.
[91] Cf. e.g. *La Fontaine,* 1861, and *Histoire de la littérature anglaise,* i. 95-6.
[92] G. Paris, *La Poésie du moyen âge,* première série, 1885, 233.

(1842), affirmed: 'La révolution française porte évidemment un caractère celtique.'[93] Henri Martin sought to persuade his readers of the pre-revolutionary character of the Arthurian legend. He dwelt with delight on the moment when 'le cycle de la Table Ronde . . . submerge le cycle de Charlemagne':[94] 'Au chevalier conquérant et politique, fils des Franks, succède le chevalier errant, fils des Gaulois, poursuivant par le monde la poésie du danger et l'idéal de l'amour . . . parmi les oiseaux fatidiques, les nains, les géants, les fées protectrices, les monstres ennemis et les animaux frères d'armes de l'homme. Tout un monde enchanté environne les héros de la Table Ronde.'[95] He praised the democratic nature of the Round Table. In the twelve peers of Charlemagne he saw 'l'esprit hiérarchique des Germains', whereas 'la Table Ronde remplace la hiérarchie germanique par l'égalité gauloise. Le nombre des chevaliers de la Table Ronde est illimité.'[96] He defended the adulterous loves which, as we shall see, were for Catholics a deplorable feature of the Arthurian legend. For Martin 'l'élan idéal qui voulait séparer l'amour des vulgarités de la vie conjugale'[97] was an admirable aspiration, justified by the sordid nature of feudal marriage: 'On en vient à déclarer nettement l'amour et le mariage incompatibles. . . . Le mariage féodal . . . méritait parfaitement cet anathème. On épousait un fief.'[97]

The misogynist republican 'enemy of Gothic' Delécluze, was, however, in his *Roland ou la chevalerie* (1845), as loud in his denunciation of Arthurian legend as Léon Gautier some twenty years later; republican and Catholic puritanism were here in accord.[98] Scandalized by 'les relations fausses et immorales d'Arthur, de Genièvre et de Lancelot . . . et celles également choquantes, sous l'influence desquelles agissent Tristan Yseult et le roi Marc',[99] Delécluze affirmed that 'le résultat de la lecture de ces romans, pendant six siècles dans l'Europe, a été d'établir dans presque tous les esprits, une préférence marquée pour les liaisons illicites.'[100] It was through these works that 'le culte presque superstitieux de la femme, exalté par les préjugés chevaleresques',[101] had been transmitted down the centuries. In his turn, the Catholic medievalist Henri

---

[93] Michiels, *Histoire des idées littéraires en France au XIXe siècle,* 1842, i. 219.
[94] H. Martin, op. cit. p. 366.
[95] Ibid. pp. 369-70.
[96] Ibid. p. 375.   [97] Ibid. pp. 383-4.
[98] Cf. Delécluze's denunciation of the *fabliaux* in 1843: 'Le laid, le laid hideux, ressort constamment de ces compositions' (*Revue de Paris,* xvii (July 1843), p. 255.
[99] Delécluze, *Roland, ou la chevalerie,* 1845, ii. 264.
[100] Ibid. i. 356.   [101] Ibid. p. xvi

d'Arbois de Jubainville denounced 'cette prédominance de l'élément érotique qui distingue les romans de la Table ronde de deux du Cycle carlovingien'. Of Paulin Paris's newly-published *Romans de la Table Ronde mis en nouveau langage* he said: 'Nous ne le conseillerons ni aux femmes ni aux jeunes gens.'[102] Léon Gautier was of the same mind: 'La création du cycle de la Table ronde fut un grand malheur pour notre poésie nationale', he states in *Les Épopées françaises.*[103] Calling the Celtic 'merveilleux antichrétien'[104] 'le fléau mortel de notre poésie du moyen âge',[105] he deplores the fact that medieval French poets had recourse to 'ces fictions inutiles autant que ridicules',[106] thereby denaturing the *chanson de geste,* wholly admirable only in its earliest form, pure of Celtic taint. 'Ayant les anges,' he laments, 'ils ont voulu avoir les fées. Ayant les saints, ils ont cru avoir besoin des nains. . . . Les nains et les fées déshonorent . . . de leur présence tous les cycles de nos épopées nationales: pénétrant partout, troublant tout, infectant tout.'[107]

It was precisely the anti-Christian element in the Arthurian legend, of course, that appealed to Renan and to celtophile republicans like Henri Martin. Renan, in an article on La Villemarqué published in 1860, urged that Chrétien de Troyes's works, in particular the *Perceval* (published by a Belgian editor in 1866-71), should be made accessible to the public without delay. Expressing regret that the government-sponsored *Anciens Poètes de la France* (1858-70) was confined to the Carolingian cycle, he confessed that '[mon] goût personnel . . . me fait trouver dans les romans de la Table-Ronde infiniment plus de charme que dans les romans carlovingiens.'[108] In 'La Poésie des races celtiques' (1854) he had extolled 'cette Table-Ronde autour de laquelle le moyen âge groupa toutes ses idées d'héroïsme, de beauté, de pudeur et d'amour'.[109] 'S'il est en poésie un merveilleux que nous puissions accepter,' he continued, 'c'est assurément celui-là.' This is because Celtic mythology, 'purement naturaliste',[110] is free from all Catholic dogma. Unaware that the version of the *Mabinogion* which he is using is an expurgated one,[111] Renan denies that the Arthurian legend, in its primitive Welsh or Breton

---

[102] *Revue des questions historiques,* vi, 1 Apr. 1869, p. 527.
[103] *Les Épopées françaises,* i (1865), 343.
[104] Ibid. p. 425.   [105] Ibid. p. 525.
[106] *Les Épopées françaises,* i (1865), 122.
[107] *Revue du monde catholique,* xx, 10 Jan. 1868, pp. 251-2.
[108] *Journal des débats,* 1 Nov. 1860.
[109] Renan, *Os. cs.* ii. 274.   [110] Ibid. p. 277.
[111] See R. Galand, *L'Âme celtique de Renan,* p. 123.

form, is immoral: 'On n'y rencontre pas une légèreté ni un mot grossier.'[112]
French imitators, such as Chrétien de Troyes, were responsible for
transforming 'la virginale pudeur des romans bretons en une galanterie
effrontée, si bien que ces compositions, si chastes dans l'original,
devinrent le scandale du moyen âge.'[112]

If Catholics and republicans were divided in their appreciation of the
fabliaux and the Arthurian romances, they were unanimous in their
enthusiasm for the *Chanson de Roland*. Patriotic feeling inspired this.
It was responsible, of course, for France's rediscovery of her medieval
literature in the late eighteenth and nineteenth centuries: intense pride
in the European supremacy of French medieval literature is expressed
throughout every volume of the *Histoire littéraire de la France*. If Sainte-
Beuve's attitude towards it is usually one of coolness and faint disdain,
there are moments when patriotic sentiment arouses a more positive
enthusiasm in him. He is moved by the *Combat de trente Bretons contre
trente Anglais*, finding in it 'un héroisme sublime et naturel'.[113] His
articles on the chroniclers — Villehardouin, Joinville, Froissart, and
Commines (read by him in Liège in 1848 in order to 'oublier, s'il se
pouvait, dans leur commerce, les sottises et les misères du présent')[114] —
are all highly enthusiastic in tone.

The loudest praise of the *Chanson de Roland* was voiced by Léon
Gautier, who declared in 1864 of the scene of Roland's death: 'Qui
n'admire pas une telle page n'a pas une goutte de sang chrétien ni de
sang français dans les veines';[115] and ended the first volume of *Les
Épopées françaises* with the defiant shout: 'ET LA CHANSON DE
ROLAND VAUT L'ILIADE',[116] addressed to all those who, like
Sainte-Beuve, considered that comparison of Greek and medieval
French literature — indulged in by ardent medievalists such as Littré
and Génin — amounted to blasphemy. Republicans were scarcely less
enthusiastic in praise of the *Roland*, exempting it from the disfavour
shown to the rest of the Carolingian cycle. Delécluze approved the
absence of Celtic 'galanterie' in it,[117] and his is the first translation

---

[112] Renan, *Os. cs.* ii. 275-6.   [113] *Causeries du lundi*, viii. 322.
[114] *Chateaubriand et son groupe littéraire*, Garnier, 1861, i , 14 (1849 Preface).
   In preparation for his course of lectures on medieval and sixteenth-century
   French literature delivered at Liège University from Nov. 1848 to July 1849.
   See Sainte-Beuve, *Ancienne Littérature (Partie médiévale)*, ed. F. Dehousse,
   1971.
[115] L. Gautier, *Études historiques pour la défense de l'Église*, 1864, p. 268.
[116] *Les Épopées françaises*, i (1865), 656.
[117] Delécluze, *Roland*, i. 38-9.

of the poem into modern French.[118] It is the only one of his trans-
lations not presented to the reader in a spirit of condemnation; for
the extracts from the *Chanson des Saisnes* and the *Roman de Lancelot
du Lac* which follow are intended to show the progress of 'la perver-
sion morale'[119] in the Middle Ages. The republican François Génin's
edition and translation of the *Chanson de Roland* followed in 1850.
Léon Gautier states the the poem's popularity dated from the publication
of this work. Génin acclaimed the *Roland* as the national epic, extolling
in it 'cette tendresse émue, ce dévouement sans bornes pour la *terre de
France*'.[120] The poem was praised by Géruzez and Demogeot, in their
respective histories of French literature, both published in 1852. In the
same year the *Revue des deux mondes* published an important article,
which attracted much attention, and was called by Guessard in 1868
'la consécration . . . donnée à la poésie du moyen âge par l'esthétique
classique'.[121] The article was by Vitet, who translated extracts from the
Roland and agreed with Génin that 'cette grande oeuvre nationale'[122]
deserved the title of epic; for, in reading certain of its best scenes, 'un
seul mot vient à l'esprit, le mot *sublime*.'[123] A supporter of Louis-
Philippe who retired from public life during the Empire, Vitet concluded
with the words: 'Quand tout s'abaisse et se ternit, n'est-ce pas le moment
de détourner les yeux pour chercher dans le passé de consolantes
splendeurs?'[124] Michelet, in his Introduction to the *Renaissance,* declared
that he heard in 'la sublime *Chanson de Roland*' 'la forte voix du peuple
et le grave accent des héros'.[125] He was convinced that the poem was of
pre-feudal origin, and could therefore be exempted from the general
condemnation of the Middle Ages which was the theme of the
Introduction: 'Ces chants', he asserted, 'ne sont pas, comme on le croit,
l'oeuvre du pesant âge féodal, qui n'a fait que les délayer. De telles choses
ne datent pas d'un âge de servitude, mais d'un âge vivant, libre
encore.'[126] Henri Martin also acclaimed the *Roland,* with only one
reservation – that the dying hero had no thought for *la belle Aude,* as
the author of the poem was ignorant of the 'nouveau monde moral'

---

[118] Published in Vol. II of *Roland, ou la Chevalerie* (1845).
[119] Delécluze, *Roland,* ii. 369.
[120] Génin, *La Chanson de Roland,* 1850, p. viii.
[121] *Recueil de rapports sur l'état des lettres et les progrès des sciences en France:
Progrès des études classiques et du moyen âge,* 1868, p. 126.
[122] L. Vitet, *Essais historiques et littéraires,* 1862, p. 81.
[123] Ibid. p. 75.
[124] Ibid. p. 82.
[125] Michelet, *Renaissance,* p. 29.
[126] Michelet, *Renaissance,* pp. 26-7.

created by the Celts, in which women were given their proper status.[127]

Only a few obdurate enemies of the Middle Ages refused to join in this chorus of approbation. Taine in his *Histoire de la littérature anglaise* quoted the scene of Roland's death as an example of the invariably pedestrian quality of medieval French writing.[128] Bernard, too, expressed disdain for the poem, complaining that '[elle]n'a point le caractère de la poésie populaire, et ne rappelle pas les chants serviens.'[129]

---

[127] H. Martin, op. cit. p. 351.

[128] Taine, *HLA*, i. 87.

[129] Bernard, *Histoire de la poésie*, p. 182. It is interesting to note that Mérimée was of the same opinion. He wrote to Damas-Hinard in 1858: 'Patriotisme à part, le Cid vaut bien mieux que le Roland. . . . Le Français est déjà un poète de salons' (*Correspondancè générale*, deuxième série, ii (1955), 444).

CHAPTER 5

THE FLIGHT FROM THE ROMANTIC MIDDLE AGES

'Reviens, reviens, bel art antique' (T. Gautier)

During the Second Empire, declares Melchior de Vogüé in an essay published at the close of the century, 'le moyen âge, bric-à-brac démodé, sombra avec le reste du bagage romantique.'[1] This is only a half-truth: during the 1850s and 60s, as we have seen, the Middle Ages, believed to be a living presence in the land, were the subject of perpetual controversy, and one would expect to find some reflection of this in the literature of the period, more especially as it so often concerned itself with re-creation of the past. It is true that the Romantic Middle Ages had faded into an object of derision long before the Empire came into being; but its place was taken by a new Middle Ages, or rather by several, owing much of their vitality and distinctive colouring to the conflicting political passions of the day. We will look at these in the next chapter; in this, we shall examine a group of writers who, following the example of Michelet, Renan, and Taine, fled from the Middle Ages into the pagan world of classical antiquity and the Renaissance. The writers in question are Gautier, Ménard, and the Parnassians.

Théophile Gautier experienced in the middle of his career a recoil from the Middle Ages comparable with that of Michelet. In later life he liked to claim that he alone had led his aberrant fellow-Romantics towards a nobler ideal. The Goncourts recorded in 1863 his famous remark: 'Nous étions le parti *mâchicoulis.* . . . C'a été une scission, quand j'ai chanté l'antiquité dans la préface de la MAUPIN.'[2] In 1867 he wrote: 'J'aimais beaucoup les cathédrales, sur la foi de Notre-Dame de Paris, mais la vue du Parthénon m'a guéri de la maladie gothique, qui n'a jamais été bien forte chez moi.'[3] Maxime Du Camp and Théodore de Banville endorse this. Du Camp, himself a life-long enemy of the Middle Ages, remarks with approval that Gautier stood aloof from the prevailing fashion: 'Il laissa le moyen âge aux autres et n'y toucha pas';[4] and

---

[1] E-M. de Vogüé, *Histoire et poésie,* A. Colin, 1898, p. 140.
[2] *Journal des Goncourt,* i. 1302.
[3] Gautier, *Portraits contemporains,* 1874, p. 12.
[4] M. Du Camp, *Théophile Gautier,* 1890, p. 129.

Banville agrees with him: 'Pour son compte, Gautier fut très-peu romantique, très-peu féru du moyen âge, car il y eut toujours en lui l'amour de la vie, de la beauté pure et sereine comme l'entendit l'antiquité hellénique.'[5] However, there is evidence in Gautier's early poetry to disclaim this. We have noted in the previous chapter that as late as 1868 he was still associated in Thalès Bernard's mind with the 'fouillis moyen âge' of the Romantics.[6] Although he was from the very beginning able to regard Romantic medievalism with ironic detachment (in *Elias Wildmanstadius ou l'homme moyen âge* (1832), and in the imaginary critic's tirade in the Preface to *Mademoiselle de Maupin* (1834),[7] we have seen that he was not above indulging in it himself in poems published at this time, such as 'Moyen Âge', 'La Basilique', 'Ballade' (1830), and 'Notre-Dame' (1831, published 1833).[8] Here he loses himself in the idéal Romantic Middle Ages in all its glory, a sun-lit world where 'Tout chatoie et reluit',[9] a 'Monde de poésie, en ce monde de prose'.[10]

In 1843, in *Tra los Montes*, Gautier is still expressing rapturous enthusiasm for Gothic architecture, aroused in him by Burgos cathedral: 'Quels hommes étaient-ce donc', he asks, 'que ceux qui exécutaient ces merveilleuses constructions . . .?La race en est-elle donc perdue?'[11] In Seville, he again laments that the Age of Faith is past: 'De notre temps . . . l'on ne comprend plus ces sublimes élancements de l'âme vers l'infini, traduits en aiguilles, en flèches, en clochetons, en ogives, tendant au ciel leurs bras de pierre et se joignant, par-dessus la tête du peuple prosterné, comme de gigantesques mains qui supplient.'[12] But in 1854, after a visit to Strasbourg, he makes it clear, in an article written for *La Presse*, that Gothic now inspires in him only repugnance and trepidation:

Autrefois, nous professions un vif enthousiasme à l'endroit des cathédrales, enthousiasme qui s'est changé en admiration douloureuse depuis que nous avons vu sur le trépied de marbre de l'acropole les purs chefs-d'oeuvre du génie grec. . . . Quel aspect sinistre présentent les hauts murs de grès rouge verdi par place comme du cuivre oxydé; avec quel effort haletant . . . la flèche se dresse vers le ciel; quel élancement rigide dans ces nervures fuselées qui montent grêles et

---

[5] From a speech delivered by Banville in 1875, quoted by E. Bergerat, *Théophile Gautier*, 1879, p. 236.
[6] Cf. *supra*, p. 97.   [7] Cf. *supra*, p. 27   [8] Cf. *supra*, pp. 15, 23.
[9] Gautier, *Poésies complètes*, ii. 147.   [10] Ibid. p. 152.
[11] Gautier, *Tra los montes*, 1843, i. 64.   [12] Ibid. ii. 233-4.

droites; quelle tristesse glaciale, quelle ombre noire sous les ogives du cloître!

Jamais nous n'avions senti à ce point l'intime souffrance, le désespoir secret et l'idéal nostalgique du moyen âge; les statuettes du porche s'allongent dans leurs niches comme des cadavres dans leur bière, dessinant à peine quelques plis cassants sous leurs draperies pareilles à des linceuls . . . pauvres vierges folles du portail, en vain vous tâchez d'être lubriques et provocantes . . . vos petits seins amaigris, vos bras fluets, vos mains diaphanes font penser à de jeunes filles atteintes de consomption et dont la beauté laisse transparaître le squelette. Votre grâce morte et vos coquetteries d'outre-tombe attristent plus qu'elles ne séduisent. . . .

Comme ceux qui ont élevé de pareils édifices devaient être mal-heureux! Quelle vie horrible, convulsée de terreurs, hantée de fantômes, suppose cette architecture sépulcrale, aux fondations cimentées d'ossements, au faîte peuplé de corbeaux, aux épouvantements com-binés pour agir sur le système nerveux! Et qu'il y a loin de là à la lumineuse sérénité grecque et aux temples blancs des bienheureux Olympiens . . .[13]

So the Middle Ages, associated with the horrors of the charnel-house, now strike terror into Gautier; and he will soon be writing the poem 'Bûchers et tombeaux' (1858), in which pagan love of life is set in opposition to medieval delectation in death. The association of Gothic art with things of the tomb had always been present to a certain extent in his work: he had never been able to contemplate cathedral crypts with the equanimity of Chateaubriand, for whom, in *Le Génie du Christianisme,* 'ces cloîtres pavés par la mort, ces sanctuaires remplis de sépulcres',[14] presented a wholly moral and edifying spectacle, in no way disturbing, or of Victor Hugo, whose imagination was captivated rather than repelled by them, as we saw in our first chapter.[15] Gautier, even in youth, regarded these things with a faint shudder. In his 'Portail' to *La Comédie de la mort* (1838), he remarked:

> Avant de s'élancer tout clocher est caveau:
> En bas, l'oiseau de nuit, l'ombre humide des tombres . . .,

but continued:

> En haut, l'or du soleil, la neige des colombes,
> Des cloches et des chants. . . .[16]

---

[13] Gautier, *L'Art moderne,* 1856, pp. 182-3.
[14] Part 4, Bk. 2, Ch. 8.   [15] Cf. *supra,* pp. 20−1.
[16] Gautier, *Poésies complètes,* ii. 3. The influence of *Notre-Dame de Paris* is evident here. Cf. *supra,* Ch. 1. p. 20.

In 1854 birds of ill-omen are perched on the topmost pinnacle of
Strasbourg cathedral; the shadow of death has engulfed the entire
structure. Similarly, Gautier remarked in his early poem 'Melancholia'
(1834), of the Campo Santo frescoes in Pisa,

> . . . chaque draperie a l'aspect d'un linceul;

but added:

> C'est que la vie alors de croyance était pleine.

Mortality is waiting to put on immortality:

> Sur tous ces fronts pâlis, sous cet air de souffrance
> Brille ineffablement quelque haute espérance;
> L'on voit que tout ce peuple agenouillé n'attend
> Pour revoler aux cieux que le suprême instant.[17]

In 1854 all hope is extinguished. As early as 1848 Gautier had been
repelled by some *tableaux vivants* of Biblical scenes at the open-air
theatre in the Champs-Élysées. As he watched them, 'une secrète
terreur s'emparait de nous.' They reminded him of

> . . . toutes ces sculptures étranges à la physionomie morte, aux
> poses suppliantes et pleines d'angoisse, aux apparences phantasmatiques,
> aux vêtements plissés en suaire, que le catholicisme a mis à la gêne avec
> une cruauté si ingénieuse dans les bizarres compartiments de son archi-
> tecture à stalactites. . . . Dans ces tristes tableaux se reproduit une
> image de la terreur secrète qui serra si longtemps le coeur du moyen
> âge.[18] C'est la Mort qui a disposé elle-même ces groupes blafards tout
> prêts pour la danse macabre.[19]

The influence of Michelet is evident in both these outbursts of
Gautier's. The words of compassion addressed by the historian to the
Gothic cathedral, seen as a woman who has adorned herself with 'une
délicieuse coquetterie' − 'Vous avez beau faire, souffrante beauté, le
bracelet flotte autour d'un bras amaigri; vous savez trop, la pensée vous
brûle, vous languissez d'amour impuissant'[20] − are repeated by Gautier
to the foolish virgins in 1854, but the 'coquetteries' are now 'des
coquetteries d'outre-tombe', arousing only disgust, and anticipating
Michelet's harsh words pronounced in 1855: 'La vieille église gothique,
in extremis, s'entoure de petits ornements, frisures, guipures, etc., elle
s'attife et se fait jolie. . . .'[21] (We shall see later on how this coquetry of

[17] Ibid. p. 85.
[18] Cf. Kotzebue, *supra,* p. 86n.
[19] Gautier, *Histoire de l'art dramatique en France,* v (1859), 271.
[20] Michelet, *Histoire de France,* ii. 688.
[21] Michelet, *Renaissance,* p. 144.

Gothic art, pathetic for the early Michelet, macabre and distasteful in the eyes of Gautier, held a powerful fascination for Gautier's friend Baudelaire.)[22]

So, just as Michelet in his scrutiny of the Middle Ages experienced the suffering and despair of his ancestors, Gautier experienced their obsessive terror of death; or rather, both writers, a prey to these desolate feelings in their own lives, projected them on to a personal vision of the Middle Ages, as a nightmare from which it was necessary to escape at all costs. 'Reviens, reviens, bel art antique. . . . Couvrir ce squelette gothique . . .! '[23] cried Gautier, and Michelet declared: 'Il faut faire volte-face, et vivement, franchement, tourner le dos au moyen âge, à ce passé morbide.'[24]

Although we have seen that he had begun to recoil from Gothic art as early as 1848, Gautier in 1854 dated his conversion to Hellenic perfection from his visit to Athens in the autumn of 1852. It is true that in an article written from Athens for the *Moniteur universel,* he had pronounced an early *Prière sur l'Acropole:* 'Là, en effet . . . rayonne immortellement la beauté vraie, absolue, parfaite; ensuite, il n'y a que des variétés de décadence.'[25] He wrote to a correspondent at this time: 'Athènes m'a transporté. A côté du Parthénon, tout semble barbare et grossier.'[26]

Numerous writers of the Second Empire agreed with Michelet and Gautier that the Romantic Middle Ages were in a state of sinister decomposition. The architectural detail — battlements, turrets, gargoyles, and legendary beasts — which had so delighted Hugo and the 'parti mâchicoulis' was recalled with a shudder by the new generation, and exposed as a menace to be swept away. There had been presages of this reaction in the early 1830s, in what Michelet called 'le brillant matin de juillet'.[27] Lamartine had pronounced his 'Adieu pour jamais au gothique' on sight of the Parthenon in 1832.[28] Béranger had declared two years later:

> Des loups-garous, des goules, des vampires,
> Du moyen âge aimables passe-temps.
> Fi des damnés, des spectres et des tombes!

[22] Cf. *infra,* pp. 181-2.
[23] Gautier, *Poésies complètes,* iii, 75 ('Bûchers et tombeaux', 1858).
[24] Cf. *supra,* p. 44.
[25] Gautier, *Loin de Paris,* 1865, pp. 230-1.
[26] Quoted by E. Bergerat, *Théophile Gautier,* p. 295.
[27] Cf. *supra,* p. 26.
[28] Lamartine, *Voyage en Orient,* ed. Lotfy Fam, Nizet, 1960, p. 280.

> Fi de l'horrible! il est contagieux.
> Chauves-souris, faites place aux colombes.[29]

Heine, of whom Barbey d'Aurevilly remarked in 1855 '[Il] a toujours une flèche empoisonnée . . . pour le noble coeur du Moyen Âge',[30] and who, a close friend of Gautier, may well have influenced him in some measure, told the French in *De l'Allemagne* (1835): 'Renoncez aux spectres et aux choses terribles.'[31]

During the 1850s and 60s various republican poets and critics recalled, in language strongly reminiscent of Michelet, the heroic struggle of their Romantic elders to break free from the Middle Ages, and reminded their readers that the struggle against the forces of reaction was far from being at an end. Laurent-Pichat, journalist, writer of republican verse and militant opponent of the Empire, said of the Romantics in 1859:

> Ces penseurs ont réagi depuis contre leurs tendresses archaïques. Ayant bien écouté, ils distinguèrent des menaces qui sortaient des monuments gothiques. Ils crurent avoir entendu la mort qui les appelait. Ces masses d'architecture fouillée et chargée de sculptures grimaçantes leur firent l'effet d'une danse macabre dressée en pierres. Les portails, les façades . . . leur criaient: Tu dois mourir! Eux, qui attestaient la vie, se retournèrent et continuèrent leur route.[32]

Thalès Bernard, as we have seen, repeatedly drew the attention of poets to Slavonic folklore as an entirely wholesome source of inspiration to replace the Romantic Middle Ages. He said of the Middle Ages in 1862: 'Il a rempli l'imagination des hommes, d'une foule de cauchemars, qui ont persisté trop longtemps. C'est à la poésie populaire . . . à détruire les sculptures monstrueuses qui grimacent aux gouttières des églises. . . .'[33] In 1869 Eugène Garcin, in a series of commendatory articles on 'Les Païens à travers les siècles', recalled the moment when the Romantics, formerly united in 'le culte du moyen âge', reached the parting of the ways:

> Les uns, les plus grands, les plus généreux, sortirent d'une route qui menait aux ténèbres; les autres . . . (puissent-ils, dans le jugement de l'avenir, trouver leur digne récompense!) c'est à ces ténèbres qu'ils ont

---

[29] Béranger, *Os. cs.* Perrotin, 1851, i. 316 ('Le Vin de Chypre').
[30] Barbey d'Aurevilly, *Littérature étrangère,* 1890, p. 162.
[31] H. Heine, *De l'Allemagne,* 1835, ii. 117.
[32] Laurent-Pichat, *L'Art et les artistes en France,* 1859, p. 19.
[33] A. Millien, *Chants agrestes* (Preface by T. Bernard), 1862, p. vi.

voulu conduire la société. Ils n'ont que trop réussi, hélas! . . . Le Romantisme apportait de superbes présents . . . mais, en principe, il contenait la mort. Nous qui arrivons, marchons à la vie.[34]

He expressed alarm at the activities of Viollet-le-Duc and his disciples: 'De toutes parts, l'ogive renaît, s'élance, rayonne, flamboie. Goules, aspioles, salamandres, vampires, nains, dragons, tarasques, gargouilles se raniment.'[35]

Théodore de Banville, whom Gautier mentioned approvingly in his *Rapport sur les progrès de la poésie* (1868) – 'introduisant la blanche Tyndaride dans le sombre manoir féodal du moyen âge, [il] ramena dans le burg romantique le cortége des anciens dieux'[36] –, declared in 1870 that he had been one of those who fled with a shiver of distaste from the Romantic Middle Ages: 'Moi . . . quoique très romantique, je ne pouvais accepter la mythologie des sabbats et des diables, ni la tristesse a l'état chronique; je désirais . . . le retour des vrais dieux de la poésie.'[37]

Minor poets of the day, especially those with Parnassian affiliations, when they came to emulate Hugo and Leconte de Lisle's re-creation of the past in 'petites épopées', heeded these voices raised in universal condemnation of the Dark Ages. As has often been remarked, many of them evoked this period only to dismiss it with a few words of abuse. Bouilhet in *Les Fossiles* (1859) passes rapidly over '[Les] siècles pleins de brume et de mélancolie', during which 'l'Homme manqua d'air, l'Homme étouffa d'ennui.'[38] 'Ô vapeur mortuaire, haleine de caverne!',[39] exclaims André Lefèvre (hailed by Gautier in 1868 as an 'étoile de première grandeur parmi la pléiade poétique de l'époque actuelle'),[40] on reaching the Middle Ages, 'dix longs siècles de nuit', in *L'Épopée terrestre* (1868).[41] Raoul Lafagette, in his Preface to *Mélodies païennes* (1873), extends 'la nuit vingt fois séculaire du moyen âge'[42] to include the modern age, still in the grip of Gothic superstition; and in one of the poems, 'Helios', a hymn to the sun, he casts a fleeting, appalled glance at 'l'horrible moyen âge,/Philippe II et Loyola,/

---

[34] E. Garcin, 'Les Païens à travers les siècles: (XIII) Le Romantisme catholico-féodal', *Revue moderne*, 10 Oct. 1869, p. 502.   [35] Ibid. p. 507.

[36] Gautier, *Histoire du romantisme*, 1905, p. 302.

[37] Banville, *Choix de critiques*, ed. Barracand, 1917, p. 132. Banville's loathing of Romantic medieval melancholy expressed itself in his contradiction of Vigny's 'Dieu! que le son du Cor est triste au fond des bois!': the 'Ballade de la joyeuse chanson du cor' (*Le Sang de la coupe. Trente-six ballades joyeuses*, n.d. pp. 265·6).

[38] L. Bouilhet, *Oeuvres*, Lemerre, n.d., p. 135.

[39] A. Lefèvre, *L'Épopée terrestre*, 1868, p. 248.

[40] Gautier, *Histoire du romantisme*, p. 375.   [41] *L'Épopée terrestre*, p. 54.

[42] R. Lafagette, *Mélodies païennes*, 1873, p. 5.

Despotisme, bûchers, carnage . . .'.[43] As late as 1897 the Vicomte de Guerne, a disciple of Leconte de Lisle continuing to write Parnassian verse out of season, says in the Preface to his *L'Orient chrétien,* the third volume of *Les Siècles morts,* that his task of recreating the vanished Orient is completed, now that he has reached the moment when 'l'Occident s'effondre dans la nuit du Moyen-Âge': 'Là, s'arrête l'oeuvre du Poète. Quels sont cependant les véritables siècles morts, sinon les huit siècles qui vont suivre, morts pour la pensée humaine, morts pour l'art et pour la Beauté?'[44]

Ancient Greece and the Renaissance received the homage withdrawn from the Middle Ages. We have already discussed four leading writers of the Second Empire who extolled the pagan at the expense of the medieval world: Michelet, Renan, Taine, and Gautier. There remains Louis Ménard, who, under the Empire which he detested, sought consolation for his disappointed republicanism in dreams of an ideal Greece, where, in the words of Barrès, 'Homère et Hésiode prononcent la condamnation de Napoléon III.'[45] Ménard's passionate celebration of his ideal in prose and verse influenced his friend Leconte de Lisle and many other writers of the day. In the poem 'Hellas' (1861), condemned to live out his live in a 'monde vieilli, plongé dans l'ombre noire' in which 'la Liberté dort d'un sommeil éternel', he pours out his inconsolable regret for the lost republican virtues of ancient Greece, 'trésors perdus que nul regret ne nous rendra'.[46] In the Greek world 'Tout est force et jeunesse, harmonie et beauté.'[47] Like Michelet, Ménard contemplates with dismay the passing of the gods and the falling of medieval night over the world.[48] 'La vie est condamnée,' he laments in the Preface to his *Poëmes* (1855), 'les dieux heureux, les dieux de la jeunesse et de l'amour, se changent en démons tentateurs.'[49] 'Les dieux de la beauté, brisés, étaient enfouis dans la terre. Les manuscrits, brûlés, perdus . . .', was Michelet's cry in his 1855 Introduction to the *Renaissance,* [50] repeated in *La Sorcière* (1862): 'Tout tombe, s'écroule, s'abîme. . . . "Le grand Pan est mort!"'[51] . . . Dieux anciens, entrez au sépulcre. Dieux de l'amour, de la vie, de la lumière, éteignez-vous.'[52] In *Rêveries d'un*

---

[43] Ibid. p. 183. [44] Vte. de Guerne, *L'Orient chrétien,* 1897, xi.
[45] Ménard, *Rêveries d'un païen mystique* (Preface by Barrès), 1909, xiv.
[46] Ménard, *Poëmes,* 2nd edn., 1863, p. 240. [47] Ibid. p. 160.
[48] German influence is probable here, in particular that of Heine's essay 'Les Dieux en exil' (*RDM,* 1 Apr. 1853, reprinted in the 2nd (1855) and subsequent editions of his *De l'Allemagne*).
[49] Ménard, op. cit. pp. xii-xiii. [50] Michelet, *Renaissance,* p. 61.
[51] Michelet, *La Sorcière,* i. 17. [52] Ibid. p. 23.

païen mystique (1876) Ménard dwells once more on this desolation
of a world from which the gods have departed: 'Le monde s'enveloppe
dans son linceul, les lumières du ciel s'éteignent une à une et tout rentre
dans la grande nuit.'[53] These elegiac lamentations recur also in poetry of
this time. In Leconte de Lisle's *Poèmes antiques* (1852), as in the writings
of Michelet, Quinet, and Ménard, night has fallen over the world with
the advent of the Second Empire, and the result is medieval desolation.
'Les Dieux sont en poussière et la terre est muette', he laments in
'Hypatie';[54] and in 'Dies Irae':

> Les lumières d'en haut s'en vont diminuées,
> L'impénétrable nuit tombe déjà des cieux. . . .
> Les âmes sans vertu dorment d'un lourd sommeil.[55]

Gautier, in 'Bûchers et tombeaux' (1858), anticipates Michelet's *Sorcière:*

> Une voix dit: Pan est mort! − L'ombre
> S'étend. − Comme sur un drap noir,
> Sur la tristesse immense et sombre
> Le blanc squelette se fait voir.[56]

In an early Romantic poem attacking the *bande noire*, 'Les Vendeurs
du Temple', Gautier had described a doomed church trembling at the
approach of the despoilers: 'Les anges et les saints pleuraient dans les
vitraux.'[57] Banville, in accord with the rest of his contemporaries, prefers
in 1866 to wring pathos from the plight of the pagan gods banished by
'les empereurs, jaloux/De leur gloire',[58] 'les grands dieux en pleurs dans
la brume évanouis'.[59]

These writers seek respite from the melancholy spectacle of medieval
darkness descending in ecstatic contemplation of the radiant Renaissance
dawn, when, in the words of André Lefèvre, 'un grand déchirement fendit
le noir miasme.'[60] 'Arrière les spectres décharnés de la mort et de la
douleur', cries Ménard in *Lettres d'un mort* (1859), 'voici les Dieux du
bonheur et de la vie; ils s'avancent vêtus des rayons de l'aurore, et
chassent devant eux les terreurs de la nuit.'[61] Gautier declared in 1851:
'L'imprimerie fit succéder au cahos barbare du moyen âge l'aurore splen-

---

[53] Ménard, *Rêveries d'un païen mystique*, p. 23.
[54] Leconte de Lisle, *Poèmes antiques*, n.d., p. 68.
[55] Ibid. pp. 311-12.   [56] Gautier, *Poésies complètes*, iii. 74.
[57] Gautier, *Poésies complètes*, ii. 112.
[58] Banville, *Les Exilés. Les Princesses*, 1890, p. 11 ('L'Exil des Dieux', first published in the *Parnasse contemporain*. 1866).
[59] Ibid. p. 16.   [60] A. Lefèvre, *L'Épopée terrestre*, 1868, p. 249.
[61] Ménard, *Lettres d'un mort*, 1895, p. 68. Cf. his *Poëmes*, p. 165; and Taine's
similar pronouncement of 1863 (cf. *supra*, p. 71).

dide de la renaissance';[62] Leconte de Lisle, in 1855: 'En général, tout
ce qui constitue l'art, la morale et la science, était mort avec le Poly-
théisme. Tout a revécu à sa renaissance';[63] and Banville, in 1861, called
sixteenth-century France 'cette terre d'affranchissement où la Vénus
de Milo aborda après mille années, triomphante de jeunesse sereine,
pour chasser les larves et les spectres du moyen âge'.[64]

Parnassian poets attempted in their work to restore some of this
radiant light of the Renaissance to the modern world, where wraiths
of medieval mist lingered. Emmanuel des Essarts voiced the conviction
they all shared: 'Il n'y a de salut que dans la tradition gréco-latine,
dans l'enthousiasme de la Pléiade. . . . Autrement on ne produit que du
chaos ou du néant.'[65]

The vanquishing of the Middle Ages, put to rout by the forces of
enlightenment, was versified at some length by two poets: Ménard, in
Euphorion (1863), and Louis-Xavier de Ricard, in *Le Crépuscule des
dieux* (written 1863-4, published 1866). Both works are heavily indebted
to Michelet and to Quinet's *Ahasvérus*. *Euphorion* is not one of Ménard's
best poems; and *Le Crépuscule des dieux*, like all Ricard's poetic output,
is turgid and pedestrian in the extreme; but both have a certain interest
as examples of one way in which opposition to the Empire expressed
itself.

Euphorion begins beneath the radiant skies of ancient Greece, and
moves to a gloomy cathedral where a chorus of lamentation is rising
from oppressors and oppressed: 'Pécheurs, courbez vos fronts', intones
the priest, while the people wail:

> Seigneur, toi qui promis aux serfs la délivrance,
> Prends pitié de nos pleurs![66]

All are on their knees, weeping 'sous les arceaux noirs des longs piliers
gothiques'; but Euphorion stands apart from the crowd, with doubt in
his heart. When the voice of his doubt mingles with the hymns of the
faithful,

> L'église frémissait sous ce blasphème impur,
> Et les anges pleuraient dans leurs niches d'azur.

'Où donc es-tu, Seigneur?', he asks, and declares with Michelet:

> Non! le nouveau calvaire où sa tombe se creuse
> N'aura pas de réveil ni de troisième jour,

[62] Gautier, *Histoire de l'art dramatique en France*, vi (1859), 287.
[63] Leconte de Lisle, *Articles, préfaces, discours*, p. 128 (Preface to *Poëmes et poésies*).
[64] Banville, 'Le Salon de 1861', *Revue fantaisiste*, ii. 15 May 1861, p. 42.
[65] Preface to M. Legrand, *L'Âme antique*, A. Colin, 1896, p. ix.
[66] Ménard, *Poëmes*, pp. 185-7.

adding:

> Mais ne le pleurons pas, et comptons ses victimes:
> Tortures, noirs cachots, gibets, bûchers en feu,
> Spectres de la nuit que chasse la lumière,
> Fuyez!

Whereupon the cathedral disintegrates and melts away:

> Le contour vacillant de la voûte étoilée . . .
> S'efface et fond en vague et bleuâtre vapeur.
> Tous les saints des vitraux, tous les anges des voûtes,
> Dispersés dans les airs, volent par mille routes.[67]

Louis-Xavier de Ricard, co-editor of the first *Parnasse contemporain* (1866), was imprisoned by the Imperial government for the seditious content of another publication edited by him: the *Revue du progrès* (1863-4).[68] His *Ciel, rue et foyer* (1866) is a volume of republican verse, in four sections dedicated to Quinet, Hugo, Gautier, and Michelet, in which he bemoans the tedium of the present, regrets the lost paradise of ancient Greece, and apostrophizes society:

> Ô marâtre! faut-il, comme aux siècles gothiques,
> Sur nos têtes de serf portant tes lourdes lois,
> Marcher?[69]

The collection includes *Le Crépuscule des dieux,* which begins with a desolate vision of a decaying cathedral. Bats and owls circle over the crumbling arches: 'Les colonnes pleuraient leurs vieux cintres gothiques.' As the poet contemplates the barren earth strewn with mouldering bones, he hears a cry: *'Pan est ressuscité!'* A shudder runs through the cathedral, and a radiant dawn spreads across the sky, 'combattant les brouillards qui résistaient encore'.[70] The spectre of Christ rises from the tomb in protestation; but the voice of Nature answers with a long harangue, recalling the sinister past:

> Jadis, perdue aux cieux, la pieuse prière
> Comme un fléau de Dieu maudissait la matière,
> Et les fouets, les bûchers, et les maux incessants
> Dévouaient à l'enfer la raison et les sens . . .,[71]

and reassuring mankind that deliverance is at hand: 'Homme! je viens enfin finir ton mauvais rêve. . . .'

[67] Ménard, *Poëmes,* pp. 189-93.
[68] For an account of Ricard's activities as a militant opponent of the Empire see Général de Ricard, *Autour des Bonaparte,* ed. L-X. de Ricard, 1891, Ch. 2.
[69] Ricard, *Ciel, rue et foyer,* 1866, p. 47.
[70] Ricard, *Ciel, rue et foyer,* pp. 153-5.   [71] Ibid. p. 164.

> Mais voici qu'aujourd'hui le passé se réveille;
> Fantôme, il veut encor combattre les vivants,

the voice continues, and rings out in stern command:

> Spectre des temps passés, retourne dans la tombe.[72]

At length the figure of Christ, vanquished, melts away —

> L'auréole de Christ fluait en plis mouvants
> Et, par larges lambeaux, s'envolait . . .[73]

— in the boundless dawn which has risen over the world.

Euphorion and *Le Crépuscule des dieux* are both versified Michelet, whose influence can also be seen at work in the splenetic gaze which poets of this time occasionally turned on the ruins which had been the object of so much Romantic veneration. An early example of this is Leconte de Lisle's 'Architecture', published in 1845. This poem is directed against the restorers of Gothic churches, who, as we have seen, were coming into their own at this time. Leconte de Lisle makes it clear, however, that his protest is not motivated by banal republican spite. While dropping a passing hint that Gothic architecture may be crumbling for lack of 'vrai ciment romain' in its structure, he declares that he is quite indifferent to its fate:

> Monte! épanouis-toi, cathédrale frivole! . . .
> Tu ne vaux point, hochet d'un labeur séculaire,
> Qu'on sue à t'ébranler de ta pierre angulaire.
> Ô murs de Babylone! ô temples vermoulus
> Dont le sens est futile et ne nous suffit plus![74]

Ménard, in his *Lettres d'un mort,* does not attempt to depreciate Gothic architecture — on the contrary — but speculates that its excellence may be due to a drop of Greek blood in the veins of its builders: 'Qui sait si . . . les artistes qui ont élevé les merveilleuses églises du moyen âge n'avaient pas dans les veines le sang de quelque esclave issu des races divines de la Grèce?'[75] A few years later medieval ruins are contemplated irreverently by Valade and Mérat in 'Vie des Ruines' (1863), a description of a castle —

> 'La nature, toujours prodigue en moqueries,
> A pris et réparé le nid des hobereaux . . .';[76]

---

[72] Ibid. pp. 166-7.   [73] Ibid. pp. 174-5.

[74] *La Phalange,* ii (July-Dec. 1845); quoted by M. A. Leblond: *Leconte de Lisle d'après des documents nouveaux,* 1906, pp. 174-5.

[75] Ménard, *Lettres d'un mort,* p. 13.

[76] L. Valade and A. Mérat, *Avril, mai, juin,* Faure, 1863, p. 111.

and, in 1877, by Laurent-Pichat, in a remarkable poem, 'Saint-Marc', which ends in an outburst of frenzied rage against the cathedral. The poet confesses that in days gone by he used to indulge in Romantic reverie beneath cathedral vaults:

> J'ai rêvé sous ces blocs tout ce qu'on y rêvait;
> J'ai cru que la forêt moyen âge vivait . . .;

but that now he is cured of his illusions:

> Je sais que tout est mort, vide, artificiel
> Sous ces mornes piliers qui montent vers le ciel. . . .[77]
> Aujourd'hui le gothique est éteint.[78]

Revisiting Venice after thirty years' absence, he was glad to see that the cathedral

> Comme un ponton rasé, s'effondrait dans les vases.[79]

He gazed for a long time upon 'Ce cadavre échoué dans la vague livide', noting with satisfaction that 'tout se disjoignait, dieux, saints, papes et rois', and reflecting that 'C'était la haine noire et la mort', while the bells 'Hurlaient la mort avec des voix vertdegrisées'. The poem ends on a gleefully sardonic note:

> Temples où sont venus des papes, des Césars,
> On va vous envoyer l'inspecteur des beaux-arts,
> Croquemort érudit des pierres endormies,
> Et vous serez classés au nombre des momies.[80]

For these writers who shared Michelet's vision of history, nothing remained of the ideal Romantic Middle Ages. All its radiance had been transferred to ancient Greece and the Renaissance. Not only was Gothic architecture abused and declared to be ramshackle and sinister; a severe and disenchanted gaze was turned on every aspect of the world in which the Romantics had delighted, where, for Musset, 'la Vie était jeune . . . la Mort espérait . . . tout venait de renaître'[81] — but where Michelet saw only 'vieillesse, subtilité, servilité, impuissance'.[82] We have seen that for medieval man, according to Chateaubriand, 'la nature est une constante merveille. Souffre-t-il, il prie sa petite image, et il est soulagé.'[83] But in Michelet's infernal Middle Ages 'toute la nature devient démoniaque. L'arbre en ses feuilles sombres est plein de terreurs et de

---

[77] Laurent-Pichat, *Les Réveils, poésies*, 1880, pp. 12-13.
[78] Ibid. p. 18.   [79] Ibid. p. 53.
[80] Laurent-Pichat, *Les Réveils*, pp. 54-7.   [81] Cf. *supra*, p. 11.
[82] Michelet, *La Sorcière*, i. 27.   [83] Cf. *supra*, p. 12.

piéges.'[84] 'On aimait, et le ciel descendait sur la terre',[85] declared Gautier in 1834 of the same world, which for Michelet, in 1847, had become 'ce monde de haine et de malédiction'.[86] 'Les hauts barons, les chevaliers bardés de fer qui étaient posés sur la terre comme des tours protectrices levant les bannières de la France au soleil',[87] whose disappearance was lamented by Vigny in his *Journal d'un poète,* were sanguinary brigands for republicans such as Eugène Bonnemère, who addressed the reader of his *Histoire des paysans* (1856): 'Voyez . . . ces fiers redresseurs de torts, ces gentilshommes "de haut lieu" s'abattre chaque jour dans la plaine et chevaucher, gorgés de vin et altérés de sang, non pas la lance, mais la broche à la main.'[88] Chivalry was for Pelletan a 'société mutuelle de bigamie'.[89] Courts of love were for Delécluze a symptom of 'la dépravation des esprits, pendant cette période de temps'.[90] Ménard was one of many who divested of their poetry those 'grandes chasses féodales' which appealed to the Romantic in Flaubert,[91] by pointing out the hardships which this 'amusement de la noblesse' inflicted on peasants whose crops were trampled down.[92] And medieval domestic life, celebrated by Marchangy as 'La Vie poétique des anciens châteaux' — a life of admirably-ordered, poetic ceremony, with women waiting at their spinning-wheel for their lord to return from the Crusades, pilgrims seeking hospitality from the storm, and minstrels beguiling the long winter evenings with their song —, was described in a very different light by André Lefèvre:

Ni réunions joyeuses, ni salons, ni livres, ni conversations. . . . Les femmes, enfermées dans l'épais donjon pendant que le baron giboye aux voyageurs ou pille son voisin absent . . . ouvrent l'étroite fenêtre, écoutent le chanteur, toutes prêtes à s'enfuir, à se jeter dans les bras du premier venu. . . . Telles étaient les moeurs de ces temps chers à l'Église.[93]

[84] *Bible de l'humanité,* 1864, p. 469.
[85] Gautier, *Poésies complètes,* ii. 85.
[86] Michelet, *Histoire de la Révolution,* i. 31.
[87] Vigny, *Os. cs.* 1948, ii. 1367.
[88] E. Bonnemère, *Histoire des paysans,* 1856, i. 115.
[89] *Paris Guide,* Lacroix, 1867, i. 17.
[90] E-J. Delécluze, *Roland, ou la chevalerie,* 1845, i. 187.
[91] Cf. *supra,* p. 58.
[92] Ménard, *Lettres d'un mort,* p. 47.
[93] A, Lefèvre, *L'Homme à travers les âges,* 1880, p. 202.

CHAPTER 6

THE MIDDLE AGES IN THE LITERATURE OF THE SECOND EMPIRE

'L'horreur est installée en nos tours féodales' (V. Hugo)

Fictional portrayal of the Middle Ages by writers of the Second Empire had to be in verse, as the historical novel was defunct. 'Le roman historique médiéval', says Berret, 'commençait en 1843 à sombrer dans les bas-fonds du roman-feuilleton.'[1] Novelists turned their attention to the modern world. Hugo wrote *Les Misérables* instead of continuing the medieval trilogy of which *Notre-Dame de Paris* was to have been the first part. Baudelaire's prose poems were inspired by Bertrand's *Gaspard de la nuit* transposed into a modern setting.[2] Flaubert, in 1850, dismissed the Middle Ages as a setting for a novel — 'c'est déjà fait.'[3] He started work on *Madame Bovary;* and in the course of his documentation he examined the Romantic Middle Ages, an important ingredient in the 'rêves de jeunes filles' indulged in by his heroine. 'Voilà deux jours', he wrote to Louise Colet in 1852, '. . . que je navigue . . . dans les océans laiteux de la littérature à castels, troubadours à toques de velours à plumes blanches.'[4] Emma Bovary in her girlhood succumbs to this most banal of Romantic maladies ('Avec Walter Scott . . . elle s'éprit de choses historiques, rêva bahuts, salle des gardes et ménestrels. Elle aurait voulu vivre dans quelque vieux manoir, comme ces châtelaines au long corsage')[5] — and so, in their turn, do Bouvard and Pécuchet in their declining years. Like all the other nineteenth-century maladies contracted by them, it is a passing enthusiasm which runs its course: 'Le goût des bibelots leur était venu, puis l'amour du moyen âge.'[6] The Middle Ages as a literary theme was for so long in eclipse that Flaubert felt obliged in 1875 to speak of *La Légende de Saint Julien l'Hospitalier* in deprecating, facetious tones. 'Ce n'est rien de tout et je n'y attache aucune importance',[7] he told one correspondent; and he called it 'une petite bêtise moyenâgeuse',[8] 'ma petite historiette (religioso-pohêtique et moyenâgeusement rococo'.[9] Among the Parnassian poets, Glatigny

---

[1] P. Berret, *Le Moyen Âge dans la 'Légende des siècles'*, p. 17.
[2] See Baudelaire, *Os. cs.* 1961, p. 229.
[3] Flaubert, *Correspondance*, ii. 255.   [4] Ibid. p. 371.
[5] *Madame Bovary*, 1955, p. 35.   [6] *Bouvard et Pécuchet*, 1965, p. 123.
[7] Flaubert, *Correspondance: Supplément*, iii. 208.
[8] *Correspondance*, vii. 279.   [9] *Correspondance: Supplément*, iii. 234.

wrote of his abandoned sequence of poems inspired by the *Chanson de Roland* and the *Romancero* (a few of which were published in *Les Flèches d'or*, 1864), half apologetically: 'J'affublerai le tout de ce titre "Chansons romantiques", car il faut avoir le courage de ses opinions';[10] and Dierx excised from the 1872 edition of his *Poèmes et poésies* (1864) all poems, such as 'Mandoline' and 'Le Cor', tainted with Romantic medievalism.[11]

These poets approached the Middle Ages with some embarrassment, producing verse uneven in tone and laboured in style, like Banville's 'La Belle Aude' and 'La Bonne Lorraine', which will be discussed later in the chapter, and are, as Max Fuchs remarks,[12] among the least successful of the poet's productions. As republicans, they were bound to find the Middle Ages repellent, and as struggling poets oppressed by the glory of Victor Hugo, they were anxious to break fresh ground untrodden by the master. 'Il y eut une recherche des continents intellectuels', says Mendès, 'dont Victor Hugo n'avait pas encore été le Christophe Colomb.'[13] Most of them, however, attempted epic sequences in emulation of Hugo or Leconte de Lisle, and were obliged to include the Middle Ages, if only for the sake of completeness; but they composed them without conviction, 'dans la manière sèche, sans effusion',[14] in the words of Cassagne. Hugo and Leconte de Lisle each provided a powerfully original and coherent vision of the Middle Ages; and we shall see that lesser poets making excursions into that period inevitably fell into imitation of one or the other, or even of both at once. Ricard wrote in an article on the Parnassians: 'Ils ne se permirent que par caprice de timides et rares explorations . . . dans les littératures médiévales. S'ils se risquèrent parfois jusqu'aux gestes du douzième et du treizième siècles, ce ne fut qu'en touristes très pressés, à la suite d'Hugo, avec en guise de Joanne et de Bebecker [sic], la *Légende des siècles*' — to which must be added, of course, the work of Leconte de Lisle, whom Ricard commends as the only poet '[qui] a su voir le moyen-âge directement'.[15]

[10] See J. Reymond, *Albert Glatigny*, 1936, p. 51.

[11] Dierx's poem 'La Soif', however — which he retained in *Poèmes et poésies* — furnishes the Parnassian champions of Art for Art's Sake with a Romantic call to arms inspired by *Le Combat des trente:* 'Champions du Beau qu'on lapide. . . . Faisons flotter notre pennon/Par-dessus la clameur stupide. . . . Buvons, ainsi que Beaumanoir/Le sang tout chaud de nos blessures!' (*Os. cs.* i (1894), 47-8). [12] M. Fuchs, *T. de Banville*, 1912, p. 254.

[13] C. Mendès, *Rapport sur le mouvement poétique français de 1867 à 1900*, 1902, p. 92.

[14] A. Cassagne, *La Théorie de l'art pour l'art en France*, 1906, p. 128.

[15] *Revue indépendante*, xxiii (June 1892), p. 333.

We will now examine these two rival Middle Ages, which ensured for the theme, despite the discredit attached to it by its Romantic associations, an important place in the poetry of the fifties and sixties.

A. *'La Légende des siècles'* (i) *Its reception by the critics*

Hugo's *Légende des siècles* will be considered here as a whole, in its three series (1859, 1877, and 1883), as most of the poems of the second and third series set in the Middle Ages were written in exile under the Empire, and belong in spirit with those published in 1859. Critical response to the medieval poems in the first series was contradictory in the extreme, a mirror of the confused and violent emotions which the Middle Ages, and their use as a literary theme, aroused in people at the time. Flaubert and Gautier remained sufficiently Romantic to acclaim this section of the *Légende* with great enthusiasm. 'J'ai trouvé cela tout bonnement énorme',[16] writes Flaubert to one correspondent; and to another he especially recommends 'les histoires de chevalerie qui sont dans le premier volume'.[17] Gautier said of these latter poems: 'Cela est grand comme Homère et naïf comme la Bibliothèque bleue.'[18] *L'Artiste*, on the other hand, to which Gautier, Banville, and some future Parnassians contributed, took exception to the *Légende*, finding it uncouth, contorted, full of disagreeable discordances: 'Le laid, l'ignoble sont . . . comme chez eux. Le dégoûtant même s'y prélasse en alexandrins' — and totally deficient in 'les qualités sculpturales et harmoniques' which modern taste required in poetry.[19] Taine dismissed the *Légende* as 'un mélange de folie et de parade'.[20] Republicans were divided in their appreciation of it. Laurent-Pichat, in a ferocious attack on 'cette retraite de l'intelligence humaine', brought about by Romantics seeking refuge in the Middle Ages, expressed regret that among those who had seen the error of their ways and broken with the past, Hugo was a case leaving much to be desired. 'Il n'a pas en lui', he lamented, 'ce feu qui dévore les erreurs comme les mauvaises herbes des champs. Il procède avec calme et sérénité. . . . Victor Hugo reste fidèle aux traditions. Il ne renverse pas les vieilles tourelles féodales aux souvenirs funestes.'[21] Eugène Pelletan, on the other hand, declared himself well satisfied with the *Légende*, which, in his opinion, exposed the horrors of feudalism in

---

[16] Flaubert, *Correspondance,* iv. 335.   [17] Ibid. p. 339.

[18] Gautier, *Histoire du romantisme,* p. 392.

[19] *L'Artiste*, 15 Dec. 1859, p. 183 (Auguste de Vaucelle).

[20] *H. Taine, sa vie et sa correspondance,* iii (1905), 249.

[21] *La Réforme littéraire,* 20 July 1862, p. 3.

all their 'lugubre laideur'. Reading the first series inspired him to launch headlong into a diatribe of his own against the Middle Ages, in *La Presse:*

> Le poète . . . entre dans le moyen-âge. Il aborde la féodalité, cette tyrannie à cent mille têtes dressée sur chaque escarpe de rocher, ce coupe-gorge à l'infini . . . la chasse, l'aventure, la chevauchée, l'escalade, la piraterie de terre ferme, le vol, le viol, le pillage, l'exaction, la prélibation, le festin homérique, le boeuf roti, le tonneau d'hydromel, la plaisanterie cynique, la poésie brutale du bouffon et du sirvente devant le cratère béant de l'immense cheminée, la joue rougie de la double flamme de l'ivresse et du foyer, le front sous le cadavre d'un ennemi pendu au créneau, et le pied sur un autre cadavre vivant précipité au fond d'une oubliette.[22]

The *Correspondant* critic also approved of the *Légende*, seeing in it 'l'horreur d'un passé qu'on a trop embelli: 'M. Hugo, le gothique, comme l'appelaient autrefois ses adversaires, s'est pris de haine aujourd'hui pour cette époque; il n'y voit que violences, injustices, meurtres, pillages. . . . Tout le moyen âge, dans la *Légende des siècles,* exhale cette *odeur de panthère. . . .*'[23]

Catholic opinion was equally divided. Barbey d'Aurevilly, on reading the first series, exclaimed in a transport of admiration: 'Il [i.e. Victor Hugo] est essentiellement Moyen Âge':

> Par la conformation de la tête, par la violence de la sensation, par l'admiration naïve et involontaire de la force, cet homme est éternellement de l'an 1000. Si aujourd'hui, dans sa *Légende des siècles,* il est relativement supérieur, même a ce qu'il fut, c'est que le Moyen Âge ou ce qui traîne encore, Dieu merci! du Moyen Âge dans nos moeurs, — la guerre, les magnificences militaires, l'impérieuse beauté du commandement, — tiennent plus de place dans les poèmes nouveaux que dans tous ses autres ouvrages.[24]

If Barbey considered that justice had been rendered to the Middle Ages in the *Légende,* Alfred Nettement took Hugo to task for his 'tableau pessimiste du moyen âge'. 'Les jeunes gens', he protested, 'apprendront à croire que cette époque, où l'Église avait une si grande puissance sur la société, était une époque de barbarie et de despotisme infâme.'[25] Gaston

---

[22] *La Presse,* 14 Oct. 1859.
[23] *Le Correspondant,* xlviii (Nov. 1859), pp. 511-13 (P. Douhaire).
[24] B. d'Aurevilly, *Les Poètes,* 1862, pp. 40-1. Cf. Gautier's remark to the Goncourts, four years later: 'Au fond, Hugo est purement Moyen Âge' (*Journal des Goncourt,* i. 1302).
[25] A. Nettement, *Poëtes et artistes contemporains,* Lecoffre, 1862, p. 212.

Paris was also displeased with Hugo: 'Il a exhumé,' he complained, 'pour en faire le fond de ses poèmes les plus longs et les plus importants, quelques traditions pleines d'horreur et imprégnées de crimes cachées dans des annales ignorées du moyen-âge, je ne jurerais pas même qu'il n'en ait inventé une bonne partie.'[26] He went on to say that he preferred to read the episodes recounted in *Le Mariage de Roland* and *Aymerillot* in the original version, imperfectly rendered by Hugo; but Léon Gautier, on the other hand, was carried away with enthusiasm for *Aymerillot* — 'Comme ils pâlissent devant ces admirables vers, tous les Mémoires des érudits!'[27] — to such a point that he neglected to record any misgivings he might have felt about other medieval poems in the *Légende*.

Émile Chasles, in the *Revue européenne*, complained that tyrants, in Hugo's medieval world, were too seductive — 'le mal, quand il le décrit si pittoresque et si énergique, cesse de nous déplaire' —,[28] and champions of the oppressed, too sinister — 'le peuple avait lieu de trembler. Il est des protecteurs et des amis qui ne rassurent pas.'[29] Good and evil were indistinguishable: 'Où commence le paladin, où finit le tyran?'[29]

The Middle Ages of the *Légende* disconcerted both republicans and Catholics, as it was the poet's personal creation. It was certainly not Catholic, but neither did it conform to the conventional republican view of the period, though some of its republican admirers managed to convince themselves that it did. Hugo does not take sides in the manner of the majority of his contemporaries: his view of history is an altogether loftier one, as Baudelaire remarked: 'Il n'a pas chanté plus particulièrement telle ou telle nation, la passion de tel ou tel siècle; il est monté tout de suite à une de ces hauteurs philosophiques d'où le poëte peut considérer toutes les évolutions de l'humanité avec un regard également curieux, courroucé ou attendri.'[30]

(ii) *Hugo and 'l'histoire idéale':*
its confrontation with reality in 'Promontorium somnii'

We have seen that republican writers of the Second Empire rejected the ideal Romantic Middle Ages in favour of what Taine called 'la

[26] *Jahrbuch für romanische und englische Literatur,* iii (1861), pp. 3-4.
[27] L. Gautier, *Les Épopées françaises,* 2nd edn., ii (1892), 744.
[28] *Revue européenne,* v. Nov. 1859, p. 777.
[29] Ibid. pp. 784-6.
[30] Baudelaire, *Os. cs.* p. 712 (article first published in the *Revue fantaisiste* (June 1861)).

vérité atroce et sale'; but Hugo, in *La Légende des siècles,* declined to do this. While others had turned against the Middle Ages after the 1830s, his 'fureur gothique' had survived his political change of heart and raged on unabated during the 1840s. *Le Rhin* (1842), *Les Burgraves* (1843), and Hugo's excitement on his discovery of Jubinal's translation of some *chanson de geste* fragments in 1846, bear witness to this. Tentatively in *Le Rhin,* and more audaciously in *Les Burgraves,* he moved away from the fantasy of the *Ballades* towards the epic vision of the *Légende.*[31]

In his Preface to the *Légende* Hugo called it 'de l'histoire écoutée aux portes de la légende . . . une tentative vers l'idéal'.[32] Most of his contemporaries shared this respect for legend. It was under the influence of German philosophers that its importance had been recognized in the first half of the nineteenth century. Heine, in 1843, praised Michelet's *Histoire de France* for its successful putting into practice of their doctrine:

> Mon grand maître . . . Hégel, me dit un jour ces mots: 'Si l'on avait noté les songes que les hommes ont faits pendant une période déter- minée, nous verrions surgir devant nous, à la lecture de ces songes recueillis, une image tout à fait juste de l'esprit de cette période.' L'histoire française de Michelet est une pareille collection de songes, un pareil livre de rêves: tout le moyen âge rêveur nous y regarde.[33]

The poetic superstitions of the Age of Faith captivated the Romantics, as we have seen.[34] They also engaged the attention of the serious historian. Guizot insisted that legend embodied a truth more valuable than the truth of history: 'Voltaire a tort d'appeler *erreur* le côté poétique de ces vieux temps';[35] and Michiels warned modern writers attempting to recreate the past that its true spirit could not be divined without taking legend and superstition into account. 'L'homme des temps féodaux', he reminded his readers, 'ne voyait pas un produit animal dans les longues soies que charrient les brises d'automne, mais un fil errant tombé du fuseau de la Vierge.'[36] Writers of the Second

---

[31] Cf. *supra,* p. 24n. Cf. also P. Albouy, *La Création mythologique chez Victor Hugo,* 1963, p. 139; and J. Gaudon, *Le Temps de la contemplation,* 1969, pp. 103-13.

[32] Hugo, *Légende des siècles,* 1950, pp. 5-6.

[33] H. Heine, *Lutèce,* 1855, p. 356.   [34] Cf. *supra,* pp. 11-12.

[35] Guizot, *Histoire de la civilisation en France,* iv (1830), 21. Vico, who affirmed in his *Scienza Nuova* (translated by Michelet in 1827) that 'le vrai poétique' and 'le vrai idéal' were superior to historical truth, was another important influence. See his remarks on Tasso's Godefroi de Bouillon in *Oeuvres choisies de Vico,* Hachette, 1835, i. 169, 358.

[36] A. Michiels, *Histoire des idées littéraires en France,* 1842, ii. 169.

Empire inherited these ideas, which were expounded at some length by Montégut, for instance, in his review of Quinet's *Merlin l'Enchanteur*. 'Il y a une histoire idéale', declared the critic, 'qui n'a jamais été écrite . . . qui est pourtant la seule vraie, la seule belle . . . et dont l'histoire prétendue réelle n'est que l'apparence et le reflet';[37] and he went on to say that the time had come for writers to record this history. We shall see how Leconte de Lisle, while adhering in theory to this doctrine, avoided in his poetic practice the re-creation of an ideal Middle Ages, in which his political allegiances forbade him to believe; but Hugo gave it a prominent place in *La Légende des siècles*. Before we examine this work, mention must be made of the one most remarkable fragment of Hugo's *oeuvre* in which the ideal Middle Ages are juxtaposed with republican reality. This is the part of *Promontorium somnii* dealing with 'le chimérisme gothique'.[38] *Promontorium somnii* was written in 1863 for inclusion in *William Shakespeare* (1864), but in fact remained unpublished until 1901.[39] Here, the Gothic world of the imagination, which the Romantics rescued from disgrace, is evoked in a vast vision prefiguring the work of the Symbolists. One hallucination melts into another:

> La diablerie commence. On voit, sur les premiers plans, des abbayes, des châteaux, des villes aiguës, des collines contrefaites, des rochers avec anachorètes, des rivières en serpents, des prairies, d'énormes roses. La mandragore semble un oeil éveillé. Des paons font la roue regardés par des femmes nues qui sont peut-être des âmes. Le cerf qui a le crucifix entre les cornes boit dans un lac, à l'écart. . . . L'oiseau bleu perche dans les arbres. Le paysage est difforme et charmant. On entend les fleurs chanter. . . .[40] Passent, glissent, flottent et chevauchent des êtres indistincts faits de la substance du songe . . . et toutes ces vierges-lys, et toutes ces femmes-tulipes, Yolande, Yseult, Griselidis, Viviane, et la belle Glynire pensant au duc Cavreuse, et la belle Esclarmonde pensant à Huon de Guyenne. . . .[41] Des épées fameuses, Durandal, Joyeuse, Courtain, Excalibar, mêlent à tout cela leur cliquetis. . . . Pas un échalier fermant un champ qui, à minuit, ne soit enfourché par un esprit. Le sabbat danse en rond sous les étoiles dans les vergers. . . . Le vent du crépuscule ploie et courbe dans les nénuphars les femmes

[37] E. Montégut, 'Un essai d'histoire idéale', *RDM,* 1 Sept. 1860, p. 176.
[38] Hugo, *Promontorium somnii,* ed. Journet & Robert, 1961, p. 46.
[39] When part of it appeared in *Post-scriptum de ma vie*. The whole was published in *William Shakespeare* (Reliquat), 1937.
[40] *Promontorium somnii,* p. 45.
[41] Ibid. pp. 48-9.

déhanchées et ondoyantes des étangs. Il y a des prés fées broutés des chèvres le jour et des capricornes la nuit.[42]

There follows at once a vision of the Middle Ages seen through republican eyes, with a compassion and indignation equalling Michelet's, and plainly inspired by the recently-published *Sorcière*.[43] This is the real world, from which the world of Gothic dream and superstition afforded occasional transitory escape:

Hélas, le moyen-âge est lugubre. Ce pauvre paysan féodal, ne lui marchandez pas son rêve. C'est à peu près tout ce qu'il possède. Son champ n'est pas à lui, son toit n'est pas à lui, sa vache n'est pas à lui, sa famille n'est pas à lui, son souffle n'est pas à lui. Le seigneur a la carcasse, le prêtre a l'âme. Le serf végète entre eux deux, une moitié dans un enfer, une moitié dans l'autre. Il a sous ses pieds nus la fatalité qui pour lui s'appelle la glèbe. Il est forcé de marcher dessus, et elle s'attache à ses talons, tantôt boue, tantôt cendre. Il est terre à demi.[44] Il rampe, traîne, pousse, porte, geint, obéit, pleure . . . ses enfants sont des petits, sa femme, hideuse d'infortune, est à peine une femelle; il vit dans le dénuement, dans le silence, dans la stagnation, dans la fièvre, dans la fétidité, dans l'abjection, dans le fumier . . . il doit aux seigneurs tout ce que les seigneurs peuvent vouloir, le respect, la corvée, la dîme, sa femme. Si sa femme est vieille et trop horrible, on prend sa fille. Tout arbre est gibet possible. . . . Il a chaud, il a froid, il a faim, il a peur.[45]

Hugo's contemporaries, however, ignoring the existence of this work, had access only to his *Légende,* in which the ideal and sinister Middle Ages are inseparable and in perpetual confrontation, just as they were in the work of his Romantic youth.[46] The Middle Ages are still, for him, 'le combat du jour et de la nuit', uniquely enthralling for the extremes of good and evil, beauty and horror, which they offer.

(iii) *Evil in the 'Légende' Middle Ages:*
'Crimes, deuils, banquets, prêtres, femmes, scandales . . . !'

The glimpses of 'le moyen âge lugubre' which Hugo offers to readers of the *Légende* bear a close resemblance to the similarly epic descriptions of the Empire in *Napoléon le Petit* and *Les Châtiments*. Berret says that under the Empire 'Hugo alla vers un moyen âge sinistre, pilori des tyrans, et tribune des vengeurs du peuple.'[47] While the Empire evoked by Michelet,

---

[42] Ibid. pp. 50-1. Cf. *Le Rhin,* Lettre XIV (Hugo, *Os. cs.,* ed. J. Massin, vi. 278-9).
[43] Journet & Robert (ibid. p. 72) see no direct influence, but I would say that it is discernible.
[44] Cf. *La Sorcière, supra,* p. 55.   [45] *Promontorium somnii,* pp. 51-2.
[46] Cf. *supra,* p. 18.   [47] P. Berret, op. cit. p. 22.

Renan, and Taine in medieval guise was an essentially empty world — Michelet's in the grip of overpowering *ennui,* and Renan's and Taine's given over to futile frivolity — Hugo's is indeed dramatically sinister, abounding in action. Workers of iniquity wade through rivers of blood, conspire in dark forests, preside over hideous orgies, and are challenged at every turn by workers of noble deeds. This world, like that of *Notre-Dame de Paris,*[48] lies in the shadow of Montfaucon,

> Tas de poutres hideux où le jour rampe et glisse . . .
> Vil bâtiment, des temps fatals fatal complice!

which, with its

> Lourd enchevêtrement de poteaux, de crampons,
> Et d'arcs-boutants pareils aux piles des vieux ponts[49]

(reminiscent of the ramshackle constructions described by enemies of Gothic architecture), is the sinister cathedral of the dark Middle Ages.

When Hugo came to write the *Légende,* he had at his disposal a world created by him several years before the *coup d'état,* which he was able, with remarkably little modification, to use afresh as the sinister Middle Ages-cum-Second Empire of the *Légende.* This is the world of *Les Burgraves* (1843), where lawlessness and treachery are the order of the day:

> On est féroce ou lâche; on est vil ou méchant . . .
> Partout le droit du poing, l'horreur, la violence.[50]

The tyrant Hatto gives orders for the hanging, pillage, and extortionate taxing of his subjects.[51] The mortification of those who retain some vestige of conscience is deepened by the memory of a glorious past putting to shame the inglorious present:

> Vos pères,
> Hardis parmi les forts, grands parmi les meilleurs,
> Étaient des conquérants; vous êtes des voleurs![52]

cries the Emperor Frederick Barbarossa. The same invective, denouncing the same sorry state of affairs, recurs in the *Légende,* with one important modification: whereas in *Les Burgraves* the Emperor appears in the role of 'justicier', freeing the innocent, punishing the guilty, and bestowing his blessing upon a world set to rights at the end of the play, in the *Légende,* emperors, with their confederates the popes, are the arch-villains, 'embusqués au détour du chemin',[53] to

---

[48] Cf. *supra,* p. 20.   [49] *Légende des siècles,* p. 113.   [50] *Les Burgraves,* Act II, Sc. i.
[51] Ibid. Act I, Sc. v.   [52] Ibid. Act II, Sc. vi.   [53] *Légende des siècles,* p. 110.

beg taxes from the poor, in 'Les Deux Mendiants', plotting the sub-
jection of the world in 'Montfaucon'. Once regarded with awe by
Hugo in *Hernani* as 'ces deux moitiés de Dieu, le pape et l'empereur',[54]
they are now the evil-doers against whom he fulminates in *Les Quatre
Vents de l'esprit:*

> Croulez, toi monstre pape, et toi monstre empereur![55]

In *Les Burgraves* the world has fallen into abjection since the
dismemberment of the Empire; in the *Légende,* since the evil hour
when emperors, popes, and kings laid their felonious hands upon it.

There is a hint in the Introduction that the Middle Ages of the
Légende will resemble the Empire of *Les Châtiments:* Hugo explains
that criminal usurpation of power occurred so frequently in the Middle
Ages that he has been obliged to devote space which might at first sight
seem excessive to tales of it. The dark side of the past is present to some
degree in all the medieval poems of the *Légende*, with the exception of 'Le
Mariage de Roland' and 'Aymerillot', both written in 1846, before the
Empire, and concerned exclusively with the ideal, legendary Middle
Ages. There is no trace of republican sentiment in either of these poems:
the world which they evoke is a serene one, far removed from that of
'les rois vautours et les princes de proie'[56] in 'Montfaucon', 'Ratbert',
and the rest. Roland in 'Le Petit Roi de Galice' (1858), and the hero of
'Éviradnus', move out of the ideal sphere of 'Le Mariage de Roland' and
'Aymerillot' into a corrupt world, where they shine as bright stars in
the encircling gloom. Emperor and King share the enslaved world between
them in 'Éviradnus': 'Le roi prend, l'empereur pille, usurpe, investit.'[57]
They indulge in the uninhibited revelation of criminal intent common
to all medieval tyrants of nineteenth-century republican fiction:

> Dès demain, j'entre en danse avec tout mon orchestre . . .
> Les impôts, cela pousse en plantant des gibets[58]

proclaims the emperor Sigismond on winning the state of Lusace with a
throw of the dice. In both their faces 'un oeil de tigre brille',[59] and both
countenances are 'lugubrement grandies/Par de rouges reflets de sacs et
d'incendies'.[60] The same 'rouge reflet' stains the mountain-tops in 'Le

---

[54] Act IV, Sc. ii.
[55] Hugo, *Os. cs.,* ed. Massin, xiv. 909.
[56] *Légende des siècles,* p. 317.
[57] Ibid. p. 240.
[58] Ibid. p. 256.
[59] Ibid. p. 254.
[60] Ibid. p. 239.

Jour des Rois', as the long line of pillagers returns home at sunset:
'Vainqueurs, sanglants, joyeux, les rois s'en retournèrent.'[61] Servitude
is universal: 'Les enfants sont manants, les femmes sont servantes';[62]
and a convent full of trembling nuns is overrun by the drunken soldiers
of one of these bandit-kings — 'Tout s'est évanoui dans un rire féroce'[63]
— in circumstances of horror that will not be surpassed even by Leconte
de Lisle, in the similar episode recounted in 'Le Lévrier de Magnus'
(*Poèmes tragiques*). Horror is also abundantly present in the legend
'Gaiffer-Jorge, duc d'Acquitaine'. Amid the bugles' 'sinistre éclat de
triomphe et de fête', the duke feasts with his barons, waiting for the
serfs digging beneath his castle to announce what they find on
reaching the foundations. At length, from their excavation, 'une lueur
sortit' — the same evil red glow:

> On la sentait venir de quelque horrible lieu;
> Tout le donjon parut sanglant comme un mystère . . .

and 'une lugubre voix' from the depths of the earth tells Gaiffer: 'Ne
creuse point plus bas, tu trouverais l'enfer.'[64] In 'Masferrer', too, the
world is given over to the forces of evil:

> Tout tremble; pas un coin de ravine où ne grince
> La mâchoire d'un tigre ou la fureur d'un prince. . . .
> Ils tiennent tout, la terre et l'homme, en leurs liens . . .
> Ils sont les grands marcheurs de nuit, rasant les places;[65]

but it is above all in 'Ratbert' (dated 1857, published 1859), and in 'Les
Quatre Jours d'Elciis' (dated 1857, published 1883), that abundance of
sinister detail builds up a world identical with the one denounced by
Hugo in *Les Châtiments*. Ratbert — 'Un tel homme suffit pour qu'un
siècle pourrisse'[66] — is first seen among his robber-barons, who have
assembled with chivalric pomp to pay him homage and give advice on
his next act of usurpation. Obsequious prelates pour flattery into his

---

[61] Ibid. p. 161. It is of course the infernal red glow which we have already encountered in *Notre-Dame de Paris* and derivative representations of the sinister
Romantic Middle Ages (cf. *supra*, pp. 19-20). In *William Shakespeare* (1864) Hugo
maintains that 'cette lueur tragique remplit le passé.' It accompanied tyrannical
rulers wherever they went: 'Ils n'éclairaient pas le ciel; ils l'incendiaient. . . . On
entendait des bruits d'écroulements dans leur gloire. Une rougeur s'y mêlait.
Était-ce de la pourpre? Était-ce du sang? Était-ce de la honte? '(*William
Shakespeare*, p. 215).

[62] Ibid. p. 158.
[63] Ibid. p. 160.
[64] Ibid. pp. 384-5.   [65] Ibid. pp. 386-7.
[66] *Légende des siècles*, p. 332.

ears: 'Ta politique est sage et ta guerre est adroite,/ Noble empereur', and counsel perfidy: 'La ruse est licite/Lorsqu'elle a glorieuse et pleine réussite.' The bishop Afranus tells him: 'L'empereur ne veut rien sans que Dieu le désire./Donc, faites!';[67] and in due course, by a perfidious *coup d'état*, Ratbert seizes the citadel of Final. He celebrates with 'une prodigieuse et ténébreuse orgie': 'Sur le bord des plats d'or on voit des mains sanglantes.' 'Presque nue au milieu des montagnes de roses', sits the courtesan Matha,

> Et sous la table, heureux, du genou la pressant,
> Le roi cherche son pied dans les mares de sang . . .

while

> Le drapeau de l'empire, arboré sur ce bruit,
> Gonfle son aigle immense au souffle de la nuit.[68]

By order of 'l'aventurier royal fait empereur par Rome', the loyal soldiers of the old marquis Fabrice are put to death:

> Trente sur les crochets et douze sur le pal
> Expirent au-dessus du porche principal.[69]

Ratbert possesses all the attributes of Louis Napoleon in *Napoléon le Petit* and *Les Châtiments:* treachery, cunning, superstitious devotion, and lasciviousness. He even possesses the moustache[70] so often mentioned in *Les Châtiments* – in 'Nox', for instance:

> Comme un loup qui se lèche après qu'il vient de mordre,
> Caressant sa moustache, il dit. – J'ai sauvé l'ordre![71]

Elciis, the fearless republican invited by the emperor Othon to speak his mind in 'Les Quatre Jours d'Elciis', reveals in the course of his four-day-long harangue the state of total degradation into which the world has fallen:

> Ah! ce siècle est d'un flot d'opprobre submergé! . . .[72]
> L'horreur est installée en nos tours féodales.
> Ah! crimes, deuils, banquets, prêtres, femmes, scandales![73]

Everywhere he sees

> . . . l'empiétement des moutiers, des couvents,
> Des hommes tonsurés et noirs sur les vivants,
> Et le frémissement du monde qui recule.[74]

---

[67] Ibid. pp. 306-9.
[68] Ibid. pp. 323-5. Cf. the orgy in 'On loge à la nuit' in *Les Châtiments:* 'Par places sur les murs on voit des mains sanglantes' (*Os. poétiques,* ii. 112).
[69] *Légende des siècles,* p. 326.   [70] See ibid. p. 328.   [71] Hugo, *Os. poétiques,* ii. 13.
[72] *Légende des siècles,* p. 362.   [73] Ibid. p. 368.   [74] Ibid. p. 363.

Hugo's last evocation of the Empire in sinister medieval guise was his very fine poem 'Coups de clairon', dated February 1870 and published after his death in *Les Années funestes*. The poet sees in vision an evil citadel:

> Quelle est cette ville
> Haute sous les cieux
> Et qui semble vile,
> Bien qu'énorme aux yeux?

A compound of Babylon, Jericho, and the Cities of the Plain, it is none the less distinctly feudal in appearance, and is variously described as 'la ville du mal', 'le donjon des loups', 'le burg lascif', and 'l'éden enfer'. Its 'tours damnées' with 'la lueur féline/De leurs soupiraux' can be seen from afar at nightfall:

> Cette cité veille
> Du haut de ses forts,
> Au dedans vermeille,
> Sinistre au dehors . . .

and from afar also can be heard the hideous merriment of its inhabitants, ruled over by a bandit-prince: 'On dirait les voix/Des bêtes féroces/ Chantant dans les bois':

> Les créneaux sans nombre,
> Le long mur dormant
> Font un monceau d'ombre
> Sur leur flamboiement.
>
> Visible en ces brumes,
> L'aigle menaçant
> Passe entre ses plumes
> Son bec teint de sang.[75]

So much, then, for the sinister Middle Ages conjured up by Hugo in exile. The demonic figures who stalk through it are, like Taine's medieval men, wild animals. Tiphaine in 'L'Aigle du casque' pounces upon the boy Angus with 'un rugissement de bête carnassière',[76] and goes into the kill 'comme un loup dans les cirques romains'.[77] Fabrice, lamenting over his granddaughter's corpse, calls Ratbert 'une bête féroce' and his henchmen 'des loups'.[78] Elciis tells Othon and the twelve kings seated on the steps of his throne:

> Plutôt que me fier à vous, je me fierais
> Aux jaguars, aux lynx, aux tigres des forêts.[79]

[75] Hugo, *Os. cs.*, ed. J. Massin, xiv. pp. 1079-91.
[76] *Légende des siècles*, p. 298.   [77] Ibid. p. 302.   [78] *Légende des siècles*, p. 331.
[79] Ibid. p. 362. Cf. Taine's pronouncement made in the same year, *supra*, p. 72.

So sinister, indeed, is this world that it might lead one to suppose that Hugo's verdict on the Middle Ages is now the same as Taine's: 'On en était arrivé . . . à l'abrutissement ignoble des Calédoniens et des Papous, au plus bas-fond du cloaque humain';[80] but this is not the case: the medieval section of the *Légende,* though vast enough to embrace, as we have seen, a vision of the dark Middle Ages in all their horror, is far from being a mere reproduction of the conventional republican view. It is not the world of total savagery which we shall encounter in the poetry of Leconte de Lisle.

(iv) *The ideal Middle Ages in the 'Légende':* *'ce grand rayonnement des anciens et des pères'*

We have seen some of the answers given to the question so often asked in mid-nineteenth-century France — who, exactly, are 'nos pères'? Hugo was not among those republicans who suggested the Greeks, or the Druids, or the men of the Renaissance, as a substitute for the discredited forefathers of the Middle Ages. In the Preface to *Les Burgraves* he held fast to the Romantic view that 'pour nous, peuples nés du moyen âge . . . ils [i.e. les burgraves] sont nos pères.' And the Middle Ages of the *Légende,* though darkened by the sinister shadow of the Empire falling over it, is still in part illumined by 'ce grand rayonnement des anciens et des pères'[81] whose memory is evoked by Elciis in the market-place. The 'souffle d'épopée'[82] of the early, heroic Middle Ages that captivated Michelet and Renan before they enveloped the whole period in the same condemnation, retains its prestige for Hugo. In fact his purpose in writing the *Légende* — according to notes for a projected preface — was to 'mêler à l'esprit contemporain un peu de ce prodigieux souffle d'audace, de persévérance, de volonté et d'abnégation qui animait nos pères, et de *doubler l'âme du temps présent avec l'âme du vieux temps'.*[83] In the *Légende* august forefathers are ever-present in the memory — 'Les grands spectres des ancêtres/Sont toujours autour de moi',[84] proclaims the Cid — or in the flesh, in the person of such heroic veterans as Fabrice. As in *Les Burgraves,* heroism has waned with each succeeding generation. This is the theme of 'La Paternité':

> Voilà quinze cents ans que le monde est chrétien;
> Les fières mœurs s'en vont; jadis le mal, le bien,

---

[80] Cf. *supra,* p. 75.   [81] *Légende des siècles,* p. 359.
[82] *Légende des siècles,* p. 359.   [83] Hugo, *Os. cs.,* ed. J. Massin, x. 671 (my italics).
[84] *Légende des siècles,* p. 102.

> Le bon, le beau vivaient dans la chevalerie. . . .
> Les paladins étaient à leurs vieux noms fidèles. . . .
> On n'est plus à présent les hommes d'autrefois[85] —

but the memory of a better world is still fresh . It is revived by Elciis in his long lament: 'Ah! deuil sans borne après les prouesses sans nombre!' he cries, and expresses disgust that 'les preux' should have been succeeded everywhere by 'les poltrons'.[86] The bishop who urges Ratbert to commit further acts of iniquity appears untroubled by the memory of a past that has been safely buried:

> Les vieux temps, qui n'ont plus d'avocats,
> Agissaient autrement; mais je fais peu de cas
> De ces temps-là; c'étaient des temps de république,[87]

he declares, and proceeds to assist his master in the poisoning of the importunate Onfroy, 'ce héros d'un autre âge',[88] but evil is by no means allowed to flourish unchecked in this world. Even in the debased and deplorable present, some of the departed glory of the past lingers on, in the heroic figures ever-active in word and deed against the forces of darkness. In the most forlorn circumstances, when the world seems condemned to an eternal reign of terror, a voice always makes itself heard to denounce those who have created this night: the beggar at the end of 'Le Jour des rois', addressing the mountains, or the eagle addressing the rivers and forests at the end of 'L'Aigle du casque', or Elciis: 'Ô Dieu qui m'entendez, ces hommes sont hideux.'[89] At the end of 'Welf, Castellan d'Osbor', when evil seems to have gained the day, as the defeated Welf is reviled by his faithless subjects, who break into a servile shout of 'Vive le pape! . . . Et vive l'empereur!', Hugo himself adds a tailpiece assuring his hero that his stand was not in vain and he will live for ever in people's memory as '[un] fantôme sublime'.[90] Usually, however, the voice of protest belongs to an agent of retribution. The eye of some 'justicier' is always upon the criminal, as in 'Éviradnus'. Ratbert is decapitated by an avenging archangel; but as a rule justice is meted out by one of those paladins forming the band of 'chevaliers errants'– the 'héros chretiens *sans peur et sans reproche'* of Chateaubriand's *Génie du Christianisme*[91] — whose very existence was of course denied by republicans such as Delécluze, convinced that 'la

[85] Ibid. p. 405.
[86] Ibid. pp. 370-1. Cf. Barbey d'Aurevilly's lament that 'les Lâcheurs' and 'les Effacés' have replaced 'les Éclatants' of yore (*supra,* p. 84).
[87] *Légende des siècles*, p. 309.   [88] Ibid. p. 313.
[89] *Légende des siècles*, p. 371.   [90] Ibid. pp. 353-5.   [91] Cf. *supra,* p. 13.

chevalerie errante n'a jamais été qu'un solennel mensonge.'[92] Hugo,
however, enlists these knights in the unceasing war against tyranny:

> Ils étaient, dans des temps d'oppression, de deuil,
> De honte, où l'infamie étalait son orgueil,
> Les spectres de l'honneur, du droit, de la justice.[93]

'Toute puissance injuste, inhumaine, usurpée'[94] had reason to tremble
when one of them appeared in the distance. These incorruptible heroes
are omnipresent in the *Légende*. protecting the innocent, heaping
curses upon crowned heads, and resisting their flattering overtures as
temptations from Satan. They inhabit enclaves of free territory out of
the reach of tyranny, such as the domain of the exiled Cid, who tells
the King:

> Il n'est pas de coeurs obliques
> Voués aux vils intérêts
> Dans nos vieilles républiques
> De torrents et de forêts . . .[95];

the lair of Masferrer, 'au-dessus des lieux bas et pestilentiels',[96] in thrall
to the petty kings he refuses to join; and the moutain, 'un coin de
paradis sauvage',[97] on which Welf's castle stands: 'Ce mont excepté,
l'esclavage est partout.'[98] The Cid, 'au coeur de flamme, à l'âme
honnête',[99] shouts somewhat monotonous defiance at the King:

> Je sens vos ruses sans nombre;
> Oui, je sens tes trahisons.
> Moi pour le bien, toi pour l'ombre,
> Dans la nuit nous nous croisons . . .

— from his place of exile, rendering him increasingly uneasy:

> Tu dis à ton économe,
> A tes pages blancs ou verts:
> — "A quoi pense ce bonhomme
> Qui regarde de travers?"[100]

---

[92] E-J. Delécluze, *Roland, ou la chevalerie*, 1845, i. 176-7.
[93] *Légende des siècles*, p. 211.
[94] *Légende des siècles*, p. 211.
[95] Ibid. p. 102.   [96] Ibid. p. 392.
[87] Ibid. p. 348.   [98] Ibid. p. 336.   [99] Ibid. p. 86.
[100] Ibid. pp. 90-1. From 'Le Romancero du Cid', which surely is addressed to
  Louis Napoleon, although the editors of *Os. cs.*, ed. J. Massin, deny this (see
  vol. x, pp. 769-70).

In 'Le Petit Roi de Galice' the ideal overwhelms the evil Middle Ages, as Roland with his shining sword rides into the sinister ravine of Ernula on his white horse, disturbing the plot to do away with the orphaned boy-King. He listens in contemptuous silence to the offer of two towns as a bribe; and the orphan whom he sets free rides into Compostella, 'son paradis natal',[101] as the cathedral bells ring out, and vows to lead a life of exemplary virtue in emulation of his deliverer. Éviradnus, 'ce juste et ce preux',[102] also foils an attempted *coup d'état:*

> Quoi, ceci règne! Quoi, c'est un césar, cela! . . .
> Hors du trône, tyrans! à la tombe, vampires![103]

Welf defies the duke, King, Emperor, and Pope who try in turn to coax him out of his mountain fastness:

> Je hais ton glaive, ô duc. Je hais ton sceptre, ô roi.
> César, je hais ton globe impérial. Et toi,
> Pape, je ne crois pas à tes clefs. Qu'ouvrent-elles?
> Des enfers. . . .[104]

Defeated heroes, who, caught in some perfidious trap, have fallen into enemy hands, are no less eloquent in their defiance. Fabrice curses Ratbert:

> Oh! sois maudit, maudit, maudit, et sois maudit,
> Ratbert, empereur, roi, césar, escroc, bandit![105]

Elciis, under suspended sentence of death, whose days are numbered to those during which breath remains in his lungs to denounce the tyrant Othon, forecasts a future *débâcle:*

> Ô princes, vous pouvez crouler subitement.
> Vous avez beau compter sur vos soldats horribles. . . .
> Un beau jour, brusquement, catastrophe, tumulte,
> Tout croule et se disperse, et dans l'ombre, les cris,
> L'horreur, tout disparaît . . .,[106]

---

[101] Ibid. pp. 230-1.
[102] *Légende des siècles,* p. 232.
[103] Ibid. pp. 261-2.
[104] Ibid. p. 346.
[105] Ibid. p. 332.
[106] *Légende des siècles,* pp. 373-4.

just as Hugo, in 'Coups de clairon', ends his description of 'la ville du mal':

> Mais les fêtes cessent
> Si soudain le soir
> Des clairons se dressent
> Sur l'horizon noir.

'Trompettes terribles', he cries, 'Chantez et sonnez!/Sur ces tours horribles . . .'; for nothing can withstand the scorching blast of their fury: 'La tour la plus fière/Sous ce vent périt', and the whole Gothic 'amas de ténèbres' — 'les murs teints de sang', 'les jardins, les cours', 'le reflet des lampes/Aux rondeurs des tours' — will disappear in one final cataclysm.[107]

(v) *Romantic aspects of the 'Légende'*

The medieval world of the *Légende des siècles,* then, is a paradise as well as an inferno; but even its infernal aspects often fail to inspire any republican spirit of condemnation in Hugo. In this respect, as in so many others, he remains a Romantic, in whom the sinister side of the Middle Ages arouses an aesthetic *frisson* rather than moral indignation.[108] Although the great hall of the castle in 'Masferrer', where the kings assemble amidst their plunder, is a place of horror, it enchants his imagination. He takes a medieval delight in descriptions of the carnage which republican historians deplored as the favourite pastime of feudal barons. In 'Le Petit Roi de Galice' mighty blows split Roland's adversaries in two; and the tumultuous excitement of the battle exhilarates the narrator:

> Tous d'un côté; de l'autre, un seul; tragique duel!
> Lutte énorme! combat de l'Hydre et de Michel! . . .
> Larges coups, flots de sang par des bouches vomis . . .
> Cris de rage; ô carnage! ô terreur![109]

The same delight of the *jongleur* addressing his audience is evident in the description of the chase in 'L'Aigle du casque': 'Et vous ne lirez

---

[107] Hugo, *Os. cs.,* ed. J. Massin, pp. 1085-92.
[108] Cf. *supra,* p. 21.
[109] *Légende des siècles,* p. 228.

plus ceci qu'en frémissant.'[110] Sinister detail is evoked for its aesthetic
value rather than its propaganda value: the *oubliettes* in 'Éviradnus',
for instance:

> On dirait une bouche obscure de l'enfer . . .
> On distingue les dents sinistres d'une herse,
> Et, plus bas, le regard flotte dans de la nuit;
> Le sang sur les parois fait une rougeâtre enduit . . .,[111]

which serve a noble purpose in the end, when the hero finds them extremely
convenient in his fight to the death against Sigismond and Ladislas; and,
conversely, many figures from the ideal Middle Ages of the *Légende* are
made to appear momentarily satanic and sinister: the 'chevaliers errants',
'ces magistrats sinistres de l'épée', 'justes, bons, lugubres, ténébreux',
some of them resembling 'des larves de l'enfer';[112] the abbess confronting
the soldiers in 'Le Jour des rois', 'la crosse en main . . . Sinistre';[113] and
Roland's sword in 'Le Petit Roi de Galice': 'Durandal flamboyant semble
un sinistre esprit. . . .'[114] Hugo even says of the 'chevaliers errants':
'Derrière eux cheminait la Mort, squelette chauve':[115] this must have
sent a shudder through Gautier, however much he may have approved of
the medieval section of the *Légende* as a whole. The apparatus of
Romantic medievalism — gargoyles taking on a semblance of life to
battle with the elements, and suits of armour doing likewise to strike
terror into the beholder —, which played an important part in *Odes et
ballades, Notre-Dame de Paris,* and *Le Rhin,* appears once more in
'Éviradnus'. The description of the suits of armour in this poem brings

---

[110] Ibid. p. 298.

[111] *Légende des siècles,* p. 257. *Oubliettes* were one of the chief properties employed by republican detractors of the Middle Ages. Cf. Pelletan's above-quoted
tirade (*supra,* p. 127), and a similar outburst from Agénor de Gasparin: 'Puis,
pensez-y, il y a des oubliettes dans tous les châteaux et dans tous les couvents. . . .
Bénissons Dieu de ne pas nous avoir fait vivre dans un pareil temps' (*Le Christianisme au moyen âge: Innocent III,* 1859, pp. 255-7). Mérimée poured scorn on
such febrile eagerness to believe the worst about the Middle Ages. In his 'Instructions du Comité Historique des arts et monuments' (1843), reprinted in Lacroix
& Seré, *Le Moyen Âge et la Renaissance,* vol. v (1851), he wrote: 'On donne
trop souvent des couleurs atroces au moyen âge, et l'imagination accepte trop
facilement les scènes d'horreurs que les romanciers placent dans de semblables
lieux. Combien de celliers ou de magasins de bois n'ont pas été pris pour d'affreux
cachots!' (Mérimée, *Études sur les arts au moyen âge,* 1875, pp. 275-6). Cf.
Viollet-le-Duc, *Dictionnaire raisonné de l'architecture française,* articles
'Château', 'Cul-de-basse-fosse', 'Latrines', and 'Oubliettes'.

[112] Ibid. p. 211.   [113] *Légende des siècles,* p. 160.   [114] Ibid. p. 228.

[115] Ibid. p. 212.

to mind Gautier's 'Le Souper des armures' (first published in 1858 and included in *Émaux et camées*). A comparison of the two poems illustrates how far apart their creators, both former members of the 'école mâchicoulis', had travelled. Hugo exploits the Romantic horror of the scene with undiminished delight, and indeed awe, which he intends the reader to share:

> Oh! ces hommes masqués sur ces chevaux voilés,
> Chose affreuse![116]

Gautier, rendered uneasy by a spectacle which in his heart he finds distasteful, adopts a light-hearted, mocking tone. The source of the poem (which may well have had its influence, too, on 'Éviradnus') is Gautier's description of a painting by Cattermole exhibited in 1855, *Sir Biorn aux yeux étincelants*. Sir Biorn – 'Âme retrospective'[117] – is a brother of Elias Wildmanstadius, 'l'homme moyen âge'. He prefers the company of the dead to that of the living, and on certain nights invites his ancestors to dine with him – a phantasmal assembly of suits of armour, 'Landgraves, rhingraves, burgraves,/Venus du ciel ou de l'enfer'[118], exactly like those in 'Éviradnus'; but whereas Hugo's ghostly warriors present an awesome spectacle in their immobility:

> Tous se taisent; pas un ne bouge; c'est terrible . . .,[119]

Gautier's rapidly lose all dignity:

> – Ils sont tous gris comme des chantres,
> Les vaillants comtes suzerains! –

and the scene ends in burlesque, as one of them sings 'Un lied, en treize cents, nouveau' and all collapse in disarray under the table.[120] Gautier describes them in the prose version as 'cette ferraille héraldique en gaieté'[121], and the term 'ferraille' is repeated in the poem; whereas in 'Éviradnus', of course, Mahaud reproves Zéno's disrespect for her ancestors when he exclaims: 'Comme je vous vendrais à l'encan ces ferrailles'[122] (just as Léon Gautier took exception in a review of Jules Quicherat's *Histoire du costume* to the republican historian's irreverent description of Carolingian armour: ' "Voici, dit-il, le barbare avec toute la *ferraille* qui composait son ornement" ').[123]

[116] *Légende des siècles*, p. 247.
[117] Gautier, *Poésies complètes*, iii. 77.   [118] Gautier, *Poésies complètes*, iii. 78.
[119] *Légende des siècles*, p. 244.   [120] Gautier, op. cit. pp. 80-1.
[121] Gautier, *Les Beaux-Arts en Europe*, i (1855), 108.
[122] *Légende des siècles*, p. 252.
[123] Léon Gautier, *Vingt Nouveaux Portraits*, 1878, p. 225.

So Hugo — who wrote most of the *Légende* in the *moyenâgeux* interior of Hauteville-House[124] — restores to the Middle Ages, in this work, much of the Romantic prestige which republicans were attempting to take from them. For him they retain their chivalric glory, and above all their mystery: the 'chevaliers errants' - 'On ne savait jamais d'où sortaient ces fantômes'[125] — are steeped in it, and the reasons — precise enough in the medieval original — are not given for the mysterious combat between Roland and Oliver in *Le Mariage de Roland.* Hugo is unable to regard the Middle Ages with the moral indignation of most of his fellow-republicans, or with the uneasy derision of Gautier. Although he creates a sinister Middle Ages bearing an ominous resemblance to the Empire, he continues to believe in an ideal Middle Ages which, like Montalembert, he uses as a counterblast to the Empire, and, like Barbey d'Aurevilly, he exalts as a world satisfyingly 'énorme' in comparison with the triviality of the present.

Before we leave Hugo, one curious detail may be added: during the years spent in exile there were moments when his anti-clericalism caused the Gothic cathedral to appear to him in a light as sinister as that in which other republicans habitually saw it. First, there is the glimpse of its 'double tour aiguë' in 'Tout le passé et tout l'avenir' (dated 1854):

> Dieu voit avec pitié ces deux oreilles d'ane
> Se dresser dans la vaste nuit . . . ;[126]

then, in *Dieu,* two years later, a more horrifying evocation of the God of the Dark Ages in his temple:

> Dieu gothique, irritable, intolérant, tueur,
> Noir vitrail effrayant qu'empourpre la lueur
> Du bûcher qui flamboie et pétille derrière . . . ;[127]

followed by Hugo's declaration in *L'Âne* that, during those centuries, to the victims of 'le prêtre epouvantail',

> La cathédrale d'ombre ouvrait son grand portail.[128]

---

[124] See P. Berret. '*La Légende des siècles*' *de V. Hugo,* 1945, pp. 69-73.
[125] *Légende des siècles,* p. 212.
[126] *Légende des siècles,* p. 566.
[127] Hugo, *Dieu* (*Le Seuil du gouffre*), ed. Journet & Robert, 1961, p. 58 (written early 1856, according to Journet & Robert, published 1891).
[128] Hugo, *L'Âne,* ed. P. Albouy, 1966, p. 119 (probably written late 1857 or early 1858; published 1880).

B. *The Middle Ages of Leconte de Lisle:*
'Siècles d'égorgeurs, de lâches et de brutes'

We will now examine the rival Middle Ages of Leconte de Lisle. Most modern critics consider his medieval poems, called by Elsenberg 'cette malencontreuse série',[129] to be the least successful of his excursions into the past, marred by strident anti-clericalism, and sterile, monotonous hatred of the world they evoke. Republican critics, of course, acclaimed them as the poet's highest achievement. Eugène Garcin, contemplating medieval society as depicted by Leconte de Lisle, asked himself: 'Mais n'est-ce pas là un mauvais rêve du rapsode, un cauchemar de l'historien?' and replied at once: 'Non, tout cela est implacable comme la réalité. On voudrait ne pas y croire: vain désir! On ne peut méconnaître ce qui fut la société d'alors.'[130] Ricard, looking back in 1892 to the days of the Parnasse, wrote: 'Un seul poète, alors, a su voir le moyen-âge directement; et en cette partie, une des plus magnifiques de son oeuvre, il ne fut pas imité, du moins comme il a dû de suite l'être; c'est . . . Leconte de Lisle.'[131]

Leconte de Lisle and his disciples shared Taine's preoccupation with '[la] divination précise et prouvée des sentiments évanouis'.[132] They too sought to recreate past societies and states of mind, to 'rendre intellectuellement la vie au passé',[133] in the words of Leconte de Lisle. Hugo, in his Preface to the *Légende,* had put their ideal into words when he spoke of 'fidélité absolue à la couleur des temps et à l'esprit des civilisations diverses',[134] but they maintained that this was merely an idle boast on his part, and that they themselves were far better equipped to reproduce the past in all its native strangeness, unclouded by modern sentiment. Leconte de Lisle, in his Academy speech (1887), complained that Hugo had failed to make himself into 'une sorte de contemporain de chaque époque'. The *Légende* was in fact 'plutôt . . . l'écho superbe de sentiments modernes attribués aux hommes des époques passées qu'une résurrection historique ou légendaire'.[135]

---

[129] H. Elsenberg, *Le Sentiment religieux chez Leconte de Lisle,* Jouve, 1909, p. 218 (cf. I. Putter, *The Pessimism of Leconte de Lisle,* 1954, p. 207; E. Estève, *Leconte de Lisle, l'homme et l'oeuvre,* Boivin, 1923, pp. 105, 115; A. Fairlie, *Leconte de Lisle's Poems on the Barbarian Races,* 1947, p. 340).

[130] *Revue moderne,* 10 Sept. 1869, p. 27.

[131] *Revue indépendante* (June 1892), p. 333.   [132] Cf. *supra,* p. 72.

[133] Leconte de Lisle, *Articles, préfaces, discours,* p. 209 (Academy speech, 1887).

[134] *Légende des siècles,* p. 5.   [135] Leconte de Lisle, op. cit. pp. 208-9.

The medieval men resurrected by Leconte de Lisle may not give utterance to modern sentiments; but this does not make them any the less familiar to the modern reader, for they are none other than the 'fous furieux', 'brutes sanguinaires', and 'bêtes féroces' of Taine and the *philosophes*. Leconte de Lisle's Middle Ages corresponds exactly to theirs. He uses all the resources at his disposal – the work of Michelet, Taine, and lesser historians, even the Gothic novel – to evoke in its full horror the hell upon earth which republicans so often told their readers they were very fortunate to have escaped, by having been born into a better world.

In our first chapter we saw that a few isolated attempts at fictional denigration of the Middle Ages were made during the Romantic period. Leconte de Lisle took up this work with a will: his implacable enmity towards the Middle Ages raged unabated during a long career, which stretched from his first medieval poem, 'Les Paraboles de Dom Guy' (1859), to the landmarks of his later years: the *Histoire populaire du Christianisme* (1871), the *Histoire du moyen âge* (1876), the poem 'Les Siècles maudits' (1883), and the Academy speech (1887), in which he spoke, in language reminiscent of Voltaire and Condorcet, of 'les noires années du moyen âge, années d'abominable barbarie, qui avaient amené l'anéantissement presque total des richesses intellectuelles héritées de l'antiquité, avilissant les esprits par la recrudescence des plus ineptes superstitions, par l'atrocité des moeurs et la tyrannie sanglante du fanatisme religieux'.[136] His friend Ménard protested against the violence of this attack,[137] forgetting that he himself had equalled it on various occasions – for example, in the vision of carnage, famine, and pestilence in the *Tableau historique des beaux-arts* (1866) written in collaboration with his brother René.[138]

It was suggested more than once during the Second Empire that the peculiarly horrific nature of the Middle Ages presented an inspiring challenge to the modern writer. The protestant Agénor de Gasparin expressed dissatisfaction with republican writing on the medieval

---

[136] Leconte de Lisle, op. cit. p. 201. Cf. his letter of 1886 to Émilie Leforestier: 'La nuit s'est faite dans l'âme humaine, et nous avons vu, pendant quinze à seize siècles, l'ignorance, la sottise et la férocité déborder sur tout l'occident . . . et nous verrions encore ces horreurs, si les mêmes fous féroces redevenaient les maîtres' (I. Putter, *La Dernière Illusion de Leconte de Lisle,* 1968, p. 112). These pronouncements were of course made at a time when the Middle Ages were – as we shall see – enjoying a return to favour.

[137] *La Critique philosophique,* 1887, p. 318.

[138] See L. and R. Ménard, *Tableau historique des beaux-arts,* 1866, p. 28.

Church in the tradition of the *philosophes* who refused to believe that fanaticism could be sincere, 'histoire frondeuse, moqueuse, qui ne voit que des hypocrites'. 'Pour elle,' he protested, 'la grandeur, l'horrible grandeur de ces temps a disparu.'[139] We have seen that Barbey d'Aurevilly called in 1855 for 'une réprobation digne de ce temps immense, quelque chose, enfin, qui aurait son éloquence, son injuste, mais réelle beauté'.[140] In 1877 he again invited enemies of the Middle Ages to seek inspiration in what they abhorred. 'La Calomnie fait des légendes aussi bien que la Vérité!' he exclaimed: 'La Haine est une fière Muse.'[141] These observations were provoked by the second series of the *Légende des siècles*, which he considered to be a disappointingly half-hearted production of Hugo, 'le poète imprécatoire et maudissant du Moyen Âge'.[141] It is both surprising and regrettable that Barbey neglected to record his opinion of Lecontre de Lisle's medieval poems.

The first of these, 'Les Paraboles de Dom Guy' (*Poésies barbares*) contains already most of the elements which recur throughout the whole sequence. The poem, a sermon delivered by a monk, Guy de Clairvaux, against the corruption of Rome in the early fifteenth century, is a vast allegorical vision encompassing the entire medieval world. Paris lies beneath the shadow of innumerable gibbets, with their 'amas de pendus'. The windows of the Louvre – 'Géhenne dont le roi Charles sixième est l'hôte' – are fired with the same lurid glow which illumines Hugo's sinister Middle Ages:

> Une rouge lueur, du fond des embrasures,
> Sortait, comme du sang qui jaillit des blessures.[142]

In the churches, the iniquitous deeds of Isabeau de Bavière cause the saints and angels to shed the bitter tears first remarked upon by Michelet:

> Et j'ai vu, tout navrés durant ces infamies . . .
> Les Anges qui pleuraient du haut des pendentifs.[143]

In the valleys of Touraine –

> Où le Jacque, épuisé de son labeur, oublie
> Sa grand'misère avec la chaîne qui le lie –,[144]

as evening falls, the sound of 'd'effroyables chansons'[144] is heard from the monasteries, the denizens of which appear to Dom Guy, who sees in vision their bestial orgy, 'autant de loups sanglants au fond des antres'.[144]

---

[139] A. de Gasparin, *Innocent III*, 1859, p. 15.   [140] Cf. *supra*, p. 44.
[141] B. d'Aurevilly, *Les Poètes*, 1889, pp. 75-6.
[142] *Poèmes barbares*, p. 337.   [143] Ibid. pp. 338-9.   [144] Ibid. pp. 343-4.

All medieval men, for Leconte de Lisle, are ravening wolves: the voice
of Christ, denouncing the abbot in 'L'Agonie d'un saint', addresses him
as a 'Loup féroce, toujours affamé de morsures',[145] and the monk put to
death by the Albigensians in 'La Mort du moine' is of the same ilk:
'Frères, voyez ce moine! Il a la face humaine,/Mais son coeur est d'un
loup, chaud de rage et de haine.'[146] Dom Guy sees also a vision of
universal carnage — the armies of every nation

> Hurlant, les yeux hagards, haletantes, meurtries,
> Se ruant pêle-mêle en tourbillons, rendant
> L'écume de la rage à chaque coup de dent.[147]

What most distresses him is that, of these furious armies, 'Sur la terre,
Jésus, que ta croix illumine . . . les plus égorgeurs, hélas, c'étaient tes
fils.'[148] Further account will be given of the Crusaders in 'Le Lévrier
de Magnus' (1883), which begins with details of their activities on the
way to the Holy Sepulchre ('Et leurs dagues gravaient la croix dans les
chairs vives',[149] etc.). 'Les Paraboles de Dom Guy' contains also Leconte
de Lisle's favourite expression 'assomme avec la crosse,/Étrangle avec
l'étole'[150] (an activity performed in this instance by the Church, seen as
an evil shepherd who is no better than a 'loup féroce' devouring his
flock), which will be repeated in 'Les Deux Glaives' (1861)[151] and 'La
Mort du moine' (1894).[152] Dom Guy ends his sermon with the cry:

> Sus! sus! La coupe est pleine et déborde. Debout,
> Les forts, les purs, les bons, car le monde est à bout![153]

urging leaders of Church and State to make their way to the Council of
Constance and re-establish order in the Church. This cry will be repeated
in subsequent medieval poems of Leconte de Lisle as a sinister call to
arms. In 'L'Agonie d'un saint' it is the signal for the massacre of the
Albigensians:

> Sus, à l'assaut! l'épée aux dents, la hache au poing! . . .
> Tuez! à vous le ciel s'ils n'en réchappent point!
> Arrachez tous ces coeurs maudits et ces entrailles![154]

The language in which Dom Guy's sermon is couched is the one which
Leconte de Lisle is to employ in all these poems. He simulates the effect

---

[145] Ibid. p. 323.   [146] *Derniers Poèmes*, p. 36.
[147] *Poèmes barbares*, p. 341. Cf. 'La Mort du moine', *Derniers Poèmes*, p. 37; and
'Les Siècles maudits', *Poèmes tragiques*, p. 60.
[148] *Poèmes barbares*, p. 341.   [149] *Poèmes tragiques*, p. 113.
[150] *Poèmes barbares*, p. 332.   [151] Ibid. p. 313.
[152] *Derniers Poèmes*, p. 36.   [153] *Poèmes barbares*, p. 350.
[154] *Poèmes barbares*, p. 321.

of a medieval voice speaking (even when, as in 'Un Acte de charité', the narrator is anonymous – presumably the poet himself, transformed into 'une sorte de contemporain' of the Middle Ages) with a blend of archaism and Old Testament imagery: words such as 'navrure', 'ouir' and 'moutier',[155] interlarded with abundant reference to the everlasting fires of hell, and weeping, wailing, and gnashing of teeth.

'Un Acte de charité' (1860), the second of Leconte de Lisle's medieval poems, tells the tale of a noblewoman who, out of compassion for their misery, burns alive a horde of her famished serfs who have taken refuge in a barn:

> – J'ai fait ce que j'ai pu, je vous remets à Dieu,
> Cria-t-elle, et Jésus vous ouvre son royaume![156]

As Leblond points out,[157] Leconte de Lisle had already recounted a prose version of the story in 1846, in the *fouriériste* newspaper *La Démocratie pacifique,* as an anecdote illustrating the evils of charity distribution: 'L'aumône . . . sanctionne le règne de l'oppression.'[158] (In the previous month, which was one of widespread famine, Lamartine had appealed to the public: 'Répandez-vous en aumônes plus abondantes',[159] angering *La Démocratie pacifique,* which had been campaigning against charity as an odious survival from the Middle Ages: 'Nous n'aimons pas ces procédés de grand seigneur à vilain.')[160] In this 1846 version, however, the story has an ending different from the one told in 'Un Acte de charité': 'Elle avait tout donné; elle n'avait rien guéri. Le désespoir la saisit. Elle convoqua tous ses pauvres dans une église, et s'y brûla avec eux.'[161] The noblewoman in the poem, shedding pious tears and uttering pious sentiments as, 'pleine de dévoûment et d'une force étrange', she barricades 'tous ses pauvres amis' into a barn and sets light to its four corners,[162] is a far more sinister figure. A version of the story corresponding exactly to the poem, and revealing the identity of the lady, is told in Eugène Bonnemère's *Histoire des paysans* (1856).[163] Here details of the famine –

---

[155] Ibid. pp. 326-7.   [156] Ibid. p. 284.   [157] M-A. Leblond, op. cit. p. 203.

[158] Leconte de Lisle, *Articles, préfaces, discours,* p. 105 (*La Démocratie pacifique,* 29 Nov. 1846).

[159] *La Démocratie pacifique,* 3 Oct. 1846.   [160] Ibid. 10-11 Aug. 1846.

[161] Leconte de Lisle, op. cit. p. 106.   [162] *Poèmes barbares,* p. 284.

[163] It seems probable that this violently republican work was one of the principal sources of Leconte de Lisle's medieval poems. It contains an account of 'de pieux cantiques' ascending during a massacre of the Albigensians (vol. i. p. 134), which is echoed in 'L'Agonie d'un saint' (*Poèmes barbares,* p. 322) and 'Les Raisons du Saint-Père' (*Derniers Poèmes,* p. 46); and on the next page there is a reference to 'ces siècles maudits de la féodalité'.

wolves roaming the countryside, and acts of cannibalism occurring among the peasantry: 'On vit des pères tuer leurs enfants, des enfants tuer leurs pères' — are given, as in 'Un Acte de charité', and the victims are herded into a barn instead of a church: 'La dame suzeraine de l'Artois, la noble comtesse Mahault, veuve d'Othon IV . . . s'il en faut croire l'annaliste flamand Meyer, n'imagina rien de mieux que de faire renfermer dans une grange tous les pauvres du pays, et par pitié, d'y mettre le feu.'[164]

It is a curious coincidence that Nodier, in the volume of his *Voyages pittoresques et romantiques dans l'ancienne France* dealing with Franche-Comté (1825), should have told this same story, seen through Romantic and royalist spectacles, as a tailpiece to his description of the ruins of Mahaut's castle, La Châtelaine, near Arbois:

> Comme elle étoit bonne et douce, l'amitié du pauvre peuple embellissoit sa solitude. . . . Il arriva un jour qu'une affreuse famine obligea tous les indigents du pays à se réfugier autour d'elle, et ce jour-là, la veuve d'Othon V [sic] n'avoit point de pain. Elle mit le feu de sa main à la salle des aumônes et de la charité. . . . Mahaut mourut sans doute avec les infortunés dont elle abrégeoit les tourmens par un dévouement tragique . . .

and that he should have proceeded to express regret that 'le martyre sublime de *la Châtelaine* n'a pas été couronné des palmes de la poésie, comme le suicide de Sardanapale.'[165] Perhaps Leconte de Lisle read this, and — fortified by Bonnemère's version — took up Nodier's challenge. The circumstance of Mahaut's perishing with her victims (as in Leconte's 1846 version), and the term 'dévouement' (employed sardonically in the poem) — neither of which occur, to our knowledge, in any other account of the episode — lend some support to this hypothesis. It is safe to assume, in any case, that Leconte de Lisle's verse rendering would not have met with Nodier's approval!

The theme of 'Un Acte de charité' — atrocities committed with pious intent — leads us back to the question of the ideal versus the real Middle Ages, already broached in connexion with Hugo. Orthodox Parnassian practice prescribed that the past should be recreated not in its reality, but in the ideal it formed of itself, which was preserved in religion, legend, and art. Leconte de Lisle spoke with pride in 1862 of 'ce génie

---

[164] E. Bonnemère, *Histoire des paysans,* 1856, i. 287. I am preparing an article on Leconte de Lisle's poem, which deals with the complicated question of this legend's actual source.

[165] Nodier, Taylor, & Cailleux, *Voyages pittoresques et romantiques dans l'ancienne France (Franche-Comté)*, Gide, 1825, pp. 141-2.

singulier, propre à notre siècle, qui reconstruit pièce à pièce les époques passées, par leurs côtés puissants et idéalement vrais'.[166] He and his disciples set out in theory to create an ideal Middle Ages far more subtle than the Romantics' trivially sentimental one. As republicans, however, they shared the detestation of that period of history which Michelet voiced with such vehemence under the Empire; and it will be remembered that Michelet, in 1846, began to feel bitter regret for having presented his readers of 1833 with 'l'idéal de cet affreux Moyen Âge'.[167] In 1869 he explained that he had recreated 'cette idée que le Moyen âge eut de lui ... son élan, son désir, son âme',[168] only to give more authority to the demonstration, effected in his later works, that in no way did the real Middle Ages measure up to the ideal one. Leconte de Lisle made use of the same stratagem. Although as a modern poet-historian he was bound to concern himself with the ideal past, he was morally obliged, as a republican, to give sinister reality pride of place. The dilemma was solved by using the 'ideal' Middle Ages to confound the 'real' one, made all the more hideous by contrast with it.[169] He sought the ideal face of the past in religion, rather than legend or art: in his Academy speech he mentioned 'les diverses conceptions religieuses dont l'humanité a vécu, et qui, toutes, ont été vraies à leur heure, puisqu'elles étaient les formes idéales de ses rêves et de ses espérances', These, he considered, should be the chief concern of poets desirous to 'rendre intellectuellement la vie au passé'.[170]

In his article on this Academy speech Ménard pointed out, reproach-fully, that his friend had in fact neglected the ideal aspect of medieval Christianity: 'Le sacerdoce, qui est l'élément diabolique des religions, l'empêche de voir le symbole, qui en est l'élément divin.'[171] However, Ménard himself, in the Preface to his *Poëmes*, had passed swiftly from the remark 'l'Humanité ne s'est jamais trompée, tous ses dogmes sont vrais, tous les dieux qu'elle a adorés sont réellement des types divins',[172]

---

[166] Letter to Flaubert, quoted by M. Ibrovac, *J-M. de Heredia*, 1923, p. 340.
[167] Cf. *supra*, p. 49.
[168] Michelet, *Histoire de France*, i (1879), 15.
[169] A device frequently employed by Taine (cf. *supra*, p. 71). Cf. also L. Gautier's defiant declaration that the real Middle Ages were more splendid even than the ideal: 'Le Charlemagne de l'Histoire est supérieur à celui de la Légende' (*Les Épopées françaises*, ii (1867), 599); 'Le Guillaume de l'Histoire est supérieur à celui de la Légende' (ibid. iii (1868), 522); 'La réalité est presque toujours supérieure à la fiction' (conclusion of *La Chevalerie*, 1884, p. 781).
[170] Leconte de Lisle, *Articles, préfaces, discours*, p. 209.
[171] *La Critique philosophique*, 1887, p. 318.
[172] Ménard, *Poëmes*, 2nd edn., 1863, p. v.

to consideration of how, in the Middle Ages, Christian ideals had been
translated into a highly unpleasant reality: 'Il prêche la douceur et le
pardon,' he said of the God worshipped in those days, 'et la terre, sous
son règne, se couvre de cachots, de gibets et de bûchers.'[173] Michelet
had pointed out this sinister discrepancy as early as 1833, when he
remarked of the clergy during the Albigensian Crusade: 'Ces hommes
de paix ne demandaient que mort et ruine, des paroles effroyables
sortaient de leur bouche. . . . Une soif horrible de sang semblait avoir
embrasé le leur.'[174] In 1846 this briefly glimpsed contradiction had
crystallized into a formula denouncing the Middle Ages as a whole:
'Le moyen âge posa une formule d'amour, et il n'aboutit qu'à la
haine';[175] and he returned to the theme in the following year: 'Je me
suis souvent demandé . . . comment la religion la plus douce dans son
principe, celle qui part de l'amour même, a-t-elle donc pu couvrir le
monde de cette vaste mer de sang?'[176]

Leconte de Lisle's medieval poems provide a dramatic illustration
of this paradox. Piety and ferocity mingle to create a powerfully
sinister effect. Holy hymns are wafted to heaven with the smoke from
the bonfires where heretics are roasting alive. 'Dieu de miséricorde, ô
justice, ô bonté', cries the abbot in 'L'Agonie d'un saint', remembering
this inferno which he helped to kindle, 'C'est vous qui m'échauffiez du
feu de votre zèle.'[177] Words of peace and love escape the lips of the
most sanguinary fanatics, at moments when their fury reaches its height.
'A l'oeuvre! Dieu le veut! à l'oeuvre! Alléluia!'[178] screams the monk at
the end of 'Hiéronymus', as he bounds on to the throne of the deposed
bishop, to prepare further onslaughts against the heretics. At the end of
'La Mort du moine' the captured monk, 'ce boucher tondu' who, 'Le
goupil d'une main et la torche de l'autre', has roamed through the
burning towns of Provence, 'le sang jusqu'aux genoux',[179] dies at the
hands of the heretics – having spewed forth a torrent of curses at them –
with 'un sourire de joie et de ravissement' on his lips:

> Et, dans un long soupir de sereine agonie,
> Il dit:
>   – Lumière! Amour! Paix! Chants délicieux!
> Salut! Emportez-moi, saints Anges, dans les Cieux![180]

[173] Ibid. p. xiii.   [174] Michelet, *Histoire de France,* ii. 556-7.
[175] Cf. *supra,* p. 49.   [176] Michelet, *Histoire de la Révolution française,* i. 33.
[177] *Poèmes barbares,* p. 322.   [178] *Poèmes tragiques,* p. 101.
[179] *Derniers Poèmes,* p. 37.   [180] Ibid. p. 40.

This is surely misinterpreted by Pierre Flottes, who cites it as proof that in later life Leconte de Lisle mellowed towards the Church of Rome: 'En ce monde adouci, il n'y a plus de place pour la haine. Dans la croisade des Albigeois, le moine catholique ne fait plus figure de tourmenteur; comme ses adversaires, il vit un rêve de foi; il meurt en pensant aux anges des cieux.'[181]

In 'Un Acte de charité' sincere Christian compassion ('Une grande pitié s'éveilla dans son âme')[182] impels the noblewoman to commit an act of atrocious cruelty. Hugo's otherwise similar tale (in *Le Rhin*) of the bishop Hatto, who herds a crowd of starving peasants into a barn and sets it on fire because he is too avaricious to feed them, lacks this element of sardonic irony.

Hugo's Torquemada, however, in the play written in 1869 and published in 1882, is inspired by the same atrocious compassion as that which burns in the breast of Leconte de Lisle's noblewoman. This was a considered choice on his creator's part: 'Les opinions des historiens', he wrote, 'sont partagées sur Torquemada. Pour les uns, c'est un sanguinaire, le bourreau par nature; pour les autres, c'est le visionnaire, le bourreau par pitié. Entre ces deux données, l'auteur a choisi celle qui lui a paru, au point de vue humain, la plus philosophique, et, au point de vue littéraire, la plus dramatique.'[183] Leconte de Lisle was very impressed by the work, though he objected that it violated historical truth:

Certes, en brûlant par milliers ses misérables victimes, le vrai Torquemada . . . ne pensait en aucune façon les mener à la béatitude céleste. Il tenait uniquement à les exterminer, en leur donnant sur la terre un avant-goût des flammes éternelles. Mais Victor Hugo a développé son étrange conception avec tant de verve, d'éloquence et de couleur, qu'il faut le remercier, au nom de la Poésie, d'avoir prêté cette charité terrible à cet insensé féroce qui puisait la haine de l'humanité dans l'imbécillité d'une foi monstrueuse.[184]

In spite of this pronouncement, Leconte de Lisle's medieval poems echo *Torquemada* here and there. 'L'Agonie d'un saint', published before the

---

[181] P. Flottes, *Leconte de Lisle, l'homme et l'oeuvre*, 1954, p. 124. Cf. I. Putter: 'His descriptions of the monks . . . show clearly enough his empathy for them. *La Mort du moine* ends in an ecstasy of religious passion, even though its subject is one of the very butchers he repeatedly condemns' (*The Pessimism of Leconte de Lisle*, 1954, p. 158).

[182] *Poèmes barbares*, p. 283.

[183] Hugo, *Os. cs.*, ed. J. Massin, xiv. 695 (Notes for a projected preface).

[184] Leconte de Lisle, *Articles, préfaces, discours*, p. 210.

play was written, may have influenced Hugo. Though the abbot in it is filled with overweening pride and hope of celestial recompense, rather than compassion for souls in danger of perdition, certain of his utterances resemble Torquemada's. In his work of extermination he was, he assures the Lord, 'dévoré de la soif de ton unique amour'.[185] Torquemada declares: 'En moi l'amour sublime/ Crie. . . .'[186] Stating 'J'ai purifié l'âme à Satan promise', the abbot relives his hour of triumph: 'Gloire au Christ! les bûchers luisent, flambeaux hurlants';[187] while Torquemada's favourite formula is 'le feu lave l'âme . . .![188] Brûler, c'est épurer',[189] and he too is roused to ecstasy at the thought of 'les bûchers sauveurs', crying: 'Gloire à Dieu! joie à tous! . . . Je couvrirai l'univers de bûchers.'[188] Leconte de Lisle's medieval poems published after *Torquemada* may in their turn have been influenced by it. Although the monk in 'Hiéronymus' (published before Hugo's play, in 1876) conforms to Leconte de Lisle's conception of the 'insensé féroce', crying:

> Que j'entende hurler les jeunes et les vieux . . .
> Et qu'ils meurent têtus, pour que tu les maudisses,
> Jésus! . . .,[190]

Pope Innocent III in 'Les Raisons du Saint-Père' (1890) tells the spectre of Christ that he is concerned only with the saving of souls:

> Vois! La nuit se dissipe à nos bûchers en flammes,
> La mauvaise moisson gît au tranchant de fer;
> Et mêlant l'espérance à la terreur des âmes,
> Nous leur montrons le Ciel en allumant l'Enfer . . .,[191]

transposing, and improving upon, Torquemada's statement:

> L'enfer dans le bûcher s'éteint et se dissipe;
> De sorte que la flamme envoie au ciel les morts,
> Et que, pour sauver l'âme, il faut brûler le corps.[192]

Finally, the exaltation of Torquemada, as he contemplates the *quemadero:*

> Autodafé! pardon, bonté, lumière, feu,
> Vie! éblouissement de la face de Dieu! . . .
> Le salut s'ouvre au fond des cieux . . .,[193]

---

[185] *Poèmes barbares*, p. 319.   [186] Hugo, *Torquemada*, Act 1, Sc. 6.
[187] *Poèmes barbares*, pp. 321-2.   [188] *Torquemada*, Act 1, Sc. 6.
[189] Ibid. Act 1, Sc. 7.   [190] *Poèmes tragiques*, p. 98.   [191] *Derniers Poèmes*, p. 45.
[192] *Torquemada*, Act 1, Sc. 7. Pierre Clarac points out, however, that Leconte de Lisle's Pope is in fact inspired by overweening pride rather than the 'cruelle charité' of his model, the Grand Inquisitor in Dostoevsky's *Brothers Karamazov*, a figure resembling Torquemada, whose desire is to 'donner le bonheur aux hommes' (*RLC*, vi (1926), pp. 512-17).
[193] *Torquemada*, Act 2, Sc. 5.

is equalled by that of the expiring monk's last words, at the end of 'La Mort du moine'.

So Leconte de Lisle, while believing that all religions had their hour of truth and reflect the noblest ideals of each civilization, is yet unable to regard Christianity with the reverence which he pays to the others. Its ideals are, in his eyes, purely sinister. Like Michelet, in fact, he detests Christianity because of its continuing vitality; for him, much of the horror of the Gothic novel still clings to it. And this horror is abundantly present in his scenes set in the days of medieval Christianity.

'Le Lévrier de Magnus' (1883), for instance — the tale of the evil Crusader whom retribution pursues in the form of a phantom hound, the ghost of one of his victims — is a Gothic tale full of Romantic elements. After a long career of crime in Saracen lands Magnus returns to his castle on the Rhine: 'Quand, comment et par où revint-il? On l'ignore.' His sinister hound — aglow with the familiar evil red 'lueur' — never leaves his side:

> L'ardeur du vaste feu brûle les dalles plates,
> Mais il n'en ressent rien, et, quoiqu'il soit tout noir,
> Il se revêt parfois de lueurs écarlates.[194]

The wind howls through the castle with its 'plainte sépulcrale'[194] in which can be heard the cackling of demons. He remembers his past exploits at the head of his 'troupeau carnassier'.[195] Confident that, in the hour of need, absolution could be bought for 'quelques sous d'or' from any 'clerc rapace ou vil moine',[196] he spread terror throughout the land, breaking one day into a convent and ravishing its abbess, Alix, who plunged a dagger into her heart and turned into the avenging hound, which, in the castle, transfixes him with 'Cet oeil féroce où flambe un reflet de l'Enfer'.[197] 'Dans son rêve sinistre à jamais enfermé', he listens to

> . . . le vent dans la tour écroulée
> Où le hibou hulule, et qu'il habite seul.[198]

He is visited by hideous nightmares:

> Quel sommeil! Plus heureux sur son grabat de sangle,
> Le misérable serf, harassé, maigre et nu,
> Meurtri par le collier de cuivre qui l'étrangle![198] —

---

[194] *Poèmes tragiques*, pp. 115-17.
[196] Ibid. p. 121.   [195] Ibid. p. 124.
[197] Ibid. p. 134.   [198] Ibid. pp. 136-7.

in which there appears the spectre of Alix with the dagger in her heart,
like the 'nonne sanglante' in Lewis's *Monk*. She commands him to
repent. He refuses, and sees the flames leaping in the fire:

> Une Griffe en jaillit, avide de sa proie,
> Saisit l'homme à la gorge irrésistiblement,
> Et rentre, au rire affreux de l'infernale Joie.

In a deafening peal of thunder and a blinding blaze of lightning,

> Le donjon, comme une nef qui sombre,
> Tressaille, se lézarde, et croule tout fumant.[199]

Leconte de Lisle's medieval poems supply the deficiency which Barbey
d'Aurevilly had lamented in Hugo's *Légende:* the absence of 'le prêtre . . .
le moine . . . le grand évêque oublié par Walter Scott lui-même . . . tout
le *personnel* de cette société si savamment hiérarchisée'.[200] His monks
think aloud, and at length, the bestial thoughts which he attributes to
them, ruminating upon past slaughter of heretics and future campaigns.
They too move in the atmosphere of the Gothic novel: the sequence
of poems devoted to them was called by Leconte de Lisle 'l'Épopée du
Moine'. The protagonist of each of these poems – 'L'Agonie d'un saint',
'Les Deux Glaives', 'Hiéronymus', 'La Mort du moine' and 'les Raisons
du Saint-Père' – is a Monk who, while sometimes possessing a precise
historical identity, also preserves much of the sinister, supernatural
anonymity of Lewis's Monk. Gone for ever is 'la paix du gothique
monastère',[201a] celebrated by Marchangy, by Musset in *Rolla,*[201b]
and by Montalembert, who marvelled in *Les Moines d'Occident* at
'cette affection mutuelle qui régnait entre les moines . . .'[202] ce pur
et profond bonheur qui régnait en eux et autour d'eux'.[203]

The old abbot Hiéronymus sits enthroned beneath 'les Saints étirés
dans les retraits de pierre', and the colossal effigy of 'un maigre
Christ'[204] – examples of Gothic art, like the figure of Christ on the
Cross in 'Les Deux Glaives' –, 'Fantôme douloureux, tout roide et
tout sanglant'[205] closely resembling those often described, with
infinite distaste, by Taine.[206] Flickering tapers cast 'des lueurs

---

[199] Ibid. p. 142. Cf. the end of Poe's *Fall of the House of Usher*.
[200] B. d'Aurevilly, *Les Poètes,* 1862, p. 42.
[201a] Marchangy, *La Gaule poétique,* ii (1813), 10.   [201b] Cf. *supra,* p. 11.
[202] Montalembert, *Les Moines d'Occident,* i, p. lxxxix.   [203] Cf. *supra,* p. 82.
[204] *Poèmes tragiques,* pp. 85-6.   [205] *Poèmes barbares,* p. 309.
[206] Cf. 'le Christ maigre du moyen âge, le misérable ver de terre déformé et
sanglant', *Histoire de la littérature anglaise,* i. 262.

funèbres' over the assembly. Before the abbot stands an errant monk returned to the fold: 'Un sourire furtif fait reluire ses dents.' Hiéronymus, the possessor of

> Dix mille manants, serfs de glèbe ou de métier,
> Plein droit de pendaison sur ces engeances viles,
> Droit d'anathème et droit d'interdit sur deux villes . . .,[204]

reprimands the monk for his desertion of the cloister in favour of 'la fange du siècle à qui l'Enfer est dû'.[207] He hurls passionate imprecations at him, telling him that 'penser est blasphème et vouloir est folie!', that 'la sainte Église a dit ce qui doit être su!', that his duty is to 'croire, obéir et se taire,/Ramper en gémissant la face contre terre', and that he is to be sealed up forthwith 'au fond de l'*In-pace*'.[208] But the monk refuses to submit: he reveals that a divine mission has been entrusted to him:

> L'extermination par Dieu même prescrite
> Du Kathare hérétique, impur, lâche, hypocrite,
> Et des peuples souillés par son attouchement,[209]

and that, furthermore, the better to carry out this task, he has been appointed by Pope Innocent III as Hiéronymus's successor.

'Les Deux Glaives' (1861) is a dramatic recreation of the penitent Emperor Henry IV's submission to Pope Gregory VII at Canossa, and of his miserable end twenty-nine years later, in poverty and solitude, cursing his ancient enemy, 'le grand Moine qui vit la force à ses genoux'.[210] This theme was of course extremely topical. Critics have remarked that the poet in his compassion for Henry's pitiable plight shows himself to be 'plus près de César que du Pape';[211] but the Pope here is possessed of a certain grandeur, and is by no means as odious a figure as Innocent III in the later poem 'Les Raisons du Saint-Père'.

In 'L'Agonie d'un saint,' published in the same year, an aged abbot on his deathbed, surrounded by his monks, a sinister 'troupeau d'ombre',[212] relives the Albigensian massacres, seeing in vision

> Ceux d'Alby, de Béziers, de Foix et de Toulouse,
> Que le fer pourfendit, que la flamme brûla . . .,

crying out once more the words with which he urged on the Crusaders:

> Je vous livre, ô guerriers, ces pourceaux et ces chiens,
> Pour que vous dépeciez leurs cadavres infâmes![213]

---

[207] *Poèmes tragiques*, pp. 85-6.   [208] Ibid. pp. 87-9.   [209] Ibid. pp. 97-8.
[210] *Poèmes barbares*, p. 314.
[211] P. Flottes, op. cit. p. 85. See also J. Vianey, *Les 'Poèmes barbares' de Leconte de Lisle*, Malfère, 1933, p. 105.   [212] *Poèmes barbares*, p. 318.   [213] Ibid. pp. 321-2.

He is surely Saint Dominic (of whom Voltaire wrote in his *Essai sur les moeurs:* 'Plusieurs historiens assurent que saint Dominique était à la tête des troupes, un crucifix de fer à la main, encourageant les croisés au carnage',[214] and Leconte de Lisle himself, in his *Histoire populaire du Christianisme* (1871): 'Saint Dominique se distingua particulièrement dans cette épouvantable boucherie'),[215] rather than, as Vianey suggests,[216] the papel legate Arnaud Amaury, who was of course never canonized. Michelet said of Dominic in 1833: 'Personne n'eut plus que lui le don des larmes', quoting the deposition of a monk who had often seen him 'baigné de larmes, qui lui courait en si grande abondance sur le visage, *qu'une goutte n'attendait pas l'autre*'.[217] Leconte de Lisle's saint cries out, imploring Christ to admit him into Paradise, 'Voyez mes yeux creusés du torrent de mes pleurs.'[218] History records, however, that Dominic died at midday, in one of his monasteries in Bologna, whereas Leconte de Lisle, faithful to the tradition of the Gothic novel, makes him die at midnight, during a raging tempest:

> Minuit sonna, lugubre, et jeta dans le vent,
> Ses douze tintements à travers les ogives;
> Le bruit sourd de la foudre ébranla le couvent,
> Et l'éclair fit blanchir les tourelles massives.[219]

The sudden doubt which overwhelms the dying saint, as the spectral figures of his victims rise before him:

> Seigneur, Seigneur! parlez, êtes-vous satisfait?
> La sueur de l'angoisse à mon front glacé fume.
> Ô Maître, tendez-moi la main si j'ai bien fait,
> Car une mer de sang m'entoure et me consume . . .[220]

is strongly reminiscent of the remorse which assails Michelet's Pope Innocent III, in the 1833 *Histoire de France,* when he falls a prey to 'cette angoisse du doute'[221] by which the medieval soul is constantly beset: 'Il lui arrivait par-dessus sa victoire un cri confus de sang versé, une plainte à voix basse, douce, modeste, et d'autant plus terrible.'[222] But the voice of Christ, unmoved by his supplications, rings out to denounce him:

> . . . Loin de moi, fou furieux! Va-t-en,
> Ô moine tout gorgé de chair et de sang d'homme!

[214] Chapter LXII.   [215] *Histoire populaire du christianisme,* 1871, p. 107.
[216] J. Vianey, op. cit. pp. 102-3.
[217] Michelet, *Histoire de France,* ii. 478.
[218] *Poèmes barbares,* p. 323.   [219] Ibid. p. 319.
[220] Ibid. p. 321.   [221] Michelet, *H.F.* ii. 638.   [222] Ibid. p. 520.

'Qui t'a dit de tuer en mon nom, assassin?' it asks, and cries: 'Arrière! Va hurler dans l'abîme éternel!' 'Je vois flamber l'Enfer, j'entends rire le Diable,/Et je meurs!' shrieks the abbot:

> Ce disant, convulsif et hagard,
> L'Abbé se renversa dans un rire effroyable.[223]

Leconte de Lisle's Innocent III, in 'Les Raisons du Saint-Père', published thirty years later (1890), is a figure resembling Michelet's revised version of the Pope (in his 1855 Introduction to the *Renaissance*), who, far from feeling remorse, recalls with gloating satisfaction the extermination of the Albigensians: 'J'ai trouvé aux archives', writes Michelet, 'deux lettres d'Innocent III, écrites bien près de sa mort, où il accepte, dans les termes d'un enthousiasme frénétique, le poids de tout le sang versé. Voilà le véritable Innocent, et non l'Innocent douteux et pleureur que moi-même, comme les autres, j'avais fait d'après ce roman [i.e. the *Chanson de la Croisade contre les Albigeois*].[224] The unwavering resolve of Leconte de Lisle's Innocent is in accord with this conception: he sternly upbraids the spectre of Christ, who has appeared in mute reproach before him — 'Laisse agir notre Foi, ne nous interromps plus' —, until at length he fades away. The Pope even sneers at Christ's Passion (which Michelet had in 1833 described with such tender eloquence, identifying with it medieval faith for ever trembling on the verge of doubt) — '. . . tu doutas, Jésus, de ton oeuvre sacrée', he reminds him, and scornfully asks him why he rejected Satan's tempting offer: 'Que ne revêtais-tu la pourpre des Césars?' The Pope himself, with his Church Militant, has taken it up with alacrity, and, in the name of Christ, has let loose 'la horde carnassière' of Crusaders to conquer the Orient: 'Et tu nous appartiens, Jésus!':

> Dans l'anathème et dans les clameurs du carnage,
> Quand nos Voix s'entendront, c'est Toi qui parleras![225]

Other figures in Leconte de Lisle's medieval world are his perfidious and cruel Cid, appearing with bloodstained hands, in each of the three

---

[223] *Poèmes barbares*, pp. 322-3. Cf. Chateaubriand's picture of the dying Trappist, in *Le Génie du Christianisme:* 'Quel spectacle que celui du Trappiste mourant! quelle sorte de haute philosophie! . . . Étendu sur un peu de paille et de cendre . . . ses frères rangés en silence autour de lui, il les appelle à la vertu, tandis que la cloche funèbre sonne ses dernières agonies' (Part 4, Bk. 3, Ch. 6).

[224] Michelet, *Renaissance,* p. 153.

[225] *Derniers Poèmes*, pp. 44-6. Again, the interpretation of Flottes, who sees in this poem evidence that Leconte de Lisle was beginning in spite of himself to sympathize with the Papacy (Flottes, op. cit., p. 124), is surely a mistaken one.

poems devoted to him in striking contrast with Hugo's model of honour
and probity;[226] and his Pedro the Cruel, to whom Mérimée, in his
Histoire de Don Pèdre Ier (one of his sources) always gives 'the benefit
of the doubt',[227] but whom the poet, with a selection of horrific detail
from several sources, embellished with his own imagination, portrays as
a sanguinary monster.[228]

Finally, there is 'Les Siècles maudits' (1883),[229] beginning

> Hideux siècles de foi, de lèpre et de famine,

and ending with a solemn curse:

> Dans chacune de vos exécrables minutes,
> Ô siècles d'égorgeurs, de lâches et de brutes,
> Honte de ce vieux globe et de l'humanité,
> Maudits, soyez maudits, et pour l'éternité!

It is a compendium of all that every nineteenth-century enemy of the
Middle Ages found most sinister in them: the lurid 'lueur' reappears as
'le reflet sanglant des bûchers'; the witches, werewolves, and 'feux
blêmes' flickering in the cemetery derive from Hugo's *Ballades,*[230a] the
Jewish merchant, who 'pour mieux suer son or cuit sur la braise ardente',
from *Ivanhoe*[230b] (a favourite novel of Leconte de Lisle's); the 'noble
sire aux aguets sur sa tour', waiting to pounce upon hapless merchants
below, from a multitude of republican history books; the carrion-crow-
infested gibbets with their corpses swaying in the wind, from Villon;
and the Albigensians 'scellés vifs dans les murs', as 'la Goule Romaine',
'ce vampire ivre de sang humain', presides over 'l'holocauste fumant sur
son autel de fer', from Leconte de Lisle's own medieval inferno.

C. *Leconte de Lisle's disciples: Bernard, Renaud, Lefèvre*

Republican allegiances required that on the infrequent occasions
when they chose the Middle Ages as a setting for their poems, minor
Parnassians should deal with them as harshly as their master, Leconte
de Lisle.

---

[226] For an account of nineteenth-century opposition to the Cid's Romantic image
see Fairlie, op. cit. pp. 304-6.

[227] A recent biographer of Pedro finds Mérimée's indulgence towards the tyrant
excessive, and attributes it to reluctance on his part to blacken unduly a king
of Castile, in a work dedicated to the Countess Montijo (F. Piétri, *Pierre le
Cruel,* Plon, 1961, pp. 229-30).

[228] For a definitive analysis of these two groups of poems see Fairlie, op. cit.
Chs. 8 and 9.

[229] *Poèmes tragiques,* pp. 59-60.   [230a] Cf. *supra,* p. 19.   [230b] Chapter 6.

Thalès Bernard, as we have seen, never lost an occasion to heap detraction on the Middle Ages. He did this in verse as well as prose: 'Élisabeth Bathory', for instance (*Poésies mystiques,* 1858) tells the story, transposed into a medieval setting, of a vampiric Hungarian noblewoman who tries to retain her youth by bathing in the blood of countless sacrificial victims from the neighbouring peasantry.[231] For their part in her crimes, her servants are all burnt at the stake, but she is merely imprisoned, because, explains the King:

> . . . on ne peut punir de même
> La noble dame et le vilain.[232]

Yet Bernard at the same time continues to celebrate in his verse the Romantic Middle Ages of the 1820s and 30s. In the same collection, he sings a hymn of praise to 'le moyen âge ardent, pittoresque, inspiré';[233] and ten years later, he is still assuring his readers: 'Devant le moyen âge, en mon coeur, je m'incline',[234] and exclaiming 'Rends-moi cette époque aux couleurs naïves',[235] while producing, side by side with these effusions, experimental samples of republican verse. This curious incongruity is most apparent in his 'Paysage féodal' (1868), which begins in the orthodox Romantic manner:

> Hier tout était grand, l'art comme la nature,
> L'Église au fin clocher, fière de sa structure.

Republican sentiment, however, soon gets the better of Bernard, and a sinister shadow falls over the bright scene, where, as silver plumes and golden banners fluttered in the breeze –

> . . . les coursiers hardis, toujours caracolant,
> Écrasaient çà et là quelque flâneur trop lent.

He ends in an explosion of fury:

> . . . pendant que partout, se gorgeant de rapines,
> Les châteaux crénelés dominaient les collines,
> Et que leurs habitants, sombres oiseaux de nuit,
> Passaient du vol au meurtre et de la table au lit,
> Que faisait donc le peuple? Il vivait dans sa bauge,
> Rongeant quelques débris comme un porc à son auge,
> N'ayant pour vêtement qu'un sordide haillon,
> Et s'il voulait parler: le fouet et le bâillon![236]

---

[231] Countess Bathory was brought to trial in 1611. See V. Penrose, *Erzsébet Báthory,* Mercure de France, 1962.

[232] T. Bernard, *Poésies mystiques,* 1858, p. 79.

[233] Ibid. p. 239.

[234] T. Bernard, *Mélodies pastorales,* septième livraison, 1869, p. 7.

[235] Ibid., cinquième livraison, 1868, p. 3.

[236] *Mélodies pastorales,* cinquième livraison, 1868, p. 4.

Armand Renaud's *Les Poèmes de l'amour* (1860) is an early example of a sequence of historical episodes, by a future Parnassian. The medieval section includes 'La Lépreuse', which tells of a 'seigneur Raymon, beau comte à l'âme affreuse',[237] adored by a wretched girl who is doubly outcast from feudal society as she is both Jewish and a leper. He employs her to murder a usurer who is pursuing him, and ignores her thereafter. Driven insane, she is pronounced a witch and condemned to death:

> L'évêque condamna la lépreuse à la flamme.
> Raymon, tout en brocart, vint pour la voir brûler . . .,[238]

whereupon she drags him into the fire for the flames to engulf them both.

André Lefèvre's republican indignation breaks out here and there in his fairy-tale 'Les Aventures de Ramon et de la Vierge aux yeux bleus' (1864). The land in which this story of ideal love takes place is — in spite of the holy fountains and magic mirrors to be found there — not an altogether enchanted one. The knight-errant hero's early life is briefly sketched:

> Il grandit au milieu des discordes civiles,
> Des meurtres, des viols de femmes et de villes . . .,[239]

and when he hears mysterious sobbing as he rides through the forest, the narrator explores, in a long digression, the possibilities of its source:

> Peut-être il est trop tard! Peut-être dans sa tour
> Le ravisseur déjà cache sa prisonnière. . . .
> Ordinaire aventure en cet âge où la règle
> Sous la force pliait, où l'ombre du donjon
> Dévorait à ses pieds la plaine. . . .[240]

In their philosophical and reflective poems these poets were addicted to imagery coloured by the republican view of the Middle Ages. Claudius Popelin, in a sonnet dedicated to Sainte-Beuve, declares that he shelters under the critic's illustrious name as

> Dans la sinistre nuit de l'âge féodal,
> Contre le roc altier que le donjon domine
> On voit Jacques Bonhomme appuyer sa chaumine.[241]

Renaud's 'Le Pauvre Pâtre' is a lengthy allegory illustrating the plight of poets deserted by their Muse, with a tale of a serf infatuated with his

[237] A. Renaud, *Les Poèmes de l'amour,* 1860, p. 151.
[238] *Les Poèmes de l'amour,* p. 153.
[239] A. Lefèvre, *La Lyre intime,* 1864, p. 45.   [240] Ibid. p. 53.
[241] C. Popelin, *Poésies complètes,* 1889, p. 284.

lord's daughter, who cruelly scorns him and makes his life unendurable:

> En vain ses compagnons, ses égaux en misère,
> Lui parlaient-ils d'amour, de danses dans les champs.[242]

Ricard laments in 1866 that the weary days of the Second Empire pass by

> Comme un morne troupeau de moines, qu'engloutit
> Le mystère béant des corridors gothiques.[243]

D. *Coppée and Mendès: disciples of both Hugo and Leconte de Lisle*

A few of the minor Parnassians who wrote historical verse in emulation of Leconte de Lisle could not bring themselves to depict a Middle Ages as dark and savage as his. They were drawn in spite of themselves towards Hugo's world, in which universal barbarism is relieved by magnanimous gestures and the presence of saintly avengers. But they were unable to achieve Hugo's grandiose effects, and their epic fragments lack both his and Leconte de Lisle's power, falling into bathos and sentimentality.

François Coppée and Catulle Mendès both produced samples of this hybrid and, more often than not, ludicrous verse. Coppée's 'Le Justicier' is a diligent attempt to create a wholly sombre Middle Ages. A sinister (though upright and on the side of republican justice) Leconte de Lisle-ian monk confronts the resurrected corpse of a sinister Hugolian baron, the 'très-haut et très-puissant Gottlob, dit *le Brutal*', who

> Après être allé voir pendre trois paysans . . .
> Mourut, les bras en croix et l'hostie à la lèvre.

His life has been devoted to persecution of his vassals:

> Vêtu de fer, ganté de fer, masqué de fer,
> Il arrivait, suivi de ses piquiers avides,
> Et d'un geste faisait garnir les gibets vides.
> Les vassaux par le fer, la corde ou le bâton
> Mouraient . . .
> Impôt toujours, et, quand on refusait, carnage.[244]

---

[242] A. Renaud, *Les Poèmes de l'amour,* 1860, p. 224.
[243] L-X. de Ricard, *Ciel, rue et foyer,* 1866, p. 46.
[244] Coppée, *Poésies, 1864-1869,* 1873, pp. 74-6.

The corpse on its bier, watched over by the monk, suddenly comes to life. The monk sermonizes it, enjoining it to profit by this reprieve and repent:

> . . . je vois des vassaux en pleurs, des champs en friches
> Et des pendus bercés par le vent des forêts[245]

he tells the baron, and goes on to speak, in the accents of Leconte de Lisle's monks, of 'le joyeux crépitement des flammes'[246] awaiting him in Hell. But Gottlob refuses to repent: with 'un rire atroce'[247] he commands the monk to be silent, and, 'haletant d'une horrible folie',[248] he is about to seize a weapon, when the monk, 'ses yeux creux et brillants comme un foyer de forge',[248] leaps upon him and strangles him. Coppée does not attempt to reproduce savagery on this scale in his later *Récits épiques* (1878). He begins them in the style of Leconte de Lisle, loses courage, and ends with gratuitous miracles. In 'Le Liseron' marauding soldiers, like those in 'Le Lévrier de Magnus', are on the point of sacking a convent, when their leader, seeing the nuns at prayer, is suddenly 'saisi par un émoi qu'il n'avait jamais eu',[249] and turns away filled with shame. Mendès's *Contes épiques* (1872) are confections similar to Coppée's. 'Tu mens! je suis damné!'[250] cries the corpse of a bishop in 'Les Deux Évêques', as it rises from its catafalque to interrupt the oration of its successor, who has just assured the congregation that their dead master is now enjoying his just reward in heaven. 'Le Landgrave de Fer' tells of a change of heart as miraculous as that in 'Le Liseron'. Overhearing one of his vassals describe him as an object of universal terror and loathing:

> Seigneur des champs féconds, de qui les mains avides
> Font que le manant pleure auprès des granges vides . . .[251]

the landgrave is moved to sudden repentance, pardons three peasants due to be hanged, revokes all the taxes he has imposed, and frees some merchants he was about to despoil.

E. *The ideal Catholic Middle Ages:*
'Jours chrétiens et bénis, si chers aux coeurs pieux . . .'

These sporadic attempts to reproduce the dark Middle Ages of Hugo and Leconte de Lisle are of negligible importance; but more insignificant

[245] Ibid. p. 81.   [246] Coppée, *Poésies, 1864-1869*, p. 81.   [247] Ibid. p. 85.
[248] Ibid. p. 88.   [249] Coppée, *Poésies, 1874-1878*, p. 118.
[250] Mendès, *Contes epiques*, 1872, p. 52.   [251] *Contes épiques*, p. 48.

still was the ideal Middle Ages of a few contemporary Catholic versifiers. An insipid dilution of the ideal Romantic Middle Ages, it is to be found in such works as Auguste and Léon Le Pas' *Légendes des litanies de la sainte Vierge* (1860), Charles Fournel's *Légendes dorées* (1862) (which provoked sharp comment from the critic of the *Revue des deux mondes:* 'Reproduire jusqu'aux *gaucheries gothiques* des oeuvres du moyen âge, c'est un peu trop d'exactitude dans l'imitation'),[252] and Joseph Boulmier's *Rimes chevaleresques* (1868). Auguste and Léon Le Pas exclaim:

> Jours chrétiens et bénis, si chers aux coeurs pieux . . .
> Âge d'or dont l'Église a consacré la gloire,
> Vous existez toujours pour ceux qui savent croire!
> Votre divin soleil pour nous n'est pas couché,[253]

and tell tales such as 'La Trêve du Sauveur' – the reverse of 'Le Lévrier de Magnus' –, in which a repentant bandit expiates the crimes he committed as a Crusader. Their collection of edifying legends celebrates the contemplative Middle Ages, while Boulmier concentrates on the martial glories of chivalry in his *Rimes chevaleresques*. He begins with a prelude, 'Le Moyen Âge':

> J'aime le moyen âge et sa robuste allure . . .
> Sa taille germanique et ses sourcils heurtés,
> Avec ses yeux de moine aux perçantes clartés . . .
> Maintes fois, spectre aimé, sa douce remembrance
> A mon chevet brûlant vient se faire entrevoir,[254]

repeating sentiments already expressed by him in 'Le Ménestrel' (1862):

> Il est une contrée où surtout je voyage,
> Un pays idéal, divin: le moyen âge – [255]

and proceeds with a series of poems which could have been dictated by Louis Veuillot himself. 'La Bataille de Poitiers' vibrates with anti-English sentiment, calling down curses upon the 'moderne Carthage'.[256] In 'Dieu le Veut' Pope Urbain II commands the French to exterminate 'les pourceaux d'Islam':[257]

> En avant donc, chrétiens! là-bas! à la rescousse! . . .
> En avant! Dieu le veut! sus aux païens infâmes![258]

---

[252] *RDM,* 1 May 1863, p. 249.
[253] A. & L. Le Pas, *Légendes des litanies de la sainte Vierge,* 1860, p. 62.
[254] J. Boulmier, *Rimes chevaleresques,* 1868, pp. 7-8.
[255] *Revue française,* 15 Oct. 1862, p. 104.
[256] *Rimes chevaleresques,* p. 64.
[257] *Rimes chevaleresques,* p. 16.   [258] Ibid. p. 19.

and they reply with one voice: 'DIEU LE VEUT!'[259] Inspired by the events of 1862, this poem, no less than the Le Pas' 'La Trêve du Sauveur', provides the exact antithesis of Leconte de Lisle's poems on the Crusades.

F. *The ferocious and macabre Catholic Middle Ages:*
Barbey d'Aurevilly and Baudelaire

There was nothing new in this persistent celebration of the Romantic Age of Faith, if one excepts the echo of Veuillot's crusading voice. The quality of Barbey d'Aurevilly's and Baudelaire's Catholic nostalgia for the Middle Ages is far more distinctive. They dare to uphold what others deplore — in Barbey d'Aurevilly's case, medieval ferocity and blood-lust, and in that of Baudelaire, medieval delectation in the macabre. The 'énorme' rather than the 'délicat' Middle Ages holds them in thrall. They take pleasure in forcing it upon the attention of the bourgeois society they despise, for nothing could be farther removed from that grey world than the magnificent enormities of medieval life and art: 'Les charmes de l'horreur n'enivrent que les forts'[260] proclaimed Baudelaire in his poem 'Danse macabre'; and we have already heard some of the emphatic praise which Barbey never tired of bestowing on 'ces époques, où la vie, cette chose inférieure pour Guizot, du moins existait!'[261]

Barbey, in his critical articles, often paused to lose himself in enraptured contemplation of the old order, which he insisted, in defiance of liberal historians, had nothing whatsoever in common with modern society: 'Le père votait seul. . . . On était épluché pour fait d'hérésie. On communiait.'[262] He was at moments tempted to glorify the Middle Ages in a work of the imagination, and did in fact write one poem about the Cid. This retelling of the legend in which the Cid gives a leprous beggar his hand to kiss was inspired by the *Légende des siècles,* and depicts a Campéador more splendid even than Hugo's — a 'radieux passant' illumined by the rays of the setting sun:

Il n'était qu'or partout du cimier aux talons.[263]

Barbey d'Aurevilly's most cherished project, however, was an historical novel on the tenth century, in which the ferocious Norman pirates whose blood he liked to imagine running in his veins and preserving him from bourgeois decrepitude, would be seen in action: 'Une épopée, *par la*

[259] Ibid. p. 22.   [260] Baudelaire, *Os. cs.* 1961, p. 93.   [261] Cf. *supra,* p. 85.
[262] B. d'Aurevilly, *De l'histoire*, 1905, p. 240 (1857).
[263] B. d'Aurevilly, *Disjecta membra*, 1925, ii. 23-4.

Splendeur de Dieu, comme disait . . . le Conquérant!',[264] he described this work in a letter of 1855. Four years later he advised Hugo to abandon *La Fin de Satan* and write instead 'quelque violente épopée du Xe siècle'.[265] His own project was never realised, although he amassed a quantity of documentation for it.[266] The Merovingian world – 'cette société effroyablement grandiose, qui n'épouvante que les faibles imaginations de son éloquente barbarie'[267] – also inflamed his imagination. He saw in 'le caractère de ces premières races, auquel on préfère les sénilités de la sienne', 'une grandeur si *grande* qu'elle va jusqu'à l'énormité toujours'.[268] Thierry's *Récits des temps mérovingiens* failed to satisfy him: he considered that they lacked 'la coloration énergique qu'on est en droit d'attendre d'un homme qui a traversé ce fleuve rouge des Chroniques et qui doit plaquer du feu et du sang sur tout ce qu'il touche!'[269] He attributed this to the fact that they were written for the timorous readers of the *Revue des deux mondes* – a publication for which he had nothing but contempt, calling it on one occasion 'ce mancenillier de l'ennui'[270] –, who would have quailed at 'des détails par trop prolongés de brutalité et d'horreur'.[269]

Cassagne states that Baudelaire was, like the Goncourts, totally in-different towards the Middle Ages.[271] This is not so, of course: it is belied by his advocacy of 'les charmes de l'horreur' embodied in the 'danse macabre' (which will be discussed later in the chapter), and by the fact that on one occasion, moved by the same awe which medieval men and their 'passions colossales'[272] inspired in Barbey d'Aurevilly, he deserted the modern world in *Les Fleurs du Mal* to regale his readers with an episode from medieval history. This was in the poem 'Châtiment de l'Orgueil' (inspired by a few lines from Michelet's *Histoire de France*),[273] in which the Middle Ages are spoken of with the utmost reverence:

> En ces temps merveilleux où la Théologie
> Fleurit avec le plus de séve et d'énergie,[274]

---

[264] B. d'Aurevilly, *Lettres à Trébutien,* iii. 303.

[265] B. d'Aurevilly, *Les Poètes,* 1862, p. 41.

[266] See *Disjecta membra,* i. 167-71, and ii. 211-15.

[267] *Sensations d'histoire,* p. 371 (1861).   [268] Ibid. p. 373.

[269] B. d'Aurevilly, *Les Historiens politiques et littéraires,* 1861, pp. 133-4.

[270] B. d'Aurevilly, *Les Philosophes et les écrivains religieux,* 1887, p. 238 (1877).

[271] A. Cassagne, *La Théorie de l'art pour l'art en France,* 1906, p. 123.

[272] B. d'Aurevilly, *De l'histoire,* p. 206 (1855).

[273] See A-M. Schmidt, 'Sur une source inconnue de Baudelaire', *NRF,* 1 Apr. 1937, pp. 602-4.

[274] Baudelaire, *Os. cs.* p. 19.

the poem begins, and goes on to tell of an extraordinary outburst of
satanic pride, on the part of a theologian, and the no less extraordinary divine retribution which followed it. Michelet gives a laconic
account of the incident: Simon de Tournai, intoxicated all of a sudden
by his powers of disputation, cries out: ' "Ô petit Jésus, petit Jésus,
comme j'ai élevé ta loi! Si je voulais, je pourrais encore mieux la
rabaisser', and forthwith loses his reason' 'Dieu le punit: il devint si
idiot que son fils eut peine à lui faire rapprendre le Pater.'[275] Baudelaire elaborates considerably upon this, magnifying both the enormity
of the blasphemy –

> "Jésus, petit Jésus! je t'ai poussé bien haut!
> Mais, si j'avais voulu t'attaquer au défaut
> De l'armure, ta honte égalerait ta gloire,
> Et tu ne serais plus qu'un foetus dérisoire!'[275] –

and the enormity of the act of God which strikes down the blasphemer:
the pitiable state into which he falls is described in twelve lines, forming
a series of statements both factual and figurative, which succeed each
other with terrible gravity.

So two Catholic Middle Ages – the one a shining example designed
to edify the reader, and the other (anticipating the dark Middle Ages
of the Symbolists) a horrific world designed to shatter his bourgeois
complacency – co-existed with the republican one, whose chief purpose was to arouse in him disgust and moral indignation.

G. *The ideal Republican Middle Ages:*
Roland, Joan of Arc, Villon, and King Arthur's court

There was also an ideal republican Middle Ages, which served to give
moral inspiration. Its creators, though writers of far greater repute than
those responsible for its Catholic counterpart – Boulmier and his companions in obscurity – relied no less than they did on the trappings of
an outworn Romanticism. Guiding spirits in this ideal universe were the
various medieval figures whom the republicans exempted from blame,
and indeed claimed as heroes fighting for their cause – and frequently
against the Second Empire. We have already spoken of them in our
discussion of attitudes towards medieval literature in Chapter 4. They
were Roland, Joan of Arc, Villon and the heroes of Arthurian legend.

---

[275] Michelet, *Histoire de France,* ii. 396.
[276] Baudelaire, *Os. cs.* pp. 19-20.

It was in 1870 that Roland and Joan of Arc came into their own —
as we shall see in the next chapter — but the former already enjoyed
considerable popularity in the 1860s. In 1864 he was the subject of an
opera — Mermet's *Roland a Roncevaux,* in which he was shown torn
between his love for 'la belle Aude' and his duty to the Emperor.
Despite the anachronistic appearance of the hero, which disturbed
several critics (e.g. Henri Blaze de Bury in the *Revue des deux mondes:*
'Pourquoi ces cheveux coupés court, cette moustache et cette barbiche
de sous-officier? . . . ce n'est plus Roland, c'est un zouave de l'empereur
Charlemagne'),[277] the work was a great success. Encouraged by the
increasing popularity of the *Chanson de Roland* at this time, both
among critics and the general public, several poets tried their hand at
producing fragments of a modern *Roland.* The results were almost
invariably disastrous.

Maxime Du Camp, an ardent republican and enemy of the Middle
Ages, campaigned in the Preface to his *Les Chants modernes* (1855)
against the use of the past — 'le fatras des choses éteintes'[278] — as
literary material; but he made an exception in the case of Roland. His
collection of verse *Les Convictions* (1858) contains a poem 'Le Cor
d'ivoire' in which the dying Roland throws his horn into the air. It
vanishes in the sky; and a rhapsody to Progress ensues, as the poet asks
where the horn is now:

> Est-il caché sous les broussailles?
> Le roc l'a-t-il dans ses entrailles?[279]

He receives the reply that it is buried at the spot where it fell, but that
one day a valiant man will disinter it and it will sound again, announcing deliverance from servitude and the advent of a better world. No less
absurd than this were Banville's two poems on the Roland theme, 'La
Belle Aude' (dated 1860) and 'Roland' (dated 1863), both published
in *Les Exilés* (1867). In 'La Belle Aude' he follows fairly closely Vitet's
1852 translation of the *Chanson de Roland,* which furnishes him with
many whole lines — 'Morte à toujours! Dieu lui fasse merci' etc. — oddly
at variance with Hugolian turns of phrase ('C'est bien le doigt farouche
de la mort') and adventitious ornament contributed by Banville himself

---

[277] *RDM,* 15 Oct. 1864, p. 1005.
[278] *Les Chants modernes,* 1855, p. 39.
[279] M. Du Camp, *Les Convictions,* 1858, p. 89.

('Ses longs cheveux, tandis qu'elle s'endort,/Tombent pareils à des branches de saule.').[280] 'Roland' begins in the style of Vigny's 'Le Cor':

> Roncevaux! Roncevaux! que te faut-il encor?
> Il s'est éteint l'appel désespéré du cor . . .,[281]

proceeds with a line taken this time from Génin's translation ('Hauts sont les puys et longs et ténébreux'),[281] and ends in entirely Hugolian style, with a description of bloodshed at Roncevaux reminiscent of the fight between Roland and the bandits in 'Le Petit Roi de Galice', and a dénouement — the descent of Saint Michael, who wipes the blood from Roland's sword so that he can continue the fight — which derives from the end of 'Ratbert'. Albert Glatigny's 'La Mort de Roland' (in *Les Flèches d'or*, 1864) is an exercise in the decasyllabic metre. Its style, though more harmonious than Banville's, also wavers uneasily between the archaic ('Car il sent bien que son temps est fini') and the Romantic ('La Mort livide emplit le val fumant')[282]

While many medieval figures were limited in their appeal (Abelard, for instance, an exclusively republican hero), Joan of Arc (like Roland) received acclaim from both royalists — such as Louis de Carné, who declared in his *Les Fondateurs de l'unité française* (1856): 'Jeanne en effet aimait le roi avec l'exaltation d'une Vendéenne'[283] — and republicans, who insisted on spelling her name without the noble *particule*. Energetic action was taken, by republicans in particular, during the Empire to enlist her in their cause. For Michelet, she was 'l'Évangile héroïque du peuple, la prophétie vivante de la Révolution';[284] for Henri Martin, 'La fille des Gaules . . .[285] le Messie de la nationalité et l'âme même de la France'.[286] The Comtesse d'Agoult (Daniel Stern), whose salon was a meeting-place for opposition writers and politicians, published in 1857 her *Jeanne Darc*, inspired by Michelet and Martin — and one in a long series of dramatic works of indifferent merit written on this theme during the nineteenth century. Rejected by the Porte-Saint-Martin theatre as insufficiently spectacular, it was performed in translation at Turin in 1860, and received tempestuous applause from an audience who saw the heroine as 'le Garibaldi de la France'.[287]

---

[280] Banville, *Les Exilés. Les Princesses*, 1890, p. 152.
[281] Ibid. p. 37.   [282] Glatigny, *Poésies*, 1870, p. 188.
[283] L. de Carné, *Les Fondateurs de l'unité française*, Didier, 1856, i. 440.
[284] Michelet, *Renaissance*, p. 83.   [285] H. Martin, *Jeanne Darc*, 1857, p. 281.
[286] Ibid. p. 3.
[287] See D. Stern, *Florence et Turin*, 1862, p. xxvi; and J. Vier, *La Comtesse d'Agoult et son temps*, iv (1961), 138-41.

Another republican hero was Villon, in whom the first generation of Romantics (with the exception of Gautier and Nerval) took little interest,[288] but who enjoyed some measure of popularity after 1850. Paul Lacroix's 1854 edition of his works — the first since that of Prompsault (1832) — was followed by Jannet's edition in 1867: and the first biography and study of the poet (Campaux's Sorbonne thesis) came out in 1859. It was the custom of all critics, in speaking of Villon, to set him in opposition to Charles d'Orléans and praise one poet at the expense of the other.[289] Villemain was severe upon Villon — 'un homme . . . dont la vie fut misérable, déshonorée, et dont l'imagination fut abaissée souvent à ce qu'il y a de plus vil'[290] — but commended the work of Charles d'Orléans, with its 'bon goût d'aristocratie chevaleresque'.[291] Nisard, on the other hand, dismissed Charles d'Orléans as 'un esprit agréable occupé de galanterie',[292] and extolled Villon as 'un enfant du peuple, né poète, qui lit dans son coeur, et qui tire ses images des fortes impressions qu'il reçoit de son temps'.[293] These preferences were dictated surely by political allegiances rather than the aesthetic considerations suggested by Edelman, who interprets disparagement of Charles d'Orléans either as 'une revanche contre les fadeurs du néo-classicisme . . . ou du genre troubadour',[294] or (in Nisard's case) as a classicist's support for Boileau's judgement that Villon is the only medieval poet worthy of mention.[295] Villon was the idol of the republicans. His 'Ballade des pendus' inspired an important feature of their Middle Ages: descriptions of gibbets with decomposing corpses swaying in the wind (e.g. in Hugo's 'Montfaucon'[296] and Leconte de Lisle's 'Les

---

[288] See L. Cons, *État présent des études sur Villon,* 1936, p. 48; and N. Edelman, *RHLF* xliii (1936), p. 329.

[289] See N. Edelman, 'La Vogue de Villon en France de 1828 à 1873', *RHLF* xliii (1936).

[290] Villemain, *Tableau de la littérature du moyen âge,* revised edn., 1855, ii. 241.

[291] Ibid. p. 202.

[292] D. Nisard, *Histoire littéraire de la France,* i (1844), 155.

[293] Ibid. p. 160. Cf. A. Campaux, *François Villon,* 1859, pp. 306, 310.

[294] Edelman, op. cit. p. 322.

[295] Ibid. pp. 331-2.

[296] Although most of Hugo's description of Montfaucon derives from Sauval (cf. Berret, op. cit., pp. 68-9; and Edelman, p. 328, who sees no trace of Villon's influence in the poem), the description of the corpses is a product of the poet's imagination, which was surely coloured by Villon in, e.g., the lines 'Et ces morts sans repos, où fourmille le ver/ Plus que l'abeille d'or dans le creux des yeuses' (*Légende des siècles,* p. 115). E. Deschanel (*Le Romantisme des classiques,* Lévy, première série, 1883, p. 394) states that Hugo greatly admired the 'Ballade des pendus', especially the line 'Plus becquetés d'oiseaux que dés à coudre'.

Siècles maudits'.) And the poet himself was a figure with whom several
writers of the Second Empire identified themselves. He was not only
an 'enfant du peuple' in their admiring eyes; he was also the Villon of
Gautier's *Les Grotesques* — picturesquely subversive, waging war against
'les bourgeois et le guet',[297] and sentimentalized: 'il avait une belle âme,
accessible à tous les bons sentiments', declared Gautier, citing the poet's
tender regard for his mother, and — led astray by the obscurity of the
text, imperfectly understood at this time — the fact that 'il soutenait
trois jeunes orphelins.'[298] This image of a subversive and sentimental
Villon was cherished by the Parnassians and persisted until the 1870s.
Murger, in the Preface to his *Scènes de la vie de bohème* (1849) included
Villon — 'Poëte et vagabond par excellence, celui-là!'[299] — in his gallery
of illustrious outcasts from bourgeois society. Campaux drew his readers'
attention to the pathetic paradox of 'un bohême qui aimait sa mère'.[300]

A section of the Parnassian group of poets — Banville and his disciples
— regarded Villon with affection as one of themselves: a carefree vagabond,
'Villon, ce bel enfant qui n'eut ni feu ni lieu',[301] and a poet scrupulously
attentive to his craft, 'Villon qui polit sa Ballade/ Au temps jadis.'[302]
Emmanuel des Essarts wrote an enthusiastic article acclaiming him as 'cet
écolâtre vagabond, cet échappé de Montfaucon, cet aïeul de la bohême'.[303]
(Outside the Parnassian circle, harsh and hostile judgement was often
passed on him: his 'tristes gaietés' gave offence to Michelet, as we have
seen;[304] Sainte-Beuve expressed distaste for both the work — 'cette oeuvre
gothique bizarre'[305] — and its author's 'vie de taverne et de crapule',[306]
as did Laprade, an enemy of both Villon and of the Parnassians.)[307]

We have seen that Banville, like Gautier, rejected the Romantic
Middle Ages — 'la mythologie des sabbats et des diables . . . la tristesse
à l'état chronique'. He prescribed, as a remedy for this morbosity, 'le
lyrisme exalté de Ronsard . . . la joie virile bue à la grande coupe de
Rabelais . . . la fleur d'esprit gaulois de Villon';[308] and during the 1860s
he composed his *Trente-Six Ballades joyeuses à la manière de François
Villon* (published collectively in 1873). The content of these ballads

---

[297] Gautier, *Les Grotesques*, 1844, i. 49 (this essay on Villon was first published
in 1834).   [298] Ibid. p. 19.
[299] H. Murger, *Scènes de la bohême*, 2nd edn., 1851, p. ii.
[300] Campaux, op. cit. p. 319.
[301] Banville, 'La Voie lactée' (1842), *Les Cariatides*, 1889, p. 22.
[302] Banville, *Le Sang de la coupe. Trente-six Ballades joyeuses*, n.d., p. 196.
[303] *L'Artiste*, 1 Nov. 1859, p. 106.   [304] Cf. *supra*, p. 103.
[305] *Causeries du lundi*, 3rd edn., xiv. 292.   [306] Ibid. p. 288.
[307] See Laprade, *Le Sentiment de la nature chez les modernes*, 1868, pp. 58-9.
[308] Banville, *Choix de critiques*, pp. 132-3 (1870). Cf. *supra*, p. 116.

could scarcely be farther in spirit from Villon: Banville regrets 'l'an mil huit cent trente',[309] reviles the uncongenial Paris of the 1860s — 'Les Dieux sont morts, et morte l'allégresse'[310] —, and celebrates the delights of rustic life. He concludes with a brief tribute to Villon, whom he addresses as a fellow 'vagabond dormant sous le ciel bleu'.[311] The expression of modern sentiment in this work was deliberate: Banville explained to the reader: 'Mon effort fût demeuré stérile si je n'eusse été de mon temps dans le cadre archaïque, et si dans la strophe aimée de Charles d'Orléans et de Villon je n'eusse fait entrer le Paris de Gavarni et de Balzac, et l'âme moderne.'[312] Only in *Les Exilés* had he attempted to recreate the past, in emulation of the more serious Parnassians. In 1870 he proclaimed: 'Toute oeuvre qui existe est et doit être néces-sairement moderne, et il ne dépend pas de son auteur qu'elle ne le soit pas. Quant aux décors et aux costumes dont il lui plaît de l'habiller, ceci ne regarde que son style et sa toute-puissante fantaisie.'[313]

Two disciples of Banville, Armand Silvestre and Albert Glatigny, shared his admiration for Villon. Silvestre flippantly celebrated a Rabelaisian Villon ('Villon, qui fut un grand chanteur,/Prisait fort les belles haulmières' etc.);[314] Glatigny — of whom Banville wrote in his memoirs 'En lui je vois renaître Villon'[315] — was, as a poverty-stricken wandering actor, more entitled than the rest of his fellow-Parnassians to be called a latter-day Villon. Some of his work — the 'Ballade des enfants sans-souci', published in the second *Parnasse contemporain* (1869-71), inviting his friends' pity for the travelling player's lot, and the *Testament de l'illustre Brizacier,* a poignant farewell to his youth, written and published (in part) in 1868 — echoed, very faintly but more faithfully than any other Parnassian production, the poetry of Villon.

Finally, there is Banville's very successful one-act play, *Gringoire* (1866), the hero of which, according to Max Fuchs, is a compound of the two poets presented in contrast to each other by D'Héricault in the Preface to his edition of Gringoire's works (1858) — Villon, carefree and subversive ('toute sa vie . . . n'a été qu'un loisir, une indocilité constante contre les moeurs reçues et la littérature reçue'),[316] and Gringoire, en-dowed with bourgeois virtues and the desire to 'prouver et instruire'.[316] Neither Villon nor Gringoire, says Fuchs, fulfilled Banville's ideal of the

[309] *Le Sang de la coupe,* pp. 197-8.   [310] Ibid. p. 207.   [311] Ibid. p. 271.
[312] Ibid. Avant-Propos, p. 170.   [313] *Choix de critiques,* p. 411.
[314] A. Silvestre, *Rimes neuves et vieilles,* 1866, pp. 95-8.
[315] Banville, *Mes Souvenirs,* 1882, p. 396.
[316] *Oeuvres complètes de Gringoire,* ed. D'Héricault and Montaiglon, i (1858), p. xiv.

poet-hero: 'Il fallait donc fondre les deux personnages en un seul, et Gringoire seul, beaucoup moins connu que Villon, pouvait donner son nom à l'être de raison créé de la sorte.'[317] But it was since his appearance in *Notre-Dame de Paris* that Gringoire had in fact attained celebrity, and Banville's creation owes more to Hugo than to any other source. He is Hugo's Gringoire, 'pâle, grelottant, et comme ivre de faim',[318] threatened with the gallows by Louis XI, and earning his pardon by a display of poetic eloquence. He is also the Gringoire of Murger, who transmuted Hugo's self-absorbed, unsentimental poet into a pathetic figure, 'maigre et affamé . . . dolent et mélancolique'.[319] He has much in common with Gautier's Villon, furthermore: the legend of the orphans (albeit exploded by Campaux) is woven into his history, told to the King by his patroness: 'Quand je le vis pour la première fois . . . il avait sur ses genoux deux petits enfants égarés qu'il avait trouvés pleurant après leur mère.'[320] And he is the modern poet, 'un nourrisson de Calliope et du saint choeur parnassien',[321] who suffers at the hands of the philistine Olivier-le-Daim. The serious side of his character – his championing of the poor, which wins Loyse's heart, and his moral, upright nature, which enables him to win her hand as well – may indeed have been suggested to Banville by D'Héricault's presentation of Gringoire as a respectable bourgeois with a republican conscience: 'Il fait la leçon aux directeurs de la société, il leur recommande la pitié, l'amour, le respect pour le pauvre peuple.'[322] (D'Héricault's friend Moland had also made painstaking attempts to divest Gringoire of his Romantic, bohemian aura, insisting that he was 'un homme sobre et rangé. . . .[323] Enfant sans souci, il ne l'était que de nom.')[324] Banville's hero, then, is a combination of the Romantic Gringoire, corrected by D'Héricault, and the Parnassian Villon – but with more of the latter than the former in his make-up: he recites in the course of the play two 'ballades à la manière de François Villon'. Presumably he is given the name of Gringoire because Villon's disreputable character debarred him from the entry into bourgeois society granted to Banville's poet.[325]

[317] M. Fuchs, *T. de Banville*, 1912, p. 399.
[318] Banville, *Gringoire*, 1866, p. 24.
[319] Murger, op. cit. p. ii. Cf. *Gringoire*, p. 52.   [320] *Gringoire*, p. 22.
[321] Ibid. p. 35.   [322] Ch. d'Héricault & A. de Montaiglon, op. cit. p. xxxiv.
[323] L. Moland, *Origines littéraires de la France*, 1862, p. 349.
[324] Ibid. p. 357.
[325] Edelman is of the opinion that Villon's criminal career was responsible for the Romantics' neglect of him: 'Il était bien difficile de voir en lui un beau bandit' (op. cit. p. 221).

Banville's play is a vehicle for republican sentiment of a mild variety.
Gringoire's 'Ballade des pauvres gens' —

> Rois, qui serez jugés à votre tour,
> Songez à ceux qui n'ont ni sou ni maille. . . .
> Le seigneur vient, toujours plus endurci.
> Sur son vassal, d'épouvante saisi,
> Il met sa main comme un aigle sa serre,
> Et lui prend tout en disant: "Me voici!"
> Aux pauvres gens tout est peine et misère![326] —

melts the heart of Louis XI, who is portrayed not as the sinister tyrant
of *Notre-Dame de Paris*, but as a benevolent despot who listens with
great forbearance to the poet's recital of his seditious 'Ballade des
pendus', and, won over by the pathetic eloquence with which he confesses his love for Loyse, pardons him, exclaiming: 'Il y a là un
homme!'[327] (Hugo's Louis XI, wearying of Gringoire's long-winded plea
for mercy, snaps out: 'Bah! lâchez-le!')[328] Louis's court in *Gringoire* is
a convivial, domesticated place, bearing little resemblance to 'le Retrait
où dit ses heures Monsieur Louis de France' in *Notre-Dame de Paris*.
Even the 'Ballade des pendus', with its refrain 'C'est le verger du roi
Louis', referring to the forest of gibbets where the King's victims
'voltigent, palpitants encore',[329] is facetious rather than horrific. For
Hugo, Louis XI was always an object of horror. In *Napoléon le Petit*[330]
and *Les Châtiments*[331] he and Louis Napoleon are companions in
infamy. *Gringoire* was performed before an enthusiastic audience at
Compiègne; Calmettes (an unreliable witness) reports maliciously that
Leconte de Lisle, a clandestine beneficiary of Imperial charity, objected
angrily to Banville's portrayal of a benevolent monarch distributing
bounty to a grateful poet: 'Le malheureux!', he is said to have mur-
mured, 'n'avoir su peindre qu'un mendiant!'[332]

Much of Gautier's frivolous condescension towards his gallery of
'Grotesques' — 'pauvres gloires éclopées, figures grimaçantes'[333] — went
into the creation, by Banville and his followers, of this Parnassian Villon.
Their light-hearted and superficial interest in the poet was very different

---

[326] *Gringoire*, pp. 55-6.
[327] Ibid. p. 38.
[328] *Notre-Dame de Paris*, p. 506.
[329] *Gringoire*, p. 30.
[330] See *Napoléon le Petit*, p. 266.
[331] See Hugo, *Oeuvres poétiques*, ii. 122.
[332] F. Calmettes, *Leconte de Lisle et ses amis*, Librairies-Imprimeries réunies, 1902, p. 37.
[333] Gautier, *Les Grotesques*, 1844, ii. 326.

from the view which later writers, such as Marcel Schwob,[334] were to take of him. As Edelman remarks, 'Après 1873, c'est un autre sujet et une autre histoire.'[335]

One last province of the ideal republican Middle Ages remains to be surveyed: the Arthurian legend, exploited by Quinet in *Merlin l'Enchanteur* (1860). The extreme archness of this prolix fantasy renders it almost unreadable today; but in its day it caused a sensation, as an audacious political satire directed against the Empire. Quinet had in his youth, twenty years before, conceived the idea of bringing legend up to date and converting tradition to serve modern ideals: he suggested in 1837 that Tristan, wearying of his solitary life in the forest, should be interpreted by the modern writer as 'le génie de la France elle-même, si promptement lassée des forêts enchantées du moyen âge, si avide de la vie active des temps modernes.'[336] In *Merlin,* he indulged to the full his capacity for this sort of fanciful speculation. He declares in the Preface that he wrote the work in order to 'renouveler l'imagination française dans les sources nationales';[337] his purpose, however, seems to have been above all one of self-aggrandizement. His choice of hero may well have been inspired by the revised edition of Henri Martin's *Histoire de France* (Volume III, 1858). Here Martin exalts Merlin as a 'prophète politique'.[338] 'Il prend des proportions immenses',[338] he declares, concluding: 'Le symbole a enfin disparu, mais l'esprit que voilait ce symbole est immortel.'[339] Quinet's Merlin is Quinet himself, and Viviane is his wife, who furnished the second edition with explanatory notes, relating each chapter to her husband's private life and the political event of the day. Quinet speaks with Merlin's voice, defying the Empire from exile. 'Dans un univers esclave, je vivrai, je mourrai libre',[340] and pacifying the nations of the world, whom he reconciles at the Round Table, the ideal federation of future republics. The action of the book, which commemorates his peregrinations through Europe during his exile, has little connection with the episode of medieval legend, although at one point Merlin's servant Jacques Bonhomme laments, in the accents of Béroul, the desolation into which Arthur's court (i.e. France under Louis Napoleon's rule) has fallen: 'Oh! Dieu! quel deuil et quel dommage!'[341] Familiar

[334] Cf. *infra,* p. 278.   [335] Edelman, op. cit. p. 339.
[336] Quinet, *Os. cs.* ix: *La Grèce moderne. Histoire de la poésie,* 4th edn., n.d., p. 406.
[337] Quinet, *Os. cs.* xvi: *Merlin l'Enchanteur,* i. 4th edn., n.d., p. (v).
[338] H. Martin, *Histoire de France,* 4th edn., iii (1858), 361.
[339] Ibid. p. 369.   [340] *Merlin l'Enchanteur,* i. 85.
[341] *Merlin l'Enchanteur,* ii (*Os. cs.* xvii), 238.

republican judgements are passed on Gothic architecture and the
Middle Ages as a whole. Merlin invents the former ('Sa foi était moins
profonde qu'il ne pensait . . . son architecture grandiose est néanmoins
grêle et chancelante'),[342] and describes the latter to Jacques Bonhomme,
in a prophecy of the fate which lies in store for him ('D'abord les pestes,
des sueurs de sang, des larmes, du fer, des geôles, des oubliettes, de
sombres manoirs pour le maître, un peu de paille et la douleur pour
toi').[343] In one curious scene Quinet divides into two and holds a
conversation with himself: Merlin descends into the limbo of what is
to be, and predicts the course of their future existence to 'les âmes
ébauchées qui n'ont pas encore vécu'[344] — Napoleon, Martin Luther,
Colombus, and Quinet himself, to whom Merlin promises a career of
honourable adversity: 'Tu adoreras la justice; elle te sera refusée. Tu
sentiras sur tes lèvres la vérité; chose cruelle! tu ne pourras la publier. . . .
A la fin viendra le long exil, et les tiens ne te connaîtront plus. . . .
Pourtant tu marcheras jusqu'à la fin, la tête droite, sans connaître le
joug.'[345] Merlin's entombment is Quinet's exile: he addresses his
contemporaries in the 'Chant de Merlin dans le sépulcre': 'J'ai choisi
la justice, et le monde l'iniquité. . . . J'ai aimé la lumière, et le monde
les ténèbres.'[346] It is also France under Imperial rule, 'un monde qui
se meurt'.[347] Merlin's greatest grief is caused by the defection of Jacques
Bonhomme, who joins a travelling circus, enticed by the bright clothes
offered to him — just as the common people of France have been seduced
by the tawdry glitter of the Empire. The book ends in triumph as the
walls of the tomb collapse and 'l'Enfer écroulé'[348] brings deliverance.

Another adversary of the Empire (and a close friend of Quinet), the
poet Victor de Laprade, was deeply impressed by *Merlin* and sent its
author a letter of fervent congratulation: 'Cette lecture . . . m'a donné
un des grands moments de ma vie intellectuelle et m'a rendu ma jeunesse.'[349]
Three years later he in his turn composed an Arthurian fantasy, *La Tour
d'ivoire* (written in 1864, published the following year in *Les Voix du
silence*), directed against the materialism of the Empire. Its hero, a
poursuivant du Graal — 'Vigilant, le coeur haut et la lance en arrêt'[350] —,
braves the world's temptations, 'des belles aux bras nus . . . d'insidieux
festins',[351] to find ideal Love awaiting him in an enchanted tower at the

---

[342] Ibid. i. 127.   [343] Ibid. p. 257.
[344] Ibid. p. 152.   [345] *Merlin l'Enchanteur*, i. 160-1.
[346] Ibid. ii. 326.   [347] Ibid. p. 300.   [348] Ibid. p. 486.
[349] Quoted by P. Bonnefon in *Le Correspondant*, 10 Mar. 1917, p. 917.
[350] Laprade, *Oeuvres poétiques*, vi (1889), 39.   [351] Ibid. p. 69.

end of his quest. Laprade's friend Laurent-Pichat disapproved of this allegory, finding it 'trop *moyen âge*'.[352]

Both these works were considered by enthusiastic critics to provide substantial proof of the nineteenth century's superiority over the Middle Ages. Speaking of *Merlin l'Enchanteur,* the Parnassian Emmanuel des Essarts exclaimed: 'Combien cette nouvelle Table ronde, ce nouveau Saint-Graal nous semblent plus poétiques et humains que les mythes et les légendes du passé!'[353] And Saint-René Taillandier praised Laprade's *Tour d'ivoire* in the *Revue des deux mondes:*

> Ce cycle efféminé, qui ne représentait que trop gracieusement l'immoralité naïve du moyen âge, acquiert entre ses mains une élégance virile. Que M. de Laprade condamne tant qu'il voudra . . . l'esprit de notre XIXe siècle, cette transfiguration des poèmes du Saint-Graal est la réponse que je lui oppose. Il a montré là, qu'il le sache ou non, combien le XIXe siècle est supérieur au XIIIe.[354]

H. *Medieval art as a source of inspiration*

Dramatic recreations of medieval history or legend, such as those which have occupied our attention so far, were all (with the exception of Hugo's *Légende*) the work of republicans or (far less frequently) Catholics, who held strong views about the Middle Ages, dictated by their political sympathies, and set out to give a picture of medieval life in accordance with these views. It remains to discuss those few writers who drew their inspiration from medieval art. We saw at the end of Chapter 3[355] how this approach to the past – contemplation of the works of art it has left to posterity – was often recommended as the one most conducive to dispassionate divination of bygone ages. We have also seen how in practice the gaze which writers turned upon medieval art was often far from dispassionate. Several of them hastened to perceive, in the grandiose forms and profuse decoration of Gothic architecture, the incompetence or irresponsibility of its builders. Théophile Gautier, having conceived a distaste for medieval sculpture, in which he saw a morbid preoccupation with death, extended his detestation to the Middle Ages as a whole. Taine, one of the principal advocates of this way of looking at the past through art, was also one

---

[352] See *Lettres inédites de V. de Laprade à Ch. Alexandre,* p. 99.
[353] E. des Essarts, *Portraits de maîtres,* Perrin, 1888, p. 284.
[354] *RDM,* 1 Aug. 1865, pp. 632-3.
[355] Cf. *supra,* pp. 85-6.

of the most eager to interpret medieval art in a prejudicial manner.
Flaubert, however, and Baudelaire, and some Parnassians, did venture
to scrutinize it afresh: and in so doing they came close to the discovery
of a new Middle Ages, which was to be exploited by the next generation.

Taine held the view that, of all the various art forms available to the
historian in his work of divination, the best was 'un document littéraire',
for 'quand ce document est riche et qu'on sait l'interpréter, on y trouve
la psychologie d'une âme, souvent celle d'un siècle.'[356] We have seen
that at this time only specialists in the field read medieval literature
in the original text. Even one as scrupulous in his documentation as
Flaubert would have been unlikely to go so far as to consult a thirteenth-
century manuscript (as has been suggested that he may have done, in
the preparation of *Saint Julien*).[357] It was to medieval art that these
writers turned for inspiration. Historians were beginning to favour
reproductions of ancient works of art in place of illustrations by modern
artists; and their example was followed by Baudelaire and Flaubert.
Baudelaire chose in 1860, as the frontispiece for a projected second
edition of *Les Fleurs du mal*, a 'squelette arborescent' from Langlois's
Essai sur les danses des morts (1851); he stipulated in a letter to his
publisher that the engraver should produce 'un FAC-SIMILE, stricte-
ment rien de moins, rien de plus . . . *la copie servile* de l'image macabre
de Langlois'.[358] Flaubert told his publisher in 1879·that the only
illustration he would allow for *La Légende de Saint Julien l'hospitalier*
was a reproduction (from the same author's *Essai sur la peinture sur
verre*, 1832) of the stained-glass window that had inspired it: 'Je
désirais mettre à la suite de *Saint Julien* le vitrail de la cathédrale de
Rouen. Il s'agissait de colorier la planche qui se trouve dans le livre de
Langlois, rien de plus.'[359]

(i) *The Dance of Death:*
'Les charmes de l'horreur n'enivrent que les forts'; statues on tombs

The Parnassians, when they devoted a poem to medieval art, usually
chose as their source of inspiration either the Dance of Death or statues
on tombs. Both these themes were exploited in the first instance by

---

[356] Taine, *HLA*, Introduction, p. xlvi.
[357] See A. W. Raitt, 'The Composition of Flaubert's *Saint Julien l'hospitalier*', *FS*, xix (Oct. 1965).
[358] Baudelaire, *Correspondance générale*, ed. Crépet, iii. Conard, 177-8.
[359] Flaubert, *Correspondance*, viii. 207.

Gautier, who was unable on each occasion to conceal the distaste for
the Middle Ages which he felt increasingly, as we have seen, in the
course of his career. Their subsequent treatment by younger poets
marks the beginning of a shift away from republican disapprobation of
the Middle Ages and towards Symbolist nostalgia for them.

Republicans saw the *danse macabre* as an invention of the Church
designed to terrorize the faithful into submission. It had been censured
even by Marchangy, who called it 'cette danse dégoûtante'.[360] Langlois
compared pagan with Christian representations of death, and left the
reader in no doubt as to where his preference lay: 'Loin d'ajouter, par
les simulacres des crânes décharnés et des hideux squelettes, à ce qu'a
de sinistre l'aspect des tombeaux, la mort n'était, chez les anciens,
figurée sur le dernier asile des hommes que sous des formes élégantes
et souvent gracieuses.'[361] This contrast is the subject of Gautier's
poem 'Bûchers et tombeaux':[362]

> Le squelette était invisible
> Au temps heureux de l'Art païen,

he begins —

> Pas de cadavre sous la tombe,
> Spectre hideux de l'être cher;

and he describes some of the 'images douces et riantes' which the ancients
devised to palliate the horrors of death, represented by Gothic art in all
its 'hideur railleuse' as a ubiquitous skeleton leading the *danse macabre:*

> A chaque pas grossit la bande;
> Le jeune au vieux donne la main;
> L'irrésistible sarabande
> Met en branle le genre humain.

The participants in the dance appear before Gautier one by one; and
the sight of them is more than he can bear: hence his cry:

> Reviens, reviens, bel art antique,
> De ton paros étincelant

---

[360] *La Gaule poétique,* viii (1817), 163.
[361] E-H. Langlois, *Essai . . . sur les danses des morts,* 1851, i. 65. A theme taken
up by successive German writers in the latter part of the eighteenth century,
notably Lessing and Schiller. See H. Hatfield, *Aesthetic Paganism in German
Literature,* 1964, Ch. 2. Little critical attention has been paid to the fact that
nineteenth-century French Hellenism — in particular that of Gautier and
Taine — is often little more than a reproduction of earlier-expressed German views.
[362] Published in *L'Artiste,* Jan. 1858, and in the 3rd edn. of *Émaux et camées* at
the end of that year.

> Couvrir ce squelette gothique;
> Dévore-le, bûcher brûlant![363]

Shortly after the appearance of this poem Gautier's friend Baudelaire turned his attention to the *danse macabre*, which he proceeded to celebrate with passionate enthusiasm: he seems at times to be joining issue with Gautier on the subject, and to be protesting at his squeamish aversion for Gothic skulls and skeletons. In January 1859 he wrote to Alphonse de Calonne: 'Vous verrez, dans le poëme du *Squelette*, le soin que j'ai pris de me conformer à l'ironie criarde des anciennes *Danses macabres* et des images allégoriques du moyen âge.'[364] This poem was the one which appeared in the *Revue contemporaine* of March that year under its new title *Danse macabre*. It was inspired by a statuette representing a female skeleton dressed for the ball in a crinoline skirt, the work of Baudelaire's friend Ernest Christophe. Certain lines from Gautier's *Comédie de la mort* (1838) seems also to have inspired Baudelaire in the composition of this poem (e.g. 'La mort fait la coquette et prend un ton de reine'[365] — describing statues on tombs); but whereas Gautier, as we have seen, regarded with the utmost repugnance the 'coquetteries d'outre-tombe'[366] of Gothic art, Baudelaire has fallen in love with his 'coquette maigre' and pays her extravagant compliments: 'Ô charme d'un néant follement attifé! . . . Tu réponds, grand squelette, à mon goût le plus cher!' He then rounds upon those less susceptible than he is to her 'funèbres appas', and tells them:

> Les charmes de l'horreur n'enivrent que les forts!

With the question 'Qui ne s'est nourri des choses du tombeau?' he turns his attention from the statue to contemplate the entire human race disporting itself beneath the ironic gaze of Death waiting to claim it as her own. A spectacle that filled Gautier with dismay fills him with sardonic satisfaction: 'Antinoüs flétris, dandys à face glabre', he tells his contemporaries —

> Cadavres vernissés, lovelaces chenus,
> Le branle universel de la danse macabre
> Vous entraîne en des lieux qui ne sont pas connus![367]

---

[363] Gautier, *Oeuvres poétiques*, iii. 72-5.
[364] Baudelaire, *Correspondance générale*, ii. (1947), 251.
[365] Gautier, *Poésies complètes*, ii. 5.   [366] Cf. *supra*, p. 112.
[367] Baudelaire, *Os. cs.* 1961, pp. 92-4.

Medieval or modern art inspired Baudelaire to celebrate 'les charmes de l'horreur' on several other occasions in *Les Fleurs du Mal*. Mortimer's picture *Death on a Pale Horse*, with its skeleton on horseback wearing 'un diadème affreux',[368] stirred his imagination ('Une Gravure fantastique', 1857); and so did Holbein's *Dance of Death* and sixteenth-century anatomical engravings – 'ces mystérieuses horreurs' – containing the figure of 'le squelette laboureur' bent over its spade, which caused him once again to see in vision his own destiny and that of his fellow-beings – 'Manants résignés et funèbres', this time, forced even in death to labour without respite.[369]

Baudelaire returned enthusiastically to the theme of the *danse macabre* more than once in his 1859 *Salon*. Praising Penguilly's *Petite Danse macabre*, he remarks: 'Les artistes modernes négligent beaucoup trop ces magnifiques allégories du moyen âge, où l'immortel grotesque s'enlaçait en folâtrant, comme il fait encore, à l'immortel horrible. Peut-être nos nerfs trop délicats ne peuvent-ils plus supporter un symbole trop clairement redoutable',[370] and pours scorn on a timorous publisher who had recently brought out a prayer-book illustrated with samples of medieval art from which all trace of the macabre had been expunged, '*comme n'étant plus du goût de ce siècle*'.[371] He praises also a statuette of a young girl in the embrace of a skeleton, commending the sculptor, Hébert, for having appreciated the skeleton's 'beauté mystérieuse et abstraite', ignored by antiquity and rediscovered in the Middle Ages. In outright contradiction of the sentiments expressed by Gautier in 'Bûchers et tombeaux', he suggests that Hébert's creation 'pourrait peut-être, exécutée dans de plus grandes proportions, faire une excellente décoration funèbre dans un cimetière ou dans une chapelle'.[372]

Baudelaire's poem 'Danse macabre' gave the theme a certain popularity among Parnassians, several of whom produced pale imitations of it.[373] An altogether new treatment of the theme was ventured by Anatole France in 'La Danse des morts' (1869).[374] Although 'les charmes de

---

[368] Ibid. p. 66.   [369] Ibid. p.89.
[370] Ibid. p. 1069.   [371] Baudelaire, *Os. cs.* p. 1069.
[372] Ibid. pp. 1093-4. Cf. Baudelaire's attack on contemporary neo-paganism in his article 'L'École païenne' (1852, *Os. cs.* pp. 623-8); and his 'Projets de lettre à Jules Janin' (1865): 'Pourquoi la tristesse n'aurait-elle pas sa beauté? Et l'horreur aussi?' (Ibid. p. 805).
[373] e.g. Coppée's 'Bouquetière' (*Poésies, 1864-9*), Henri Cazalis's 'Figurines macabres' and 'Danse macabre' (*L'Illusion*, 1875), and Dierx' 'La Mort coquette' (*Les Amants*, 1879).
[374] Published in 2nd *Parnasse contemporain*, 1869-71.

l'horreur' are not entirely absent from this poem, there is none of Baudelaire's sardonic delight in the macabre. Neither is there any republican moral indignation: the poet, far from expressing horror at the Dance, distils consolation from it, seeing in the procession led by the figure of Death only the orderliness and calm of the medieval social hierarchy, and its touching faith in a future existence, for which he feels envy and nostalgia:

> Je crois que cette image édifiante et sainte
> Mettait un peu d'espoir au fond du désespoir,
> Et que les pauvres gens la regardaient sans crainte.

With insistent irony he repeats that any form of immortality is preferable to extinction:

> Sous les pas des danseurs on voit l'Enfer béant,
> Le branle d'un squelette et d'un vif sur un gouffre;
> C'est bien affreux, mais moins pourtant que le néant –

that an elegiac tranquillity, 'la paix du monastère', was infused into the Dance by those anonymous artists who painted it on church walls and in manuscripts, and that in these works,

> On sent communier en Dieu toute âme humaine,
> On sent encor la foi, l'espérance et l'amour.[375]

He concludes, in flagrant defiance of Leconte de Lisle:

> Oh! bienheureux ceux-là qui croyaient à l'Enfer.[376]

Parnassians seeking inspiration in medieval art also turned towards recumbent stone statues on tombs. Their worship of sculptural form predisposed them towards these figures, evoked for the first time by Gautier in *La Comédie de la mort:*

> Les chevaliers couchés de leur long, les mains jointes,
> Le regard sur la voûte et les deux pieds en pointes.[377]

Charles Cros's 'La Dame en Pierre' –

> Joignant les mains, les yeux heureux
> Sous le voile des paupières[378] –

appeared in the second *Parnasse contemporain;* and France's 'La Vision des ruines' was included in his collection *Les Poèmes dorés* (1873). This poem is a vision of Paris reduced to devastation by some future cataclysm.

---

[375] A. France, *Poésies,* n.d., pp. 108-9.   [376] Ibid. p. 113.
[377] Gautier, *Poésies complètes,* ii. 3.   [378] Ch. Cros, *Os. cs.* 1964, p. 16.

Among the ruins which bear witness to each stage of the city's history lie
the broken figures in the wreck of the cathedral, who

> Les mains jointes, suivent en paix
> Le rêve qui clôt leur paupière.[379]

Each of these poets strove to discern behind the form the state of mind
from which it had sprung. Gautier's statues cover and conceal, yet at the
same time perpetually recall, the death and decay which haunted the
minds of their creators. They lie in a lugubrious crypt watching

> L'eau qui suinte et tombe avec de sourds frissons.[380]

Cros and France restore to theirs an ideal beauty free from all funereal
associations:

> Sur ce couvercle de tombeau
> Elle dort. L'obscur artiste
> Qui l'a sculptée a vu le beau
> Sans rien de triste,[381]

Cros begins his poem; and Anatole France's statues — both those in 'La
Vision des ruines' and the participants in 'La Danse des morts', who

> S'en sont allés dormir sans révolte et sans bruit:
> Ils comptent bien qu'un jour le lévrier de pierre,
> Sous leurs rigides pieds couché fidèlement,
> Saura se réveiller et lécher leur paupière[382] —

await with serene and enviable confidence the joys of the life to come;
while Cros's 'Dame en pierre' is absorbed in more worldly preoccupations:

> Elle a des rêves amoureux
> Dans ses prières.[381]

(ii) *Parnassian 'sonnets gothiques'; Heredia:*
'La rose du vitrail toujours épanouie'

The Parnassians were also concerned with an ideal Middle Ages, preserved in stained glass, sculpture, and illuminated manuscripts, when
they attempted to present, in an occasional short poem, what Pierre
Moreau calls 'le *quadro* symbolique où se résume, en une rapide

---

[379] A. France, op. cit. p. 39.
[380] Even the house of Elias Wildmanstadius, 'l'homme moyen âge', described with
such light-hearted jocularity by Gautier in *Les Jeunes-France,* has the same
sinister, graveyard humidity oozing from its walls: 'Les murs suaient à grosses
gouttes' (*Les Jeunes-France,* 1881, p. 319).
[381] Ch. Cros, op. cit. p. 16.   [382] A. France, op. cit. p. 112.

perspective, une civilisation, un peuple'.[383] This ambition haunted for
a time even Rimbaud, who in 1871 expressed his disgust with Parnassian
attempts to 'reprendre l'esprit des choses mortes'.[384] Delahaye records
that about this time Rimbaud showed him some prose poems entitled
'la Photographie des temps passés', including one 'Moyen-Âge', which
he describes as 'de la photographie qui reproduirait une synthèse, le
portrait physique et moral d'une collection humaine au cours de
plusieurs générations: idées, passions, mouvements, décor'.[385]
Parnassian poems of this type, dealing with the Middle Ages, were
Coppée's 'Vitrail' (*Poèmes divers*, 1867), Frédéric Plessis' 'Sonnet
gothique' (*Parnasse contemporain* 1869-71), and Heredia's 'Vitrail'
(1892). The first two are dutiful and undistinguished exercises.
Heredia's sonnet — entirely Parnassian in spirit, of course, although it
was published in 1892 — is the only one of these works to achieve
distinction. Inspired by a few lines from Gautier's 'Portail' to *La
Comédie de la mort* — and also, perhaps, by reminiscences of Hugo
and Leconte de Lisle[386] — 'Vitrail' restores to the Middle Ages their
Romantic splendour. Once a numerous company, 'étincelants d'azur,
d'or, de flamme et de nacre', receiving benediction on the eve of
departure for exploits in far-off lands, the 'hauts barons' now lie
changed to stone, 'les seigneurs auprès des châtelaines', beneath 'la
rose du vitrail toujours épanouie'. This is the ideal Middle Ages, which
should in theory have been the exclusive concern of Parnassians when
they undertook to recreate the past, but which in practice, as we have
seen, was a sphere which they seldom reached. The past is in 'Vitrail'
and the other medieval *Trophées* — 'Épiphanie' and 'Le Huchier de
Nazareth' — ideal and splendid, yet seen as it were from a distance,

---

[383] P. Moreau, *L'Histoire en France au XIXe siècle*, n.d., p. 127.
[384] Rimbaud, *Oeuvres*, ed. S. Bernard, 1960, p. 349.
[385] E. Delahaye, *Rimbaud*, Reims, 1905, p. 111.
[386] See M. Ibrovac, *J-M. de Heredia: Les Sources des 'Trophées'*, 1923, pp. 93-5.
Ibrovac suggests as a possible source of the last line, 'La rose du vitrail toujours
épanouie' (which according to Barrès took Heredia ten years to find), Gautier's
words (from 'Portail') 'cette floraison toujours épanouie'. Cf. also *Notre-Dame
de Paris:* 'Il [Quasimodo] ne rêvait pas d'autres espaliers que les vitraux toujours en fleur' (p. 180); Gautier's subsequent flippant mention of 'les roses des
vitraux toujours épanouies', which sent Wildmanstadius into a transport of
admiration (*Les Jeunes-France*, p. 325); and 'les cathédrales avec leurs rosaces
toujours épanouies et leurs verrières en fleurs' which sent into a frenzy of
exasperation the imaginary critic in the Preface to *Mademoiselle de Maupin*
(p. 19). Heredia exacts once more a full measure of respect for them, and
reinvests 'toujours' with new poetic force.

without any hint of praise or blame. There is no moral significance
in 'Vitrail'[387] – only a distant sense of elegiac regret. This brings it
close to the work of the Symbolists; the Middle Ages are epitomized
in a few haunting gestures, to produce a purely decorative and melancholy effect. A Catholic critic complained in 1905 that 'Vitrail' failed
to bring out the proper significance of the stained-glass window, whose
purpose was to provide Christian consolation. 'Le vers est beau, certes,'
he wrote of the last line, 'mais je ne puis supporter cet enthousiasme
archéologique d'où naît une si profonde indifférence pour les beautés
de la vie morale. Puisque les héros et les chrétiennes ne sont plus, que
nous importe l'éclat de cette rose toujours épanouie?'[388]

So Baudelaire, Anatole France, and Heredia, approaching the Middle
Ages through art, rediscovered many of their Romantic enchantments,
which had turned to poison for writers such as Michelet and Gautier:
Baudelaire found in them 'les charmes de l'horreur', Anatole France 'la
paix du gothique monastère', and Heredia, the visual splendour of 'la
rose du vitrail toujours épanouie'.

(iii) Flaubert's Saint Julien: 'un rêve, farouche et tendre tour à tour'

The most carefully-wrought and most original product of this
approach to the past remains to be discussed. It is Flaubert's Légende
de Saint Julien l'hospitalier, which was begun (in its documentary stage)
in 1856, abandoned for twenty years and finally written during the
autumn and winter of 1875-6, appearing in 1877 as one of the Trois
Contes. Flaubert's friend Taine was disconcerted by Saint Julien. With
scarcely concealed regret he wrote to its author: 'Julien est très vrai,
mais c'est le monde imaginé par le moyen âge, et non le moyen âge
lui-même; ce que vous souhaitiez, puisque vous vouliez produire l'effet
d'un vitrail . . . tout [est] du pur idéal de l'an 1200.'[389] So Flaubert
had, in Taine's eyes, fallen into the sin with which Michelet bitterly
reproached himself: he had given 'l'idéal de cet affreux Moyen Âge'.[390]
Like Walter Scott, he had fled from 'la vérité pure, telle qu'elle est,
atroce et sale'.[391] Saint Julien proved nothing about the Middle Ages;

---

[387] Cf. Heredia's early sonnet, 'Les Scaliger' (in the 1866 Parnasse contemporain),
a description of the Scaliger tombs in Verona, bearing some resemblance to
'Vitrail', yet containing a political message: protest at Austrian domination
over Italy.

[388] L-C. Delfour, Catholicisme et romantisme, Soc. française d'imprimerie et de
librairie, 1905, p. xxiv.

[389] See Flaubert, Trois Contes, Conard, 1910, pp. 226-7.   [390] Cf. supra, p. 49.

[391] Cf. supra, p. 72.

and in this of course lay its power and originality. The most scrupulous documentation went into its composition: all the medieval arts of peace and of war, details of which were gleaned from a multitude of specialists including Sainte-Palaye and Viollet-le-Duc, are encompassed in the life of Julien. As warrior and saint he fulfils his parents' hopes, kindled by the prophecies made at his birth, that he will be a far-famed conqueror or a pillar of the Church – and also provides confirmation of Taine's view that the Middle Ages were 'un âge de moines et de chevaliers';[392] but the work is not an earnest attempt to recreate the true Middle Ages according to the methods prescribed by Taine, who, realizing this, gave it only faint praise and reserved his highest commendation for *Hérodias*.

Aloof from political preoccupations, Flaubert saw Catholics and republicans as 'les deux masques alternés de la bêtise humaine',[393] in the words of Thibaudet. Their perpetual wrangling over the Middle Ages diverted him, as we have seen. He found equally comic M. de Faverges's pious regard (in *Bouvard et Pécuchet*) for '[le] moyen âge, époque de foi religieuse et de dévouements chevaleresques'[394] and Homais's emphatic denunciation of 'ces temps monstrueux du moyen âge'.[395] *Saint Julien* seems at first to be a negation of the republican Middle Ages. Peace, prosperity, and contentment reign in the home of Julien's parents. They live in the unspoilt Romantic Middle Ages of Hugo's 'La Fée et la péri' ('Tu verras les barons, sous leurs tours féodales/ De l'humble pèlerin détachant les sandales').[396] Julien's father, in summer and winter alike, 'rendait la justice à ses vassaux, apaisait les querelles de ses voisins'.[397] In the summer he strolls through his domain giving paternal advice to his vassals; and when merchants appear in the neighbourhood, they are – by contrast with those hapless victims of the 'noble sire aux aguets sur sa tour'[398] so often depicted in republican histories and poems – treated with every respect and sent on their way 'avec un gros profit, sans avoir enduré aucune violence'.[399] But this unearthly peace is short-lived; it is a state of innocence from which, all too soon, Julien's sanguinary instincts and rage to destroy emerge. He soon becomes a wild animal, bent only on the pursuit of his kind – one of Taine's 'brutes sanguinaires' and 'bêtes féroces', in fact: '. . . il rentrait au milieu de la nuit, couvert

[392] Taine, *Philosophie de l'art*, 1865, p. 131.
[393] A. Thibaudet, *Gustave Flaubert*, Gallimard, 1935, p. 158.
[394] *Bouvard et Pécuchet*, 1965, pp. 132-3.   [395] *Madame Bovary*, 1955, p. 319.
[396] Cf. *supra*, p. 18.   [397] *Trois Contes*, 1961, p. 79.
[398] Cf. *supra*, p. 160.   [399] *Trois Contes*, p. 84.

de sang et de boue, avec des épines dans les cheveux et sentant l'odeur
des bêtes farouches. Il devint comme elles.'[400] On the hunt which leads
him to the encounter with the stag, his casual cruelty as he forges on his
way, striking out at the sleeping wood grouse – 'Julien, d'un revers
d'épée, lui faucha les deux pattes, et sans le ramasser continua sa route'[400]
– recalls that of the monster Tiphaine in Hugo's 'L'Aigle du casque',
pouncing upon the child Angus at the end of his epic pursuit of him: 'Et
d'un revers de hache il abat ces deux mains/ Qui dans l'ombre élevaient
vers les cieux la prière.'[401] On his last hunt, when all the animal kingdom
conspires to humiliate him, Julien's bestial instincts take possession of
him once more: 'Sa soif de carnage le reprenait; les bêtes manquant, il
aurait voulu massacrer des hommes';[402] and when in the dark he comes
upon his sleeping parents and mistakes them for his wife in the arms of a
lover, 'il trépignait, écumait, avec des hurlements de bête fauve.'[402] And
after he commits the act of parricide, he wanders through a world of
total desolation – 'Le soleil, tous les soirs, étalait du sang dans les nuages;
et chaque nuit, en rêve, son parricide recommençait'[403] – recalling the
guilt-laden world of Hugo's sinister *Légende des siècles* Middle Ages, and
Empire of *Les Châtiments,* where 'La lune chaque nuit se lève en un
suaire,/Le soleil chaque soir se couche dans du sang.'[404]

So an ideal and a sinister Middle Ages follow each other here in
sequence. At times they bear a fleeting resemblance to the Catholic and
republican Middle Ages; but in reality they have nothing to do with either.
They are 'le Moyen Âge énorme et délicat', exploited for purely aesthetic
purposes. 'Le monde n'est qu'un clavecin pour le véritable artiste,'
Flaubert wrote in a letter of 1842, 'à lui d'en tirer des sons qui ravissent
ou qui glacent d'effroi.'[405] So it was with the Middle Ages of *Saint Julien,*
praised by Jules Lemaître as a perfect rendering of 'le moyen âge, violent
et mystique',[406] and called by Émile Blémont 'un rêve, farouche et tendre
tour à tour'.[407] In 1853, three years before he began to prepare *Saint
Julien,* Flaubert wrote to Louise Colet: 'Tu sais que c'est un de mes vieux
rêves que d'écrire un roman de chevalerie. Je crois cela faisable, même
après l'Arioste, en introduisant un élément de terreur et de poésie large
qui lui manque.'[408] Although in his letters he makes several jocular

---

[400] Ibid. pp. 92-3.   [401] *Légende des siècles,* p. 302.
[402] *Trois Contes,* pp. 118-19.   [403] Ibid. p. 125.
[404] Hugo, *Oeuvres poétiques,* ii. 41.   [405] Flaubert, *Correspondance,* i. 97.
[406] See *Trois Contes,* Conard, p. 247.
[407] E. Blémont, *Artistes et penseurs,* Lemerre, 1907, p. 242.
[408] *Correspondance,* iii. 245.

references to the supposedly anodyne, milk-and-water nature of his tale, calling it 'cette oeuvre édifiante, qui me fera passer pour "tourner au cléricalisme"',[409] there is in fact a full measure of terror in the story, much of which takes place in the 'énorme' Middle Ages which captivated Barbey d'Aurevilly. 'Les charmes de l'horreur' are not absent from it either, from the moment the leper makes his appearance to Julien. At the same time, it has its reassuring, picturesque and poetic side: 'Cela me met dans un milieu plus propre que le monde moderne et me fait du bien',[410] Flaubert told George Sand while he was writing it. In 1856 he reported to Bouilhet on the progress of his documentation: 'Je lis des bouquins sur la vie domestique au moyen âge et la vénerie. Je trouve des détails superbes et neufs. Je crois pouvoir faire une couleur amusante. Que dis-tu "d'un pâté de hérissons et d'une froumentée d'écureuils"?'[411] This quest for what Flaubert called 'particularités cocasses'[412] — a legacy of his Romantic origins[413] — was judged with severity by Valéry.[414] In *Saint Julien* the greatest number of these details are concentrated in the passage dealing with Julien's hunting-dogs and the various methods of pursuing quarry. The danger in this self-conscious use of the picturesque is that a patronizing note of false naïveté may creep into the narrative and trivialize it; in Flaubert's story one of the few hints of this ironic condescension occurs in the mention of Julien's father's reluctance to take a bath (a medieval trait which was one of the main points of contention between republicans and Catholics):[415] 'Il y avait même, dans un endroit écarté, une étuve à la romaine; mais le bon seigneur s'en privait, estimant que c'est un usage des idolâtres.'[416]

Saint Julien, then, a vision of the Middle Ages both ideal and horrific, owes nothing to conventional Catholic or republican views of the period; neither is it merely a 'Moyen Âge énorme et délicat' exploited for the Romantic extremes of horror and perfection it offers: the originality of this work lies in the personal experience which informs it. We saw in

---

[409] *Correspondance: Supplément*, iii. 238. Cf. *supra*, p. 124.

[410] *Correspondance*, vii. 279.

[411] Ibid. iv. 104.

[412] *Correspondance: Supplément*, i. 246.

[413] *Notre-Dame de Paris* abounds in such 'particularités'. Cf. also Hugo's 'Légende du beau Pécopin' (*Le Rhin*).

[414] See Valéry, *Oeuvres*, i (1957), 618.

[415] Cf. e.g. Michelet, *La Sorcière* (*supra*, p. 57), and Lecoy de la Marche's reply (*Revue du monde catholique*, xiv (1866)).

[416] *Trois Contes*, p. 79.

speaking of Renan that Flaubert was conscious at times of a medieval self stirring within him.[417] When he was visited by 'le frisson historique',[418] the memory of all his previous existences returned to him. Several of these were medieval: 'Je suis mort, pendant la croisade, pour avoir mangé trop de raisin sur la plage de Syrie. J'ai été pirate et moine.'[419] And Julien is clearly Flaubert, in a large measure: his ferocity is Flaubert's,[420] and also his solitude. When, after the catastrophe, he drifts without purpose through an alien world ('Il s'en alla, mendiant sa vie par le monde'), his suffering is unmistakably Flaubertian: 'Le besoin de se mêler à l'existence des autres le faisait descendre dans la ville. Mais l'air bestial des figures, le tapage des métiers, l'indifférence des propos glaçaient son coeur.'[421]

An important letter written to Hennique in 1880 reveals Flaubert's intentions in his recreation of the past:

> Dieu sait jusqu'à quel point je pousse le scrupule en fait de documents, livres, informations, voyages, etc. . . . Eh bien, je regarde tout cela comme très secondaire et inférieur. La vérité matérielle . . . ne doit être qu'un tremplin pour s'élever plus haut. Me croyez-vous assez godiche pour être convaincu que j'aie fait dans *Salammbô* une vraie reproduction de Carthage, et dans *Saint Antoine* une peinture exacte de l'Alexandrinisme? Ah! non! mais je suis sûr d'avoir exprimé *l'idéal* qu'on en a aujourd'hui.[422]

He had remarked many years before, in 1864: 'L'histoire n'est que la réflexion du présent sur le passé, et voilà pourquoi elle est toujours à refaire.'[423] This preoccupation with today's ideal of the past − in place of the past's ideal of itself, sought after by orthodox Parnassians, and which Taine mistakenly believed to be Flaubert's sole object in *Saint Julien* − is a new and sophisticated one, which marks the beginnings of the Symbolist era. (Marcel Schwob, in his famous article published in *Spicilège* (1896), had nothing but praise for the story and for its hero,

---

[417] Cf. *supra,* p. 58. Sartre corroborates this! See *L'Idiot de la Famille,* Gallimard, 1971, i. 196, 513, 515, 609.

[418] *Correspondance,* iii, 19.

[419] Ibid. v, 240.

[420] He wrote to Popelin in Sept. 1870: 'J'ai une envie démesurée de me battre − oui! "Une soif de carnage"' (*Times Litt. Supp.,* 13 June 1968, p. 615).

[421] *Trois Contes,* pp. 123-4. Cf. *L'Éducation Sentimentale,* where Frédéric Moreau is similarly cast adrift: 'Il voyagea./ Il connut la mélancolie des paquebots . . .', etc. (Part 3, Ch. 6), and where at an earlier stage he experiences the same *ennui:* 'Quelquefois, l'espoir d'une distraction l'attirait vers les boulevards . . . Mais . . . il se sentait tout écoeuré par la bassesse des figures, la niaiserie des propos . . .' (Part 1, Ch. 5).

[422] *Correspondance,* viii, 374.

[423] *Correspondance: Supplément,* ii, 19.

'un Julien cruellement passionné, dont l'âme est tout près de la nôtre'.)[424]
Flaubert holds fast to his scrupulous work of documentation; but he has
pronounced the words which emancipate writers from the need to engage
in such labours. The true face of the past is no longer sought; and the
Symbolist imagination will soon create, from any chance materials that
take its fancy, a diversity of new and extravagantly subjective Middle
Ages.

[424] M. Schwob, *Spicilège,* 2nd edn., 1896, p. 182.

SECTION TWO: AFTER 1870

CHAPTER 7

'Roland, c'est la France faite homme' (Léon Gautier)

The ever-changing fortunes of the Middle Ages during the nineteenth
century took a new turn in 1870. Their return to favour at this time
forms a curious interlude, quite distinct, of course, from the Symbolist
return to favour which immediately followed it, and deserving some
mention, despite the fact that it bore no fruit in literature other than
the most mediocre and ephemeral.

The war, the Commune, and the Prussian occupation all served to
focus attention on the Middle Ages. As in 1851, they were enlisted in
the work of national regeneration; but whereas then only the Imperial
government had been concerned in their promotion, now almost everyone, Catholic and republican alike, took a part in it. Léon Gautier, as
one might expect, was in the forefront of the national task-force.
Republican poets joined in no less: their outraged patriotism dispelled
their aversion for the Middle Ages, which were invoked both in battle —

> Restés sans peur et sans reproche,
> Jacques Bonhomme avec Roland,
> Amadis de Gaule et Gavroche
> Vont ensemble au combat hurlant . . .[1]

proclaimed Banville in November 1870 — and in defeat: hopes of an
eventual *revanche* were nurtured by meditation upon the stories of
Roland and Joan of Arc, as we shall see.

The attention of everyone was redirected towards national tradition,
neglect of which was declared to be a major cause of the disasters which
had befallen France. Even Renan and Taine relented in some measure
towards the Middle Ages. Renan's *La Réforme intellectuelle et morale
de la France* (November 1871) prescribed as a remedy for the nation's
ills return to the 'Germanic' spirit of the *ancien régime*. 'La France du
Moyen Âge est une construction germanique',[2] he declared. Progressive
elimination of Germanic elements, the last of which had been swept away
by the Revolution, had weakened the nation and brought her to her

---

[1] Banville, *Idylles prussiennes*, 1872, p. 84.   [2] Renan, *Os. cs.* i. 347.

present extremity: 'Corrigeons-nous de la démocratie. Rétablissons la royauté, rétablissons dans une certaine mesure la noblesse',[3] was Renan's advice. Taine's *Origines de la France contemporaine* protested against the demolition of tradition by classical reason. In the first volume, *L'Ancien Régime* (1876), he spoke with the utmost warmth of the medieval Church's civilizing influence: 'C'est dans ce monde doux et divin que se réfugie le coeur attristé, affamé de mansuétude et de tendresse.'[4]

Fustel de Coulanges published a series of articles in which he re-examined, in the light of recent events, the present import of France's medieval past. In August 1871 he went as far as to say that wrong thinking about the Middle Ages was responsible for the tragic state of dissension resulting in the Commune:

> Chacun se façonne un moyen âge imaginaire . . . et chacun se fait sa foi et son *credo* politique suivant l'erreur à laquelle il a donné sa pré-férence ou à laquelle son éducation première l'a enchaîné. Autant de façons d'envisager le moyen âge, autant de partis en France: ce sont nos théories historiques qui nous divisent le plus. . . . Ne disons pas que l'un nie le droit du seigneur parce qu'il est royaliste, et que l'autre en affirme l'existence parce qu'il est républicain; le contraire est plus vrai; c'est parce que l'un n'a pas vu dans l'histoire le droit du seigneur et les autres choses semblables qu'il est royaliste, c'est parce que l'autre a cru les y voir qu'il est républicain. Ainsi l'histoire forme nos opinions.[5]

He pleaded for a saner approach to the past:

> A l'observer attentivement, nous reconnaîtrons d'abord qu'il ne mérite ni tant d'enthousiasme ni tant de colères; alors, loin de nous irriter, il nous calmera peut-être, et il éteindra ces mêmes passions qui aujourd'hui s'allument en son nom et prétendent s'autoriser de lui.[5]

'La connaissance du moyen âge,' he concluded, 'mais la connaissance exacte et scientifique, sincère et sans parti-pris, est pour notre société un intérêt de premier ordre.'[5] In May 1872 he denied that France was essentially Germanic in origin, putting forward the theory, to be developed in his *Histoire des Institutions politiques de l'ancienne France* (Vol. I, 1875), that the Frankish invasions were not in the nature of a conquest and had no lasting effect upon the nation.[6] The

---

[3] Ibid. p. 373.
[4] Taine, *Les Origines de la France contemporaine:* (1) *L'Ancien Régime*, 1876, p. 8.
[5] *RDM*, 1 Aug. 1871, pp. 537-8.
[6] *RDM*, 15 May 1872, F. de Coulanges, 'L'Invasion germanique au cinquième siècle'.

following September he contended that of those warring historians engaged in 'une sorte de guerre civile en permanence', the most culpable were on the republican side: 'Être patriote, pour beaucoup d'entre nous, c'est être ennemi de l'ancienne France.' They more than anyone else provided fuel for France's enemies: 'Le véritable patriotisme', Fustel proclaimed, 'n'est pas l'amour du sol, c'est l'amour du passé, c'est le respect pour les générations qui nous ont précédés. Nos historiens ne nous apprennent qu'à les maudire.'[7]

So republican denigration of the Middle Ages was for the time being outlawed. Henri Martin suggested to his fellow-countrymen that in their hour of need they should seek 'un véritable appui moral' in the Druids;[8] but it was to the heroes of medieval epic – in particular to Roland – that most Frenchmen turned for consolation. Léon Gautier gives 1870 as the starting date for a new phase of revived interest in them;[9] in the Introduction to his 'édition classique' of the *Chanson de Roland* (1875) he stated that 'la réaction en faveur du moyen âge a marché plus vite que les plus téméraires n'eussent osé le désirer.'[10] During the Siege of Paris, Charles Lenient lectured at the Sorbonne on 'la Poésie patriotique en France', and Gaston Paris, at the Collège de France, on 'la *Chanson de Roland* et la nationalité française'. Lenient (a fervent republican) interrupted his course of lectures to consider patriotic poetry, beginning with the Carolingian epic cycle. The *querelle des anciens et des modernes,* he declared, could scarcely provide 'l'alimentation morale' urgently needed by his audience: 'Aussi mes regards se sont-ils tournés malgré moi d'un autre côté, vers des temps moins heureux, moins brillants, mais plus conformes aux nôtres.' He added that 'les âmes, énervées et amollies par vingt ans de servilité et d'affaissement sentent le besoin de se retremper aux sources des grandes pensées et des grands sentiments.'[11] In early December he presented to his audience the characters of the *Chanson de Roland*. Ganelon – by tradition a descendant of Doon de Mayence – was 'le Mayençais, personnage morose, susceptible, ombrageux, comme le sont volontiers les gens d'outre-Rhin.' Roland, 'franc, ouvert, sans arrière-pensée, sans détour, incapable de mensonge et de duplicité', was set in opposition to the fraudulent figure of Siegfried, 'enveloppé de son bonnet magique qui le rend invisible, et

[7] *RDM,* 1 Sept. 1872, pp. 243-4.
[8] H. Martin, *Études d'archéologie celtique,* 1872, p. iv.
[9] See *Les Épopées françaises,* 2nd edn., ii (1892), Ch. XVI.
[10] *La Chanson de Roland,* ed. L. Gautier, 1875, p. xlix.
[11] *Revue des cours littéraires,* 15 Oct. 1870, pp. 721-3.

devenu invulnérable depuis qu'il s'est baigné dans le sang du dragon Fafnir. . . . L'un est le héros des ténèbres, l'autre, le héros de la lumière.'[12] Mention was made at this point of the King of Friesland's perfidious weapon in Ariosto, a 'tube de fer' which Roland throws into the sea: 'Les canons Krupp sont sortis de là.'[13] About the same time Gaston Paris gave his opening lecture at the Collège de France (8 Dec.). Its theme was 'la solidarité indissoluble qui nous rattache moralement à nos pères des temps féodaux'.[14] The *Chanson de Roland* was chosen as the principal text: 'Douce France!' he exclaimed, 'Les Allemands nous ont envié ce mot, et ont vainement cherché à en retrouver le pendant dans leur poésie nationale.' On the same day Léon Gautier finished the Introduction to his edition of the *Chanson de Roland* (published in 1872), in which he expressed the hope: 'Puissent les beaux vers de ce Chant national consoler ceux qui pleurent aujourd'hui sur leur pays; puisse ce récit du passé nous rendre la confiance en l'avenir!'[15] 'Où étaient-ils, quand notre Chanson fut écrite . . . nos orgueilleux envahisseurs?' he asked: 'Ils erraient en bandes sauvages sous l'ombre de forêts sans nom: ils ne savaient . . . que piller et tuer. Quand nous tenions d'une main si ferme notre grande épée lumineuse . . . qu'étaient-ils? Des Mohicans ou des Peaux-Rouges . . .'[16] Looking forward to *la Revanche* − 'Nous n'avons encore, il est vrai, assisté qu'à la défaite; mais il n'est pas sans quelque gloire, ce Roncevaux du XIXe siècle, et demain nous saurons bien le réparer par quelque grande et belle victoire de Saragosse' − he concluded with the quotation: '*Damnes Deus pere, n'en laiser hunir France!*'[16] Some embarrassment was caused to Gautier by the fact that in the first edition of *Les Épopées françaises* (1865-8) he had, as a fervent *germaniste* engaged in perpetual skirmishes with *romanistes* such as Paul Meyer, dwelt at some length upon 'la *germanicité* de nos poëmes'.[17] The *Chanson de Roland* in particular, he had insisted, 'présente essentiellement le caractère germanique'.[18] In 1870 he modified this assertion to 'notre *Roland* . . . est le chant roman des Germains christianisés.'[19] Clinging to his belief in the superiority of

---

[12] Ch. Lenient, *La Poésie patriotique en France au moyen âge*, 1891, pp. 44-5.
    Cf. the felonious warrior in Hugo's 'Chant du Tournoi' (1824), *supra*, pp. 18-19.
[13] G. Paris, *La Poésie du moyen âge*, première série, 1885, 111.
[14] Ibid. p. 108.
[15] *La Chanson de Roland*, ed. L. Gautier, 1872, p. viii.
[16] Ibid. pp. cc-cci.
[17] *Les Épopées françaises*, i (1865), 10.
[18] Ibid. p. 83.
[19] *La Chanson de Roland*, 1872, p. xxix.

the German race, in which he continued to include the French nation, he made a distinction between good Germans and bad: 'Nous appartenons à la race des Germains qui ont fait halte, et nous ne sommes pas de ceux qui perpétuent les invasions!'[20] He claimed Charlemagne for the French: 'L'Allemagne prétend que Charlemagne lui appartient et n'a rien de français. . . . C'est nous, Franks, qui avons gardé le souvenir vivant du grand Empereur . . . c'est nous qui l'avons aimé et chanté: donc il nous appartient, donc il est à nous.'[21] Gautier's *Chanson de Roland* ran into seven editions between 1872 and 1879, and in 1878 the poem was put on the syllabus for the *agrégation des lettres* and *agrégation de grammaire*. In the same year Rochet's colossal statue of Charlemagne, attended by Roland and Ogier — which we encountered in our second chapter, at the 1867 Exposition Universelle[22] —, was placed in front of Notre-Dame, 'couronne en tête, superbe, vainqueur',[23] in the words of Léon Gautier.

Enduring results came from the upsurge during the Siege of patriotic regard for medieval literature. In 1872 Gaston Paris and Paul Meyer founded *Romania*, with its epigraph from Wace:

> Pur remembrer des ancessurs
> Les diz et les faiz et les murs,

as a rival to the enemy publication *Germania*. They wrote in the Prospectus: 'L'oeuvre que nous voulons entreprendre, si elle est avant tout scientifique, est en même temps nationale, et nous avons la ferme conviction que la rupture trop brusque et trop radicale de la France avec son passé, l'ignorance de nos véritables traditions . . . doivent être comptées parmi les causes qui ont amené nos désastres.'[24] In 1875 the Société des Anciens Textes Français was founded. Its programme (published in 1874) stated that it would be in the national interest to follow Germany's example and teach medieval literature in schools. Appealing for support to 'tous ceux qui aiment la France de tous les temps', the Society declared: 'Nous pensons qu'il n'est pas d'oeuvre plus vraiment nationale que celle à laquelle nous voulons nous consacrer.'[25] A similar declaration was made in the prefatory note to the first number of the *Revue historique*, founded by Monod and Fagniez in 1876: 'L'étude du passé de la France . . . a aujourd'hui une

---

[20] Ibid. p. xxxii.   [21] Ibid. p. cxx.   [22] Cf. *supra*, p. 40.
[23] *Les Épopées françaises*, 2nd edn., i (1878), 549.
[24] *Bibliothèque de l'École des Chartes*, xxxii (1871), p. 231.
[25] Ibid. xxxv (1874), p. 629.

importance nationale. C'est par elle que nous pouvons rendre à notre pays l'unité et la force morales dont il a besoin.'[26]

This climate of opinion brought forth a vast amount of hastily-improvised patriotic verse and drama, presenting in the main the image of a resplendently heroic Middle Ages. Some poets, however, continued to regard the feudal past as thoroughly sinister; and for them the Prussian invasion represented the unleashing upon France's Athenian civilization of Taine's wild beasts and tattooed savages, or Leconte de Lisle's 'loups à face humaine' and Crusading 'horde carnassière'.[27] Banville's *Idylles prussiennes* appeared each week in *Le National* during the siege of Paris. One of them was entitled 'Cauchemar' (Oct. 1870):

> Oui, venez tous! Goths et Vandales
> Graissés de suif, sortez encor
> De vos tanières féodales,
> Avec vos casques tachés d'or!
>
> Ainsi que des sauvages ivres,
> Brûlez le passé radieux
> Et les monuments et les livres!
> Brisez les images des Dieux![28]

Leconte de Lisle himself declared in 'Le Sacre de Paris' (Jan. 1871):

> Tous les loups d'outre-Rhin ont mêlé leurs espèces:
> Vandale, Germain et Teuton . . .[29]

Auguste Lacaussade hurled imprecations at the enemy in 'Le Siège de Paris' (1871):

> Sous le savant en vous gît la brute première,
> Le sauvage en vous n'est pas mort. . . .
>
> Votre instinct carnassier, loups à faces humaines,
> Se trahit à vos cruautés! . . .
>
> En des jours de progrès ramenant les ténèbres,
> Le moyen âge et ses terreurs,
> Vous avez rallume par vos forfaits célèbres
> Du passé les sombres fureurs.[30]

[26] *Revue historique,* i (1876), p. 4.
[27] For the Romantics, of course, Germany had always represented 'le moyen âge perpétué' (F. Baldensperger, *Études d'histoire littéraire,* première série, 1907, 164) — that is, in their eyes, the domain of poetry and romance.
[2b] Banville, *Idylles prussiennes,* 1872, pp. 36-7.
[29] *Poèmes tragiques,* p. 79.   [30] A. Lacaussade, *Poésies,* i (1896), 265-7.

Hugo told the Assemblée Nationale in the same year that the declaration of Papal infallibility coinciding with the Prussian invasion had brought back the Dark Ages: 'A côté du pape gothique, qui essaye de revivre, l'empereur gothique reparaît.'[31] In 1872 he called the German victory 'le moyen-âge qui met la griffe sur la révolution';[32] and in *L'Année terrible* he described the Prussian armies, 'le flot des bandes féodales',[33] closing in upon Paris, as the seven Saxon tribes — 'Hideux, casqués, dorés, tatoués de blasons'[34] —descending upon Athens. (However, as in *La Légende des siècles,* behind the sinister latter-day Middle Ages, a better world, which they replaced, is discernible: the Prussians are unworthy of their glorious forefathers, the Burgraves of old, and Hugo denounces their 'exploits louches et singuliers/ Dont se fût indignée au temps des chevaliers/ La magnanimité farouche de l'épée' — 'Rois teutons,' he tells them, 'vous avez mal copié vos pères'.[35])

Other writers — and these were in the majority — found relief for their wounded patriotic feelings in the contemplation of an ideal medieval France triumphing over her enemies. Coppée's play *La Guerre de cent ans* (written in collaboration with Armand d'Artois in 1872, published 1877, never performed), shows a noble family helping Du Guesclin in his work of *revanche* after the defeat of Crécy and the humiliating treaty of Brétigny. The dying Enguerrand de Mauny addresses his sons: 'Les hontes d'aujourd'hui mes enfants, lavez-les!'[36] They set forth to fight the English:

> Vêtus de fer de pied en cap, la lance droite,
> Fermes sur leurs chevaux bardés de fer comme eux . . .[37]

Vestiges of republican sentiment linger here and there — Du Guesclin sermonizes Enguerrand's son Oliver on the wretched lot of his serfs: 'Pauvre Jacques, sa vie est comme un mauvais rêve'[38] — but the world in which the characters move is in every other respect a Romantic

---

[31] Hugo, *Os. cs.*, ed. J. Massin, xv (1970), 1261.
[32] Ibid. p. 1330. Cf. also Paul de Saint-Victor, *Barbares et bandits,* Lévy, 1872, pp. 26-7, 179-80.
[33] Ibid. p. 57.
[34] Ibid. p. 45. Here again, Heine had shown the way to the French. Cf. *Germania* (1844): 'Cette chevalerie en uniforme prussien, hideux mélange de superstition gothique et de moderne mensonge . . .' (*Poëmes et légendes,* 1855, p. 243).
[35] Hugo, *Os. cs.* xv. 51.
[36] Coppée & D'Artois, *La Guerre de cent ans,* 1878, p. 26.
[37] Ibid. p. 7. Cf. Gottlob le Brutal, the evil baron in Coppée's earlier 'Le Justicier', who set forth each day, 'Vêtu de fer, ganté de fer, masqué de fer', to persecute his vassals (*supra,* p. 163).
[38] *La Guerre de cent ans,* p. 50.

elysium. The young soldier Alain evokes in loving detail his childhood home, as he leaves to join Du Guesclin:

> Adieu, donjon, tourelles,
> Créneaux où sont les nids des blanches tourterelles,
> Où le lierre grimpant s'émaille de fleurs d'or,
> Grands bois où, vers le soir, passe le son du cor . . .
> Longs reflets des vitraux sur les vieilles armures . . .[39]

(In later life, Coppée's admiration for the Middle Ages grew with each passing year, and he extolled them on numerous occasions in his verse as 'Jours de géniale innocence',[40] when the poor were 'libres d'angoisse',[41] concluding at the end of his career, now an ardent Catholic and member of the Ligue de la Patrie Française, that 'Notre pire démence, en ce siècle orgueilleux,/ C'est l'horreur du passé, le mépris des aïeux.'[42])

In the second edition of *Les Épopées françaises* Léon Gautier recalls that 'l'ennemi n'avait pas encore quitté notre territoire que déjà nous nous tournions en larmes vers ces deux figures lumineuses, Roland et Jeanne d'Arc, en leur demandant à la fois des consolations et des espérances.'[43] Gautier had, as a disciple of Veuillot, looked forward in 1865 to a crusade against the English, 'ces révolutionnaires . . . ces hérétiques'. In that fortunate event, he declared, 'Jeanne saurait bien marcher à notre tête, guerrière invisible; et grâce à elle, nous chasserions de leur insolente prépondérance dans les conseils de l'Europe ceux que la Pucelle a si glorieusement chassés d'Orléans.'[44] After 1870 Joan of Arc was often invoked, in the same tone of voice, by patriotic poets; but now the enemy was English only in name and Prussian in reality – 'le dur Teuton d'Allemagne aux yeux clairs',[45] against whom Banville enlisted the national heroine's aid at the end of his poem 'La Bonne Lorraine' (1872).

> O Jeanne! lègue-nous ta haine héréditaire;
> Marche avec nous à l'ennemi![46]

cried Jules Barbier in 1870; and three years later his play *Jeanne d'Arc* was performed in Paris, with choruses set to music by Gounod –

> Nous délivrerons la patrie! . . .
> Dieu le veut![47]

[39] Ibid. p. 59.   [40] Coppée, *Poésies, 1886-90,* p. 134.
[41] Coppée, *Dans la prière et dans la lutte,* 1901, p. 79.
[42] Coppée, *Des vers français,* 1906, p. 12.
[43] *Les Épopées françaises,* 2nd edn., ii (1892), 745.
[44] *Études littéraires pour la défense de l'Église,* 1865, p. 413.
[45] Banville, *Les Exilés. Les Princesses,* p. 191.
[46] J. Barbier, *La Gerbe: Poésies, 1842-83,* 1884, p. 251.
[47] J. Barbier, *Jeanne d'Arc,* 1874, p. 84.

The heroine defies her captors at the end:

> Je connais mon pays; il m'a donné son âme!
> Il se redressera comme moi sous l'affront! . . .
> Noyez-le tout entier dans le sang et les larmes!
> Reculez sa frontière, ivre de vos succès! . . .
> La France renaîtra dans le dernier Français![48]

The same sentiments were expressed in Laprade's poem written for the inauguration of Frémiet's statue in the Place des Pyramides (1874):

> Nous attendons, ô Jeanne! une autre délivrance:
> La race d'où tu sors n'est pas près de périr.[49]

Laprade published a considerable amount of patriotic verse at this time; Frédéric Mistral wrote of him in 1870: 'Les races qui trouvent de tels bardes pour glorifier leurs défaites ne sont pas près de mourir. Quand Théroulde chantait le désastre de Roland, n'affirmait-il pas aussi la vitalité française?'[50] The appeal of Roland and the glorious defeat of Roncevaux was in fact more powerful even than that of Joan of Arc during the seventies. 'Roland, c'est la France faite homme',[51] proclaimed Léon Gautier in 1870; and Gaston Paris told his audience at the Collège de France: 'Faisons-nous reconnaître pour les fils de ceux qui sont morts à Roncevaux et de ceux qui les ont vengés.'[52] Gautier said of the *Chanson de Roland* in *Les Épopées françaises:* 'Il a fallu la guerre de 1870 pour nous en donner l'intelligence et l'amour. Sedan a fait comprendre Roncevaux',[53] and he further explained the *Chanson*'s popularity at this time: 'En attendant Charlemagne, nous nous consolâmes avec Roland.'[54] Michelet's reflections during the Siège of Paris were more bitter in tone: 'Il m'est souvenu de Roland, que Ganelon de Mayence se garda bien de combattre, mais qu'il sut mettre dans un cirque des Pyrénées. . . . Il périt. Qui ose dire l'avoir vaincu? . . . Il périt de son propre effort, de l'appel désespéré que son cor fit aux nations, — sourdes alors, comme aujourd'hui.'[55]

Roncevaux was the principal theme of an insignificant offshoot of *La Légende des siècles: La Légende des paladins* (1875), by Joseph Autran, a close friend of Laprade. Léon Gautier was captivated by this work and called its author 'un *revigoureur*'.[56] It is a collection of insipid

---

[48] J. Barbier, *Jeanne d'Arc*, p. 179.   [49] Laprade, *Oeuvres poétiques*, vi. 250.
[50] See E. Biré, *Victor de Laprade*, 1886, p. 342.
[51] *La Chanson de Roland*, 1872, p. vii.   [52] G. Paris, *La Poésie du moyen âge*, i. 118.
[53] *Les Épopées françaises*, 2nd edn., ii (1892), 725.
[54] Ibid. p. 746.
[55] Michelet, *La France devant l'Europe*, 2nd edn., Florence, 1871, p. 74.
[56] *Les Épopées françaises*, ii (1892), 763.

apocryphal anecdotes concerning Roland and his peers. 'A ce récit, peuple de France,' proclaimed Autran, 'si ton coeur bat, tu peux revivre!',[57] and he deplored the state of disunion into which France had fallen, whereas in the Middle Ages her people were

> Fiers et suivant au loin leur étoile qui brille,
> Ils marchaient triomphants;
> Ils ne formaient alors qu'une seule famille
> Avec tous ses enfants.[58]

In conclusion he looked forward to the day when

> Nous serons de nouveau, sans peur et sans reproche,
> La race des vainqueurs.[59]

Much more important than this was Henri de Bornier's play *La Fille de Roland* (1875), the most remarkable — for the extraordinary sensation it caused, if not for its literary merit — of all the medieval evocations inspired by the events of 1870. The play was written eleven years before its performance. The Théâtre Français refused it in 1865, because, according to Bornier, it was feared that it might give offence to the Emperor. 'Eh quoi!' he was told, 'vous voulez mettre en scène Charlemagne, un empereur humilié, la France vaincue! . . . Y songez-vous? Est-ce qu'un empereur peut être humilié? Est-ce que la France peut être vaincue?'[60] The only later addition was the 'Chanson des épées' in the second act (referring to 'L'étranger frémissant de rage,/ Sarrazins, Saxons, ou Danois,/ Tourbe hurlante et carnassière'),[61] but the entire play proved to be astonishingly in keeping with the mood of the 1875 audience. With Sarah Bernhardt and Mounet-Sully in the leading roles, it ran for 115 consecutive performances. Its success was, in the words of Banville, 'immense, complet, retentissant'.[62] On the first night the audience were moved to tears by lines such as 'Ô vainqueurs, prenez garde aux enfants des martyrs!',[63] 'Tout homme a deux pays, le sien et puis la France!',[64] and Charlemagne's speech after Gérald's victorious combat with the Saracen:

> Ô France! douce France! ô ma France bénie!
> Rien n'épuisera donc ta force et ton génie!
> Terre du dévoûment, de l'honneur, de la foi;
> Il ne faut donc jamais désespérer de toi.
> Puisque, malgré tes jours de deuil et de misère,
> Tu trouves un héros dès qu'il est nécessaire![65]

---

[57] J. Autran, *Os. cs.* v (1877), 161.   [58] Ibid. p. 257.   [59] Ibid. p. 260.
[60] H. de Bornier, 'L'Héroïsme au théâtre', *Le Correspondant*, 10 Feb. 1900, p. 539.
[61] *La Fille de Roland*, 1930, p. 33.   [62] *Le National*, 25 Feb. 1875.
[63] *La Fille de Roland*, p. 18.   [64] Ibid. p. 57.   [65] *La Fille de Roland*, p. 65.

In the 'Chanson des épées', according to Mounet-Sully, they saw 'une allusion frémissante à l'Alsace et à la Lorraine'.[66] Charlemagne's line 'Quand ils n'ont plus la gloire, il reste aux rois la mort!'[67] was applauded to the echo as an allusion to Sedan. Ganelon was identified with Marshal Bazaine, who had been brought to trial for treason in 1873.[68] The intensity of the patriotic emotion aroused in the audience was such that they were prepared to overlook any shortcomings in the plot and characterization of the play. These were not inconsiderable: Ganelon was presented as a virtuous *père de famille* who had escaped death and vanished into obscurity, to repent of his crime and rear a son of exemplary courage and virtue – Gérald, who falls in love with Berthe, the daughter of Roland and Aude, whom his sense of honour forbids him to marry when he learns the secret of his father's identity. Certain critics raised their voices against this play: Auguste Vitu, writing in *Le Figaro*, was one of those who objected that Charlemagne was German rather than French;[69] and Banville was outraged at Bornier's violation of legend – 'J'aimerais mieux un viol fait à l'histoire!' – and, in particular, at his conversion of Aude into a wife and mother. This he called 'un crime de lèse-poésie'.[70] Paulin Paris, however, gave *La Fille de Roland* his entire approval, and told its author: 'Courage donc, monsieur de Bornier, vous nous avez rendu la tragédie nationale.'[71]

---

[66] Mounet-Sully, *Souvenirs d'un tragédien,* Lafitte, 1917, p. 117.
[67] *La Fille de Roland,* p. 59.
[68] See Lenient, *La Poésie patriotique en France dans les temps modernes,* 1894, ii. 416.
[69] See A. Vitu, *Les Mille et une nuits du théâtre,* 2nd edn., Ollendorff, iii (1886) 255.
[70] *Le National,* 25 Feb. 1875.
[71] *Polybiblion littéraire,* deuxième série, i (1875), p. 528.

CHAPTER 8

THE 1880s AND 1890s: I. THE CLIMATE OF OPINION

'Seule la littérature mystique convient à notre immense fatigue'
(R. de Gourmont)

A. *Respect for tradition: 'N'assombrissons pas nos antiquités nationales';
the 'foyer inspirateur' of legend*

The events of 1870 had their part in forming the climate of opinion of
the eighties and nineties which brought forth the works of the Symbolists,
whose infatuation for the Middle Ages was such that Heredia declared in
1905: 'Le mouvement symboliste a été surtout un retour vers le Moyen-
Age.'[1] This climate was one of renewed respect for 'nos pères' and pride
in the national tradition.

Republican historians continued to let fly at the Middle Ages during
these years;[2] and we have seen that Leconte de Lisle's denunciation of
'les siècles maudits' entered its most active phase in the 1880s. Voices
of protest were raised against him, however. 'Non, non, il ne faut point
maudire le moyen âge', wrote Jules Lemaître in an article published two
weeks after the appearance of 'Les Siècles maudits' (Dec. 1883). He
insisted that modern man owed less to the ancient Greeks than to his
medieval Christian ancestors, who had endowed him with 'une compli-
cation de la conscience morale, un approfondissement de la tristesse et
un enrichissement de la sensibilité'.[3] Four years later Anatole France
predicted in *Le Temps,* a few days before Leconte de Lisle delivered his
Academy speech, that it would contain 'un morceau sur le moyen âge'.
'M. Leconte de Lisle poursuit le moyen âge de sa haine', he continued,
and proceeded to defend his forefathers at some length:

---

[1] G. Le Cardonnel & Ch. Vellay, *La Littérature contemporaine,* Mercure de
France, 1905, p. 284.

[2] e.g. Marc Bonnefoy: 'Ô moyen âge! ô époque infernale!' (*Histoire du bon
vieux temps,* Librairie centrale des publications populaires, 1884, p. 206). Cf.
also Raoul Rosières's portrait of the feudal baron: ' "Armez-vous, dit-il à ses
routiers, il me faut de l'argent, fouillez ces cabanes, frappez ces serfs,
emprisonnez-les, tuez-les s'il le faut!" ' (*Histoire de la société française au
moyen-âge,* i. 359); and Henri Bouchot's portrait of his lady:
'Fières et brutales comme leurs seigneurs, les dames féodales ont mieux à
tenter que de tirer l'aiguille ou de chanter leur ami sur un rythme dolent.
Montées sur des roncins de bataille, elles tiennent les routes, armées jusqu'aux
dents' (*La Famille d'autrefois,* Lecène & Oudin, 1887, p. 13).

[3] J. Lemaître, *Les Contemporains,* i (1886), 160. Cf. Mme de Staël, *supra,* pp. 3, 16.

Ils préparèrent le monde meilleur dont nous jouissons aujourd'hui. . . .
Ils portèrent au plus haut degré de l'héroïsme les vertus militaires, qui
sont les vertus fondamentales sur lesquelles tout l'ordre humain repose
encore aujourd'hui. Ils apportèrent au monde ce qui l'honore peut-être
le plus: l'esprit chevaleresque.[4]

Increasing emotion overcame him, and he concluded with a solemn
benediction:

Tandis que j'écris, mille images éparses de la vie de nos pères brillent
et s'agitent à la fois dans mon imagination . . . je vois partout les saintes
choses du travail et de l'amour, je vois la ruche pleine d'abeilles et de
rayons de miel. Je vois la France et je dis: Mes pères, soyez bénis; soyez
bénis dans vos oeuvres qui ont préparé les nôtres, soyez bénis dans vos
souffrances qui n'ont point été stériles, soyez bénis jusque dans les
erreurs de votre courage et de votre simplicité.[4]

Two years later, in an article on French folk songs, he returned to the
theme: 'N'assombrissons pas à plaisir nos antiquités nationales. De tout
temps, la France fut douce à ses enfants';[5] and he declared shortly after-
wards: 'Le respect du passé est la seule religion qui nous reste, et elle est
le lien des esprits nouveaux.'[6]

Both Lemaître and France praised the work of Gaston Paris. Lemaître
was moved by the first volume of *La Poésie du moyen âge* (1885) to write
an article overflowing with gratitude to the eminent medievalist, for his
demonstration that 'le moyen âge, c'est bien nous-mêmes . . . les hommes
de ces temps anciens sont bien réellement nos pères.'[7] Speaking of this
personal appeal of the Middle Ages which antiquity lacks, Lemaître
declared:

Rien ne me touche plus que de savoir ce qu'ont été mes pères lointains,
ce qu'ils ont dit, ce qu'ils ont écrit, ce qu'ils ont pensé, ce qu'ils ont
souffert, comment ils ont songé le songe de la vie − et de retrouver leur
âme en moi. C'est le passé qui fait le prix du présent et qui donne au
présent sa forme. C'est dans le passé qu'il faut vivre, fût-ce pour en avoir
pitié: en nous attendrissant sur nos ancêtres, c'est sur nous-mêmes que
nous nous attendrissons.[8]

He concluded: 'Ce livre nous fait aimer M. Gaston Paris: il nous fait aimer
aussi le moyen âge.'[7] Anatole France was similarly moved by Gaston

---

[4] A. France, *Oeuvres complètes illustrées,* Calmann-Lévy, vi. 93-5.
[5] A. France, *Os. cs.* vii. 121.   [6] Ibid. p. 336.
[7] Lemaître, *Les Contemporains,* iii (1887), 235. Cf. once more the *groupe de
Coppet, supra,* p. 3.   [8] Ibid. pp. 226-7.

Paris's *Manuel d'ancien français* (1888). As he read it in the shade of a venerable oak-tree, it evoked for him 'les figures de tous ceux qui, dans la douce France, aux âges de chevalerie et de clergie, parlèrent de combats, d'amour et de sagesse'.[9] The voice of the oak-tree spoke to his imagination:

> Lis, lis à mon ombre les chansons gothiques dont j'entendis jadis les refrains se mêler au bruissement de mon feuillage. L'âme de tes aïeux est dans ces chansons plus vieilles que moi-même. Connais ces aïeux obscurs, partage leurs joies et leurs douleurs passées. . . . Sois pieux, vénère la terre de la patrie. N'en prends jamais une poignée dans ta main sans penser qu'elle est sacrée.[10]

We have seen[11] the controlled but ever-present patriotic fervour that informed Gaston Paris's lectures during the sixties and seventies; his work reached a wider public in the eighties and nineties, with the publication of *La Poésie du moyen âge* (2 vols., 1885-95) and the *Manuel* (1888). The first of these works contained his 1869 lecture, 'Les Origines de la littérature française', in which he spoke of the mysterious poetry of Celtic place-names: 'Ils gardent sous leur enveloppe usée mais tenace les premières émotions de nos pères à la vue du sol où tant de générations se sont couchées avant la nôtre',[12] with the same emotion that had filled Barbey d'Aurevilly, introducing his Abbaye de Blanchelande, with its 'nom si pittoresque, si poétique et presque virginal', to the readers of *L'Ensorcelée* (1852) — 'le nom, ce dernier soupir qui reste des choses!'[13] Medieval studies flourished during these two decades. Gaston Paris declared in 1881 that 'les rares protestations qu'il arrive parfois d'entendre encore à ce propos font l'effet de ces projectiles oubliés qui viennent tout à coup, maniés par une main maladroite, à faire explosion sur un champ de bataille depuis longtemps abandonné.'[14] Among important

---

[9] A. France, *Os. cs.* vi. 572.   [10] Ibid. p. 579.

[11] Cf. *supra*, pp. 89, 198, 203.

[12] G. Paris, *La Poésie du moyen âge,* première série, 1885, 46.

[13] B. d'Aurevilly, *L'Ensorcelée,* 1966, p. 41.

[14] G. Paris, *La Poésie du moyen âge,* première série, 1885, 221. He was referring to the cry of alarm let forth by Brunetière in 1879 (*RDM*, 1 June). This extremely querulous article protested against the increased momentum of medieval studies during the 1870s, 'cette glorification systématique de la langue et de la littérature du moyen âge'. Taking up the position adopted by Sainte-Beuve, Brunetière warned that the medievalists' activities threatened to bring about a dangerous decline in taste: 'Redevenus en quelque sorte barbares à mesure qu'ils enfonçaient plus avant dans le moyen âge, c'est vers la barbarie qu'ils nous tirent insensiblement' (F. Brunetière, 'L'Érudition contemporaine et la littérature française au moyen âge', in *Études critiques sur l'histoire de la littérature française,* première série, 1880, 13, 70).

works published in the field were Petit de Julleville's history of medieval French theatre (1880-6), Godefroy's *Dictionnaire de l'ancienne langue française* (1881-1902), the *Cours de littérature celtique* (8 vols., 1883-99) by D'Arbois de Jubainville, who had been given the newly-created Chair of Celtic Language and Literature at the Sorbonne in 1882, Léon Gautier's *La Chevalerie* (1884), Jeanroy's *Origines de la poésie lyrique au moyen âge* (1889), Clédat's *Rutebeuf* (1891), Longnon's edition of Villon (1892), *Les Fabliaux* (1893) by Joseph Bédier, who had occupied the Chair of Medieval French Literature at Fribourg since 1889, Clédat's *La Poésie lyrique et satirique en France au moyen âge* (1893), and the first two volumes of the *Histoire de la langue et de la littérature française des origines à 1900,* published by Armand Colin under the editorship of Petit de Julleville. In 1880 medieval French literature was added to the prescribed syllabus for lycées (classes de deuxième et troisième). Elementary notions of the subject were to be acquired from 'une Chrestomathie du Moyen Âge'; and many such 'Chrestomathies' were duly published to this end (e.g., those of Godefroy (1883), Aubertin (1883), Constans (1884), Petit de Julleville (1886), and Clédat (1887), followed by that of Gaston Paris and Ernest Langlois in 1897).

Inspired by the same reverence for national tradition, French folk-lorists were no less active during these years. According to Maurras, Jean-François Bladé, the collector of *Poésies populaires de la Gascogne* (3 vols., 1881-2) and *Contes populaires de la Gascogne* (3 vols., 1886), unable to fight in 1870 because of poor eyesight, 'prit le parti de guerroyer contre l'Allemagne sur le champ de la science'.[15] The most active of all these folklorists was Paul Sébillot, at whose instigation the series 'Les Littératures populaires de toutes les nations' was begun in 1881. The 'Dîner de ma mère l'Oye', founded in 1882 by Sébillot and a few friends, evolved three years later into the Société des Traditions Populaires, which began publication of its *Revue des traditions populaires* in 1886. The periodical *Mélusine* was revived in 1884; and E. Rolland's six-volume *Recueil de chansons populaires* (1883-90) was perhaps the most notable of the many collections of folk-songs published at this time.

The movement for the recognition of medieval French art, culminating in the 1904 Paris Exposition des Primitifs français, must also be mentioned in this connection.[16] Louis Courajod was the most zealous

---

[15] Ch. Maurras, *Barbarie et poésie,* Nouvelle Librairie nationale, 1925, p. 125.
[16] For an account of this movement see G. Lafenestre, *Les Primitifs à Bruges et à Paris,* 1904.

campaigner in this field. From 1874 he was in charge of medieval and Renaissance sculpture at the Louvre, where he worked on the reclassification of the collection. The department of medieval and Renaissance sculpture was opened at the Louvre in 1893. Émile Mâle's *L'Art religieux du XIIIe siècle en France* was published in 1898.

The national tradition in all its manifestations provided balm for the wounded patriotic feelings of this generation. Mendès, in his article 'De la légende',[17] bewailed the destruction of legend, which he saw withering in the inclement air of positivist science:

> Elle [i.e. la légende] se disperse, s'évanouit, se meurt. Tout bon élève de l'École des Chartes a discuté Charlemagne, douté de Roland et nié Turpin . . . perdre toute illusion, voir s'écrouler une à une toutes les renommées légendaires, en arriver à croire que les hommes d'autrefois ne valaient pas mieux que les hommes d'aujourd'hui, cela est-il bien salutaire? Nous avons tant besoin d'exemples, hélas![18]

'Aucune pitié pour aucun rêve,'[19] he sighed, and impressed upon his fellow-poets that they must minister to a world sorely in need of consolation:

> Ah! les historiens dédaignent les chevaliers anciens, les preux, les héroïnes, les combats fantasques, les aventures miraculeuses? Eh bien! prenons tout entier ce passé fabuleux qu'ils répudient. . . . A nous tout ce qui n'est pas, c'est-à-dire la plus prestigieuse des opulences.[20]

The Wagnerian critic Édouard Schuré also dwelt upon the consoling power of legend in the Introduction to his *Les Grandes Légendes de France* (1892). The Celtic soul, he declared, 'la glorieuse vaincue qui toujours rebondit de ses défaites', was the indestructible soul of France; and Celtic legend, forged in this 'foyer inspirateur', possessed a mysterious regenerative virtue.[21]

---

[17] First published in *La République des lettres* (Jan. 1877), reprinted in Mendès's *Légende du Parnasse contemporain*, 1884.

[18] Mendès, *La Légende du Parnasse contemporain*, 1884, pp. 265-6. Cf. Nodier's remarks of 1830 on the consoling power of legend after the Revolution ('Du fantastique en littérature', *Oeuvres*, v (1832), 78).

[19] Ibid. p. 268.

[20] Ibid. pp. 270-1. Mendès was, of course, not in any sense of the word a Symbolist; but his one-act play *La Part du roi* (1872), with its banal Romantic intrigue, presents a few curiously pre-Symbolist features. Its setting is 'dans un château, autrefois', and its heroine 's'efforce de garder le maintien un peu roide des peintures sur fond d'or, auxquelles elle ressemble' (Mendès, *Théâtre en vers*, 1908, pp. 62-3).

[21] E. Schuré, *Les Grandes Légendes de France*, 1892, pp. i-ii.

Preoccupied with heroism incarnated in a martyred race, various writers of this period espoused the cause of one or other of the nation's constituent races, deemed by them to be the most worthy to survive. In 1881 Gobineau wrote *La Cour d'amour*, one of a planned but never executed collection of *Nouvelles féodales*, in which – in the words of Roger Béziau – the ageing writer 'se plaît à transposer ses amours dans une époque chère à son coeur'.[22] It was in the course of the same year that he finished his poem *Amadis* (published posthumously in 1887), and wrote two chapters of an *Histoire des mérovingiens*. All these works were vehicles for his belief in the superiority of the Aryan race. Chivalry and courts of love were of Germanic origin, he maintained, and Gallo-Roman Reason, in the person of the *légistes*, plotted the destruction of both. Its modern representatives were 'la canaille gallo-romaine qui, en ce moment, tourne à Monsieur Grévy et à Monsieur Gambetta'.[23] Certain other writers championed the Latin races. Paul Adam in his novels traced through history the conflict between Latin 'Idées-Forces' and Nordic barbarism; while the 'Sar' Joséphin Péladan's twenty-one-volume 'éthopée', *La Décadence latine* (of which the first volume, *Le Vice suprême*, appeared in 1884), was, in the words of Henri Mazel, permeated with 'cette angoisse de la décadence *finis Latinorum*! qu'ont ressentie si douloureusement tous ceux qui grandirent sous le signe maléfique de la Défaite'.[24] 'A la race latine qui va mourir', declared Péladan in 1891, 'nous préparons une dernière splendeur.'[25]

So the climate of these years was one of concern with tradition, and past deeds of valour enshrined in legend. We shall see that these preoccupations were not without their effect upon the writing of the Symbolists, almost all of whom were, like Bernard Lazare in his *Miroir des légendes* (1892), 'épris des gloires abolies'.[26]

B. *The upsurge of idealism: 'Il faut revenir aux Primitifs . . .'*

More important still, it was one of return to the past in protest against the modern world. Mazel wrote in 1891: 'L'atmosphère actuelle est . . . saturée d'idéalisme religieux. . . . Cette période peut dater ses origines,

---

[22] R. Béziau, '*La Cour d'amour*, dernière nouvelle de Gobineau' *RHLF* (Oct.-Dec. 1963), p. 663; see also R. Béziau, 'Une Opinion inédite sur les cours d'amour', *Revue des sciences humaines* (Jan.-March 1964). (For the tale itself see *MF* (Feb. 1963).)

[23] *RHLF* (Oct.-Dec. 1963), p. 654 (from the *Histoire des Mérovingiens*).

[24] *Nouvelle Revue du Midi* (Dec. 1924), p. 43.

[25] J. Péladan, *Salon de la Rose+Croix: Règle et monitoire, 1891*, pp. 28-9.

[26] B. Lazare, *Le Miroir des légendes*, 1892, p. 6.

au moins en France, de nos grands désastres.'[27] Idealism, or 'mysticism' — much of it of a somewhat spurious nature — took the place of the repudiated Second Empire positivism. Reviews such as Emmanuel Signoret's *Le Saint-Graal* (founded in 1892) — which enrolled under its banner forty contributors designated 'les Quarante chevaliers du Saint-Graal'[28] —, the Belgian Catholic *Durendal* (1894), and *La Trêve-Dieu* (1897), which declared in its first number: 'Sus aux banalités dont s'angoisse le Rêve',[29] testify to this prevailing climate, as does the immense popularity of such works as Paul Sabatier's *Vie de saint François d'Assise* (1894), which ran into nine editions in the year of its publication.

The English Pre-Raphaelites, derided in the 1850s,[30] now came into their own in France. Gabriel Sarrazin praised the noble idealism of Rossetti, 'un des seuls à oser réarborer, en parfaite sincérité de coeur, le grand Amour extatique des moines et des chevaliers'.[31] (Four years later, he acclaimed Tennyson's *Idylls of the King*[32] as 'un puissant coup d'aile vers le Sublime'.[33])

The French followed their example in preferring to the art of the Renaissance, glorified by Taine's generation, 'les beautés plus pâles, l'éclat moins superbe et plus pénétrant, du XIIIe siècle, par exemple, ou du XVe . . . l'âge magique, mystérieux et si complexe qui s'appela le moyen âge'.[34] A pamphlet was published entitled *De l'influence néfaste de la Renaissance* (by Marcel Reymond, 1890). In *Le Latin mystique* (1892) Remy de Gourmont borrowed the language once used by enemies of the Middle Ages to call their revered Renaissance

---

[27] H. Mazel, 'Tendances religieuses de l'art contemporain', *L'Art*, 1 Aug. 1891, p. 46.

[28] See L. Guichard, *La Musique et les lettres en France au temps du wagnérisme*, 1963, pp. 68-70.

[29] *La Trêve-Dieu*, no. 1 (Le Havre, Jan. 1897) (prefatory sonnet by Marcel Béliard).

[30] Maxime Du Camp referred to Millais's *Ophelia* as 'cette poupée en cire qui se noie . . . composition étrange, presque ridicule et assurément puérile' (*Les Beaux-Arts à l'Exposition Universelle de 1855*, 1855, p. 301). Henri Delaborde fulminated against the P.R.B. in the *RDM* (15 July 1858): 'Rien de plus malencontreux, rien de moins sympathique que l'effort pour paraître ingénu' (p. 244).

[31] G. Sarrazin, *Poètes modernes de l'Angleterre*, Ollendorff, 1885, p. 245.

[32] Also derided in France when they first appeared (1859). One critic asked: 'Pourquoi la poésie [anglaise] répète-t-elle des cantilènes surannées par la bouche de son lauréat? . . . pourquoi M. Tennyson n'a-t-il pas laissé là le vieil Arthur et ses chevaliers de la Table Ronde?' (*Revue internationale*, i (1859), p. 329. E. Gaulhiac).

[33] G. Sarrazin, *La Renaissance de la poésie anglaise*, Perrin, 1889, p. 170.

[34] *Revue bleue*, xlviii, 22 Aug. 1891, p. 243 (Pierre Gauthiez).

'cette époque indécise que l'on dénomme la Renaissance et qui fut l'un des reculs les plus mémorables en l'histoire de la civilisation'.[35] The Italian, Flemish, and French Primitives, for so long in disfavour (except with Catholics, such as Ozanam, who praised their serene and wholesome piety) were now prized by aesthetes for their 'decadent' qualities.[36] Young painters, such as Maurice Denis, Émile Bernard, Armand Point, and Andhré des Gachons, imitated their techniques. Maurice Denis, at the age of fifteen a fervent Catholic and disciple of Fra Angelico, noted in his diary (1886): 'Les médiévistes se multiplient. On s'arrache les Primitifs.'[37] His friend Émile Bernard told a reporter from the *Écho de Paris* in 1892 that medieval and modern were now synonymous: 'Je rêverais de créer un style hiératique qui s'élèverait au-dessus de la modernité. . . . Comme procédés et comme inspiration, il faut revenir aux Primitifs. . . . Il faudrait, en un mot, créer un style qui serait celui de notre époque.'[38] Armand Point announced in 1895 that this return to the Primitives was everywhere under way: 'Nous revenons, par une marche naturelle, à un état d'âme identique.'[39] In 1896 he founded at Marlotte a *phalanstère* called 'Hauteclaire' (a name found for him by his friend Élémir Bourges, who also suggested 'Blanc-Moutier' as a possibility).[40] In this Ruskinian colony medieval arts such as enamel-work and the painting of frescoes, were revived. Andhré des Gachons, who displayed on his door 'une pancarte à fond bleu, effroi du bourgeois: *L'imagier Andhré des Gachons*',[41] was declared by his friend Léon Maillard in 1892 to have rediscovered the 'état d'âme' of 'les artistes délicieux des temps échus'. His paintings possessed the same 'attitudes chèrement gauches' and 'allongement si suggestif des traits et des lignes'.[42] Three years later another of his admirers remarked that 'les hideurs de la vie moderne n'ont pas atteint son âme; il vit dans le passé radieux du Moyen Âge.'[43]

This return to favour of medieval art soon degenerated into the shallowest of vogues. Jules Lemaître remarked at the end of the century that among the more tiresome of 'les snobs des vingt dernières années'[44] were 'les snobs de Botticelli, de saint François d'Assise et de l'esthétisme

---

[35] R. de Gourmont, *Le Latin mystique,* 2nd edn., 1892, p. 255.
[36] See M. Praz, *The Romantic Agony,* 1833, p. 339.
[37] M. Denis, *Journal,* i (1957), 63.
[38] *La Wallonie,* vii (1892), p. 74.   [39] *L'Ermitage,* vi (July 1895), p. 11.
[40] See E. *Bourges: Correspondance inédite avec A. Point,* ed. G. Marie, 1962, p. 121.
[41] L. Maillard, *Notes pour demain: (1) L'Imagier Andhré des Gachons,* 1892, p. 10.
[42] Ibid. pp. 7-8.   [43] *La Plume,* 1 Dec. 1895, p. 542 (Félicien Pascal).
[44] Lemaître, *Les Contemporains,* vii (1899), 98.

anglais'.[45] Francis Poictevin, whose now unreadable work enjoyed considerable popularity during the 1880s and 90s, could certainly be placed in this category. *Presque* (1891), for instance, records in the jargon of the day the fugitive aesthetic sensations provoked in the author by the works of Fra Angelico and Memling, Botticelli's *Primavera,* and Burne-Jones's *Cophetua and the Beggar Maid;* his obsession with Tiphaine Raguenel, the first wife of Du Guesclin; and his daily 'pèlerinage ogival' to Notre-Dame.[46]

(i) *The 'Sar' Péladan: 'Soyons le Tout-Passé . . .'*

Strong individual voices of protest against the modern world were raised by several leading writers of the day, most of them Catholic, and all enraptured by medieval mysticism.

The most vociferous of these – and the one with least literary merit – was the 'Sar' Joséphin Péladan. A disciple of Barbey d'Aurevilly – 'Je crois à l'Idéal, à la Tradition, à la Hiérarchie',[47] he proclaimed at the beginning of his career in 1883 –, he was inspired by a performance of *Parsifal* at Bayreuth in 1888 to found his new Order of Chivalry – 'la Rose+Croix, le Temple et le Graal'. Despite his graniose profession of humility, 'Péladan n'est rien, Péladan n'est que l'écho des Voix du Passé' (1892),[48] self-advertisement played a large part in his activities. The aesthetic manifesto of his Order appeared in the *Figaro* in 1891. 'Soyons le Tout-Passé en face de Tout-Paris', it proclaimed, 'soyons des patriciens en face de la canaille.'[49] It was 'une manifestation de l'Art contre les arts, du Beau contre le laid, du rêve contre le réel, du Passé contre le présent infâme.'[50] The purpose of the Rose+Croix Esthétique was to 'insuffler dans l'art contemporain et surtout dans la culture esthétique l'essence théocratique',[51] and, above all, to *'ruiner le réalisme'*, and set up in its place 'l'Idéal catholique et la mysticité'.[52] Péladan's *Comment on devient mage* (1892), addressed 'au jeune homme contemporain', earnestly exhorted him: 'Agenouille ta vie devant un Graal, une précieuse relique du passé; sois son chevalier pieux et vaillant.'[53] The

[45] Ibid. p. 95.
[46] F. Poictevin, *Presque,* 1891, p. 93.
[47] Péladan, *La Décadence esthétique: (1) L'Art ochlocratique, salons de 1882 et de 1883,* 1888, p. 45.
[48] Reported in *Revue indépendante,* xxiv (July 1892), p. 116.
[49] Péladan, *Salon de la Rose +Croix: Règle et monitoire,* 1891, p. 36.
[50] Ibid. p. 25.   [51] Ibid. p. 33.   [52] Ibid. pp. 7-8.
[53] Péladan, *Comment on devient mage,* 1892, p. 268.

Constitutions of the Order, published in 1893, predicted that 'la chevalerie du Graal sera comme un intermonde, attendri encore des parfums souffrants de la terre et déjà baigné des encens paisibles et rayonnants du ciel.'[54] It gave a programme of activities including 'des auditions de musique sublime. Et des conférences propres à éveiller l'idéalité des mondains',[55] and concluded with a request for the donation of 'un coin de terre, dans un pays où la vie soit facile et peu chère, et de préférence une ruine, quelque église abandonnée ou quelque moustier ancien et inoccupé, afin d'y commencer Monsalvat'.[56] This particular dream was never in fact realized; but concerts and lectures were given at Rose+Croix Soirées; the Théâtre de la Rose+Croix was founded in 1890; and in the spring of 1892 the first Salon de la Rose+ Croix was held. At these Salons works by the young disciples of the Primitives were exhibited, including (in 1895) Andhré des Gachons's *Sara de Maupers*, in medieval costume, holding in her pale hands the Rose and the Cross.

(ii) *Remy de Gourmont: 'se plonger jusqu'au cou dans l'idéal'*

Remy de Gourmont was another writer who set out to publicize medieval mysticism. In 1885 he recommended to his contemporaries the poetry of Dante and his circle. 'Cette fréquentation d'esprits pleins d'une douce mysticité' would furnish them with an opportunity to 'se plonger jusqu'au cou dans l'idéal',[57] he told them. He then published his *Latin mystique* (1892), in which he revealed to them the splendours of medieval Latin poetry. Barbey d'Aurevilly had long ago been a connoisseur of 'le robuste latin des moines dans lequel palpitaient l'âme et le génie du Moyen Âge',[58] which, some twenty years later, was given pride of place in the library of Huysmans's Des Esseintes. It was his reading of *A Rebours* that had introduced Gourmont to it. In *Le Latin mystique* he announced: 'Seule, que l'on soit croyant ou non, seule la littérature mystique convient à notre immense fatigue, et pour nous qui ne prévoyons qu'un au delà de misères de plus en plus sûrement, de plus en plus rapidement réalisé, nous voulons nous borner à la connaissance de nous-mêmes et des obscurs rêves, divins ou sataniques, qui se donnent rendez-vous en nos âmes de jadis.'[59] In the same year he and his friend

---

[54] Péladan, *Constitutions de la Rose+Croix, le Temple et le Graal*, 1893, p. 11.
[55] Ibid. p. 37.   [56] Ibid. p. 43.
[57] R. de Gourmont, 'La Béatrice de Dante et l'idéal féminin en Italie à la fin du XIIIe siècle', *Revue du monde latin*, vi (Aug. 1885), p. 451.
[58] B. d'Aurevilly, *Les Historiens politiques et littéraires*, 1861, pp. 377-8.
[59] R. de Gourmont, *Le Latin mystique*, p. 12.

Albert Aurier published four instalments of *Le Livret de l'imagier* in the *Mercure de France*. These were brief descriptions of selected Primitive paintings, introduced by Aurier's 'Frontispice' (February 1892), recounting the discovery

en de bien oubliées petites salles innombrables endormies sous des voûtes, et mal éclairées par les verrières de rares ogives [of] l'album de voyage . . . d'un de ces naïfs et glorieux Imagiers . . . qui, bien que, déjà, hélas! vivant en pleine Renaissance, avait pourtant conservé dans son coeur la foi tenace du Moyen-Âge, l'ardent spiritualisme de l'art gothique, la haine du matérialisme et du classique pastichisme de la nouvelle école!

This little vellum notebook had, explains Aurier, inspired his partner and himself with

la fantaisie de nous métamorphoser pour quelques semaines, aujourd'hui, en ce pauvre Imagier du passé . . . de pieusement rechercher, parmi les usines et les casernes du maintenant, les débris méprisés des choses qu'il aimait, lui, pour, nous aussi, avec sa naïve émotion de bon artisan, noter, sur un livret pareil au sien, nos réflexions de dociles écoliers devant les chers rêves éternisés des magistraux ancêtres de ces âges si péremptoire-ment défunts.[60]

So the aesthetic standards of an earlier generation were reversed. Taine and his followers had proclaimed themselves men of the Renaissance, whose lost paradise shone forth in resplendent contrast with the return of medieval obscurantism they witnessed all around them. To the writers of the eighties and nineties the Middle Ages were the lost paradise, and the Renaissance — the base materialism of their bourgeois contemporaries — was the enemy.

(iii) *Huysmans and Bloy:*
'Le beau moyen âge qui vous prend aux entrailles'

There was of course an element of pose in both Péladan's and Gourmont's worship of the Middle Ages. The quality of their idealism is somewhat suspect: Péladan's chief concern was to attract publicity to

[60] *Mercure de France,* iv (Feb. 1892), pp. 168-9. Aurier died at the end of the year; Gourmont continued their joint enterprise with *L'Ymagier* (2 vols., 1894-6), which published fifteenth- and sixteenth-century woodcuts of saints, monsters, demons, etc., and modern imitations of them by artists such as Émile Bernard. To the pictures were added epigraphs from Latin and vernacular medieval literature. A 'texte modernisé' of Rutebeuf's *Miracle de Théophile* appeared in the Oct. 1895 number, and Sainte-Palaye's version of *Aucassin* in Dec. 1896.

himself, while Gourmont's – in *Le Latin mystique* – was with the erotic
content of the literature which he was exhuming (temptations of the
flesh, the perversity of womankind, tortures inflicted on female saints,
etc.). The works of J. K. Huysmans and Léon Bloy reflect a far more
heartfelt nostalgia for the Middle Ages, and a far more profound disgust with the modern world, to which both Péladan and Gourmont
were paying court, but which Huysmans and Bloy lost no opportunity
to denounce in the most vituperative terms.

Huysmans remarked sarcastically in his Preface to Gourmont's *Latin
mystique:* 'Il paraît que la jeunesse littéraire devient mystique.'[61] Dis-
missing with scorn the works exhibited at the first Rose+Croix Salon,
'de froides singeries, de faux décalques des Primitifs',[62] he declared that
mysticism without faith was meaningless. His novels show a progression
from 'un catholicisme salé d'un peu de magie . . . [un] mysticisme dépravé
et artistement pervers',[63] of the same brand as Gourmont's, – to which
Des Esseintes is attracted in *A Rebours* (1884), and which Durtal practises
in *Là-Bas* (1891) – to the orthodox glorification of medieval faith and
art in *En Route* (1895), *La Cathédrale* (1898), and *L'Oblat* (1903). The
Benedictine revival of medieval liturgy and plain-song (which had already
soothed the tortured nerves of Des Esseintes, who called it 'le verbe de
l'antique Église, l'âme du moyen âge')[64] was acclaimed in the latter three
novels. All Huysmans's work is a paean of praise to medieval art –
whether of cathedral builders,[65] painters (Durtal calls the works of the
Primitives 'une échappée hors des sens, sur d'infinis lointains'),[66] or
Latin poets, 'les vieux mystiques qui nous enlèvent loin du cloaque
pestilentiel de ce temps, qui nous permettent d'oublier les vaines ou les
malpropres journées que nous vécûmes'[67] – and to the Middle Ages
themselves, 'le beau moyen âge qui vous prend aux entrailles',[68] as he
was once heard to describe them. *Là-Bas,* the story of Durtal's researches into the life of Gilles de Rais, was conceived as 'l'éloge du
moyen âge opposé à cette fin de siècle'.[69] Gourmont on reading it

---

[61] Gourmont, *Le Latin mystique*, p. vii.   [62] Ibid. p. xi.
[63] Huysmans, *A Rebours*, 1965, pp. 263-4.   [64] Ibid. p. 248.
[65] The enduring influence of Michelet can be seen in Huysmans's descriptions of
Chartres in *La Cathédrale*: '. . . l'aspect suppliant de l'édifice . . . les bras levés
de ses tours . . . les mains jointes de ses clochers' (*La Cathédrale*, 1898, p. 480).
[66] Huysmans, *Là-bas,* 1891, p. 9.
[67] *Le Latin mystique*, p. xvi.
[68] J-H. Rosny, *Torches et lumignons,* La Force française, 1921, p. 57.
[69] Letter from Huysmans to Boullan, quoted by L. Deffoux & E. Zavie, *Le Groupe
de Médan,* Payot, 1920, p. 266.

exclaimed: 'L'âme du moyen âge est en ce livre.'[70] Wandering in the
ruins of Tiffauges, Durtal arrives at the conclusion that 'la société n'a
fait que déchoir depuis les quatre siècles qui nous séparent du Moyen
Âge . . . la noblesse, le clergé, la bourgeoisie, le peuple, avaient, dans
ce temps-là, l'âme plus haute.' The medieval clergy, 'qui . . . fut admirable, s'élança en des transports surhumains et atteignit Dieu!', are set
in opposition to their faint-hearted modern descendants.[71] In *La
Cathédrale* 'l'époque où nous vécûmes le plus près de Dieu, le Moyen
Âge',[72] and 'les flamboyantes extases de la mystique gothique',[73] are
set beside 'cette Renaissance, tant vantée à la suite de Michelet par les
historiens . . . la fin de l'âme mystique, la fin de la théologie monumen-
tale, la mort de l'art religieux, de tout le grand art en France!'[74]

Bloy was similarly contemptuous of Symbolist aesthetic dabblings
in the Middle Ages, 'ces démarquages d'un passé brûlant de foi, au profit
des ambitions marécageuses d'une esthétique de mécréants'[75] (although
he paid tribute to *Le Latin mystique,* 'le glorieux livre de Remy de
Gourmont qui paraît être, après Verlaine, le démarcateur le plus
péremptoire de l'évolution des âmes, en cet instant').[76] In *Le Désespéré*
(1886) his fictional self, Caïn Marchenoir, hurls imprecations against
the modern world: 'Tout est avachi, pollué, diffamé, mutilé, irréparable-
ment destitué et fricassé',[77] and against 'La République des Vaincus' in
particular: 'Nous descendons spiralement, depuis quinze années, dans
un vortex d'infamie.'[78] Like Huysmans, he despises the watered-down
Catholicism of his day, and desires to see the ferocious Catholicism of
the Middle Ages restored in its full rigour. In *La Femme pauvre* (1897)
Marchenoir dreams of a Pope with fire in his veins, a Gregory VII or
Innocent III, to excommunicate the Republic: 'Voyez-vous Léon XIII,'
he asks, 'jetant l'Interdit sur les quatre-vingts diocèses de France, un
Interdit absolu, *omni appellatione remota,* jusqu'à l'heure où tout ce
grand peuple sanglotant demanderait grâce . . .?'[79] His friend the artist
Pélipodas Gacougnol, on being asked by Clotilde (to whom he has just
read Verlaine's sonnet from *Sagesse*) 'Qu'est-ce que le Moyen Âge?', is
roused to heights of eloquence, ending his portrait of the Age of Faith
with a reminiscence of Hugo's 'Chevaliers errants'. Here Bloy, like Barbey

[70] *Mercure de France,* ii (June 1891), p. 323.
[71] *Là-bas,* pp. 169-70.   [72] *La Cathédrale,* p. 121.
[73] Ibid. p. 169.   [74] Ibid. p. 154.
[75] L. Bloy, *Oeuvres,* ed. Bollery & Petit, ii (1964), 323 (1891).
[76] Ibid. p. 313 (*MF* vii (Mar. 1893)).
[77] Bloy, *Oeuvres,* iii, 149.   [78] Ibid. p. 175.
[79] *La Femme pauvre,* Mercure de France, 1962, p. 190.

d'Aurevilly, triumphantly acknowledges the Middle Ages to have been the 'reign of terror' denounced by Gautier and Leconte de Lisle, the kingdom of suffering which evoked an answering anguish in Michelet:

> Le Moyen Âge, mon enfant, c'était une immense église comme on n'en verra plus jusqu'à ce que Dieu revienne sur terre, − un lieu de prières aussi vaste que tout l'Occident et bâti sur dix siècles d'extase qui font penser aux Dix Commandements du Sabaoth! C'était l'agenouillement universel dans l'adoration ou dans la terreur. Les blasphémateurs eux-mêmes et les sanguinaires étaient à genoux, parce qu'il n'y avait pas d'autre attitude en la présence du Crucifié redoutable qui devait juger tous les hommes. . . . Les pauvres gens des campagnes labouraient le sol en tremblant, comme s'ils avaient craint d'éveiller les trépassés avant l'heure. Les chevaliers et leurs serviteurs de guerre chevauchaient silencieusement au loin, sur les horizons, dans le crépuscule. Tout le monde pleurait en demandant grâce.[80]

(iv) *Maeterlinck and Rodenbach:*
'compliquer la mysticité, agrandir les musées . . .'

The Belgian Symbolists added their voice to this chorus of protest against the modern world. The rapid advance of industrialism was threatening to disfigure their ancient cities; and their nostalgia for the Middle Ages, whose last vestiges they saw disappearing all around them, was of an especially impassioned variety.

A Rebours, which had led Gourmont to medieval Latin literature, led Maeterlinck to the discovery of the fourteenth-century Flemish mystic Ruysbroeck l'Admirable.[81] He communicated this overwhelming experience (which did more than anything else to transform him from a Parnassian into a Symbolist) to a friend in 1885: 'Jamais je n'ai éprouvé une joie ni un étonnement pareils, c'est l'homme *de génie absolu*.[82] The Introduction to his translation of Ruysbroeck's *Ornement des noces spirituelles* (written 1887-8) was published in the *Revue générale* (Brussels) in 1889. The 1891 edition of his Introduction and translation is a modified version of the *Revue générale* articles. He declared in the first version:

> Je vois en elle [dans la sincère histoire de cette âme] toute l'*existence* du beau moyen âge noir, au moment où Dieu a été le plus surnaturellement

---

[80] *La Femme pauvre,* p. 109.
[81] For a full account of Maeterlinck's debt to Ruysbroeck see J. Hanse, 'De Ruysbroeck aux *Serres chaudes* de Maurice Maeterlinck', in *Le Centenaire de M. Maeterlinck (1862-1962),* 1964.
[82] *Annales de la Fondation M. Maeterlinck,* v (1959), p. 47.

aimé dans l'absence de tout ce qui n'était pas Dieu seul. Ç'a été réellement alors l'unique été des coeurs, et à nous que sommes en hiver, hélas!, et peut-être plus loin . . . ces ardeurs semblent à présent de fiévreuses ténèbres où notre pauvre âme périrait comme une plante du pôle au soleil.[83]

Georges Rodenbach celebrated Bruges as a survival from the Middle Ages in his immensely popular novel *Bruges-la-morte* (1892). An article of his written in 1894 inveighed against the project to turn the city into a modern industrial port: 'Bruges-port-de-mer . . . il faudrait réaliser Bruges-Porte de l'Art! c'est-à-dire continuer à restaurer les palais, les antiques demeures, achever les tours, parer les églises, compliquer la mysticité, agrandir les musées.'[84] His novel *Le Carillonneur* (1897) ends with the defeat of the hero, Joris Borluut, who has dedicated his life to the restoration of ancient Bruges, and the triumph of the Ligue du Port-de-Mer and vulgar modernity, as a procession led by 'le Cercle des vélocipédistes' parades rejoicing through the condemned medieval city.[85]

In our next chapter we shall examine some varieties of the Symbolist literary product which this remarkable return to favour of a once-despised Middle Ages brought forth.

[83] Article in *Revue générale,* 50 (1889), quoted by J. Hanse, op. cit. p. 105.
[84] Rodenbach, *Évocations,* 1924, pp. 109-10.
[85] Rodenbach, *Le Carillonneur,* 1897, p. 311.

CHAPTER 9

THE 1880s AND 1890s:
II. THE SYMBOLIST MIDDLE AGES

'. . . les obscurs rêves, divins ou sataniques, qui se donnent rendez-vous en nos âmes de jadis' (A. Aurier)

A. *Four precursors*
(i) *Verlaine: 'Moi rêvant toujours de ce Moyen Âge-là'*

The Symbolist rediscovery of the Middle Ages is prefigured in the work of four great precursors of the movement: Verlaine, Rimbaud, Villiers de l'Isle-Adam, and Mallarmé. Verlaine and Villiers were especially instrumental in the creation of this new Middle Ages.

Verlaine, in the Parnassian 'Prologue' to his *Poëmes saturniens* (1866), which Y-G. Le Dantec calls 'a deliberate pastiche of Leconte de Lisle',[1] departs from Leconte de Lisle in one significant respect: in his review of the great ages of epic he gives an honourable mention to 'les Francs tumultueux, nos pères', and to their 'chant de geste sans rivaux/De Roland et de ceux qui virent Roncevaux'.[2] The poem 'Effet de nuit' in the same collection, inspired by *Gaspard de la nuit* and Hugo's 'Montfaucon',[3] is an original variant on the well-worn theme of the gibbet 'plein de pendus rabougris . . . dansant dans l'air noir des gigues nonpareilles', for the mysterious spectacle of the 'gros de hauts pertuisaniers' with their spears gleaming 'à contre-sens des lances de l'averse' finally steals the scene from the familiar dance of the corpses.[4]

In his study of Verlaine's style Claude Cuénot remarks that 'le moyen âge n'est pas une époque où le génie de Verlaine, bien qu'admirateur de Villon, se[meut] aisément.'[5] This is true, inasmuch as the poet's attempted reconstructions of the period ('La Pucelle' and 'La Grâce', *Jadis et naguère*) fall very flat; but leaves out of account the fact that he initiated a fresh use of the Middle Ages, distinct from the exhausted genre of historical re-creation, in *Sagesse* (Dec. 1880, dated 1881). Another critic

[1] Verlaine, *Oeuvres poétiques complètes,* 1962, pp. 1074-5.
[2] Ibid. p. 59.
[3] See J-H. Bornecque, *Les 'Poèmes saturniens' de Paul Verlaine,* 1967, pp. 217-18.
[4] Verlaine, op. cit. pp. 67-8.
[5] C. Cuénot, *Le Style de Paul Verlaine*, 1963, p. 131.

contends that in this work Verlaine's 'élan vers le moyen âge "énorme et délicat" est une manifestation tardive et très limitée',[6] attributable to 'l'engouement des Symbolists français et des Préraphaélites anglais pour un moyen âge factice'.[7] This also does Verlaine far less than justice: the medieval imagery in *Sagesse* (to which could be applied the remark made by Antonin Artaud of Maeterlinck's Middle Ages, that it was 'pas seulement un décor, mais une façon profonde de sentir')[8] is wholly original − antedating by a decade the poetry of the Symbolists − and of central importance in Verlaine's work. Any debt incurred was on the Symbolist side rather than Verlaine's.

Sagesse contains the well-known sonnet in which Verlaine, in a sudden access of Ultramontane fervour, veers away from contemplation of the Catholic seventeenth century towards a more exemplary age of faith, 'le Moyen Âge énorme et délicat':[9]

> Quel temps! Oui, que mon coeur naufragé rembarquât
> Pour toute cette force ardente, souple, artiste!
>
> Et là que j'eusse part − quelconque, chez les rois
> Ou bien ailleurs, n'importe, − à la chose vitale,
> Et que je fusse un saint, actes bons, pensers droits,
>
> Haute théologie et solide morale,
> Guidé par la folie unique de la Croix
> Sur tes ailes de pierre, ô folle Cathédrale![10]

It also contains the poems, written in the same year (1875), in which he opposes the Republic in the accents of a conventional Catholic upholder of tradition:

> Nous tenons pour l'honneur jamais taché
> De la Tradition, supplice et gloire!

'Ils ont dit tout', he says of his forefathers; and he exhorts the new generation:

> Redevenez les Français d'autrefois,
> Fils de l'Église, et dignes de vos pères![11]

But Verlaine also wrote in the course of that year (most of which he spent in England, after his release from prison in January) some immeasurably more interesting poems, in which medieval imagery is a

[6] G. Zayed, *La Formation littéraire de Verlaine,* 1962, p. 74.
[7] Ibid. p. 52.
[8] See R. Bodart, *Maurice Maeterlinck,* Poètes d'aujourd'hui, Seghers, 1962, p. 89.
[9] Cf. *supra,* pp. 9-10.
[10] Verlaine, op. cit. p. 249.   [11] Ibid. pp. 251-3.

vehicle for personal emotion. These are 'Bon chevalier masqué qui chevauche en silence . . .', 'J'avais peiné comme Sisyphe . . .', and 'Écrit en 1875' ('J'ai naguère habité la meilleur des châteaux'), which, although it features in the first manuscript of *Sagesse,* was not published until 1885.[12] Here Verlaine has discovered a fresh source of Catholic inspiration. Reverses of fortune, interior tumult, and struggle with temptation are rendered in terms of feudal warfare. The moral climate in which the poet lived during and after his imprisonment is translated into an Arthurian landscape in which allegorical beings strive with one another. The chief sources are Tennyson and Bunyan;[13] the result is powerfully original. In the extraordinary poem 'Bon chevalier masqué . . .' Verlaine creates a haunting, mysteriously medieval 'état d'âme' – pursuing the vein discovered by Nerval and Baudelaire.[14]

Many different sources[15] have been suggested for his 'chevalier Malheur' –

> Bon chevalier masqué qui chevauche en silence,
> Le Malheur a percé mon vieux coeur de sa lance –,

who restores to the poet 'tout un coeur pur et fier' with the touch of his icy gauntlet, and rides away with the same parting words that a Belgian *gendarme* called after him, as he left the prison at Mons: 'Au moins, prudence! Car c'est bon pour une fois.'[16] 'Le meilleur des châteaux', in 'Écrit en 1875', –

> Ô lieu presque aussitôt regretté que quitté,
> Château, château magique où mon âme s'est faite –

belongs to the same universe. It is the Mons prison, to which the repentant Verlaine looks back with nostalgia as an ideal refuge from the world's temptations. V. P. Underwood identifies it with Arthur's castle in *Gareth and Lynette,* and points out Bunyan's influence in the concluding lines:

> Ô sois béni, château d'où me voilà sorti
> Prêt à la vie, armé de douceur et nanti
> De la Foi. . . .[17]

---

[12] In *Le Zig-Zag,* 1885, and *La Vogue,* 1886. Finally included in *Amour* (1888).

[13] A more lowly source of Verlaine's inspiration was Adelaide Anne Procter's *A Knight Errant.* For a full discussion of all these influences see V. P. Underwood's edition of *Sagesse,* 1944, pp. 56-7, and his *Verlaine et l'Angleterre,* 1956, pp. 237-43, 246-8, and 377-9.

[14] Cf. *supra,* pp. 25-6.

[15] See Underwood, *Verlaine et l'Angleterre,* pp. 238-41; Zayed, op. cit. p. 149, pp. 177-8.

[16] Verlaine, op. cit. p. 240.   [17] Ibid. pp. 408-9.

A medieval aura clung to Verlaine throughout his subsequent career. He struck medieval attitudes ('Moi le Chevalier qui saigne sur azur'[18] (*Amour*); 'Oxford est une ville qui me consola,/Moi rêvant toujours de ce Moyen Âge-là'[19] (1893)); he took a keen interest in the Symbolists' medievalizing activities, asking Moréas in 1890 to send to the Hôpital Broussais 'soit un Rabelais, soit quelque étude sur quelque poete moyenâgeux, renaissant ou antique, enfin quelque chose qui me sorte un peu de la crasse ignorante où croupis',[20] and in 1892 exhorting Emmanuel Signoret, the founder of *Le Saint-Graal*, to make a stand against the newly-formed École Romane: 'En présence des menaces d'une Renaissance factice, d'un paganisme brutal . . . restez Moyen-âge, gothiques, si l'on veut, par la conviction, par la grandeur, par, aussi, le subtil et le délicat.'[21] His 'Moyen Âge énorme et délicat' sonnet was repeatedly quoted; he was commended by Bloy for his 'miraculeux atavisme de sentiment',[22] and hailed by many as a reincarnation of a medieval poet — usually Villon.[23] 'A travers les siècles', Huysmans said of him, 'il a retrouvé ces accents d'humilité et de candeur, ces prières dolentes et transies . . . oubliés depuis ce retour à l'orgueil du paganisme que fut la Renaissance.'[24]

(ii) *Rimbaud: 'Je n'en finirais pas de me revoir dans ce passé'*

A very different Middle Ages haunted the imagination of Arthur Rimbaud. Like Verlaine, he wrote an early poem on the Parnassian gibbet theme, 'Bal des pendus'.[25] This is an unimportant exercise, however; the Middle Ages reappear in a far more interesting guise in poems such as 'La Rivière de Cassis', and in *Une Saison en Enfer* and *Illuminations*. They are (in fugitive glimpses) the republican Middle Ages. As

---

[18] Ibid. p. 425.   [19] Ibid. p. 1007.
[20] Verlaine, *Correspondance,* ed. Van Bever, iii (1929), 249-50.
[21] Ibid. pp. 326-7.   [22] Bloy, *Oeuvres,* ii. 278 (1889).
[23] See Valéry's essay 'Villon et Verlaine', in *Oeuvres,* i (1957), 427-43.
[24] Huysmans, *En Marge,* ed. L. Descaves, 1927, p. 214 (1894). Cf. Maeterlinck's description of Ruysbroeck's *Livre des douze béguines:* 'des tristesses transies, semblables un peu à celles de Villon ou de Verlaine' (Introduction to *L'Ornement des noces spirituelles' de Ruysbroeck l'Admirable,* 1891, p. xxix).
[25] Rimbaud, *Oeuvres,* ed. S. Bernard, Garnier, 1960, pp. 48-9. According to Izambard (*Rimbaud tel que je l'ai connu,* Mercure de France, 1946, pp. 60-1), it was inspired by his lending Rimbaud a copy of Banville's *Gringoire.* E. Starkie calls it 'pure Banville' (*A. Rimbaud,* 1961, p. 53); while Gengoux (*La Pensée poétique de Rimbaud,* 1950, pp. 101-2), says that it derives from Gautier's 'Bûchers et tombeaux.' But the tone is sardonic ('Presque tous ont quitté la chemise de peau/Le reste est peu gênant et se voit sans scandale' etc.) and far closer to Baudelaire's 'Danse macabre' than to Banville or Gautier.

several critics have remarked, there is an unmistakable flavour of Michelet (whom the poet greatly admired) in Rimbaud's work. The dramatic urgency and hectic impatience of Michelet's second, Middle-Ages-denouncing manner is Rimbaud's also; the annihilation of old worlds and discovery of new ones beyond the horizon are prospects which enchant them both. In 'Adieu' (*Une Saison en Enfer*) – 'Tous les souvenirs immondes s'effacent. Mes derniers regrets détalent, – des jalousies pour les mendiants, les brigands, les amis de la mort, les arriérés de toutes sortes. . . . Il faut être absolument moderne'[26] – Enid Starkie detects the influence of *La Bible de l'humanité*.[27] She also points out that the violent excitement kindled in Rimbaud at the thought of 'le temps des *Assassins*', which he imagines to be close at hand in 'Matinée d'ivresse' (*Illuminations*), was communicated to him by his reading of Michelet's account of this eleventh-century sect's activities in the *Histoire de France*.[28] Suzanne Bernard compares the hallucinatory chaos evoked in 'Villes' I (*Illuminations*) with Michelet's description of medieval Nuremberg in his *Introduction à l'histoire universelle*.[29] Gengoux[30] believes that Rimbaud derived much inspiration from *La Sorcière*, and sees in 'Enfance' II and III (*Illuminations*) ('. . . la haute mer faite d'une éternité de chaudes larmes'; 'Il y a une cathédrale qui descend et un lac qui monte')[31] Michelet's cathedral dissolving in the 'sea of tears' shed by medieval humanity. This does seem a most likely source.

'La Rivière de Cassis' is an evocation of the Semoy at Bouillon:

> Tout roule avec des mystères révoltants
> De campagnes d'anciens temps;
> De donjons visités, de parcs importants:
> C'est en ces bords qu'on entend
> Les passions mortes des chevaliers errants:
> Mais que salubre est le vent![32]

Suzanne Bernard goes as far as to say that here Rimbaud's 'haine pour l'époque féodale' is unleashed, as he rejoices in the salubrious wind

---

[26] Rimbaud, *Oeuvres*, p. 241.
[27] Starkie, op. cit. p. 304. Their temperamental affinity is also shown in Michelet's diary (1841): 'Tout a péri pour moi, l'antiquité, le Moyen Âge; je me sens profondément moderne, en ce moment' (cf. *supra*, p. 47).
[28] Ibid. p. 207.
[29] Rimbaud, *Oeuvres*, p. 502. It is also – like much of the rest of *Illuminations* – curiously akin to Hugo's *Promontorium somnii* (cf. *supra*, pp. 130-1).
[30] Gengoux, op. cit. pp. 14-15, 514.
[31] Rimbaud, *Oeuvres*, p. 256.
[32] Ibid. p. 150.

bearing away evil memories.[33] The ideal Middle Ages appear only once in his work, in a fleeting vision of

> la soie, en foule et de lys pur, des oriflammes
> sous les murs dont quelque pucelle eut la défense.[34]
>
> ('Mémoire')

Elsewhere, Rimbaud, subject like Flaubert to 'le frisson historique' —[35] 'Je n'en finirais pas de me revoir dans ce passé', he exclaims in 'Mauvais Sang' (*Une Saison en Enfer*) — relives the republican Middle Ages as the eternal 'manant':

> Je me rappelle l'histoire de la France fille aînée de l'Église. J'aurais fait, manant, le voyage de terre sainte; j'ai dans la tête des routes dans les plaines souabes, des vues de Byzance, des remparts de Solyme; le culte de Marie, l'attendrissement sur le crucifié s'éveillent en moi parmi mille féeries profanes. — Je suis assis, lépreux, sur les pots cassés et les orties, au pied d'un mur rongé par le soleil. . . .
>
> Ah! encore: je danse le sabbat dans une rouge clairière, avec des vieilles et des enfants.[36]

Whereas less inspired republican historians anathemized the Middle Ages from a safe distance, Michelet lived through them in the act of passing judgement on them. There is the same flavour of personal experience in Rimbaud's work (and in Flaubert's). It results in something far more suggestive than conventional historical recreations, which both anticipates and surpasses the work of the Symbolists. Rimbaud's 'Alchimie du verbe', in which he looks back to a self which he has already impatiently repudiated, is a clear prophecy of all that will preoccupy them for a long time to come:

> J'aimais les peintures idiotes, dessus de portes, décors, toiles de saltimbanques, enseignes, enluminures populaires; la littérature démodée, latin d'église, livres érotiques sans orthographe, romans de nos aïeules, contes de fées, petits livres de l'enfance, opéras vieux, refrains niais, rhythmes naïfs.
>
> Je rêvais croisades, voyages de découvertes dont on n'a pas de relations, républiques sans histoires, guerres de religion étouffées, révolutions de moeurs, déplacements de races et de continents: je croyais à tous les enchantements.[37]

---

[33] Rimbaud, *Oeuvres,* p. 431.
[34] Ibid. p. 177.
[35] Cf. *supra,* p. 190.
[36] Rimbaud, *Oeuvres,* p. 214.
[37] Rimbaud, *Oeuvres,* p. 228.

(iii) *The 'énorme' Middle Ages of Villiers de l'Isle-Adam*

In the spring of 1872 Edmond de Goncourt recorded a conversation
with Victor Hugo:

Puis il parle de sa famille, de sa généalogie lorraine, d'un Hugo, grand
brigand féodal, dont il a dessiné le château près de Saverne, d'un autre
Hugo, enterré à Trèves, qui a laissé un missel mystérieux, enfoui sous
une roche appelée la Table, près de Saarburg, et qu'a fait enlever le roi
de Prusse. Il raconte longuement cette histoire, la semant de détails
bizarres, de cette archéologie moyenâgeuse, qu'il aime et dont il fait si
souvent emploi dans sa poésie et sa prose.[38]

This same Romantic 'archéologie moyenâgeuse' is employed by Villiers
de l'Isle-Adam in *Axël* (published between 1872 and 1886). Villiers's
passionate devotion to the Middle Ages set an example to the Symbolists.
Teodor de Wyzewa expressed their admiration for him in the *Revue
indépendante* (1886): 'M. de Villiers est un prince, perdu au travers
de nos démocraties. Ces lointains héroïsmes passionnés, d'instinct
il les conçoit réels. Il ignore notre vision moderne des choses.'[39] For
Villiers, who had set his face against the republican ideal of Progress, it
was not the Middle Ages, but the nineteenth century (incarnated in
Tribulat Bonhomet) that was thoroughly sinister. His nineteenth-century
heroes belong in spirit to the Middle Ages, like the Duke of Portland (of
one of the *Contes cruels*), who on his return from the East vanishes from
Queen Victoria's court to live entombed in his 'massif manoir à créneaux,
construit en de vieux âges',[40] having caught 'la grande lèpre antique . . . la
Lèpre-sèche et sans remède' from its 'dernier dépositaire', a beggar whose
hand he clasped in 'une seconde de bravade — un mouvement *trop* noble,
plutôt!'[41] — and like Axël himself, who also inhabits a castle situated in
the 'énorme' Middle Ages. The stage directions for the second part, 'Le
Monde tragique', indicate

une haute salle au plafond de chêne. . . . Au fond, grande porte
principale . . . surmontée de l'écusson d'Auërsperg, supporté de ses
grands sphinx d'or. A gauche, grande fenêtre gothique — laissant voir . . .
d'immenses et brumeuses forêts. . . . La salle est d'une profondeur qui
donne l'impression d'une bâtisse colossale datant des premiers temps

---

[38] *Journal des Goncourt*, ii. 888.
[39] T. de Wyzewa, *Nos Maîtres*, 1895, p. 150.
[40] Villiers de l'Isle-Adam, *Contes cruels. Nouveaux Contes cruels*, ed. P-G. Castex,
1968, p. 82.
[41] Ibid. pp. 89-90. (cf. the identical gesture made by Barbey d'Aurevilly's Cid
(*supra*, p. 166), in his poem published four years after Villiers' tale (Jan. 1887).

du moyen âge. A droite, vaste cheminée où brûle un grand feu. . . . Sur
les murs . . . entre des armures sarrasines, d'énormes vautours et de
grands aigles fauves sont cloués.[42]

Axël belongs to the ideal Middle Ages. He is full of paternal solicitude
towards his vassals. His cynical cousin the Commandeur d'Auërsperg
marvels at this, murmuring 'Comme tu les soignes!'[43] He himself descends from the sinister Middle Ages: nostalgic memories of the good
old days well up in him as dusk descends over the castle:

> Ha! ah! c'est l'heure où le marchand va dormir, 'la conscience tran-
> quille': les bons aïeux ne sont plus là, pour détrousser un peu sur les
> chemins. . . . En vérité, je me blâme pas outre mesure ces façons d'agir,
> chez les devanciers! De tout temps, ne fut-ce pas le droit du chasseur
> d'ôter le gibier d'entre les crocs de ses chiens?[43]

He sternly disapproves of the Middle Ages recreated by Axël, however.
The confrontation between the cousins is most impressive. The Commandeur begins by trying to coax Axël out of his feudal fastness, in
the manner of kings and their emissaries from the *Légende des siècles:*
'Ah! mon cher, si tu quittais l'exil et daignais me suivre en ce monde
de fêtes, de luxe et d'amours . . .'[44] (Axël later refers to himself in
similarly Hugolian terms as 'un songeur assez peu commode, qu'il
serait peut-être sage, à vos rois, de ne point braver').[45] He then un-
wittingly reveals the extent of his fatuity in a long harangue:

> Tu te laisses endoctriner par un halluciné qui vit chez toi [he
> begins (alluding to Maître Janus)] — Que tu joues au moyen âge, —
> soit! Ici, c'est fait exprès; la chose est innocente, et non, même, sans
> quelque grandeur. Mais pousser le travestissement jusqu'à rénover les
> souffleurs du Grand-Oeuvre! . . . Allons! . . . Imite-moi. Saisis-toi de la
> vie, telle qu'elle est. . . . Je m'appelle *la vie réelle,* entends-tu? Est-ce
> donc en se montant l'imagination (et ceci dans des manoirs à créneaux
> qui n'ont plus le sens commun et ne représentent, désormais, que des
> curiosités historiques tolérées pour la distraction des voyageurs), qu'on
> peut arriver à quelque chose de tangible et de stable? Sors de ce
> tombeau suranné![46]

[42] V. de l'Isle-Adam, *Axël,* 1960, pp. 81-2.
[43] Ibid. pp. 134-6.
[44] *Axël,* p. 132.
[45] Ibid. p. 179. Cf. Hugo's Welf, Castellan d'Osbor: 'Le vieux songeur n'est pas
     d'humeur accommodante' (*Légende des siècles,* p. 339).
[46] Ibid. pp. 139-40.

(iv) *Mallarmé: 'Ô fermoirs d'or des vieux missels!'*

Mallarmé in his famous lecture of 1890 paid tribute to the medieval quality of Villiers' rare distinction, alluding to the 'haute ruine inexistant'[47] where he dwelt in Paris, to his ancestral home, 'le mystère par lui quitté jadis, la vague ruine à demi écroulée sur un sol de foi',[48] enumerating his illustrious forbears, from the eleventh to the fifteenth century,[49] and insisting that Villiers, far from being born out of his true time, had fulfilled his destiny by transmitting the past into the future as a magnificent afterglow:

Si! à considérer l'Histoire il avait été ponctuel, devant l'assignation du sort . . . car ce n'est pas contemporainement à une époque, aucunement, que doivent, pour exalter le sens, advenir ceux que leur destin chargea d'en être à nu l'expression; ils sont projetés maint siècle au-delà, stupéfaits, à témoigner de ce qui, normal à l'instant même, vit tard magnifiquement par le regret, et trouvera dans l'exil de leur nostalgique esprit tourné vers le passé, sa vision pure.[50]

Mallarmé himself, a fervent admirer of Poe, Wagner, and Tennyson (and of Bertrand's *Gaspard de la nuit*),[51] helped to bring to his contemporaries' notice these important sources of the Symbolist Middle Ages. And his own early poems − those published in the first *Parnasse contemporain* (1866), such as 'Les Fleurs', and those written in the early sixties but published later ('Apparition', written 1863, published 1883; 'Sainte', written 1865, published 1883) −, with their Pre-Raphaelite lilies and languors, exerted a powerful influence on the Symbolist poets. E. Noulet claims (with some exaggeration) that they alone were responsible for 'l'ornementation surchargée de 1880, ses draperies, ses banderoles, son fer forgé'.[52] Certain aspects of the Symbolist Middle Ages were conjured into being by Mallarmé in the early sixties: his call in 1862 for recognition of poetry as a sacred rite guarded from the profane − 'Ô fermoirs d'or des vieux missels! ô hiéroglyphes inviolés des rouleaux de papyrus!',[53] and Aubanel's praise of his 'Sainte' in 1865 − 'cela ressemble à une vieille peinture de missel, à un vitrail ancien'[54] − are harbingers of things to come. Mallarmé spoke his final word on the Middle Ages in the *Revue blanche*, towards the end of his career (1895). After an evening spent with 'le

[47] Mallarmé, *Os. cs.* 1961, p. 482.   [48] Ibid. p. 494.
[49] Ibid. p. 490.   [50] Mallarmé, *Os. cs.* pp. 495-6.
[51] See Mallarmé, *Correspondance,* i (1959), 188, 196-9.
[52] E. Noulet, *L'Oeuvre poétique de Stéphane Mallarmé,* Droz, 1940, p. 83.
[53] Mallarmé, *Os. cs.* p. 257.   [54] Mallarmé, *Correspondance,* i. 183.

livre exceptionnel d'Huysmans' (he does not specify which one), he
was moved to exclaim:

> Le Moyen-âge, tout-de-même, reste à jamais notre incubation . . . en
> deça, ainsi que commencement de monde, le moderne pourrait abdiquer
> le regard: au seuil d'une ère dispensatrice, je veux, du bienfait terrestre
> ou la condition plénière − tout, par souci que la projection de sainteté
> ne suffît pas et manquât court, se ramassa au noir de nous pour filer
> véritablement si c'est possible, en joie, quelque chose comme durant
> les siècles des siècles, oh! que ce soit.[55]

B. *The Symbolist relationship with the past: 'Ce qui, normal à l'instant même, vit tard magnifiquement par le regret'*

Mallarmé's 'ce qui, normal à l'instant même' leads us to what must
be our next concern (before the Symbolist past itself) − the Symbolist
approach to the past. Various remarks scattered through Anatole
France's critical essays illustrate how this approach differs from that of
the previous generation. Anatole France's attitude to the past remains
that of a Parnassian. He fails to understand the new generation, and
protests at Péladan's worship of the thirteenth century:

> Je crois que son grand mérite à nos yeux est de ne plus exister. C'est
> une jouissance d'artiste que de vivre par l'imagination dans le passé;
> mais il faut bien se dire que le charme du passé n'est que dans nos rêves
> et qu'en réalité le temps jadis, dont nous respirons délicieusement la
> poésie, avait dans sa nouveauté ce goût banal et triste de toutes les
> choses parmi lesquelles s'écoule la vie humaine.[56]

(He also protests at Flaubert's illusion that 'les personnages antiques
jouissaient eux-mêmes de l'impression d'étrangeté qu'ils nous
donnent.')[57] He stops short after 'ce qui, normal à l'instant même';
'vit tard magnifiquement par le regret' is a concept which means nothing
to him, but which conveys exactly the Symbolists' relationship with the
past. The previous generation had claimed that they were able to see it
(in Taine's words) 'avec nos yeux, *avec les yeux de notre tête'*;[58] but
for them the past was past, something from which they stood aloof, even
while their gaze was directed upon it. The Symbolists turned to it self-
consciously and overlaid it with contemporary sensibility, recognizing

---

[55] 'Variations sur un sujet: (III) Catholicisme', *Revue blanche*, viii. 1 Apr. 1895,
pp. 320-1. See *Os. cs.* p. 392, for the slightly modified version published in
Divagations (1897).

[56] A. France, *Os. cs.* vii. 229 (Jan. 1890).

[57] Ibid. vi. 354.   [58] Cf. *supra*, p. 72.

the need for it as a modern malady. Claudel summed up their attitude in a letter written in 1900 to Marcel Schwob, who had sent him *La Croisade des enfants:* 'Si quelqu'un pouvait connaître le passé d'une vue directe et certaine, et comme avec les yeux mêmes, ce ne serait pas là l'aimer en *tant que passé*; et ce goût amer et subtil, cette secrète sensibilité, cette pitié de ce qui n'est plus, qui m'a fait aimer *Mimes,* me font aimer plus encore la *Croisade des enfants.'*[59] Anatole France was right; the Symbolists did love the past precisely because it was dead as Rodenbach declared in *La Jeunesse blanche* (1886):

> Le Passé, c'est un cher enseveli qu'on pleure,
> Que nous aimons surtout maintenant qu'il est mort.[60]

Rodenbach luxuriated in the death-agony of the Middle Ages, best seen in Bruges — 'Grande gloire finie!'[61] — and its decaying houses — 'Le moyen âge mort se réfugie en eux.'[62] The restorer Joris Borluut, hero of *Le Carillonneur,* feels 'la joie de sculpter son tombeau' as he goes about his work of preserving Bruges's decrepitude. He is eventually supplanted by a restorer of the school of Viollet-le-Duc: 'Chaque jour les dissonances s'accrurent, les profanations, les anachronismes, les vandalismes. . . . C'étaient des bâtisses neuves, la parodie du passé.'[63] Disapproval of Viollet-le-Duc was universal at this time: Bourget in 1891 looked forward to the day when 'on défendra aux archéologues de nettoyer une ruine';[64] Huysmans deplored his treatment of Notre-Dame: 'Le fameux Viollet le Duc l'a rajeunie, lui a râclé l'épiderme, l'a poncée de telle sorte qu'elle a complètement perdu sa patine de prières';[65] and France was no less condemnatory in *Pierre Nozière* (1899): 'Vraiment il y a trop de pierres neuves à Pierrefonds . . . les vieilles pierres, les vieux témoins, ne sont plus là, et ce n'est plus le château de Louis d'Orléans. . . . Et l'on a détruit des ruines, ce qui est une manière de vandalisme.'[66]

The Symbolists' return to the Middle Ages differed from that of the Romantics, in that they were unable to inhabit the past forgetful of the present, or wilfully to turn the present into the past. They gazed with

[59] Quoted by P. Champion, *Marcel Schwob et son temps*, 1927, p. 270.
[60] Rodenbach, *Oeuvres*, i (1923), 22.
[61] Rodenbach, *Le Carillonneur*, p. 22.
[62] Rodenbach, *Oeuvres*, i. 78 ('Dimanches', Apr. 1885).
[63] *Le Carillonneur*, pp. 299-300.
[64] P. Bourget, *Sensations d'Italie*, Lemerre, 1891, p. 115.
[65] Huysmans, *De tout*, 1902, pp. 75-6.
[66] A. France, *Os. cs.* x. 403 (cf. pp. 454-7). These protests repeat Hugo's early words of warning in *Le Rhin* (1842). See Hugo, *Os. cs.*, ed. J. Massin, vi. 259, 360.

longing at the past while remaining rooted in modern life. Their novels about the Middle Ages were not of the thoroughgoing historical sort: heroes of these works were men of the nineteenth century born out of their true time, in accordance with Huysmans's contention (in his essay on Gustave Moreau) that

La théorie du milieu, adaptée par M. Taine à l'art est juste – mais juste à rebours, alors qu'il s'agit de grands artistes, car le milieu agit sur eux alors par la révolte, par la haine qu'il leur inspire; au lieu de modeler, de façonner l'âme à son image, il crée dans d'immenses Boston, de solitaires Edgar Poe; il agit par retro, crée dans de honteuses Frances des Baudelaire, des Flaubert, des Goncourt, des Villiers de l'Isle Adam . . . des êtres d'exception, qui retournent sur les pas des siècles et se jettent, par dégoût des promiscuités qu'il leur faut subir, dans les gouffres des âges révolus, dans les tumultueux espaces des cauchemars et des rêves.[67]

They were often the last of an ancient line; sometimes a family curse, or prophecy from time immemorial, brooded over their destiny. (Poe's Roderick Usher was their prototype in fiction.) Villiers de l'Isle-Adam – as Mallarmé made clear in his memorable tribute to him – was in his life the most splendid example that there ever could have been of the last of an ancient line; and the destinies of Axël, who bears 'un nom qui résume sept siècles de hauts faits',[68] and Sara, the last daughter of the Princes of Maupers – mysteriously linked since the twelfth century – are correspondingly grandiose: to the Commandeur, who has been exhorting him to 'faire son chemin', Axël retorts: 'Mon chemin? voici des siècles qu'il est tracé.'[69]

Mallarmé's *Igitur* (written 1869-70) takes up Poe's theme of the intolerable oppression which weighs down upon the last of an ancient line: the hero, *projeté hors du temps par sa race*[70] like Villiers, feels within his castle the presence of innumerable ancestors, whose mysterious 'grimoire' – 'l'étincelle d'or du fermoir héraldique de leur volume' – glitters faintly in the gloom.[71]

Numerous heroes of novels published during the eighties and nineties lived a life dedicated to retrospection.[72] First there was Des Esseintes – again the debilitated last incarnation of his race – meditating on ancient

---

[67] Huysmans, *Certains*, 1904, pp. 21-2. Cf. *A Rebours*, p. 224.
[68] *Axël*, p. 160.   [69] Ibid. p. 151.
[70] Mallarmé, *Oeuvres*, p. 440.   [71] Ibid. p. 437.
[72] Their ancestor was Gautier's 'Elias Wildmanstadius ou l'homme moyen âge' (1833). Although this is a piece of light-hearted satire, there is a curious, ambiguous pathos about Wildmanstadius, 'cette âme du quinzième siècle au dix-neuvième', who shuts himself away in 'un moyen âge de quelques toises

heresies, solacing his nerves with plain-song, stagnating in 'une studieuse décrépitude'.[73] Then there was Péladan's Mérodack (a self-portrait of the 'Sar') in *Le Vice suprême,* published in the same year as *A Rebours* (1884), similarly absorbed in 'la vie rétrospective, cette habitude des intelligences décadentes':[74] 'L'archaïsme de ses préoccupations le ferma à la contemporanéité. A s'isoler du siècle, il contracta l'habitude de la vie artificielle rétrospective, et comme son corps d'éphèbe jurait avec l'habillement actuel, ses cogitations portèrent toutes des dates lointaines.'[75] Next, Bloy's Marchenoir, 'une espèce d'homme du Moyen Âge,'[76] who

fut orné, dès son premier jour, de la déplorable faculté . . . de porter, autour de son intelligence, comme une brume de choses anciennes et indiscernables, comme un halo de rêveries antérieures qui ne lui permirent longtemps qu'une vision réfractée du monde ambiant. . . .[77] Depuis son enfance, il avait cette impression d'être beaucoup plus le contemporain des Croisades ou de l'Exode que de la racaille démocratique.[78]

Marchenoir is depicted in the act of escaping from the modern to the medieval world. The forays he makes into the Middle Ages are short ones; the modern world presses in upon him and cannot be ignored for long. On his visit to the Grande-Chartreuse he feels with a shock of delight that he is re-entering the Middle Ages: 'Il suffit de franchir les limites de ce célèbre Désert pour sentir l'absence soudaine du dix-neuvième siècle et pour avoir, autant que cela est possible, l'illusion du douzième.'[79] The life of Saint Radegonde which he is writing affords him moments of similar satisfaction.

Hubert d'Entragues, the hero of Remy de Gourmont's *Sixtine* (1890) is seen writing a novel about himself transposed into a fifteenth-century setting, with characters refined into 'de purs symboles',[80] in order to assuage the pangs of unrequited love. The modern and medieval worlds

---

[73] Huysmans, *A Rebours,* p. 33.
[74] Péladan, *Le Vice suprême,* 13th edn., 1896, p. 58.   [75] Ibid. p. 121.
[76] Bloy, *La Femme pauvre,* p. 111.
[77] Bloy, *Oeuvres,* iii. 52.   [78] Ibid. p. 131.
[79] Ibid. p. 93. Cf. Huysmans' disillusionment in 1891. See *Là-haut,* 1965, pp. 242 sqq.
[80] Gourmont, *Sixtine, roman de la vie cérébrale,* 1890, p. 88.

---

carrées' (*Les Jeunes-France,* p. 317). 'Comme beaucoup d'autres,' his creator says of him, 'il avait manqué son entrée en ce monde, il n'était qu'une espèce de fou; il eût été un des plus hauts génies, sa vie eût été pleine et complète: il était obligé de se créer une existence factice et ridicule, et de se jouer lui-même de lui' (pp. 324-5).

alternate, as the story of the prisoner Guido, in love with a statue of the Madonna, keeps pace with that of Entragues, infatuated with the faithless Sixtine.

Huysmans' *Là-bas* (1891) is the chronicle of Durtal's excursion into the fifteenth century:[81] 'Ah! s'écrouer dans le passé, revivre au loin, ne plus même lire un journal, ne pas savoir si des théâtres existent, quel rêve!'[82] is his cry as he embarks upon a life of Gilles de Rais, to the immediate enrichment of his own: 'Le jour où Durtal s'était plongé dans l'effrayante et délicieuse fin du Moyen Âge, il s'était senti renaître.'[83] He and his friends, including Carhaix the bell-ringer of Saint-Sulpice – 'une créature caduque et rétrograde'[84] in the eyes of modern society, commended by another of the group, Des Hermies: 'Vous êtes, Dieu merci! si loin de votre époque, si fervent des choses qu'elle ignore ou qu'elle exècre . . .'[85] – take refuge in divers esoteric occupations, attempting to transport into the late nineteenth century (which is never left for long) some of the aristocratic singularities and practices of the Middle Ages: 'Sonner les cloches en les adorant, et se livrer aux besognes désuètes de l'art féodal,' exclaims Des Hermies, 'ou à des labeurs monastiques de vies de Saints, ce serait complet, si bien hors de Paris, si bien dans les là-bas, si loin dans les vieux âges!'[85] Durtal strolls through the ruins of Tiffauges, savouring his nostalgia: 'A n'en pas douter, ce fut une singulière époque que ce Moyen Âge, reprit-il, en allumant une cigarette.'[86] And after an evening spent discussing astrology, demoniacal possession, and the black arts with his friends –

'C'est égal,' pensait, une fois de plus, Durtal, en regardant cette salle à manger si tépide et si seule, et en se rappelant les extraordinaires conversations qui s'étaient tenues dans cette tour, 'ce qu'on est loin ici des idées et du langage du Paris moderne! – Tout cela nous réfère au Moyen Âge', dit-il, en complétant sa pensée tout haut.[87]

There is, however, no perfect sanctuary from the cruel intrusions of the modern world: as Durtal reaches the end of his account of Gilles de Rais's life, and tells his friends how the weeping crowd surged around the penitent criminal on his way to the scaffold, praying for his soul's repose, 'une voix enrouée, énorme, une voix d'écaillère, de pousseur de charrette' – the voice of the ignoble Parisian populace of 1889 –, reaches

---

[81] Inspired by Huysmans' own visits to the ex-abbé Boullan in 1890: 'On vivait là dans un plein surnaturel du Moyen Âge' he told a friend (*Là-haut*, p. 225).

[82] *Là-bas*, p. 20.　　[83] Ibid. p. 24.

[84] Ibid. p. 57.　　[85] Ibid. pp. 433-4.

[86] Ibid. p. 169.　　[87] *Là-bas*, p. 397.

their Saint-Sulpice tower, crying: 'Vive Boulanger! . . . Boulange! Lange!'[88]

The brooding presence of the past — which appears to Verhaeren as a mysterious figure holding a sword and prophesying:

> Tu seras nul, et pour ton âme inoccupée
> L'avenir ne sera qu'un regret du passé[89] —

is everywhere now; and all poets see themselves as the character described by Henri de Régnier in his tale *Le Chevalier qui dormit dans la neige*, 'celui qui n'a pas eu d'aventures pour avoir été par trop aussi le contemporain de l'époque qui n'est pas'.[90]

Ludwig of Bavaria, who committed suicide in 1886, appealed irresistibly to their imagination. Homage was paid to him by Verlaine, in his sonnet 'Roi, le seul vrai roi de ce siècle' (1886),[91] and by Louis le Cardonnel in 1892:

> Suprême Chevalier des légendes d'azur
> Obstinément fidèle à leur splendeur pâlie,
> Vous tourniez vers les jours évanouis d'Arthur
> Des yeux couleur de mer et de mélancolie.[92]

Just as the modern characters created by these writers were more often than not obsessed with the Middle Ages, their medieval characters were in many cases endowed with modern complexity and sophistication. 'A nous de rendre à cette matière la vie moderne et complexe',[93] declared the poet Moréas in 1891, speaking of his experiments with medieval literature. In the same year he stated that his aim was to 'évoquer l'âme moderne dans son apparat héréditaire'.[94]

Laforgue's 'moralité légendaire', *Lohengrin, fils de Parsifal* (1886), is the first work of this kind that comes to mind. A satire on bourgeois marriage and the modern *jeune fille*, the dialogue between the two lovers is peppered with acid anachronisms (Elsa: '. . . à votre merci, ô Prince

---

[88] Ibid. pp. 439-40.

[89] Verhaeren, *Poèmes*, ii (1896), 81 (*Les Débâcles*, 1888).

[90] H. de Régnier, *La Canne de jaspe*, 3rd edn., 1897, p. 287. (This tale was first published in *L'Ermitage* (Nov. 1893), and in *Contes à soi-même*, 1894.)

[91] Verlaine, op. cit. p. 426.

[92] L. Le Cardonnel, *Poèmes*, 6th edn., n.d., p. 52 (first published in *L'Ermitage*, Aug. 1892). See also Barrès's tribute to Ludwig of Bavaria in Ch. 4 of *L'Ennemi des lois*, 1893.

[93] W. G. C. Byvanck, *Un Hollandais à Paris en 1891*, 1892, p. 74.

[94] J. Huret, *Enquête sur l'évolution littéraire*, 1891, p. 428. Precursors of the Symbolists here were, on a frivolous level, Banville (cf. *supra*, p. 173), and, on a serious level, Flaubert (cf. *supra*, pp. 190-1).

Charmant! Et je saurai vous tisser des armures de rechange. . . . L'adorable Chevalier me laissera-t-il vieillir aveugle et paria dans cette société
bourgeoise?'[95] . . . Lohengrin: 'Je suis Lohengrin, le Chevalier-Errant,
le lys des croisades futures pour l'émancipation de la Femme. Mais, en
attendant, j'étais trop malheureux dans les bureaux de mon père' etc.)[96]

More or less deliberate projections of modern sensibility on to the
Middle Ages were of frequent occurrence in subsequent years. Even
Anatole France, in his insistence that 'le temps jadis, dont nous respirons
délicieusement la poésie, avait dans sa nouveauté ce goût banal et triste
de toutes les choses parmi lesquelles s'écoule la vie humaine',[97] was
indulging in this practice. The Gilles de Rais conjured up by Huysmans's
Durtal is a modern aesthete:

> Car il est presque isolé dans son temps, ce baron de Rais! Alors que
> ses pairs sont de simples brutes, lui, veut des raffinements éperdus d'art,
> rêve de littérature térébrante et lointaine . . . adore la musique d'église.
> . . . Ses goûts d'ameublement étaient solennels et bizarres; il se pâmait
> devant les étoffes abbatiales, devant les soies voluptueuses, devant les
> ténèbres dorées des vieux brocarts. . . . Il était le Des Esseintes du XVe
> siècle![98]

The women in Gourmont's medieval plays – *Théodat* (1889), in which
Maximienne wins back her husband from his episcopal vow of chastity
('Elle se dresse, et comme une chatte s'étire les membres . . .[99] enfan-
tinement elle gigotte'[100] etc.), and the *Histoire tragique de la Princesse
Phénissa* (1893) – are modern Parisian temptresses, as is Mélissinde, the
heroine of Rostand's pseudo-Symbolist drama *La Princesse lointaine*
(1895).

C. *The vogue for medieval domestic interiors:*
'finir par se croire vivre au moyen-âge . . .'

This desire on the part of 'la littérature de tout à l'heure' to give
modern life a medieval aura soon communicated itself to the bourgeois public of the day. The 1880s and 90s witnessed a resurgence of
the 'fureur gothique' which was rife during the twenties and thirties.[101]

---

[95] Laforgue, *Os. cs.* iii (1924), 113.
[96] Ibid. p. 116. See L. Guichard's commentary in *La musique et les lettres en France au temps du wagnérisme*, 1963, pp. 124-7.
[97] Cf. *supra*, p. 230.
[98] *Là-bas*, pp. 67-8.
[99] Gourmont, *Théodat*, 1893, p. 43 (first published in *Revue indépendante*, June 1889).
[100] Ibid. p. 49.   [101] Cf. *supra*, p. 26.

The tide of Romantic bric-à-brac, swollen with the new Pre-Raphaelite contribution, returned in force.

The Chat Noir, opened by Rodolphe Salis in 1881, described itself as a 'Cabaret Louis XIII. Fondé en 1114 par un fumiste.'[102] In its sham-medieval setting — stained glass, tapestries, massive tables and chairs — poets and artists congregated, and were entertained in 1891 with a lantern-slide performance of the death of Roland at Roncevaux.[103]

In 1888, at Rochefort, Pierre Loti gave a 'dîner quinzième siècle' comparable with the Bal des Truands held at the Impasse du Doyenné by Nerval and his friends in 1835. It was held in the Gothic wing of Loti's house, which boasted 'une couche de poussière artificielle, habilement répandue'.[104] Hydromel and hippocras were drunk; a jester rose out of a pie; pilgrims, minstrels, and Saracen prisoners arrived in ceaseless procession for the diversion of the guests. One of these, Marcel Sémézies, relived the scene for the readers of the *Nouvelle Revue:* 'C'est vraiment le Passé, ce *passé mort* cher à Loti, qui se réveille tout d'un coup. . . . Plus forte que l'admiration, une émotion quasi-religieuse — où se mêle un rien de vague tristesse — plane au-dessus des têtes.'[105] It was still talked about years after the event: Maurice d'Ocagne entertained Edmond de Goncourt in 1894 with a description of the 'mangeaille archaïque' that was eaten, the 'vieux français des CONTES DROLATIQUES de Balzac, à défaut de l'autre' that was spoken, and the distribution of leftovers to 'd'authentiques mendiants de la Charente-Inférieure, que Loti avait fait costumer en mendiants du XVe siècle'.[106]

An increasing volume of protest testifies to the rapid extension of the vogue for medieval domestic interiors during the eighties and nineties. An article in the *Revue illustrée* (1886) complained that

. . . nos intérieurs, où la lumière est nécessaire à cause du travail, sont obscurcis par l'abus des vitraux colorés . . . nos petits foyers s'encombrent de grands landiers en fer forgé, faits pour le vaste manteau des cheminées féodales . . . nos sièges, au lieu de s'accommoder par leurs courbes aux grâces souples de la femme contemporaine . . . affectent

[102] E. Goudeau, *Dix ans de bohème,* Librairie illustrée, n.d., p. 256.
[103] See Byvanck, op. cit. p. 33, and *Revue d'art dramatique,* 1 Mar. 1891. Cf. Jean Lorrain (*Modernités,* 1885, p. 105): 'Au fond des Brasseries/Moyen âge aux vitraux de lys enluminés,/Des messieurs de talent aux gestes avinés,/Déclament à leurs bocks des vers pleins de furies.'
[104] P. Delix, 'Le Dîner quinzième siècle de Pierre Loti', *Revue de Paris et de Saint-Pétersbourg,* iii (May 1888), p. 123.
[105] *Nouvelle Revue,* lii. 1 May 1888, p. 215.
[106] *Journal des Goncourt,* iv. 643-4.

les formes rigides des hautes cathèdres du Moyen âge, et font d'une Parisienne de cette fin de siècle une Blanche de Castille malgré elle, une châtelaine en pénitence.'[107]

Gabriel Mourey spoke in 1895 of 'des intérieurs du plus douteux moyenagisme . . . d'épais vitraux, parmi des meubles jus de chique, au coin de cheminées de stuc à gargouilles'.[108] In the following year Ottin remarked in his monumental work on stained glass that 'la vitromanie' had reached its height: 'Il n'est pas une maison bourgeoise qui se respecte aujourd'hui dans laquelle on ne rencontre de haut en bas des vitraux factices';[109] and Bloy in *La Femme pauvre* fired a passing shot at 'les vitraux postiches dont s'honore l'archaïsme des limonadiers'.[110] Zola's interior provoked much comment at this time. Hennique's description of 'son épatant faux mobilier moyenâgeux' amused Edmond de Goncourt in 1890;[111] and soon after this he was able to inspect it himself during a visit to Zola, and record with malicious delight the details of this 'mobilier de parvenu fastueux': 'des chaises à dossier doré de sept pieds, où on est reflété dans des glaces aux cadres faits de chasubles d'or et d'argent, où on aperçoit la rue de Paris à travers le coloriage archaïque d'un vitrail, où on évoque le ménage dormant dans une ruelle défendue par une grille de fer forgé. . . .' 'Tout ce décrochez-moi-ça *cathédraleux'*, he concluded, 'fait un drôle d'entour à l'auteur de l'ASSOMMOIR et de NANA.'[112] The *naturiste* poet Saint-Georges de Bouhélier, recalling this same spectacle in his memoirs, was shocked rather than amused: 'Le réalisme de Zola', he wrote, 'n'était en rien d'accord avec ces antiquailles dont par conséquent la présence ne s'expliquait pas.'[113]

Now, as in 1830, when the 'robe à la châtelaine' and the 'toque à créneaux' were all the rage, women of fashion dressed to match these settings: Edmond de Goncourt recorded in 1893 the 'apparition ce soir chez Daudet de Mme Barrès, en costume de Marguerite de Bourgogne, dans sa robe blanche de mariage, arrangée en surcot moyenâgeux, avec des enguirlandements de velours bleu'.[114]

This vogue is reflected in a multitude of Symbolist prose-poems, such

---

[107] *Revue illustrée*, i. 1 Apr. 1886, p. 283.
[108] G. Mourey, *Passé le détroit*, 1895, p. 285.
[109] L. Ottin, *Le Vitrail*, H. Laurens (1896), p. 100.
[110] *La Femme pauvre*, p. 97.
[111] *Journal des Goncourt*, iii. 1112.
[112] Ibid. iv. 70.
[113] S-G. de Bouhélier, *Le Printemps d'une génération*, Nagel, 1946, p. 285.
[114] *Journal des Goncourt*, iv. 346.

as Gustave Stevens' 'Profils perdus' (1891), an evocation of a woman:

> Ses robes étaient faites toujours de folles drapées . . . adamantinées
> d'une grecque d'or ancienne ou de quelque ceinture à fermoir gothique;
> tout son rêve cher était là d'ailleurs: finir par se croire vivre au moyen-
> âge en n'ayant autour d'elle que des choses anciennes et des fleurs rigides
> et des croisées à portraits et jusqu'à des manuscrits qu'elle ne savait
> lire.[115] —

and in several popular novels written for bourgeois consumption. Henri
de Noussanne's *Jasmin Robba* (1894) is the tale (decked out with
copious documentation from Léon Gautier's *La Chevalerie*) of an Elias
Wildmanstadius of the 1890s who acquires Pierrefonds from the state to
recreate the Middle Ages within its walls: 'Le grand mur à couronne
crénelée fermait son horizon. C'est là qu'il vivait son rêve étrange et
fastueux, sans que rien détonnât autour de lui.'[116] The heroine of *Mon
Chevalier* (1893), by 'Gabriel Franay' (Mme Louis Quioc), is a Madame
Bovary whose dreams are realised. She marries Renaud, a reincarnation
of the knights of old: 'Comme il serait beau sous le casque et l'armure,'
her reverie runs, 'et comme je le vois bien dans cette parure guerrière!
Mais sans le vouloir, je me vois en même temps à côté de lui, très belle
aussi, en robe de brocart d'or, tenant à la main une couronne de roses
dont je m'apprête à le couronner.'[117] Together, in a castle buried deep
in the forest, they spare no effort to give their existence 'la couleur
moyen âge.'[118]

D. *The Symbolist preference for medieval atmosphere:*
'L'action se passe n'importe où, et plutôt au moyen âge'

Fin de siècle nostalgia for the Middle Ages having reached this pitch
of intensity, it is not surprising that a discreetly medieval décor was
generally felt to be the most suitable for inducing the desired Symbolist
état d'âme in poetry and drama. In theory, of course, these writers held
that 'Fables' and 'Fictions' should be given a neutral, timeless setting,
with no hint of 'race', 'milieu', or 'moment'. The ideal Hero was 'la
Figure que Nul n'est' (Mallarmé, 1885);[119] the ideal poem was 'la
Fiction symbolique, libérée aussi bien de la géographie que de l'histoire'
(Morice, 1889),[120] attaining 'une vérité qui ne connaît les siècles'

---

[115] *La Jeune Belgique,* x (Dec. 1891), p. 435.
[116] H. de Noussanne, *Jasmin Robba,* 1894, p. 93.
[117] G. Franay, *Mon Chevalier,* 1893, p. 38.
[118] Ibid. p. 152.
[119] Mallarmé, *Os. cs.* p. 545 ('Richard Wagner: Rêverie d'un poëte français').
[120] Ch. Morice, *La Littérature de tout à l'heure,* 1889, p. 359.

(Mockel, 1890).[121] In practice, however, the ideal world created by writers such as Maeterlinck — whose characters moved in what he termed 'une atmosphère divine'[122] — was more often than not an ideal Middle Ages. The action of Saint-Pol-Roux's *Épilogue des saisons humaines* (1893) takes place in the dying hero's brain, metamorphosed for scenic purposes into a 'Salle circulaire dans une Tour. Aux murailles, tapisseries de gloire.'[123] 'L'action se passe n'importe où' was the stage direction for Pierre Quillard's *Fille aux mains coupées* (1886), 'et plutôt au moyen âge'.[124]

These writers called their plays 'mystères',[125] their poems 'chante-fables', 'cantilènes', 'enluminures', 'vitraux', 'naïves légendes', 'chevaleries sentimentales'.[126] They called each other 'ymagiers', 'trouveurs', and 'jongleors': for Henri Ghéon, Paul Fort was essentially 'l'imagier',[127] while Gourmont saw in him 'le véritable type des derniers *jongleors*';[128] Vielé-Griffin told Verhaeren: 'Ton art/Est comme un gonfanon, beau chevalier/Debout dans l'étrier';[129] and Mockel — who had in 1890 called Régnier 'un nonchalant et si noble trouvère'[130] — expanded this tribute four years later into a remarkable flight of fancy which bears out Martino's statement that the Symbolists' ambition was to 'faire plus moyen âge que nature'.[131] Régnier, declares Mockel, closely resembles Thibaut de Champagne, but his soul is nobler than Thibaut's, for he would not have sought out his former love after her husband's death to settle down with her in prosaic contentment:

S'il avait aimé la comtesse de Moha . . . il n'aurait point cherché celle qu'on lui avait ravie . . . dans la solitude il l'aurait évoquée et se serait fortifié de son illusoire présence. Pour elle il eût donné d'imaginaires et magiques tournois . . . maintes merveilles somptueuses, maintes prouesses d'héroïsme comme en une haute-lisse assemblées en leurs images, seraient devenues un tapis idéal pour les pieds de la Fiancée et cela, combats,

[121] A. Mockel, *Esthétique du symbolisme,* ed. M. Otten, 1962, p. 238.

[122] Maeterlinck, *Le Trésor des humbles,* 1896, p. 276.

[123] Saint-Pol-Roux, *Épilogue des saisons humaines,* 1893, p. 7.

[124] P. Quillard, *La Lyre héroïque et dolente,* 1897, p. 124.

[125] Mallarmé introduced the conception of the theatre as 'Mystère' to the Symbolists. See H. M. Block, *Mallarmé and the Symbolist Drama,* 1963, pp. 85-8.

[126] e.g. Mockel, *Chantefable un peu naïve* (1891); Moréas, *Cantilènes* (1886); Elskamp, *Enluminures* (1898); Tailhade, *Vitraux* (1891); Ch.-H. Hirsch, *Légendes naïves* (1894); F. Hérold, *Chevaleries sentimentales* (1893).

[127] *La Critique,* 5 Apr. 1897, p. 69.

[128] Gourmont, *Promenades littéraires,* iv (1912), 111.

[129] Vielé-Griffin, *Oeuvres,* ii (1926), 149.

[130] *La Wallonie,* 1890, p. 230.

[131] P. Martino, *Parnasse et symbolisme,* 10th edn., 1958, p. 163.

trésors, gloires et joies, eût formé le poème de son âme tout entière, −
pur, vaste et noble drame, mélancolique comme l'attente, mystérieux
comme la forêt . . . mais triste surtout et résigné, parce qu'Elle n'était
point là et ne devait jamais venir.[132]

E. *The Symbolist Middle Ages: its efflorescence in the 1880s and 90s*

Michaud selects the dates 1886 and 1891 as the two most important
in the history of the Symbolist movement: 'En 1886, la révolution de la
sensibilité était faite; en 1891, la révolution intellectuelle est con-
sommée.'[133] The fortunes of the Symbolist Middle Ages correspond
faithfully with those of Symbolism itself: 1886 marked the hour of its
first flowering, with the publication of Moréas' *Cantilènes,* Quillard's
Fille aux mains coupées, and Ephraïm Mikhaël's 'Dame en deuil',
'Infidélités', and 'Impiétés' in *La Pléiade,* and many of Gustave Kahn's
medieval *Palais nomades* poems in *La Vogue;* while in 1891 − with
Maeterlinck's translation of Ruysbroeck, Péladan's Rose+Croix
manifesto, Huysmans' *Là-bas,* Retté's *Thulé des brumes,* Schwob's
Coeur double, Mockel's *Chantefable un peu naïve,* Merrill's *Fastes,* and
Tailhade's *Vitraux* − the apogee was reached, after which the inevitable
decline set in. For some years, however, the Symbolist Middle Ages
continued to flourish, even while dissident voices began to be raised
against it. A single number of *L'Ermitage* (April 1894) is representative
of the period. It contains an article on Mikhaël by Edmond Pilon, who
proclaims that 'La croisade idéale sera bientôt gagnée; la Jerouschalaim de
Demain érige, dans la vespérale et brumeuse fin de ce long siècle, ses tours
d'ivoire où s'éploient des bannières de conquête';[134] a review by Saint-
Antoine of Paul Sabatier's *Vie de saint François d'Assise* approving his
comment, 'le moyen-âge n'était pas triste';[135] a prose poem by Henri
Mazel, 'Les Alyscans':

Nom sonore, nom funèbre, syllabes tristes qui glissent, et qui douces,
chutent, si sourdes, Alyscans. . . .
Appels d'oliphants par les grands bois, chansons de geste, multitudes
sarrazines que martèlent les paladins, Alyscans;[136]

and a sequence of poems, *Progression wagnérienne* by 'Sinocim' ('Le
vieux sire époux songe à sa peine, et boit/Dans sa coupe l'effroi de ses
noces gothiques' etc.).[137]

---

[132] A. Mockel, *Propos de littérature,* 1894, pp. 127-8.
[133] G. Michaud, *Message poétique du symbolisme,* 1947, ii. 399.
[134] *L'Ermitage,* v (Apr. 1894), p. 195.
[135] Ibid. p. 206.   [136] Ibid. p. 211.   [137] Ibid. p. 217.

'Ce moyen âge imaginaire,' Pol Neveux recalled in a speech given in 1929 at a gathering in memory of Stuart Merrill, 'nous l'avons chéri éperdûment . . . notre amour lui a conféré pour jamais une réalité, une vérité historique.'[138] Forgetting their mission to seek out hidden truth, poets were tempted to linger in this world. They joined in a chorus of elegiac lamentation for the passing of the Middle Ages:

Les cloches d'autrefois, dites, où sonnent-elles?
L'antan naïf est mort.   (Samain, 1885)[139]

Mais les heures sont passées
De la joie et du décor
Et dans nos âmes lassées
C'est un grand silence après le chant du cor. (Quillard, 1891)[140]

Tout est mort à jamais pour les mémoires d'hommes:
le chant de l'olifan triomphant lors des sacres,
les chasses quand au soleil de la journée en fête
vers la joie du soleil partaient du haut castel
les palefrois parés comme des archevêques. (Mockel, 1891)[141]

Some of them — Mikhaël, Ferdinand Hérold, Quillard, and (for a short time) Gustave Kahn — even received professional training at the École des Chartes; some emerged from the Middle Ages as taste began to change in the course of the nineties, while others, such as Kahn, Hérold, and Tristan Klingsor, remained absorbed in them for the duration of their poetic career, and two were to end their days in neo-Gothic fastnesses (Maeterlinck's Orlamonde and Saint-Pol-Roux's Manoir de Cécilian) built to protect their owners from the encroachments of the twentieth century.

Although the Symbolist Middle Ages soon became the common property of a multitude of writers who borrowed freely from each other — and was quickly 'banalisé' in consequence, as Fontainas points out[142] — individual varieties of it, in the work of the better poets, differ widely from one another. Moréas's is wild and bizarre, Mockel's elegiac and evanescent, Samain's languorous, Klingsor's airily iridescent and

---

[138] *Commémoration de Stuart Merrill à Versailles*, 1930, p. 36.

[139] A. Samain, *Au jardin de l'infante* (1893), 1922, p. 129 (*Le Chat noir* (Dec. 1885)).

[140] P. Quillard, *La Lyre héroïque et dolente*, 1897, p. 22 (*Mercure de France* (Aug. 1891)).

[141] A. Mockel, *Chantefable un peu naïve*, 1891, p. 64.

[142] A. Fontainas, *Mes Souvenirs du symbolisme*, Édns. de la Nouvelle Revue Critique, 1928, p. 202.

'troubadour', Merrill's mysteriously gem-encrusted, Rodenbach's pervaded with musty religiosity.

F. *Character of the Symbolist Middle Ages:*
(i) *Imprecision and subjectivity*

We must now turn our attention to the exact nature of the Symbolist Middle Ages. How, for instance, does it differ from that of the previous generation? The poets of the eighties and nineties had in common, first of all, a predilection for melting imprecision, '[un] décor de jadis et de songe'.[143] In reaction against naturalism, as a contemporary critic put it, 'l'art se rejeta vers les sujets de rêve et de légende.'[144] 'Pour la matière des oeuvres,' declared Kahn in 1886, 'las du quotidien, du coudoyé et de l'obligatoire contemporain, nous voulons pouvoir placer en quelque époque ou même en plein rêve (*le rêve étant indistinct de la vie*) le développement du symbole.'[145] Adolphe Retté, looking back on this time, recalled: 'Nous faisions l'effet de troubadours moyenâgeux égarés dans une usine.'[146] And in reaction against the Parnasse, the past in which these 'troubadours' delighted was nebulous and subjective. Earnest Parnassian attempts at historical re-creation were abandoned in favour of the enraptured contemplation of 'ce qui fut peut-être' (Jacques des Gachons, 1894).[147] Even where the apparatus of historical erudition was used (as in the tales of Marcel Schwob), it was to produce a *frisson* in the modern reader, and not to recreate the past for its own sake. Poets selected 'un temps écoulé', in the words of Kahn, 'pour y dérouler, en une tapisserie décorative, l'essence toute moderne de leur pensée.'[148]

Taine's 'rendons-nous le passé présent' evoked no response from this generation. Poets such as Kahn were commended by their fellows for having produced '[des] légendes . . . délicieusement vieillies et comme usées en les mémoires'.[149] Distance was of supreme importance: there was to be nothing precise or particular in Symbolist evocations of the

---

[43] Ch.-H. Hirsch, *Légendes naïves,* 1894, p. 68.

[44] Saint-Antoine, 'Qu'est-ce que le symbolisme?', *L'Ermitage,* v (June 1894), p. 337.

[145] 'Réponse des symbolistes', *L'Événement,* 28 Sept. 1886.

[146] A. Retté, *Le Symbolisme,* 1903, p. 16.

[147] J. des Gachons, 'Ma mie Jehanne', *L'Album des légendes.* 1894, p. 4.

[148] G. Kahn, *Symbolistes et décadents,* 1902, p. 97 (*Revue indépendante* (May 1888)). Cf. Mallarmé's treatment of the Parnassian theme of statues on tombs in 'Contre un poëte parisien' (1862). According to A. Gill (*Revue de linguistique romane,* xxxii (1968), p. 299), 'Il en a fait un symbole du poète moderne qui "distrait" de sa vie charnelle tout juste assez de feu pour animer son rêve éperdu.'

[149] R. Ghil, *Les Dates et les oeuvres: Symbolisme et poésie scientifique,* Crès (1923), p. 87.

past. 'Point d'archéologie ni de couleur historique', declared Saint-Antoine, the *Ermitage* critic, in 1894.[150] History was proscribed and legend came into its own. Those same writers who disapproved of Viollet-le-Duc's restorations spoke out against Taine's historical method: Anatole France (though no Symbolist) came to lose faith in the nineteenth century's much-vaunted scientific recreation of history,[151] and Huysmans proclaimed it to be 'le plus solennel des mensonges, le plus enfantin des leurres': 'Il ne reste donc qu'à se fabriquer sa vision.'[152]

Wagner (in his *Lettre sur la musique*, 1860) had been the first to insist that the subject of a dramatic poem must be taken from legend rather than history.[153] Painters desiring to exhibit their work at Péladan's Salon de la Rose+Croix were invited to send in representations of 'La Légende, le Mythe, l'Allégorie, le Rêve'.[154] 'La peinture d'histoire, prosaïque, et illustrative de manuel', together with 'la peinture patriotique et militaire' and 'toute représentation de la vie contemporaine ou privée ou publique', were rigorously excluded from the Salon. History, lamented Morice in 1889, had destroyed 'l'illusion de la reculée dans le temps'[155] as the steam-ship and the railway had destroyed distance in space; but poets still had the resource of legend, '[ces] admirables prétextes à fiction'.[156] For Mockel, contemptuous of '[les] sèches précisions du Parnasse et . . . ses bons devoirs d'histoire versifiée',[157] legend was 'le territoire sacré . . . où la poésie manifeste librement sa nostalgie de la Beauté', [158] 'le climat naturel du rêve'.[159]

So an atmosphere of time immemorial was prescribed for the Symbolist 'Fiction' — that atmosphere conjured up by Poe in a parenthesis of his poem 'The Haunted Palace':

> (C'était, — tout cela, c'était dans le vieux,
> Dans le très-vieux temps);[160]

---

[150] *L'Ermitage*, v (Sept. 1894), p. 155.
[151] See e.g. *Le Crime de Sylvestre Bonnard*, 1881 (*Os. cs.* ii. 499); the Preface to *Les Désirs de Jean Servien* (1882); and *Pierre Nozière*, 1899 (*Os. cs.* x. 400-1).
[152] *Là-bas*, pp. 25-6.
[153] See L. Guichard, op. cit. p. 12.
[154] Péladan, *Salon de la Rose+Croix: Règle et monitoire*, 1891, pp. 8-9.
[155] Ch. Morice, op. cit. p. 373.
[156] Ch. Morice, op. cit. p. 364.
[157] A. Mockel, 'Stuart Merrill', *Mercure de France*, 1 Feb. 1916, p. 402.
[158] Ibid. p. 406.
[159] A. Mockel, 'La Jeunesse de Maeterlinck ou la poésie du mystère', *Annales de la Fondation M. Maeterlinck*, vi (1960), p. 39.
[160] Baudelaire's translation, *Os. cs.* Conard, 1933, p. 103.

and Kahn invited the reader of his *Palais nomades* (1887):

> Et puisque tout est semblable, tous les soleils des années, toutes les souffrances des jours, écoute flotter et bruire l'âme de la légende.
>
> Le vieux rêve se meut dans une atmosphère aimante, aux douleurs lointaines les pardons faciles; écoute dans le temps sourire tes frères morts.[161]

Régnier explained the distinction between Parnassian and Symbolist use of legend in a lecture published in 1900:

> Ils [i.e. Hugo and the Parnassians] se font les contemporains volontaires de ce passé fabuleux. Ce sont pour eux des anecdotes grandioses et séculaires. . . . Les Dieux et les Héros demeurent pour eux des personnages du passé. . . .
>
> Les Poètes récents ont considéré autrement les Mythes et les Légendes. Ils en cherchèrent la signification permanente et le sens idéal; où les uns virent des contes et des fables, les autres virent des symboles.[162]

Whereas writers of the Second Empire had held that legends each possessed their hour of truth and then faded, to be resurrected only by modern erudite poets such as Leconte de Lisle, preferably at the moment of their fading, as a pathetic curiosity, the Symbolists sought a fresh, personal meaning in legend. They condemned the Middle Ages evoked by their elders as insufficiently haunting, disturbing, and intoxicating. The *Légende des siècles* was found wanting by Rodenbach:

> On désirerait parfois plus de recul, un éclairage lunaire, les tuniques pâles et mauves de la légende. . . . C'est trop de l'histoire, de la peinture d'histoire . . . .[163]

Heredia's 'Vitrail' by Laurent Tailhade:

> La *'Verrière'* d'Heredia est belle . . . plus que mes vers, seulement, elle n'est pas du tout pathétique. Et c'est ce qu'il faut: être pathétique, sans gueulade ni pleurnicherie pathétique, en profondeur, comme les émeraudes sont vertes . . . .[164]

and Flaubert's *Saint Julien* by Huysmans:

> Tout y est, tout, — sauf l'accent qui eût fait de cette nouvelle un vrai chef d'oeuvre . . . il y manque . . . la flamme qui devrait circuler

---

[161] G. Kahn, *Premiers Poèmes,* 1897, p. 107.
[162] Régnier, *Figures et caractères,* 1901, pp. 335-6.
[163] Rodenbach, *L'Élite,* 1899, p. 96 (1893).
[164] Tailhade, *Lettres à sa mère,* 1926, p. 199 (1891).

sous ces magnifiques phrases; il y manque le cri de l'amour qui défaille, le don de l'exil surhumain, l'âme mystique![165]

This new Middle Ages was made visible for all in the Symbolist theatre – the temple of 'le rite de la Religion esthétique' (Ch. Morice).[166] 'Je rêve, quant au décor,' wrote Mockel in 1890, 'je rêve de scènes très au loin, où, parmi les chansons du choeur populaire, de naïfs personnages immobiliseraient un geste sur fond d'or.'[167] His dreams were abundantly realized in the years that followed. 'Hieratic' beings moving against a 'fond d'or' appeared with increasing frequency in the small Symbolist theatres which came into being during the nineties.

This theatre described itself as *'un prétexte au rêve'* (P. Quillard, 'De l'inutilité absolue de la mise en scène exacte', 1891).[168] Stage directions were in keeping: 'Cela se passait autrefois' for Gourmont's *Histoire tragique de la Princesse Phénissa* (1893), 'Dans un prieuré de Moines blancs, à l'époque étrange des légendes' for Saint-Pol-Roux's *L'Âme noire du prieur blanc, naïve légende* (1893), and 'L'action se passe vaguement entre le XIe siècle et le XIIe siècle' for Rostand's *Princesse lointaine* (1895).

The first of these small theatres was Henri Signoret's Petit Théâtre des Marionnettes, opened in the Galerie Vivienne in 1888, for which Maurice Bouchor wrote his popular 'mystères' (didactic rather than Symbolist in intention, however). Paul Fort's Théâtre Mixte (later the Théâtre d'Art) was founded in 1890 as an idealist challenge to Antoine's Théâtre Libre. In March 1891 Quillard's 'mystère' *La Fille aux mains coupées* was performed there, most successfully, behind a gauze curtain and against a background painted by Paul Sérusier:

> Sur le fond d'or des Primitifs, [wrote the *Mercure de France* critic] un fond d'or au semis d'icônes naïves d'anges en prières, les figures se meuvent, lentes, rythmiques; elles disent, ou plutôt elles *chantent* leur âme, et, quand elles se taisent, une *récitante* (debout, à gauche de la scène et en deçà du rideau de gaze) les explique d'une voix uniforme et monotone, ou bien le *choeur* épand une musique suave de paroles: la voix de l'Invisible.[169]

Gourmont's *Théodat*, for which 'toute la famille de Paul Fort s'occupa à découper des lions rouges sur fond d'or'[170] (to a design devised by

[165] Huysmans, *En route.* 1895, p. 32.   [166] Morice, op. cit. p. 290.
[167] A. Mockel, *Esthétique du symbolisme*, p. 240.
[168] *Revue d'art dramatique*, xxii. 1 May 1891, p. 182.
[169] *Mercure de France* (May 1891), p. 302.
[170] D. Knowles, *La Réaction idéaliste au théâtre depuis 1890*, 1934, p. 243.

Maurice Denis), was performed at the Théâtre d'Art in December 1891.
On the same programme was *Le Geste du Roi*, dramatized fragments
from three *chansons de geste:* the death of Roland, in Merrill's archaic
translation, the death of the Émir from *Fierabras*, adapted by Mauclair,
and the wanderings of Berthe *au grand pied* in the forest, very freely
adapted by Retté. Mauclair, who, as we shall see, was one of the first
to defect from the Symbolist Middle Ages in the mid nineties, later
called this enterprise 'une fumisterie'.[171] In 1891 the brothers Andhré
and Jacques des Gachons founded their Théâtre Minuscule. Here
Jacques's 'luminocontes' were performed. The 'Imagier', Andhré,
painted backgrounds for them on transparent paper lit from behind
by lamps with coloured glass. His brother's poems (read slowly, 'sur un
ton de mélopée')[172] included 'Amants-lys, rêve mystique', 'Le Prince
Naif, héritier d'une race maudite' (1893), and 'Ma Mie Jehanne' ('une
moyenâgerie'), published in *L'Album des légendes* (1894).[173] Finally,
the décor for *Pelléas et Mélisande* (the first performance given by
Lugné-Poe's Théâtre de l'Oeuvre, founded in 1893 to continue Fort's
Théâtre d'Art) was inspired by Memling and Walter Crane. Maeterlinck
sent suitably indefinite instructions to Lugné-Poe for the costumes —
'XIe — XIIe siècles, ou bien selon Memling (XVe) comme vous
voudrez et selon les circonstances'.[174]

(ii) *Naïveté and melancholy*

Besides being nebulous and subjective, the Symbolists' 'moyens âges
imaginaires' were almost without exception naïve and melancholy (or
'dolents', a favourite word of theirs).

Naïveté, for so long in eclipse (Taine had contemptuously dismissed
'les voix enfantines ou nasillardes du moyen âge')[175] now came into its
own. The Symbolists not only savoured medieval naïveté, but they took
it upon themselves, became naïve themselves. Here again, while the
Parnassians stood aloof from the Middle Ages — viewing them in their
narrative poems as remotely deplorable, and in their 'Sonnets
Gothiques' as remotely picturesque — the Symbolists were attempting
to revive them as a living principle. Once applied disparagingly to
medieval literature,[176] the term 'balbutiement' was now often used by
these poets in commendation of each other's work. 'Tout cela est juste,

[171] See J. Robichez, *Le Symbolisme au théâtre*, 1957, pp. 132-3.
[172] See *La Plume*, 1 Dec. 1895, p. 539.
[173] L. Maillard, *Notes pour demain: (1) L'Imagier Andhré des Gachons*, 1892, p. 21.
[174] Robichez, op. cit. pp. 164-5.   [175] Taine, *HLA* i. 258.   [176] Cf. *supra*, p. 99.

naïf, balbutié, comme un portail de cathédrale', wrote Vielé-Griffin of Elskamp's *Salutations dont d'angéliques* (1893);[177] and Mockel in a letter to Elskamp described the same work as 'doux balbutiements qui tiennent de la chanson que l'on fredonne et de la prière qui se chuchote'.[178] Schwob's Preface to Henry Bataille's *Chambre blanche* (1895) introduced it as 'un petit livre tout blanc, tout tremblant, tout balbutiant'.[179] Maeterlinck's characters, in particular, communicate with each other in carefully-wrought 'balbutiements', like Mélisande's 'Je ne sais pas ce que je dis. . . . Je ne sais pas ce que je sais. . . . Je ne dis plus ce que je veux.'[180]

The world of Maeterlinck is also 'dolent' in the extreme. Arkel's famous cry (in *Pelléas et Mélisande*): 'Mais la tristesse, Golaud . . . mais la tristesse de tout ce que l'on voit . . .'[181] could be applied to the entire Symbolist Middle Ages. The 'immense tristesse' of the Middle Ages, which, after appealing to the Romantics,[182] had so repelled Michelet and his fellow republicans,[183] was now back in favour. It was in accord with the Symbolists' own profound pessimism (for which Michaud gives the explanation: 'La génération de 1885 est une génération de vaincus').[184] A lecture given by Émile Gebhart in December 1869, 'La vie réelle et la poésie chez les peuples d'Occident au moyen âge', marks the point of transition between two eras. It begins with a conventional republican survey of the Dark Ages:

> Le soir venu . . . la sonnerie du couvre-feu enveloppait la ville noire et muette de son bourdonnement mélancolique. C'était l'heure du recueillement et des méditations amères pour ceux qui, dans les logis bourgeois groupés à l'ombre des cathédrales, dans les manoirs féodaux ou les monastères, ne dormant pas, repassaient en revue les angoisses et les calamités du temps où ils vivaient.[185]

And yet — Gebhart goes on to say — these privations and atrocities fostered in men's souls 'un sentiment exquis que l'antiquité païenne avait à peine connu avant Épicure et Lucrèce, la mélancolie.' He concludes:

> A vrai dire, la mélancolie en [i.e. du moyen âge] a été la grâce la plus précieuse. Elle a pénétré intimement le moyen âge entier, telle

---

[177] *Entretiens politiques et littéraires*, 25 June 1893, p. 534.
[178] H. Davignon, *L'Amitié de Max Elskamp et d'Albert Mockel*, 1955, p. 8.
[179] H. Bataille, *La Chambre blanche*, 1895, p. 7.
[180] Maeterlinck, *Théâtre*, ii (1902), 102.
[181] Maeterlinck, *Théâtre*, ii. 112.   [182] Cf. *supra*, pp. 16-17.
[183] Cf. *supra*, p. 79.   [184] Michaud, op. cit. ii. 264.
[185] *Revue des cours et conférences*, vii. 25 Dec. 1869, p. 56.

qu'une mélodie plaintive qui monte et chante sous les voûtes des cathédrales, s'enfonce dans la nuit des hautes ogives.[186]

So the republican Middle Ages were now felt to have produced one desirable by-product: poetic melancholy. The elegiac mood of the Romantics and of Michelet's *première manière* was recreated. The Symbolist poets and their audience could not have enough of medieval melancholy. Gabriel de la Morandière's 'Ceux qui pleurent' (1897) is a representative lower-grade product of the fashion:

> Ils sont, enclos d'un grand crêpe, les coeurs dolents.
> L'angoisse flue en eux d'amères stalactites. . . .
>
> En leur peine immense et féodale, murés . . .
> Au scintillant dehors des choses, éplorés,
> Ils veillent, doux vassaux du Destin qui les broie.[187]

Bernard Lazare extolled Régnier's poetry in 1895: 'Il se dégage des légendes de M. de Régnier une touchante et indicible mélancolie, car l'âme de ses héros est dolente; on les aime à cause des douleurs qu'ils décèlent, à cause de leur morne et élégante tristesse.'[188]

We shall encounter the host of Régnier's defeated warriors later on. Other notable exploiters of this mood were Maeterlinck, the expert creator of an atmosphere of brooding melancholy (with sobbing rain,[189] nuns intoning the *Miserere*,[190] etc.); Rodenbach, obsessed with his *Agonies de villes* ('. . . quais taciturnes, rivières dolentes, chapelles aux vitraux pâles, on les a détruits, fermés, bouchés, comblés, tués'),[191] who proclaimed that the overpowering melancholy of the Middle Ages in small towns 'parmi le Nord où tout est mort' had stolen for ever into his soul:

> Or, moi, j'ai trop vécu dans le Nord; rien n'obvie
> A cette ombre à présent des Beffrois sur ma vie.
>
> Partout cette influence et partout l'ombre aussi
> Des autres tours qui m'ont fait le coeur si transi . . . :[192]

and Gustave Kahn, whose poems teem with dolorous images:

> Des châteaux . . .
> Si pâles, si tristes qu'au fond

---

[186] Ibid. pp. 60-1. [187] *MF* (May 1897), p. 296.
[188] B. Lazare, *Figures contemporaines*, 1895, p. 154.
[189] *Les Sept Princesses*, 1891, p. 29.
[190] At the end of *La Princesse Maleine*, 1889.
[191] Rodenbach, *Évocations*, p. 79. Cf. Hugo's lamentations in *Le Rhin* (*Os. cs.*, ed. J. Massin, vi. 360, 483).
[192] *Oeuvres*, i. 235-6 (*Le Règne du silence*, 1891).

> On savait des malheurs profonds,
> Misères par force venues . . . (*Les Palais nomades,* 1887),[193]

and reverberate with the sound of 'old, unhappy, far-off things':

> Les voix de la ballade . . .
> le récital de peines amères d'enfants
> le coeur navré de grière peine,
> les oliphants tristes du héros malade,
> les jonchées de colloques épars sur la peine
> universelle de l'amour mourant . . . (*Domaine de fée,* 1895).[194]

Gradations in the degree of this Symbolist melancholy are infinite, from the gently elegiac:

> Toute la belle histoire est finie,
> L'ancien faste et la mer baignant le pied des tours
>   (Rodenbach: *Le Miroir du ciel natal,* 1898)[195]

to a more clamorous distress that expressed itself in images of feudal desolation and *désarroi,* deriving from certain lines of Baudelaire: 'Mon coeur est un palais flétri par la cohue'; 'Mon esprit est pareil à la tour qui succombe/Sous les coups du bélier infatigable et lourd';[196] '. . . l'Espoir,/Vaincu, pleure, et l'Angoisse atroce, despotique,/Sur mon crâne incliné plante son drapeau noir';[197] and Verlaine (himself influenced by Baudelaire): 'L'espoir a fui, vaincu, vers le ciel noir';[198] 'Le Malheur a percé mon vieux coeur de sa lance'.[199] Lugubrious utterances:

> Sous la rouille des temps je suis un vieux blason . . .
> — Voici l'heure, male heure, et la male saison (Moréas, 1885)[200]

> Notre âme, elle n'est plus qu'un haillon sans couleurs
> Comme un drapeau mouillé qui pend contre sa hampe!
>   (Rodenbach, 1886),[201]

> Toutes les châtelaines sont mortes de faim, cet été, dans
> les tours de mon âme!
>   (Maeterlinck, 1889),[202]

[193] G. Kahn, *Premiers Poèmes,* p. 53.
[194] Ibid. p. 322.
[195] Rodenbach, *Oeuvres,* ii (1925), 185.
[196] Baudelaire, *Os. cs.* pp. 54-5.
[197] Ibid. p. 71.
[198] Verlaine, *Oeuvres poétiques complètes,* p. 121 ('Colloque sentimental', 1868).
[199] Cf. *supra,* p. 223.
[200] Moréas, *Oeuvres,* i (1923), 127.
[201] Rodenbach, *Oeuvres,* i. 76.
[202] Maeterlinck, *Poésies complètes,* ed. J. Hanse, 1965, p. 114.

> Je ne sais ce qui meurt en moi,
> Mais je sens la Mort qui passe,
> Et le Désastre est le roi
> Morne de mon âme lasse
>
> (Yvanhoé Rambosson, 1891);[203]

and desolate visions of battles long ago:

> Hélas! et la débâcle à travers leurs maisons,
> Le deuil de la débâcle en des nuits de tueries,
> Et les funèbres sonneries
> Cassant la destinée en or de leurs blasons
>
> (Verhaeren, *Les Preux*, 1889),[204]

> ... un désastre cassa les rondaches et les armes;
> les panaches de gloire et les cimiers d'orgueil
> avec les cris du bronze exaltant l'étendard
> les brocarts fastueux roidis aux chars des rois
> les fanfares épandant par cataractes l'or
> avec les cimiers d'or s'abîmèrent en l'histoire
>
> (Mockel, 1891),[205]

> La tête du Roi ricane du haut d'une pique;
> Les étendards fuient dans la nuit, et c'est la panique
>
> (Moréas, 1886),[206]

> C'est la fuite des étendards
> Le long de la mauvaise route
> Aux cris des barbares hagards
> Traquant mon armée en déroute
>
> (Merrill, 1895)[207]

these express an *état d'âme* shared by all except two poets – Vielé-Griffin and (from 1891 onwards) Verhaeren, who forge cheerful feudal imagery to counteract the pessimism of their fellows. Defeat is never mentioned in Vielé-Griffin's work, from his early *Joies* (1889):

> Un oiseau chantait d'espérance et de joie,
> Chantait la vie et ses tournois
> Et la lance qu'on brise et la lance qui ploie[208]

to his *Chevauchée d'Yeldis* (1893), a parable illustrating the rewards of optimistic enterprise: Martial, the only member of a company of knights

[203] Y. Rambosson, *Le Verger doré*, 1895, p. 31.
[204] Verhaeren, *Poèmes*, i (1895), 46.
[205] *Chantefable un peu naïve*, 1891, p. 64.
[206] Moréas, op. cit. p. 130.
[207] Merrill, *Poèmes, 1887-1897*, 1897, p. 123.
[208] Vielé-Griffin, *Oeuvres*, i (1924), 60.

who is without trace of faint-heartedness, wins the beautiful Yeldis, symbol of 'la Vie et toute joie'.[209] Verhaeren in 1891 moved out of the shadow of *Les Débâcles* with his poem celebrating Saint George, the antithesis of Verlaine's 'chevalier Malheur', who descends to earth with the gift of hope, 'un intime et pur cordial d'or', and takes his leave:

> . . . m'imposant la vaillance
> Et, sur le front, la marque en croix d'or de sa lance.[211]

G. *Return to a medieval mentality:*
(i) *Gothic souls in a Gothic kingdom*

So, in reaction against the pedantic precision of the Parnasse, the Middle Ages of Symbolist poets and dramatists was nebulous and subjective, and in reaction against the bourgeois vulgarities of naturalism, their plays presented 'hieratic' characters against a 'fond d'or'. They luxuriated in the medieval naïveté which had repelled Taine, and in the 'immense tristesse' which had revolted Michelet and Gautier. The whole mentality of the eighties-and-nineties writers was moreover a consciously medieval one, in reaction against the positivism of their elders. Guiding spirits in this reaction were of course the writers of the Catholic revival. Claudel's famous letter to Jacques Rivière describes the 'révélation du surnaturel' granted to him by his reading Rimbaud's *Illuminations* in 1886: 'Je sortais enfin de ce monde hideux de Taine, de Renan et des autres Moloch du dix-neuvième siècle, de ce bagne, de cette affreuse mécanique entièrement gouvernée par des lois parfaitement inflexibles.'[211] Huysmans's Durtal humbly returned to the school of 'le Moyen Âge qui savait que sur cette terre tout est signe, tout est figure, que le visible ne vaut que par ce qu'il recouvre d'invisible.'[212]

Novelists and playwrights of the Symbolist movement, renouncing the positivist, mechanical calculations of naturalism, sought a fresh, mysterious relationship between people and events, inspired in part by the world of chivalric romance. Two of the most notable examples are Maeterlinck's restoration of Fate, ruling over a world whose inhabitants live in the shadow of future events,[213] and Schwob's restoration of 'le Hasard' in human affairs, a sense of which is borne in upon him as he

[209] Ibid. p. 265.
[210] Verhaeren, *Poèmes,* iii (1896), 129-30.
[211] *Jacques Rivière et Paul Claudel: Correspondance, 1907-1914,* Plon-Nourrit, 1926, pp. 142-3.
[212] *La Cathédrale,* p. 476.
[213] See *Trésor des humbles,* Ch. 3.

contemplates the inscrutable face of the past, which, for him if not for Taine, obdurately refuses to yield up its secret.[214]

(On a more frivolous level, these writers' attitude to women was thoroughly and often self-consciously medieval: they were deified as ideal presences, 'Beata Beatrix' figures, 'princesses de songe', and 'dames des lys', or reviled as 'la Bête vénéneuse et nue, la mercenaire des Ténèbres, la serve absolue du Diable' (Huysmans),[215] or 'cet être si naïvement immoral, jouet favori du primordial Démon' (Gourmont).)[216]

The Symbolists never tired of proclaiming that their soul was a medieval one: Max Elskamp, while preparing his first book of poems *Dominical,* spoke to a friend about his 'âme très enfant dans un château, au milieu de belles Dames et sans usage du monde, presque maladroite, qui se sent heureuse de canoter sur l'étang où les cerfs viennent se noyer',[217] and this state of his soul duly appeared as the theme of one of the poems:

> Dans un beau château,
> Seigneur auprès de sa dame,
> Mon coeur cause avec mon âme
> En échangeant des anneaux,
> Dans un beau château.[218]

Paul Gérardy declared in 1892:

> Mon âme est tel vitrail gothique
> Où vont des saintes à jointes mains
> Tout lentement, au rythme lent
> Des ferveurs que leur âme égrène.[219]

These Gothic souls inhabit a Gothic Kingdom:

> J'ai fleuri mon royaume de lys frêles
> Comme les vierges et comme les joies;
> Mon palais clair a de grêles tourelles,
> Et j'ai drapé mes cieux de pâles soies,[220]

sighed Vielé-Griffin, while Merrill proclaimed:

> Mon royaume est plein de cavalcades
> Caracolant vers des plaines d'or
> Aux fanfares magiques d'un cor
> Qui décèlera les embuscades.[221]

---

[214] See his Preface to *Coeur double* (1891).
[215] Huysmans, *Certains,* 1904, p. 118.
[216] Gourmont, *Le Latin mystique,* p. 219. They were excluded from Péladan's Ordre de la Rose+Croix (see *Constitutions de la Rose+Croix,* 1893, p. 35).
[217] Quoted by R. Guiette, *Max Elskamp* (Poètes d'aujourd'hui), 1955, p. 46 (1890).
[218] Elskamp, *Os. cs.* 1967, p. 6.   [219] P. Gérardy, *Roseaux,* 1898, p. 115.
[220] Vielé-Griffin, *Oeuvres,* i. 57.   [221] Merrill, *Poèmes. 1887-1897,* p. 168.

(ii) *Event in this kingdom: the Crusader's return*

Most of the event which takes place in this kingdom revolves around the 'troubadour' and Romantic theme of the Crusader's (or pilgrim's) return.[222] Knights and princes depart for the wars; their lamenting loved ones await them; and after long years they return to their ancestral home. This cycle of events generally symbolizes the soul's desertion of the ideal for the real world, with its fatigues and deceptions which are in the end renounced in favour of the re-embraced ideal.

The subtlest and most suggestive poetic variations on this theme are undoubtedly Maeterlinck's, in his *Chansons*. Departure is foretold in a whisper:

> On est venu dire,
> (Mon enfant, j'ai peur)
> On est venu dire
> Qu'il allait partir.[223]

Waiting is the theme of his most famous song, which derives from (and is an immeasurable improvement upon) Rossetti's ballad 'An Old Song Ended':[224]

> Et s'il revenait un jour
> Que faut-il lui dire?
> — Dites-lui qu'on l'attendit
> Jusqu'à s'en mourir.[225]

The vigil theme is a favourite one of all the Symbolists. Their heroines' ancestresses are many: Hugo's 'Fiancée du timbalier', Tennyson's Mariana and Lady of Shalott, Wagner's Elsa, Rossetti's Blessed Damozel. And they themselves are legion: Kahn's 'dame Bertrade', praying

> Pour le retour du cavalier
> Du cavalier qui n'est point venu
> Las! et ne viendra jamais . . . ;[226]

---

[222] Laforgue gives this theme characteristically 'moderniste' treatment in his 'Petites misères de mai':

> Oh! ces toquades
> De Croisades! . . .
>
> Et retour louche . . .
> — Ah! tu découches! (*Os. cs.* ii (1922), 87).

[223] *Poésies complètes*, p. 189.
[224] See W. D. Halls's article in *Annales de la Fondation M. Maeterlinck*, i. 1955.
[225] Maeterlinck, op. cit. p. 181 (1893).
[226] Kahn, *Premiers Poèmes*, p. 114.

the anonymous lady who is interrogated in *Chansons d'amant:*

> Des chevaliers qui sont partis
> dès longtemps, pour plus loin, pour la vie . . .
> Dame, savez-vous morts ou vies?

and who replies:

> — Ils partaient en douce croisade
> pour longtemps, pour plus loin, pour la vie . . .;[227]

Grégoire Le Roy's 'douce châtelaine' whose gaze is for ever fixed upon the road — 'Les bien aimés s'en sont allés par là' — in 'Où s'en vont les chemins';[228] Merrill's 'Princesse qui attend', bent over her sun-dial, murmuring 'le nom d'un prince qui partit jadis à la croisade',[229] and his queen plucking petals from 'des rhododendrons roux, des lilas et des roses', sending them downstream 'Vers le Prince parti pour d'âpres épopées',[230] Hérold's Maguelonne,[231] Floriane, and 'Dame parmi les Lys',[232] all waiting for the ideal Fiancé, sighing, 'Oh, le Héros ne viendra-t-il jamais . . .?';[233] Paul Gérardy's 'reine Alyse', lisping in 'genre troubadour' accents:

> Beau prince va venir au loin,
> Beau prince viendra tôt . . .;[234]

Fontainas's virgins, sisters of the Lady of Shalott, gazing in their magic mirrors for a glimpse of 'les Rois de notre espoir';[235] and Klingsor's 'princesse Esmérée' in her 'étrange tourelle', taking up her distaff 'pour attendre Celui qui ne viendrait pas'.[236]

The theme of the warrior's return has as many variations as the vigil theme. He returns triumphant, as in Merrill's 'Triomphe':

> Car voici revenir le Prince,
> Avec trompettes et tambours . . .
> Parmi pennons et pertuisanes
> Il caracole en casque d'or . . .,[237]

[227] Ibid. p. 194.
[228] G. Le Roy, *La Chanson du pauvre,* 2nd edn., 1907, p. 108.
[229] Merrill, *Prose et vers,* 1925, p. 58.
[230] Merrill, *Poèmes, 1887-1897,* p. 90.
[231] In *La Joie de Maguelonne* (1891), *Images tendres et merveilleuses,* 1897, pp. 13-78.
[232] *Chevaleries sentimentales,* 1893, pp. 79-93.
[233] 'Floriane et Persigant', *Images tendres,* p. 106.
[234] Gérardy, op. cit. p. 105.
[235] A. Fontainas, *Crépuscules,* 1897, p. 94.
[236] T. Klingsor, *Filles-fleurs,* 1895, pp. 25-6.
[237] Merrill, *Poèmes, 1887-97,* pp. 212-13.

or — more often — weary and sick at heart, having renounced as utterly vain the victor's laurels. The hero of Régnier's *La Gardienne* (1891) returns to die, with 'le regret mal fermé de quelque plaie obscure' in his heart.[238] His temporal life has been wasted upon the field of battle, but his faithful 'Gardienne' greets him — 'N'étais-je point toujours près de toi, moi, ton Âme?' — and leads him into 'le château de songe et de sagesse'.[239] Ferdinand Hérold (a disciple of Régnier, who, says Mazel, 'comme un chevalier banneret . . . semblait se plaire dans la compagnie de ce silencieux écuyer')[240] takes up this theme in his *Joie de Maguelonne* (1891): the shade of the dead Maguelonne appears to the dying Count Pierre and tells him that all his victories have been false ones — 'Ta fougue t'a rué vers l'inutile vie.'[241] Fontainas, in the 'Retour au Manoir' section of his *Vergers illusoires* (1892), embroiders further upon this theme. In Régnier's 'Quelqu'un songe de soir et d'espoir' (*Tel qu'en songe*, 1892) the warriors return defeated and broken in spirit:

> Et le retour s'en vient, par le soir et les chemins . . .
> En cuirasses saignant par le crible des trous . . .
> Sous le vol sinistre des oiseaux de souci,
> En cors où se sont tus les grands souffles hautains,
> Et le soleil est noir en les écus ternis.[242]

As joyless and bitter is the return of Louis Le Cardonnel's 'Chevaliers qui ne sont pas morts en Palestine'. They raise their voices in a long lament: 'Tous nous avions l'espoir de ne pas revenir.' Having failed to conquer Jerusalem,

> Nous reviendrons sans joie à l'ombre de nos tours,
> Et nous devrons porter, ainsi qu'un anathème,
> Jusqu'au terme inconnu, l'ennui pesant des jours.[243]

Some poets refrain from lofty symbolism and treat the theme in purely human, quasi-'genre-troubadour' terms. Merrill's 'Princesse qui attend' recoils from the embrace of 'celui qu'elle a pleuré tant de longues années', feeling upon his face 'les hideuses balafres de mille batailles';[244] and Paul-Armand Hirsch's 'Chevalier revenant de la guerre' returns 'ivrogne, vieux déjà' to a wife who weeps in secret for the gentle troubadour she has had to send away.[245]

---

[238] Régnier, *Poèmes, 1887-92*, p. 199.   [239] Ibid. pp. 209-10.
[240] Mazel, *Aux beaux temps du symbolisme*, Mercure de France (1943), p. 139.
[241] Hérold, *Images tendres*, p. 75.   [242] Régnier, op. cit. p. 188.
[243] Le Cardonnel, *Poèmes*, pp. 96-8 (*La Plume* (Aug. 1892)).
[244] Merrill, *Prose et vers*, pp. 59-60.
[245] P.-A. Hirsch, *Prélude: Vers et proses inédits*, Librairie de l'Art Indépendant, 1893, pp. 12-14.

Vigil and Return are combined in the theme of the Sleeping Beauty. Sometimes deliverance comes — symbolizing the soul's acceptance of life — and sometimes not: never in the songs of Maeterlinck, in which, once again, the theme finds its most memorable expression. An evil queen seals a young girl into a grotto:

> Elle attendit les jours d'été:
> Elle attendit plus de sept ans,
> Tous les ans passait un passant.

Her shining hair, which has escaped through the cracks, attracts the attention of one of them, but

> Il croit que c'est un signe étrange,
> Il croit que c'est une source d'or,
> Il croit que c'est un jeu des anges,
> Il se détourne et passe encore.[246]

'Les filles aux yeux bandés', having emerged into the light of day,

> Ont salué la vie,
> Et ne sont point sorties.[247]

'Les sept filles d'Orlamonde', groping through their prison, each carrying a lamp,

> Ont ouvert quatre cents salles,
> Sans trouver le jour.

They find a door with a key in the lock, but seeing the ocean through the cracks,

> Ont peur de mourir,
> Et frappent à la porte close,
> Sans oser l'ouvrir.[248]

Other captives sing in chorus:

> Je vois le soleil par les fentes,
> Ouvrez les portes du jardin!

but are told:

> Les clefs sont tombées de la tour,
> Il faut attendre, il faut attendre,
> Il faut attendre d'autres jours.[249]

The seventh of *Les Sept Princesses* (1891) falls into an eternal slumber as her sisters, whom the prince has awoken, call to her in vain: 'Ursule! Ursule! Il est revenu! Il est là!'[250]

---

[246] *Poésies complètes,* pp. 179-80 (1893).
[247] Ibid. pp. 185-6 (1893).   [248] Ibid. pp. 191-2 (1893).
[249] Ibid. p. 203 (1891).   [250] *Les Sept Princesses,* 1891, p. 61.

Ephraïm Mikhaël also treated this theme with success. His 'Dame en deuil' (1886), wandering through her garden plucking petals from lilies, meets 'un cavalier portant des roses et des palmes', who sings to her:

> Viens, ô dame en deuil, vers les vallons
> De joie et de paix; allons ensemble
> Cueillir aux jardins des Avallons
> La fleur en exil qui te ressemble . . .,

but she tells him:

> Va-t-en! je veux rester la veuve taciturne
> De mes rêves d'antan que j'ai tués moi-même . . .,[251]

and returns to her stately solitude. Mikhaël's 'Florimond' (1889) is one of the finest Symbolist medieval poems. Florimond is a captive prince held in thrall by 'l'inavouable amour de la Reine sorcière'. His former companions in arms call to him:

> Ô frère, nous venions rompre l'enchantement,
> Te sauver des jardins et des honteuses roses,
> Mais nous sommes vaincus mystérieusement;
> Toi seul, tu peux ouvrir les belles portes closes . . .,

but he waves them on their way, choosing to remain in his 'atroce paradis'.[252]

Most Symbolists devoted at least one poem to the Sleeping Beauty theme. In the earlier ones she spurns her deliverer, or else he fails to arrive. Kahn's *La Belle au château rêvant* (1887) is a long-drawn-out drama crowded with symbolic presences. The 'Passant', a 'piéton des chemins d'idéal', gives an account of himself to the 'Veilleur des Tours' ('Je suis le frère aigri des crépuscules similaires . . . l'amer passé délétère/gît à mon diaphragme amer' etc.);[253] but when he is admitted to the presence of 'la Belle', she shrinks away from him: 'Ah! reprends-moi, sommeil, scelle-toi sur ma bouche', and 'le château retombe dans le mutisme séculaire.'[254] Régnier's *Motifs de légende et de mélancolie* (1890) begin:

> Dormez, Princesses au manoir, nul cor, ô Mortes,
> N'éveillera vos rêves et nul glaive clair
> Ne heurtera de son pommeau vos hautes portes
> Où le béryl magique incruste son éclair.'

Successive sections are entitled 'Et la Belle s'endormit', 'Et le Chevalier ne vint pas', 'Et la Belle mourut.'[255] Later, a joyous outcome (less

---

[251] E. Mikhaël, *Oeuvres*, 1890, p. 38.
[252] Ibid. pp. 97-9.   [253] G. Kahn, *Premiers Poèmes*, pp. 158-60.
[254] Ibid. p. 172.   [255] Régnier, *Poèmes, 1887-1892*, pp. 54-6.

effective poetically) was preferred: Hérold's 'Belle au Bois Dormant'
(1892) wakes to greet her 'Conquérant couronné de lumière',[256] and
Klingsor's, 'le Chevalier Printemps son beau Prince au rêve'.[254]

H. *Sub-varieties of the Symbolist Middle Ages*

It is time to examine some particular varieties of the Symbolist Middle
Ages. Many influences came together in its creation. Two or more were
often intermingled in the work of one writer, or even in one poem.
Different forms of *fin de siècle* 'moyenâgeux' borrowed their colour
from Gustave Moreau, the Pre-Raphaelites, Tennyson, Poe, Wagner,
Catholic liturgy and ritual, medieval literature, and the *chanson
populaire*. As in the Romantic era, a sinister Middle Ages coexisted
with the ideal one.

(i) *The influence of Gustave Moreau:*
'Des fuites de paons, de lynx et de licornes'

The painting of Gustave Moreau was largely responsible for the more
ornate of the trappings which bedeck Symbolist queens and princesses,
and for the unicorns and peacocks abounding in their mysterious gardens
and magic forests. This décor is associated above all with Régnier, who
had a particular predilection for unicorns and peacocks, and Merrill, all
of whose queens are laden with gems. It was a favourite one in the early
days of Symbolism. René Ghil, in *Légende d'âmes et de sangs* (1885)
announced his intention of painting

> dans l'insapide,
> Dans le mauve et le glauque, et l'azur et les ors.[258]

Moréas in his *Cantilènes* (1886) evoked 'les bêtes fabuleuses des
simarres',[259] and magic forests:

> — Nous allions par les bois pleins de monstres hybrides,
> Toi de pourpre vêtu et moi bardé de fer.[260]

Régnier's second volume of verse, *Apaisement* (1886), recreated 'le luxe
défunt des fastes accomplis':[261]

> Vous auriez bien porté les robes blasonnées
> Dont les roides brocarts parsemés d'écussons

---

[256] *MF* (Feb. 1892), p. 128.   [257] Klingsor, *Filles-fleurs,* 1895, p. 8.
[258] R. Ghil, *Os. cs.* 1938, iii, 20.   [259] Moréas, *Oeuvres,* i. 65.
[260] Ibid. p. 76.   [261] Régnier, *Premiers Poèmes,* p. 73.

> A champ d'azur chargé de guivres contournées
> Glissent sur les pavés en somptueux frissons.[262]

In his *Épisodes* (1888) 'le palais d'onyx pavé de malachite' re-echoes with 'l'appel guttural henni par la Licorne.'[263] Denizens of the magic forest in his *Poèmes anciens et romanesques* (1890) are 'La Licorne d'argent, la Guivre et le Paon noir'.[264] Unicorns and peacocks attend his Sleeping Beauty; and his invocation to the mysterious 'Dame merveilleuse' in *Le Songe de la forêt* (1890) ends:

> En ta robe j'entends piétiner la licorne
> Qui brise les rubis au bris de ses sabots.[265]

There followed Merrill's *Fastes* (1891):

> Ce sont des craquements de béryls sur les dalles,
> Des paons girant en jeux d'amour sous les portails . . .[266] –

with its procession of queens: the unhappy one in 'Rêverie' with 'ses doigts ensanglantés de bagues',[267] and the evil one in 'La Mauvaise Reine' with 'ses doigts virides d'émeraudes'.[268] In 'Les Noyées', a prose poem published by him in the same year, an evil princess, 'blonde en sa simarre violette chamarrée de licornes d'or', gloats over her captive lovers 'tandis qu'à gestes hiératiques elle avive du sang du soleil les gemmes magiques de ses bagues'.[269]

(ii) *The Pre-Raphaelite influence: 'La dame lasse de la terrasse'*

Pre-Raphaelitism was reponsible for a still more important province of the Symbolist Middle Ages, in which almost all the poets of the movement had a stake. We have seen that the Pre-Raphaelites – and also Tennyson, who, according to Gabriel Mourey – 'distilla pour eux tout ce qu'il y a de plus sain et de plus noble dans le monde du moyen âge'[270] – were universally revered at this time. Samain discovered Rossetti's poems in 1887. He wrote to a friend that he found them 'd'une suavité d'imagination et d'une poésie de rêve extraordinaires'. 'The Blessed Damozel' in particular he found 'd'une inspiration exquisement blanche, d'une atmosphère diaphane et idéale. . . . Au fond de tout cela, un flux de tristesse continue et monotone.'[271] As early as

---

[262] Ibid. p. 57.   [263] Ibid. pp. 237-8.
[264] Régnier, *Poèmes, 1887-1892*, p. 28   [265] Ibid. p. 112.
[266] Merrill, *Poèmes, 1887-97*, p. 116.
[267] Ibid. p. 90.   [268] Ibid. p. 109.
[269] *Prose et vers*, p. 57 (first published in *La Plume* (Oct. 1891)).
[270] G. Mourey, *Passé le détroit*, 1895, p. 151.
[271] Samain, *Des lettres*, 5th edn., 1933, pp. 2-3.

1882 Jean Lorrain paid tribute to Tennyson's heroines, 'filles adorables du rêve',[272] devoting a sonnet to each of them in his *Sang des dieux;* and the following year he published his *Brocéliande* in *La Forêt bleue.* This dramatic scene, an abridged adaptation of Tennyson's *Merlin and Vivien,*[273] was performed at the Théâtre de l'Oeuvre in 1896.[274] Then there came the full spate of Symbolist Pre-Raphaelitism: Moréas (although some years later he vigorously denied that the Pre-Raphaelites had influenced him, telling Byvanck 'Je ne sais pas l'anglais')[275] evoked in his first volume of verse (*Les Syrtes,* 1884) 'la sainte Forêt/Où, dans le chant des luths, Viviane apparaît':[276] poets produced 'Diptyques' and 'Triptyques';[277] Albert Samain cried 'Formons des rêves fins sur des miniatures',[278] and Karl Boès declared in the same year (1893):

> Je veux bâtir sur les Sommets la Forteresse
> Que salueront de loin les pâles Chevaliers.
> La Forteresse de Noblesse et de Détresse.[279]

These palely loitering knights throng the pages of Symbolist verse. They derive from the paintings of Burne-Jones, of whom Robert de la Sizeranne remarked in 1895: 'Les bras de ses chevaliers ne sont jamais raidis . . . la main retombant souvent inerte, comme une parure. On ne se les figure pas courant, travaillant, combattant.'[280] It is the same with the Symbolist knights, whether those of Kahn:

> Si pâle il est venu, que ma soeur pense
> 'n'a-t-elle pas bu son sang, son âme et sa fiance,
>   et n'est-il pas
> l'ombre de ses sandales et la trace de ses pas . . .' (1889),[281]

or Moréas:

> De mourir − ah! qu'il est las! −
> Le chevalier aux blanches armes (1891),[282]

---

[272] Lorrain, *Le Sang des dieux,* 2nd edn., 1920, p. 25.
[273] The ending differs inexplicably from Tennyson's, and is far more banal: Viviane finds out Merlin's secret charm while feigning sleep. (In Tennyson's Idyll, he tells her the charm during a thunderstorm, won over by her wiles.)
[274] Before a hostile and hilarious audience, See *Journal des Goncourt,* iv. 899.
[275] Byvanck, op. cit. p. 71.
[276] Moréas, op. cit. p. 44.
[277] e.g. Vielé-Griffin's 'Diptique' in *La Chevauchée d'Yeldis,* 1893; Klingsor's *Triptyque des châtelaines,* 1892.
[278] Samain, *Au jardin de l'infante,* 1922, p. 46.
[279] *L'Ermitage,* iv (Feb. 1893), p. 97.
[280] R. de la Sizeranne, *La Peinture anglaise contemporaine,* 1922, p. 189.
[281] Kahn, *Premiers Poèmes,* 1897, p. 217.   [282] Moréas, op. cit. p. 166.

or Régnier:

> Lui qui vécut parmi le tumulte, il est seul . . .
> Et lui qui fut dès toujours pâle, il est plus pâle (1892),[283]

or Klingsor:

> Les Chevaliers sont venus cueillir des fleurs, —
> des fleurs de rêve de leurs pâles doigts frêles. . . .
> Et devant Celle de Légende aux mains pures,
> les Chevaliers enfantinement troublés
> en leurs âmes folles, laissèrent crouler
> les marjolaines de leurs doigts — et moururent (1892).[284]

And the pale knight is often the poet himself, who murmurs 'Comme une ombre au manoir rétrospectif, nous sommes . . .' (Moréas),[285] or 'Moi je suis là comme un vague vassal'[286] (Retté), or laments:

> Je fus le banneret lassé, que nul espoir ne tente. . . .
> Je ne courus ni vers les guerres, ni vers la femm. . . .
> Je fus le banneret banal sans rêve et sans espoir. . . .
> Je suis le banneret banni de son manoir natal
> Par l'ennui même de son sceptre (Fontainas),[287]

or

> Le seigneur du domaine, c'est moi
> Qui traîne au fond des anciennes salles,
> Au pied des armures colossales,
> Sa honte de ne pouvoir être roi (Merrill).[288]

A crescendo of despair is reached by Gérardy in 'Dolence' (1891):

> Et puis ces rêves qui nous tuent,
> Ces rêves de gloire et d'amour . . .
> Et l'impuissance de notre âme,
> Notre impuissance qui les tue!
>
> Rêver une épée en sa main,
> Rêver en sa main un lourd glaive . . .
> Et n'avoir qu'une plume en main,
> Rien qu'une plume trop lourde encore![289]

The narrator of Régnier's tale *Le Chevalier qui dormit dans la neige* (1893) is obsessed with the portrait which hangs in his father's castle of

[283] Régnier, *Poèmes, 1887-1892*, p. 137.
[284] Klingsor, *Triptyque des châtelaines*, 1892 ('Celle de Légende').
[285] Moréas, op. cit. p. 61.   [286] Retté, *Une Belle Dame passa*, 1893, p. 24.
[287] Fontainas, *Crépuscules*, pp. 65-7.   [288] Merrill, *Poèmes, 1887-97*, p. 199.
[289] P. Gérardy, op. cit. pp. 59-60.

a knight leaning on his sword: 'Méditative face de désir et de mortification d'accord avec ces mains qui cramponnent leur lassitude à la poignée cruciale de la haute épée. Les faibles mains mélancoliques ne la lèveraient plus. . . . Il est, sous un air d'emblème et de songe,' he comes to realize, 'la figure d'un Destin. C'est en lui que j'ai vu le plus profondément en moi-même.'[290]

These knights have their female counterpart: 'la dame lasse de la terrasse' (Fontainas),[291] or 'Dame des lys languissants et fanés' (Retté),[292] a multitude of lily-sceptred damsels and dispossessed queens. They include Ghil's Dame en son manoir: 'Très pâle et longue dame, elle parle, l'exsangue/Sous les lis';[293] Le Cardonnel's queen in 'Le Rêve de la Reine' (1886), who 'mord son exsangue main de sa bouche sanglante';[294] the inhabitants of Grégoire Le Roy's 'manoir des songes':

> Quelles sont ces âmes mystiques
> Qui, dans des salles monastiques . . .
> D'un air indolent, alangui,
> Tissent des toiles pâles, pâles?
> Et pour qui? . . .;[295]

the heroine of Gérardy's 'ballade naive', 'Ce fut un Trouvère qui chanta et une Dame qui en mourut', who expires as the strings of the Trouvère's lyre break one by one:

> La dame mourut à la fenêtre,
> La dame mourut avec les lys,
> Si pâle et frêle comme un lys . . .;[296]

Klingsor's Yseult, 'un grand lys pâle de Thulé'[297] Samain's Galswinte – 'Vase mélancolique, ô Galswinte, ma soeur,'[298] and Yvanhoé Rambosson's captive queen floating downstream, like Millais's Ophelia:

> Son geste frêle et las s'éplore sur les flots
> Où se mirent ses yeux de pâles lobélies.[299]

Merrill's 'Princesse qui Attend', 'laissant ruisseler hors du filet de perles les boucles rousses de sa lourde chevelure', with her sundial, and her lips 'qui semblent avoir humé le sang des grenades blessées'[300] – a cross between Rossetti's *Beata Beatrix* and his *Prosperine*; Mikhaël's 'Dame en

---

[290] Régnier, *La Canne de jaspe*, pp. 288-9.   [291] Fontainas, op. cit. p. 35.
[292] Retté, op. cit. p. 21.   [293] R. Ghil, op. cit. pp. 12-13.
[294] A poem first published in *Le Scapin,* Jan. 1886, quoted by N. Richard, *Louis Le Cardonnel*, 1946, p. 109.
[295] G. Le Roy, op. cit. pp. 175-6.   [296] Gérardy, op. cit. pp. 95-7.
[297] Klingsor, *Triptyque des châtelaines,* 'Yseult'.
[298] Samain, *Au jardin de l'infante*, p. 100.
[299] Y. Rambosson, op. cit. p. 92.   [300] Merrill, *Prose et vers*, p. 58.

Deuil', 'regardant en ses mains pâlir des fleurs blessées', and 'saccage[ant] en passant des lys et des verveines'[301] (an activity common to all these women, and indulged in also by Florimond, 'effeuillant des glaïeuls frêles et des jasmins' with his hands which have let fall both sword and shield)[302] – all these heroines are nothing if not Pre-Raphaelite. So are the multiple female presences – sisters of the five handmaidens of Mary in Rossetti's 'Blessed Damozel', of Swinburne's 'ten maidens in the green corn' from 'The King's Daughter', and of the troop of damsels descending Burne-Jones's *Golden Staircase* – which appear in the work of so many of these poets: Merrill's

> Élise, Liliane,
> Gertrude, Viviane
> Et soeur Isabelle![303]

Klingsor's 'Filles-Fleurs', and Maeterlinck's *Sept Princesses* – 'Ursule, Geneviève, Hélène et Christabelle . . . Madeleine, Claire et Claribelle avec des émeraudes.'[304]

Maeterlinck owed much to Tennyson and the Pre-Raphaelites. His Arthurian names – which, he told Gustave Cohen, were taken from Malory[305] – are adaptations or compounds of those in the *Idylls of the King.* His *Sept Princesses,* slumbering on the steps strewn with cushions of pale blue silk, and palely reflected in the great mirror behind them, are pure Burne-Jones. But Villiers de l'Isle-Adam[306] and Poe were even more important influences. They both furnished him with the background of Gothic terror reproduced in all the plays of his first period: perilous subterranean passages, the brooding presence of supernatural forces. The castle of Ysselmonde in *La Princesse Maleine,* built upon pestilential marshes, with its tower falling into the lake, its chapel cross falling into the moat, its tapestries moving in the wind, is particularly reminiscent of the *Fall of the House of Usher.* Subsequent plays all take place in the same 'kingdom by the sea'.

---

[301] Mikhaël, *Oeuvres,* pp. 37-9.
[302] Ibid. p. 97.
[303] Merrill, *Poèmes, 1887-97,* p. 157.
[304] *Les Sept Princesses,* p. 25.
[305] G. Cohen, *Ceux que j'ai connus,* Montreal, Édns. de l'Arbre, 1946, p. 23.
[306] In his memoirs he states that 'La princesse Maleine, Mélisande, Astolaine, Sélysette et les fantômes qui suivirent attendaient l'atmosphère que Villiers avait créée en moi pour y naître et respirer enfin' (*Bulles bleues, souvenirs heureux,* 1948, p. 201).

(iii) *Wagner*

The influence of Wagner on the Symbolists is one that has been fully discussed[307] and need not for long detain us here. Less profound than that of the Pre-Raphaelites, it was responsible for the bric-à-brac – oliphants and oriflammes, helmets and hauberks, heralds sounding bugles to the four corners of the horizon – that appeared in the work of certain among these writers (notably Régnier's early work, Mockel's *Chantefable* and Merrill's *Fastes*), and is at its most banal in the verse of Ferdinand Hérold.

(iv) *The liturgical influence: 'decadent' verse and prose:*
'Mon Âme se meurt du regret de l'encens . . .'

Another species of Symbolist 'moyenâgeux' was liturgical bric-à-brac, the perverse association of sacred and profane, the ecclesiastical and the erotic – all that Bloy would have put under the heading of 'ces démarquages d'un passé brûlant de foi au profit d'une esthétique de mécréants'.[308] Modern desire took on medieval colouring, from Catholic ritual and the works of the Primitives; and medieval ecclesiastics – like Gourmont's Théodat – were shown racked by pagan temptations. It was the 'decadent' school of the eighties – Tailhade, Lorrain, Moréas – who started this fashion, mentioned with disapproval by Huysmans in his Preface to Gourmont's *Latin mystique* (1892): 'L'on s'empara des formes liturgiques pour les appliquer aux passions humaines'[309] (Gourmont himself was of course one of the chief practitioners of this genre).

Elskamp wrote to a friend in 1895: 'Quant au *décor,* le culte catholique est le plus merveilleux qui soit au monde';[310] and Rodenbach declared in the same year: 'Toute la liturgie catholique avec ses décors et ses accessoires, dont chacun est une invention de génie, suffit à ceux que tourmente obscurément un conflit d'idéal et de sensualité.'[311]

Many writers had been of this persuasion for some time. Jean Lorrain wrote in 1883:

> De mon coeur vide et froid j'ai fait un grand ciboire
> D'or fauve, rehaussé d'améthyste et d'émail.[312]

---

[307] By L. Guichard, op. cit.
[308] Cf. *supra,* p. 218.
[309] Gourmont, *Le Latin mystique,* p. vii.
[310] *Bulletin de l'Académie Royale de Langue et de Littérature Françaises,* Brussels, xxxvi (1958), p. 46.
[311] Rodenbach, *La Vocation,* 1895, p. 47.
[312] *La Forêt bleue,* 1883, p. 25.

The 'étrange Évêque' in Mikhaël's 'Impiétés' (1885) — closely related to Baudelaire's 'mauvais Moine' and Simon de Tournai[313] — says Mass with unholy pride:

> Il songe, en son âme infidèle et vide,
> Qu'il est beau, tenant ainsi l'ostensoir . . .,[314]

just as the poet exalts his love only so that others may be dazzled by the splendour of his verse.

The ecclesiastical interior of Des Esseintes's house, with its curtains 'taillés dans de vieilles étoles'[315] and sham-monk's-cell bedroom, is matched by the Princess Leonora d'Este's lily-filled boudoir, 'cette crypte mondaine',[316] in Péladan's *Vice suprême,* published in the same year (1884). In 1885 Maeterlinck promised to send a friend some prose poems 'extraits d'une plaquette "Manuel de la Mort" . . . appelés à valoir surtout je pense, par la typographie gothique, rouge et noire dont je compte les habiller en un format de petit livre d'heures' (which was never in fact published).[317] Rodenbach declared in the following year: 'Mon Âme se meurt du regret de l'encens';[318] Jean Rembrandt, the hero of his first novel *L'Art en exil* (1889), ends his life as an etiolated recluse: 'Ainsi peu à peu Rembrandt retombe, non pas à la dévotion, mais au mysticisme, un mysticisme de coeur, d'imagination, d'art. Pour s'illusionner mieux et vivre en une atmosphère toute liturgique, il a maintenant un encensoir. . . . Il a installé aussi chez lui un orgue, et passe des soirs entiers à en tirer des musiques vagues.'[319] Liturgical imagery and lines such as 'Je rêverai comme rêvent dans leurs niches les saints de pierre'[320] abound in Retté's *Cloches en la nuit* (1889). The hero of Gourmont's *Sixtine,* Hubert d'Entragues, is received by the heroine: 'Elle avait l'air assez quatorzième siècle, prisonnière en sa chaise abbatiale. Vêtus de rouge, ses pieds foulaient un coussin noir . . . vers la boiserie sculptée, fleur pâle, la tête se penchait; l'ombre de l'ogive encadrait l'auréole blonde.'[321] His fictional self, Guido, pours out extravagant worship to the image of the Madonna with whom he has fallen in love: 'Ah! beauté thauma-turge, beauté tabernaculaire!'[322]

Profane passion expressing itself in these liturgical effusions (deriving from Baudelaire's 'Franciscae meae laudes'), and identification of its

[313] Cf. *supra,* pp. 167-8.   [314] *Oeuvres,* p. 35.
[315] *A Rebours,* p. 45.   [316] *Le Vice suprême,* p. 1.
[317] *Annales de la Fondation M. Maeterlinck,* v (1959), pp. 46-7.
[318] *Oeuvres,* i. 30 (*La Jeunesse blanche*).
[319] *L'Art en exil,* 1889, p. 252.   [320] *Cloches en la nuit,* 1889, p. 58.
[321] *Sixtine,* 1890, p. 61.   [322] Ibid. p. 291.

object with medieval Madonnas and saints (deriving also from the 'Satanic' poems of *Les Fleurs du mal,* such as 'A une Madone', and from Mallarmé's 'Sainte'), were a commonplace in *fin de siècle* verse. Armand Silvestre (a surviving Parnassian who was not without influence on the Symbolists) cultivated the genre assiduously. His sonnet 'Te Deam', in which he speaks of his love as 'un parfum tremblant d'encens et de cinname', appeared in the *Nouvelle Rive-Gauche* in 1883.[323] Moréas exclaimed in *Les Syrtes* (1884):

> Tes mains aux doigts pâlis semblent des mains de Sainte
> Par Giotto rêvée et pieusement peinte
> En un coin très obscur de quelque basilique
> Pleine de chapes d'or, de cierges, de reliques,
> Où je voudrais dormir tel qu'un évêque mort,
> Dans un tombeau sculpté, sans crainte et sans remord.[324]

In Retté's poems published in *La Wallonie* (1890), he tells his loved one: 'Vous êtes une église aux voûtes de silence/Pleine d'encens mourants et de cierges éteints';[325] and she tells him: 'Je suis la fleur étrange éclose aux manuscrits.'[326] Laurent Tailhade (a disciple of Silvestre) gives his love an ecclesiastical setting in *Vitraux* (1891):

> Verrières d'or! Camails de pourpre! Orgueil fêté
> Des tabernacles, sous la pompe des courtines!
>
> J'ai rêvé de t'aimer ainsi qu'une Madone
> Qui, très pure, aux baisers mystiques s'abandonne.[327]

So Gourmont's invocations to 'Les Saintes du paradis' ('Sainte Gudule, embaumez la chanson de nos âmes',[328] etc.) and his *Oraisons mauvaises* (1900) are very late products of the genre.

This bric-à-brac was frequently drawn upon to help provide a suitably 'hieratic' atmosphere for Symbolist plays. Seven *béguines* intoning Latin hymns wander through Maeterlinck's *Princesse Maleine*. Gourmont's *Théodat* is a positive orgy of ritual converted to erotic purposes. Quillard's *Fille aux mains coupées* (first published in 1886, and performed in 1891) was hailed ecstatically by Régnier in 1890. He drew the attention of the readers of *La Wallonie* to 'la publication, sous une

---

[323] *La Nouvelle Rive-Gauche* (Feb.-March 1883), p. 2.
[324] *Oeuvres,* i. 21 (*Lutèce,* Nov. 1883).
[325] *La Wallonie,* 5 (1890), p. 276.
[326] Ibid. p. 281.
[327] Tailhade, *Poèmes élégiaques,* 1907, pp. 176-8.
[328] Gourmont, *Divertissements,* 1912, p. 56.

couverture en blanc papier spongieux, comme d'hostie, d'un mystère: *la Fille aux Mains coupées,* oeuvre singulière, précoce trouvaille, figurines d'une cire pieuse et légendaire, roides et exaltées, sur des fonds joaillés, en un choeur invisible de voix angéliques et perverses et de dolentes orgues!'[329]

Quillard, a disciple of Leconte de Lisle, took the subject of his play from a legend briefly recounted by Puymaigre in his volume of essays *Folklore* (1885) — the story, invented to explain the origin of the Hundred Years' War, of the daughter of a Duc de Guienne who orders a servant to cut off the hands which her father has covered with incestuous kisses, whereupon the wrathful Duke casts her adrift in a rudderless boat. She prays to the Virgin, who restores her hands and guides the ship to England, where she meets and marries the King's brother, whose claim to the duchy starts the war. Quillard overlaid this legend with much Symbolist ornamentation, and gave it a pagan interpretation. The girl is first seen praying, 'en sa blancheur adorable de lys':

Le large bliaud damassé, broché de calices d'argent, qui neige sur sa poitrine et l'étoile, est à peine agité par le souffle du corps pâle sculpté dans un marbre vivant.

Elle lit dans le lourd missel incrusté de joailleries.

She prays in the language of Leconte de Lisle's medieval poems: 'Ô Jésus, écartez les griffes du Malin. . . . Ô monde, ô vie, ô sens, évanouissez-vous!',[330] whereupon a chorus of perverse angels advises her to yield to earthly desires, for 'l'enfer des baisers vaut notre paradis.'[331] After her father's advances she lays her hands for the sacrifice 'sur une table de porphyre aux mosaïques de chimères'. He casts her adrift with the words of Leconte de Lisle's Countess Mahaut to her starving peasants about to be roasted alive:

Allez! au nom de la Très Sainte Trinité,
Et que Jésus vous prenne en votre éternité.

Upon the ocean she experiences mystic visions:

Dans le lilas de leurs rosaces vespérales,
Je vois s'épanouir, là-haut, des cathédrales . . . .

her hands are restored; she meets 'LE POÈTE-ROI': 'LA JEUNE FILLE s'abandonne à la volupté des caresses. Hymen! Ô hymen!',[332] but soon

[329] *La Wallonie,* 6 (Dec. 1890), p. 82.
[330] Quillard, *La Lyre héroïque et dolente,* 1897, pp. 124-5.
[331] Ibid. p. 127.   [332] Ibid. pp. 130-2.

shrinks from his embrace, 'Car je me damnerais peut-être en t'écoutant.' The perverse angels repeat their advice: 'Le Seigneur t'a rendu des mains pour les étreintes', and all ends happily.[333] The play — which met with great success when it was performed -- is a curious fusion of the Parnassian and Symbolist Middle Ages.

(v) *The orthodox Catholic influence*

Side by side with this 'decadent' Catholic Middle Ages of the Symbolists, deriving from the aesthetic blasphemies of Baudelaire, there existed its orthodox counterpart, a legacy of Verlaine's glorification of the Age of Faith. It is to be found in Verhaeren's early work *Les Moines* (1886), which extols medieval monks, 'Astres versant le jour aux siècles catholiques', for the very ferocity and inflexibility of purpose which had so appalled Leconte de Lisle: 'Étendards embrasés, armures de l'Église', he calls them, 'Abatteurs d'hérésie à larges coups de croix':[334]

> Tout ce qui fut énorme en ces temps surhumains
> Grandit dans le soleil de leur âme féconde.[335]

Verhaeren's orthodoxy, however, is aesthetic rather than heartfelt; one critic calls his attitude in *Les Moines* 'valedictory . . . a record of the poet's loss, or rather change of faith'.[336] A more uncomplicated nostalgia is present in the poetry of Louis Le Cardonnel, who felt in himself 'l'âme d'un constructeur de mystiques églises',[337] and who took Orders in 1896; in that of Max Elskamp, 'imagier à Anvers',[338] whose *Salutations dont d'angéliques* (1893) were intended as 'une nouvelle légende dorée':

> A présent c'est en vous, Madame la Vierge,
> Ma nouvelle légende un peu plus dorée . . .;[339]

and in the Symbolists' celebration of stained glass — which Taine[340] and the Parnassians had appreciated before them — and which Tailhade, in his *Vitraux*, exalted in terms scarcely different from theirs:

> Le vitrail que nul art terrestre ne profane
> Jette sur le parvis d'incandescentes fleurs . . .;[341]

[333] Ibid. pp. 134-5.   [334] Verhaeren, *Poèmes*, i. 179-80.   [335] Ibid. p. 187.
[336] P. Mansell Jones, *Verhaeren*, 1957, p. 18.
[337] Le Cardonnel, *Carmina sacra*, 1912, p. 81.
[338] Elskamp, *Os. cs.* p. 132 (*Alphabet de Notre-Dame la Vierge*, 1901).
[339] Elskamp, *Os. cs.* p. 25.   [340] Cf. *supra*, p. 68.
[341] Tailhade, op. cit. p. 170.

while Rodenbach in his *Miroir du Ciel Natal* (1898), preferred to dwell on the mysterious symbolism of

> Les vitraux sans nul or
> Et sans nuls personnages
> Qui les imagent . . .,

who, he divined,

> Ont des rêves dont à leur guise ils se décorent.
> Vitraux récompensés d'avoir bien renoncé![342]

(vi) *The influence of medieval literature: Moréas:*
'Il faut que le verbe reparaisse dans toute sa splendeur ancienne . . .'

How far, we must now ask, were the Symbolists influenced by medieval literature itself? In 1887 Léon Clédat had ventured to suggest, in the Preface of his 'traduction archaïque et rythmée' of the *Chanson de Roland,* that some of the words he had retained in his translation might be received back into the language.[343] Darmesteter, in an essay on medieval literature published during the nineties, repeated Nerval's injunction to his fellow writers: 'Le moyen âge n'a point su dire sa poésie, mais il la porte partout avec lui; à vous, artistes, de la retrouver . . . de la dire pour eux si vous êtes poètes.'[344] And yet, in spite of all the 'Chrestomathies' published during the eighties, Symbolist poets were in the main just as ignorant of medieval literature as their Romantic predecessors. Régnier told Huret in 1891: 'Je considère, historiquement, l'époque romane comme intéressante et féconde, mais vraiment les sources m'en sont fermées. Je n'en comprends pas le langage et je ne saisis pas l'utilité de l'apprendre.'[345] Quillard, swayed by his republican sympathies, referred in the same year to 'la canaille médiévale des trouvères et des troubadours'.[346] There were some exceptions: Merrill, according to M. L. Henry, had on his shelves the entire collection of the Société des Anciens Textes, as well as the works of Gaston Paris;[347] and Mockel assured Paul Champagne: 'La poésie médiévale a eu sur ma formation de poète une influence pénétrante';[348] but there is in fact little trace of the influence of medieval

---

[342] Rodenbach, *Oeuvres,* ii. 261-2.
[343] Clédat, *'La Chanson de Roland', traduction archaïque et rythmée,* Leroux, 1887, p. vii.
[344] J. Darmesteter, *Critique et politique,* Lévy, 1895, p. 127. Cf. *supra,* p. 92.
[345] J. Huret, op. cit. p. 95.
[346] Tailhade, *Poèmes aristophanesques,* 1904, p. 183.
[347] M. L. Henry, *Stuart Merrill.* 1927, p. 74.
[348] P. Champagne, *Essai sur Albert Mockel,* 1922, p. 44.

literature discernible in the work of either of these poets. Lip-service
was often paid to it in Symbolist reviews: the first number of *Le
Symboliste* (1886) extolled 'le vocabulaire si riche de Rabelais, de
Villon, de Montaigne, des Chansons de geste . . . les grandioses sim-
plicités de la mort de Roland',[349] and H. Degron spoke proudly in
Portraits du prochain siècle of 'la nouvelle Réaction dont les ancêtres
héroïques vont de Théroulde à Olivier de Magny',[350] but that was all.
It is true that much Symbolist verse is punctuated with 'las' and
'oncques'; that Charles Vignier exclaimed in a love-poem of his *Centon*
(1886): 'Ô la pure, ô la soëve, ô l'alme!',[351] and — in the course of a
Pre-Raphaelite flight of fancy —

> Il défaille emmi l'air des parfums tant amènes,
> Qu'on croirait respirer l'âme d'un cyclamen . . . —[352]

that Joseph Declareuil in *Prestiges* (1893) envisaged the hour 'Quand
nous viendra l'alme Agonie';[353] that Klingsor framed his 'Marguerite à
la fleur' (1894) 'emmi l'ovale moyen-âge et mignon';[354] but this
archaizing presupposed no extensive acquaintance with medieval
literature.

The one writer who did make a claim to this — more than a claim,
a widely-publicized boast — was Jean Moréas, inventor in 1886 of the
term 'symbolisme' and founder in 1891 of the École Romane.

In 1886 (the year in which he published his *Cantilènes*) his Symbolist
manifesto appeared in *Le Figaro:*

Il faut au symbolisme un style archétype et complexe: d'impollués
vocables . . . les mystérieuses ellipses, l'anacoluthe en suspens, tout trope
hardi et multiforme: enfin la bonne langue — instaurée et modernisée —
la bonne et luxuriante et fringante langue française d'avant les Vaugelas
et les Boileau-Despréaux, la langue de François Rabelais et de Philippe de
Commines, de Villon, de Ruteboeuf et de tant d'autres écrivains libres
et dardant le terme acut du langage.[355]

Anatole France's ironical 'examination' of this manifesto, published in
Le Temps, contained a slighting reference which immediately provoked
a dignified rejoinder from Moréas: 'Quant à Ruteboeuf, souffrez que je
m'étonne de votre indifférence: "Je ne parle pas de Ruteboeuf . . . que

---

[349] P. Adam, 'La Presse et le symbolisme', *Le Symboliste,* no. 1, 7-14 Oct. 1886,
p. 2.
[350] *Portraits du prochain siècle,* Girard, 1894, p. 38.
[351] Ch. Vignier, *Centon,* Vanier, 1886, p. 17.   [352] Ibid. p. 67.
[353] Declareuil, *Prestiges,* p. 80.   [354] *MF* (Mar. 1894), p. 220.
[355] *Les Premières Armes du symbolisme,* Vanier, 1889, p. 34.

je n'ai guère pratiqué." Il me semblait cependant que le "doux trouvère" avait droit à l'estime de tout bon poète.'[356]

In his École Romane manifesto (1891) he repeated: 'Il nous faut une poésie franche, vigoureuse et neuve, en un mot, ramenée à la pureté et à la dignité de son ascendance.' The École Romane was to take as its model 'le principe gréco-latin . . . qui florit aux onzième, douzième et treizième siècles avec nos trouvères, au seizième avec Ronsard et son école, au dix-septième avec Racine et La Fontaine', restoring 'la chaîne gallique' broken during the fourteenth, fifteenth, eighteenth, and nineteenth centuries.[357] He told Byvanck in that year: 'Il faut que le verbe reparaisse dans toute sa splendeur ancienne . . . dans ce domaine-là je me sens supérieur à tous parce que je connais les richesses cachées de notre langue';[358] and to Huret, who had asked him to elucidate his 'théorie de l'archaïsme', he proclaimed: 'Là, c'est mon domaine exclusif. Je suis le seul à réclamer un renouveau de la langue poétique, un retour aux traditions, un style retrempé aux sources de l'idiome roman.'[359] So Moréas built himself up a reputation as a connoisseur of Old French literature, which he declaimed — causing a sensation wherever he went — in the cafés of the Latin Quarter. Maurras reported that whenever he met a fellow-poet, 'd'une belle voix de gorge, où les muettes s'accentuent de sorte bizarre, il aggrave les strophes de Ronsard et de la Fontaine, de Thibaut de Champagne et d'Alfred de Vigny';[360] Merrill, that 'Pendant longtemps il épouvanta les gens en leur demandant à brûle-pourpoint: "Que pensez-vous de Gace-Brulé?"'[361] For a time he claimed the Middle Ages as his personal property; as a Greek he was proud of being better informed than the French themselves about their medieval literature. The use he made of it as a literary model was the way through which, as it were, he broke into French poetry — the beginning of his apprenticeship and evolution —, and at the same time his flamboyant assumption of a current fashion, soon left behind when it had served its initiatory purpose. As a gesture to attract notice to himself it was most efficacious. He earned the respect and awe of many of his contemporaries. One critic called him a 'lecteur assidu des plus compréhensifs de nos vieux poëmes du moyen âge';[362] Mauclair reported

[356] Ibid. p. 49.
[357] *Cent soixante-treize lettres de J. Moréas,* ed. R. Jouanny, 1968, p.148 (*Figaro* (Sept. 1891)).   [358] Byvanck, op. cit. p. 73.   [359] J. Huret, op. cit. p. 79.
[360] Quoted by J. de Gourmont, *Jean Moréas,* Sansot, 1905, p. 7.
[361] Merrill, *Prose et vers,* p. 167.
[362] *La Vogue,* v. 13 May 1886, p. 169 (Léo d'Orfer).

in 1891 that on many an evening in the Bibliothèque de la Sorbonne he had seen him engrossed in medieval literature;[363] in the same year Anatole France acknowledged that he was 'nourri de nos vieux romans de chevalerie';[364] and Barrès also paid tribute to *Le Pèlerin passionné,* speaking of 'les *Chansons de geste* et les *Fabliaux* qu'il connait . . . comme aucun spécialiste'.[365] He also attracted a great deal of adverse criticism, ranging in tone from the light-hearted derision of 'Pierre l'Ermite' in *L'Ermitage,* proposing in 1891 to set up a new 'ordre de chevalerie esthétique' in rivalry with Péladan's — 'Qu'on se hâte, qu'on se hâte, car l'affluence sera bientôt telle qu'il nous faudra imposer aux néophytes les épreuves les plus abstruses. . . . Aoi! comme on dit en Romanitas'[366] —, to the righteous indignation of the medievalist C-V. Langlois, who in 1891 launched an attack on Moréas and his fellow-Symbolists for their ignorant misappropriation of medieval literature:

L'ignorance des bacheliers . . . est incroyable. . . . Elle s'étale . . . d'une manière offensive dans la 'littérature de tout à l'heure', dont les 'petites revues' nous régalent. Si certains chefs d'écoles juvéniles prétendent, sans rire, à 'retremper notre style moderne aux sources de l'idiome roman' . . . c'est qu'ils n'ont point la moindre teinture de philologie.[367]

Huret's *Enquête sur l'évolution littéraire,* undertaken in the same year, collected numerous hostile opinions from Moréas's fellow-writers, including Huysmans, who burst out with: 'Moréas! qui a repris les anciens fabliaux français, et qui les a démarqués! Savez-vous l'effet qu'il me fait? Imaginez une poule (et encore! une poule de Valachie) qui picorerait des verroteries dans le Lacurne de Sainte-Palaye. . . . Avec cela si, au moins, il picorait les jolis mots! Mais non! c'est qu'il a un goût de Caraïbe!'[368] The rival Symbolist medievalist Marcel Schwob also attacked Moréas, comparing him unfavourably with Verlaine: 'Les vrais poètes ne sont ni théoriciens, ni grammairiens. Ils s'écoutent vivre . . . sans qu'ils aient besoin d'affubler la vie d'oripeaux décrochés à l'étalage du douzième ou du treizième siècle.'[369]

And yet, when one divorces them from all the publicity which surrounded them, and reads them for their own sake, Moréas's medieval poems, in *Les Cantilènes* (1886) and *Le Pèlerin passionné* (1891), consisting of Verlaine *poussé à outrance,* or poetry in a courtly and precious vein — alembicated sentiments expressed in archaic language, like the

[363] *Revue indépendante,* xx (July 1891), p. 75.
[364] *La Plume,* 1 Jan. 1891, p.1.   [365] Ibid. p. 13.
[366] *L'Ermitage,* ii (Oct. 1891), p. 636.
[367] *Revue bleue,* xlviii. 7 Nov. 1891, pp. 596-7.
[368] Huret, op. cit. p. 180.   [369] *L'Événement,* 5 Apr. 1891.

section of *Le Pèlerin passionné* entitled 'Étrennes de Doulce' –, are not without merit. They stand out as a refreshingly original contribution to the Symbolist Middle Ages. The criticisms of André Barre, who calls *Les Cantilènes* 'des essais malheureux', and of R. Georgin, who speaks of 'un art savant et froid',[371] are unjust. The best of these poems possess a startling quality, an authentic strangeness, which sets them in a class apart from all other Symbolist verse inspired by the Middle Ages, and which fulfils the promise in the epigraph from Adenes le Rois which Moréas chose for *Le Pèlerin passionné*:

> L'estoire iert si rimée, par foi le vous plevi,
> Que li mesentendant en seront abaubi,
> Et li bien entendant en seront esjoï.[372]

Although Merrill claimed that Moréas went no further than Bartsch's well-known *Chrestomathie* for his medieval models,[373] he did in fact, for *Les Cantilènes*, venture as far as the glossary of Célestin Hippeau's edition of *Le Bel Inconnu, ou Giglain fils de Messire Gauvain et de la fée aux blanches mains,* by Renaud de Beaujeu (1860). He paid no attention to the text (except to extract from it two names, that of the dwarf Tidogolain, whom he makes into the hero of a ballad, attributing to him a poignantly-expressed passion for a 'Dame en robe grivelée';[374] and that of La Belle Esmérée, which he uses for the heroine of another of his poems, 'La Comtesse Esmérée'), but took from the glossary words such as 'papemor' (a species of bird), 'diaspe', 'caldonie' and 'jaconce', and 'spicpètre' (a spice), which he placed in his poems, in positions of arresting prominence, converting them into bizarre snatches of local colour; the introductory stanza of one of the poems reads:

> Les papemors dans l'air violet
> Vont, et blonds et blancs comme du lait.
> Blonde suis, blanche comme du lait,
> En gone de velours violet . . .,[375]

and the last one of 'Tidogolain':

> (Dans l'air tiédi de la venelle
> Fluaient des senteurs de cannelle,
> De spicpètre et de serpolet.)
> Et la Dame dit: Ce me plaît.[376]

---

[370] A. Barre, *Le Symbolisme,* Jouve, 1911, p. 224.

[371] R. Georgin, *Jean Moréas,* La Nouvelle Revue Critique, 1930, p. 68. For a more sympathetic appreciation of Moréas's early poetry see M. Coulon's article 'Moreas, rhénan', *Revue rhénane* (Mar. 1924), and J. D. Butler, *Jean Moréas,* 1967, Ch. 4.

[372] Moréas, *Oeuvres,* i. 147.   [373] Merrill, *Prose et vers,* p. 167.

[374] Moréas, op. cit. p. 133.   [375] Ibid. p. 139.   [376] Ibid. p. 135.

(vii) *Influence of the 'chanson populaire'*

Many Symbolist poems on medieval themes were modelled on the *chanson populaire*, a source of inspiration far more readily accessible than medieval literature. A full discussion of this influence is beyond the scope of our study.[377] An earlier generation – poets such as Millien, Theuriet, and Blémont, and the group of 'Vivants' (Gabriel Vicaire and Maurice Bouchor) who broke away from the Parnassian 'impassibles' – had written moralizing, rustic verse influenced by folk poetry. Blémont said in 1890 that the duty of the state as a promoter of folklore studies and popularizer of *chansons populaires* was to 'répandre le goût des plaisirs salubres et sensés . . . moraliser et . . . poétiser l'existence'.[378] The Symbolists had other ambitions. Robert de Souza dismissed the efforts of Theuriet and his fellows as 'tableaux de genre': 'Cela est plus peint que chanté.'[379] Symbolist *chansons populaires* aspired to be sybilline incantations, seeking after a primitive apprehension of elemental truth, in accordance with current folklorist theory. Rimbaud's songs, such as the 'Chanson de la plus haute tour', were the first of these. Schuré came to seek in folk poetry 'le sens du mystère infini qui nous enveloppe, de l'invisible au-delà . . . des paroles sybillines, des cris de Pythonisse.[380]

Symbolist poets who tried their hand at this genre were Vielé-Griffin, Ghil, and Mockel, all of whom incorporated snatches of *chansons populaires* into their verse (Mockel spoke excitedly of a revival of the *chanson*, 'des mots purs, doux et vastes, la cantilène enfin trouvée');[381] Moréas (the *Airs et récits* from *Les Cantilènes* – strongly original ballads full of startling *péripéties*, such as 'Agha Véli'); Kahn (the *lieds* and *chansons* – 'Fils de roi, fils de roi',[382] 'nous étions trois cavaliers',[383] etc. – included in all his collections of verse); Elskamp; and, of course, Maeterlinck, commended by Souza for having achieved the pure *cantilène* free from all adventitious elements.[384]

(viii) *The sinister Symbolist Middle Ages: 'un passé hanté de mystères mauvais'*

So far, in our exploration of the Symbolists' work, we have encountered an ideal Middle Ages – or, at least, a Middle Ages melancholy rather

---

[377] See P. Bénichou's interesting remarks on this subject in *Nerval et la chanson folklorique*, 1970, pp. 344, 358-62.

[378] Blémont, *Esthétique de la tradition*, 1890, p. 89.

[379] *La Poésie populaire et le lyrisme sentimental*, 1899, p. 33.

[380] *Histoire du lied*, 3rd edn., Perrin, 1903, p. 24. Cf. *supra*, pp. 97-8.

[381] *Propos de littérature*, 1894, p. 121.   [382] From *La Pluie et le beau temps*, 1896.

[383] From *Limbes de lumières*, 1897.   [384] R. de Souza, op. cit. pp. 75-80.

than sinister. But, like the Romantics, they were keenly susceptible to 'les charmes de l'horreur' as well as to the pleasures of melancholy, and the dark side of the medieval world is present in much of their poetry and prose.

Before we explore it — in Schwob's short stories first of all — we will examine briefly those of Anatole France, published at the same time, and totally different in spirit and intention.

Anatole France saw no mystery in the Middle Ages. His reading of Gaston Paris left him with the impression that medieval men were essentially children with a child-like conception of the world: 'Leur monde, par rapport au nôtre, était tout petit.' This world, he said, 'pourrait être représenté, à la rigueur, par une vieille horloge un peu compliquée, comme celle de Strasbourg. Il suffirait de trois étages de marionnettes, que des rouages feraient mouvoir.'[385] This simplicity he found reassuring and wholesome. Those atrocities which provided fodder for republican history books he called 'les illusions de la peur qui les rendaient parfois cruels',[386] or (in the invocation addressed to his fore-fathers at the end of his article on Leconte de Lisle) 'les erreurs de votre courage et de votre simplicité'.[387]

France looks back on the past from the position of a civilized man sampling each portion of mankind's heritage. His indulgent eclecticism was shared by Lemaître, who remarked in his article on Gaston Paris that 'une âme antérieure à la nôtre dort en nous et . . . il n'est pas impossible de la réveiller et de jouir de ces réveils avec une demi-sincérité.'[388] It is an attitude of mind which leads to the condescension and false naïveté avoided by Flaubert in *Saint Julien*,[389] but present in all France's medieval tales. M. Bergeret is enchanted by a medieval sculptor's representation of the Last Judgement: 'Cette idée naïve de l'univers, qu'avaient exprimée là des ouvriers morts depuis plus de cinq cents ans, l'attendrissait. Il la trouvait aimable dans son absurdité.'[390] His creator regards medieval men with the same smiling indulgence, retelling their tales — such as *Le Jongleur de Notre-Dame*,[391] one of

---

[385] A. France, *Os. cs.* vi. 573-4. Cf. 'la cosmogonie du petit Pierre Nozière' in his autobiographical novel of 1899. The six-year-old Pierre regards the world as 'une sorte de jeu très compliqué et très amusant': 'Je me représentais la création comme une grande boîte de Nuremberg' (*Os. cs.* x. 275, 284).

[386] Ibid. p. 579.   [387] *Os. cs.* vi. 95.

[388] J. Lemaître, *Les Contemporains,* iii. 238.

[389] Cf. *supra,* p. 189.

[390] *Os. cs.* xii. 268 (*L'Anneau d'améthyste,* 1899).

[391] In *L'Étui de nacre* (1890).

several in which, in the words of Louis Reynaud, 'il rivalise d'ingénuité croyante, — en apparence du moins —, avec ses sources'[392] — and sometimes adding pagan endings of his own. He does this in the story of Saint Scholastica (*L'Étui de nacre*), who persuades her husband to remain with her until death in a state of holy chastity. The miraculously twining rose shoots which unite their graves are interpreted as a symbol of sanctity by all except Silvanus, a surviving pagan who knows that the god Eros caused the roses to flower, as a message to the living from the dead woman's unhappy shade: 'Aimez, vous qui vivez. Ce prodige nous enseigne à goûter les joies de la vie, tandis qu'il en est temps encore.'[393]

Marcel Schwob also regarded medieval men as children, but as children with an instinct towards wanton destruction, like Blanche la Sanglante, the child-wife who abets the grisly murder of her husband in a tale of *Le Roi au masque d'or* (1893). In the naïveté which Anatole France found engagingly 'aimable par son absurdité', he saw a mysterious perversity[394] — sometimes sanguinary like that of Blanche, sometimes innocent like that of the boy Alain in *L'Étoile de bois* (1897), who, determined to light a star of his own, finds the sign of a wooden star hanging outside a wood-carver's workshop, sets it on fire, and, with it, the whole town, which perishes in a conflagration predicted by its astrologers.

This perversity gave Schwob an intense aesthetic *frisson,* which he sought to communicate to his readers. 'Je vous l'avoue franchement,' he told Byvanck, 'le mal a un attrait pour moi; la perversité me charme.'[395] The records of singular crimes which he exhumed from fifteenth-century archives (Clouard calls his work 'une érudition devenue source de grand guignol')[396] provide what Flaubert once called 'haschich historique'.[397] His friend Samain told him that certain sentences of the *Vies imaginaires* and the *Croisade des enfants* had

[392] L. Reynaud, *La Crise de notre littérature,* Hachette, 1929, p. 84.

[393] *Os. cs.* v. 283. Cf. Francis Poictevin's ecstatic account of a similar marriage entered into by Saint Catherine of Sweden: 'Ces époux ne se touchant qu'en Dieu affolent de leur rare et réelle poésie. Les plus beaux poèmes chantés ne vaudront pas cette simplicité profonde, uniment vécue au XIVe siècle' (*Heures,* 1892, p. 9).

[394] Cf. A. Filon in the *Revue bleue,* 13 Sept. 1890, p. 346: 'Comme dans un bain rafraîchissant, on se plonge dans la vie ancienne, où les sentiments étaient plus intenses, plus durables, où tout était plus naïf, même le crime.'

[395] Byvanck, op. cit. p. 298.

[396] H. Clouard, *Histoire de la littérature française du symbolisme à nos jours,* Albin Michel, i (1947), 140.

[397] *Journal des Goncourt,* i. 687 (1860).

affected him in the manner of 'des graines pleines d'une essence violente, qui se répand soudain à travers l'esprit, et l'emplit tout entier'.[398] Plagues fascinated Schwob; and late-fifteenth-century criminals — *Faux-Visages, écorcheurs,* and *routiers;* and in particular the life of Villon, 'cette vie si mystérieusement compliquée'.[399] Meaningless horror was his speciality, as in his tale *Les Faulx-Visaiges:* 'Ils avaient avec eux des fillettes prises le long des cimetières, qu'on entendait hurler dans la nuit. Personne ne savait s'ils parlaient. Ils surgissaient du mystère et massacraient en silence.'[400] There is, of course, no trace of republican anger (though a contemporary Catholic critic complained of him that 'il assimile, mais pour les mépriser et les maudire . . . aux cruelles moeurs orientales, les rudes façons de notre moyen âge, dont il ne saurait soupçonner les tendresses cachées').[401] The horror is intensified by the archaic, faintly legal, flavour of his style (communicated to him by his sources), the tone of a painstaking, pedantic recorder, laconically relating horrific singularities. And his tales sometimes end with enigmatic flourishes, reminiscent of the closing lines of Bertrand's prose poems in *Gaspard de la nuit* (much admired by Schwob): the end of *Nicolas Loyseleur, juge* (*Vies imaginaires*) is an example:

Sur le pont de bois, entre les maisons pointues, couvertes de tuiles striées en ogives, et les poivrières bleues et jaunes, il eut soudain un éblouissement devant la lumière du Rhin; il crut qu'il se noyait, comme le moine lubrique, au milieu de l'eau verte qui tourbillonnait dans ses yeux; le mot de Marie s'étouffa dans sa gorge, et il mourut avec un sanglot.'[402]

One of his most popular works was *La Croisade des enfants* (1896). The children cry: 'Ce sont des voix blanches qui nous ont appelés dans la nuit';[403] and the pathetic 'balbutiements' of the aged and feeble Innocent III (of whom Gourmont had written in 1892 that he was 'exquis et pur entre tous, probe et doux . . . doué de science et de poésie')[404] present a remarkable contrast with Leconte de Lisle's 'Raisons du Saint-Père':

Seigneur, je suis très vieux, et me voici vêtu de blanc devant toi, et mon nom est Innocent, et tu sais que je ne sais rien . . . écoute ce chuchotement chevrotant qui monte hors de cette petite cellule de ma

---

[398] Samain, *Des lettres,* p. 102. [399] Schwob, *Spicilège,* 1896, p. 6.
[400] *Le Roi au masque d'or,* 1893, p. 105.
[401] *Libre Parole,* 28 Nov. 1892 (F. Pascal).
[402] *Vies imaginaires,* 6th edn., 1957, pp. 147-8. [403] *La Lampe de Psyché,* p. 89.
[404] *Le Latin mystique,* p. 253.

basilique et conseille-moi. . . . Bien que leur foi soit ignorante, puniras-
tu l'ignorance de sept mille innocents? Moi aussi, je suis Innocent.
Seigneur, je suis innocent comme eux. . . . Seigneur, ce sont tes petits
innocents. Et moi, Innocent, je ne sais pas, je ne sais pas. . . .[405]

Huysmans also saw beauty in medieval criminality, though of a very
different kind. Barbey d'Aurevilly had said in his article on Villon that
'l'atrocité du supplice' gave dignity to medieval criminals;[406] and he had
also been moved to transports of enthusiasm by the mentality of the
feudal baron, imbued with 'la conscience et l'orgueil de la liberté
humaine, se posant envers et contre tous, et, si cela lui plaît, même
contre Dieu!'[407] This is the theme of Durtal's life of Gilles de Rais contained in *Là-bas*. The climax is reached when Gilles repents and implores
the people's forgiveness, readily granted to him by 'la naïve et miséricor-
dieuse plèbe du Moyen Âge':[408] 'Alors, en sa blanche splendeur, l'âme
du Moyen Âge rayonna dans cette salle.'[409]

Paul Adam's novel *Être*, published in the same year, was also set in
the fifteenth century, 'un des plus beaux temps de détraquement
général',[410] according to Kahn in an enthusiastic review. This is another
offering of 'haschich historique'. The heroine Mahaud, 'la fille folle de
son corps',[411] is a sister of Gilles de Rais with an insatiable urge to
destroy: 'Elle conçut de raser le monde, de raser le monde de toute vie,
de rester unique, dans l'immensité vide.'[412] The local colour, however,
is of a decidedly inferior grade, consisting of Symbolist embellishment
('Haute parmi les candeurs de sa simarre blanche, Mahaud se fige
hiératiquement dans le cercle qu'inscrivit le glaive magique au pulvérin
d'argent'),[413] occultist bric-à-brac, — pentagrams, tetragrams, Chaldean
spells, and primordial vibrations — and a few details from the stock-in-
trade of republican history manuals ('Un tisserand franchit la ligne des
milices et témoigna que l'on avait coupé à son fils les pieds et les mains
pour un chevreuil pris dans les chasses épiscopales'),[414] with some crude
imitations of Leconte de Lisle ('Et la tête livide au bout du bras du
varlet, la tête terreuse qui pleure de ses yeux révulsés, sanglote de ses
lèvres troussées . . .').[415]

[405] *La Lampe de Psyché*, pp. 83-8.
[406] B. d'Aurevilly, *Les Critiques*, 1885, p. 304.
[407] *De l'histoire*, 1905, p. 233.   [408] *Là-bas*, p. 438.   [409] Ibid. p. 354.
[410] G. Kahn, *Symbolists et décadents*, 1902, p. 98 (*Revue indépendante* (May
1888)).
[411] P. Adam, *Être*, 1891, p. 3.   [412] Ibid. pp. 242-3.
[413] Ibid. p. 72.   [414] Ibid. p. 38.   [415] Ibid. p. 41.

The sinister side of the Middle Ages also has a place in Symbolist drama and poetry. The subject of Henry Bataille's *La Lépreuse* (performed with great success in 1896) is taken from a Breton folk-song about a leper-woman who invites passers-by to drink from her glass, thereby signing the doom of all those who have cruelly cast her out from society — 'D'une goutte de sang, j'en tuerais cent, j'en tuerais mille.'[416] Bataille perceived in this song, which he heard one day in the forest of Huelgoat, 'un souffle barbare d'une grandeur tragique.' 'La terreur médiévale', he said in his Preface, 'me semblait avoir inspiré ces chants qu'un enfant hystérique soupirait encore plusieurs siècles après, sur les lieux mêmes où ils avaient été conçus.'[417] He wrote the play in reaction against 'le pré-Raphaélisme de Burne-Jones ou même de Gustave Moreau . . . tous ces crimes artistiques perpétrés au nom des primitifs' by his fellow-Symbolists.[418]

In Maeterlinck's *Princesse Maleine* the lurid red glow that has for so long been a feature of the sinister Middle Ages[419] illumines the guilty couple at the end. One of the *béguines* opens the chapel door and 'une grande clarté rouge provenue des vitraux et de l'illumination du tabernacle inonde subitement le roi et la reine Anne.'[420]

Glimpses of this Middle Ages occur frequently in the poetry of Merrill, Kahn, and Verhaeren.

Merrill's richly ornate past is also 'un passé hanté de mystères mauvais'.[421] In *Les Fastes,* for instance (1891), he places one of his wild-eyed Pre-Raphaelite queens

> Au centre du pompeux charroi
> Qui fuit la rouge pestilence.[422]

Kahn has many horrific tales to tell. His page Kunrad, who runs away 'pour rencontrer sa destinée', seems at first destined for the conventional 'troubadour' adventure with the châtelaine; but the love which he encounters is that of a vampire, who

> . . . prit le page dans ses bras
> et lui donna un seul baiser
> qui le vieillit de trente années
>
> D'une caresse de ses mains
> elle lui décharna la face
> et la frappa de cécité

[416] H. Bataille, *Théâtre complet,* i (1922), 11.   [417] Ibid. p. 14.
[418] Ibid. p. 16.   [419] Cf. *supra,* Ch. 1, p. 20; Ch. 6, pp. 134n, 147, 155.
[420] Maeterlinck, *Théâtre,* i (1901), 175.
[421] Merrill, *Poèmes, 1887-97,* p. 94.   [422] Ibid. p. 101.

> Au pont de l'Ill la charité
> de ceux qui dans les jardins vont aimer
> nourrit parfois le pauvre aimé.[423]

Agonies' tells the tale of a servant girl driven forth by 'le maître féroce à coups de fouet' to bear her child in the wilderness:

> J'ai passé près de la porte
> D'une large ville abondante
> Mais le couvre-feu de fer dit qu'on apporte
> Passé dix heures
> Ès-villes aux pécunes abondantes
> Les malheurs.[424]

Some of his *Images* in *Le Livre d'images* (1897) are from the same world: e.g. 'Le Vieux Mendiant':

> Il fut le fils des assassins; lors une pierre
> (la marmaille jouait) lui creva la paupière
> et le mire ne guérissant qu'honnêtes gens,
> l'autre oeil se détruisit, dans son masque d'enfant
> pareil dès lors à un mur blanc.[425]

Verhaeren at the beginning of his career was obsessed with a sinister and sanguinary Middle Ages: 'Je songe quelquefois avec envie à ces flagellants du moyen âge,' he wrote in 1890, 'à ces messes nocturnes . . . à ces trépidations folles et rouges pour à tout jamais là-bas, dans le passé barbare.'[426] His contribution to the elegiac Symbolist lament for the passing of the Middle Ages was the poem 'Les Preux' (1889):

> En un très vieux manoir, avec des javelots
> Et des pennons lancéolés sur ses murailles,
> Une rage de bataille
> Rouge éclatait en tableaux. . . .
>
> Hélas! tous ces cerveaux qui rêvèrent de gloire,
> Fendus! et tous ces poings, coupés![427]

Minor poets emulate these visions of carnage and catastrophe. Albert Aurier's 'Massacre des rêves' (1890) tells of a 'Baronne, en son morne

[423] Kahn, *Premiers Poèmes,* pp. 226-8.
[424] Kahn, *Limbes de lumières,* 1897, pp. 58-9.
[425] Kahn, *Le Livre d'images,* 1897, p. 17.
[426] Verhaeren, *Impressions,* i (1926), 13.
[427] Verhaeren, *Poèmes.* i (1895), 45.

manoir', who on a night of moaning wind, 'une nuit de guerre et de
désastre', cries

> Gai Troubadour! Ô mon gai Troubadour!
>
> Racontez donc, à votre douce dame ...
> Une histoire d'amour! —

but the tale which he tells scarcely complies with her request:

> Pour l'effroi des hameaux de ces terres novales
> Que protéger ne sut le Moine nonchalant,
> Des Ducs velus, juchés sur d'étiques cavales,
> Ont passé, dans la nuit, comme un songe sanglant! ...
>
> Ils ont passé, dressant leurs féroces bannières! ...
>
> Des Ducs que Dieu voulut sevrer des apanages ...
> Éclaboussant le ciel du sang de leurs carnages
> Et comblant les vallons d'Évêques égorgés![428]

(ix) *Traces of political sentiment in Symbolist 'Fables'*

One can detect Kahn's ardently republican sympathies in the above-
quoted extracts from his poetry. His Middle Ages was in general much
darker than that of his fellow-Symbolists. Although many of these were
of extreme left-wing or anarchist sympathies (the *Entretiens politiques
et littéraires* and the *Revue blanche,* for example, were politically very
far to the left), they managed most of the time to suppress their political
allegiances while the fashion for an ideal Middle Ages was at its height.
'En ce temps', explains Kahn in an article on Tailhade written in 1901,
'vers 1884 ou 1885, aucun problème ne se posait impérieusement. Dans
une paix molle, les consciences, qu'aucun heurt n'avait réveillées,
pratiquaient une large tolérance. . . . On se choisissait un terrain de
rêverie, on y demeurait.' ('Mais ceci est passé', he goes on to say, referring
to the Dreyfus case.)[429]

Laurent Tailhade, the poet of *Vitraux* (1891), was called a 'poète
catholique' by Bernard Lazare in 1895: 'Il adore l'éclat des ostensoirs,
la senteur lourde des cierges, la somptuosité des reliquaires et des
chapes.'[430] 'Tailhade s'abusa quelque temps sur sa façon de sentir les
pompes religieuses et crut s'intéresser à leurs mobiles. Cela dura peu . . .'[430]
is how Kahn refers to this phase of his career. He made up for his passing

[428] *Oeuvres posthumes ae G.-Albert Aurier,* 1893, pp. 165-6 (first published in
  MF (Aug. 1890)).
[429] *Revue blanche,* xxvi (Oct. 1901), pp. 186-7.
[430] B. Lazare, *Figures contemporaines,* p. 213.

idolatry of stained glass by frequent reference in his subsequent writing
to 'ce turpide et sanglant Moyen Âge dont se délecte le catholicisme
belge du R.P. Huysmans',[431] 'Le Moyen Âge, centre de toute ânerie et
de toute hideur',[432] etc. – and as part of his atonement he wrote an old-
style republican poem entitled 'Résurrection', in which Christ returns
to earth and visits Paris:

> Le cardinal de pourpre, et le juge insolent . . .
> Cependant que vibrait un carillon hurlant,
> Conduisirent Jésus devant la cathédrale.

'N'entre pas dans le lieu de ténèbre et de mort!' Tailhade cries to him.
He will find there only the clergy, 'Vêtus d'or, ululant des hymnes
violentes'; 'Viens avec nous, avec le Pauvre qui t'aima!'[433]

There are occasional incongruous traces of political sentiment in
some Symbolist poems and plays written when nostalgia for the Middle
Ages was at its height. Gourmont's *Histoire tragique de la Princesse
Phénissa* (1893) is one of these curious mixtures. The young princess,
a typical Gourmont heroine who twines her arms around her middle-
aged husband Phébor: 'Toute ma peau blanche est à toi. Oh! J'ai envie
de me mettre nue! Je t'aime!',[434] is also a symbol of the future, 'où les
fils des pauvres d'aujourd'hui marcheraient dans la vie tels que des
seigneurs, – et où le fouet aurait changé de mains'.[435] Her evil mother,
jealous of her beauty, persuades Phébor to strangle her, and proclaims
in triumph: 'Tu as délivré le monde de la tyrannie de l'espoir.'[436]

One or two Symbolist 'Fables' present a political moral in heraldic
and hieratic disguise. Quillard's *L'Errante* (1896) is the most notable of
these. In the first part 'De Sable et d'Or', l'HOMME songe dans le soir
somptueux et morne',[437] alone in his 'manoir de silence et d'ombre
inviolée'.[438] 'L'Errante' then appears, a symbol of suffering humanity:
'Ses haillons brochés d'or illusoire par les astres dénoncent les routes
hostiles, les morsures du vent, peut-être l'agression de mains brutales.'
The man spurns her at first: 'Tu viens des carrefours vulgaires', he tells
her. His soul craves only regal solitude; but as she turns away he relents
and implores her to stay. Her voice has revived in him 'une fleur de jadis
aux pistils oubliés'. She is the 'dolente ombre d'une ombre que j'aimais'.[439]

---

[431] Tailhade, *Imbéciles et gredins*, 1900, p. 254.
[432] Tailhade, *Plâtres et marbres*, 1913, p. 151.
[433] Tailhade, *Poèmes aristophanesques*, pp. 92-3.
[434] Gourmont, *Le Pèlerin du silence*, 1896, p. 30.
[435] Ibid. p. 36.   [436] Ibid. p. 56.
[437] Quillard, *La Lyre héroïque et dolente*, 1897, p. 45.
[438] Ibid. p. 53.   [439] Ibid. pp. 47-50.

In the second part, 'De Gueules', he receives her into his castle, loads her with his ancestral riches, and sends her forth into the world:

> Viens et regarde: là de houleuses forêts
> Où les pasteurs de porcs se vautrent dans les bauges;
> Puis des plaines, rumeurs des blés, parfum des sauges,
> Et les paysans nus courbés sous les sillons
> A jamais . . .

in order to share this wealth. 'L'Errante' goes on her way 'auréolée par la gloire du matin, vers les plaines et vers les villes orientales, tandis que sa voix dans la solitude chante les batailles futures'.[440]

Le Victorieux, by Ferdinand Hérold (a friend of Quillard's, who campaigned for Dreyfus with him) is a pacifist 'Fable'. The melancholy Queen Irène wins the love of the warrior Yehl, a splendid Wagnerian figure —

> Sur les mailles éclatantes de son haubert
> Flotte un manteau d'or somptueux et de brocart[441] —

but pitiless to his enemies. Gloatingly he relives his past battles:

> J'ai fauché de viles moissons de vies humaines. . . .
> Je suis Yehl, Héros du crépuscule vermeil.

> Le Héros que vêt le crépuscule vermeil [he boasts]
> Est sourd à la dolente voix de la pitié.[442]

Irène's love turns to reproach:

> Ô Yehl, oh, ta victoire est sanglante et mauvaise. . . .
> Tu as paru parmi des lueurs sanglantes.[443]

She effects a miraculous change of heart in him: he discards his armour and appears before her as a purified, Tannhäuser figure, 'vêtu de rude bure'.[444] They resolve to go through the world promulgating 'les paroles aimées/Par qui mourront un jour les sanglantes erreurs'.[445] (A hint of pacifist sentiment had similarly crept into Mockel's elegiac evocation of battles long ago in *Chantefable un peu naïve:*

> les destriers bardés qui bondissaient, les dents au mors
> les pesants paladins qui bondissaient, clamant la mort,
> ils sont morts à jamais pour les mémoires d'hommes. . . .

> une ombre a dévoré les chevaliers de proie . . . ;[446]

---

[440] Ibid. pp. 53-4.
[441] Hérold, *Images tendres et merveilleuses,* p. 170.
[442] Ibid. pp. 203-4.   [443] Ibid. pp. 225-7.
[444] Ibid. p. 244.   [445] Ibid. p. 256.
[446] Mockel, *Chantefable un peu naïve,* pp. 64-5.

and in Saint-Pol-Roux's *Épilogue des saisons humaines* (1893) the dying prince recoils from his sword, calling it 'pistil du Malin, écharde de la Haine', and proclaiming: 'Maudites soient les Patries'.)[447]

(x) *The pseudo-Symbolist Middle Ages:*
Zola's Le Rêve; Rostand's Princesse lointaine

Several former Parnassians and fugitives from Naturalism fell in with the prevailing fashion, creating a spurious reflection of the Symbolist Middle Ages. Their productions were ignored or received with derision by the Symbolists themselves.

The first of these works was *Le Rêve* (1888), by Zola, who in the 1860s and 70s had subscribed to the republican view of the Middle Ages as 'une époque de terreur et d'angoisse',[448] sharing Taine's distaste for 'le Moyen Âge chrétien [qui] frissonne et gémit au fond de ses cathédrales',[449] and reproving the Romantics for their 'tendresse excessive pour . . . les vieilles cathédrales, les armures, toute la ferraille et les guenilles des siècles passés'.[450] In *Le Rêve,* however, the heroine Angélique resembles 'une petite vierge de vitrail'.[451] Abandoned as a child in a cathedral porch, she is taken in by a couple who teach her their craft of embroidering Gothic saints and lilies on altar-cloths and church vestments. Her guardian, Hubert, teaches her the history of the craft as well, in its glorious medieval heyday: 'Ces temps anciens, c'était si magnifique! Les seigneurs portaient des vêtements tout de broderies. . . .Ah! c'était beau, il y a longtemps!'[452] Her sequestered adolescence in this ideal milieu subdues 'le démon héréditaire' in her; and her soul becomes that of a 'chrétienne de la primitive Église, nourrie des lectures de *La Légende*',[453] totally untouched by the modern world: 'Cela lui semblait fou, de s'imaginer le monde comme une mécanique, régie par des lois fixes.'[453] She falls in love with Félicien d'Hautecoeur, the last of an ancient line. He appears to her as the ideal Saint George who has always haunted her dreams, 'riche comme un roi, beau comme un Dieu'.[452] He returns her love, and they while away their days in idyllic converse, reliving the Middle Ages which hold them both in thrall. But his father forbids them to marry, and Angélique pines away with grief. Consent to the marriage, when it comes, is too late to save her. Félicien tries in vain to restore her on her deathbed with a radiant

[447] Saint-Pol-Roux, *Épilogue des saisons humaines,* 1893, p. 17.
[448] Zola, *Os. cs.,* ed. Mitterand, x (1968), 50.
[449] Ibid. p. 150.   [450] Ibid. xii. 296.
[451] Ibid. v. 1173.   [452] Ibid. p. 1201.   [453] Ibid. p. 1214.

vision of their future together – his ancestral home converted into an ideal Pierrefonds: '... nous relèverons les murs du château d'Haute-coeur, et nous y achèverons nos jours. ... De nouveau, le donjon commandera aux deux vallées. Nous habiterons le logis d'honneur, entre la tour de David et la tour de Charlemagne. ... Nos murailles de quinze pieds d'épaisseur nous isoleront, nous serons dans la légende.'[454]

This novel was referred to in acid tones by the critic of *La Revue indépendante* as 'cette surprenante fantaisie chez l'Haussmann de la littérature moderne d'édifier une cathédrale gothique'.[455] In 1893 it featured – alongside Bornier's *Fille de Roland* – in the *Mercure de France's* list of 'les vingt-cinq plus mauvais livres du siècle'.[456]

In the same category in Symbolist eyes – and as coolly received by them – were the Naturalist Hennique's play *Amour,* performed at the Odéon in 1890, the Parnassian Armand Silvestre's *Grisélidis* (1891) and *Les Drames sacrés* (1894), both written in collaboration with Eugène Morand, and his *Tristan de Léonois* (1897). A childhood companion of the heroine, who causes her a fleeting moment of temptation, was introduced into the story of Grisélidis by its authors, who feared that a modern audience might find her conjugal fidelity incredible.[457] The critic of *La Plume* condemned the play out of hand: 'Point de naïveté dans la facture, point de cette saveur si particulière et si pénétrante des vieux mystères'.[458]

But the most important play set in a pseudo-Symbolist Middle Ages was of course Rostand's *Princesse lointaine,* the great popular success of 1895.[459]

Rostand's ambition in writing this play was to 'plonger dans le Bleu et le Rose'.[460] Its subject is the dying troubadour Joffrey Rudel's love for Mélissinde of Tripoli, whom he has never seen, and his voyage – 'Plus nous nous approchons, plus je sens que je meurs'[461] – to set eyes upon her and declare his love before he dies. A friend sent before him as an emissary falls in love with her – and she with him –, but duty prevails in the end, and they renounce their love, ashamed of their

[454] Ibid. p. 1298.
[455] *Revue indépendante,* xix (June 1891), p. 387.
[456] See *MF* (May 1893), p. 72.
[457] See *Grande Revue* (Oct. 1891), E. Morand, *'Grisélidis:* Quelques mots sur la pièce'.
[458] *La Plume,* 1 June 1891, pp. 191-2.
[459] The original title of Maeterlinck's *Princesse Maleine* was *La Princesse lointaine.* See A. Pasquier, *M. Maeterlinck,* 1963, p. 220.
[460] See Knowles, op. cit. p. 219.
[461] Rostand, *La Princesse lointaine,* 1901, p. 15.

betrayal of the blameless Rudel: 'La dame qu'il voulut me croire, je veux être!' cries Mélissinde.[462] Rudel dies in her arms, radiantly happy with his illusion. Mélissinde's conclusion is:

> Mon étreinte est pour toi d'une telle douceur
> Parce que l'Étrangère est encore dans la Soeur!
> Tu n'auras pas connu cette tristesse grise
> De l'idole avec qui l'on se familiarise;
> Je garde du lointain, par lequel je te plus.[463]

She becomes a Carmelite and Bertram a Crusader. There is an undeniable element of vulgarity in this play, which stems from its pseudo-Symbolist pretensions. Sermons on 'l'idéal' are delivered by a figure from the Romantic Middle Ages, Frère Trophime: 'Tout rayon qui filtre, d'idéal,/Est autant de gagné dans l'âme sur le mal',[464] and so forth. 'J'ai renié la pâle fleur des songeries/Pour la fleur amoureuse', sighs Mélissinde as she seduces Bertram.[465] The Symbolists seldom deigned to mention this play: Kahn made a passing reference in the year of its performance to 'la belle légende moyen-âge que M. Rostand a noyée de vers incertains'.[466]

I. *The decline of the Symbolist Middle Ages*

It only remains for us to chart the decline of the Symbolist Middle Ages. This began early: Robichez dates 'le retour au bon sens . . . le temps des palinodies' from 1894,[467] but in fact it was already well under way by then. One by one the Symbolists tired of their Middle Ages and turned to other preoccupations. The youthful Valéry (whose letters are interesting documents on the mentality of this period), obsessed in 1889-90 with 'tout un univers de vibrations artistes et rares'[468] afforded to him by contemplation of the early Middle Ages — 'la vie à travers un vitrail d'église, considérée'[469] —, by the autumn of 1891 had emerged from 'la forêt mystique' and was asking Gide: 'Où trouverai-je une magie plus neuve?'[470] The watchword of the nineties became 'la Vie', set in opposition to the fading world of dreams. The 'moyenâgeux' element was considered by many to be the most perishable part of Symbolism, as well as of Romanticism. Individual inventions were soon vulgarized by those whom the *Revue indépendante*

---

[462] Ibid. p. 90.   [463] Ibid. p. 96.   [464] Ibid. p. 11.   [465] Ibid. p. 69.
[466] *La Société nouvelle,* June 1895, p. 820.
[467] Robichez, op. cit. p. 348.
[468] *Paul Valéry — Gustave Fourment: Correspondance, 1887-1933,* 1957, p. 69.
[469] Ibid. p. 218.
[470] *André Gide — Paul Valéry: Correspondance, 1890-1942,* p. 126.

called in 1892 'l'haïssable troupeau des imitateurs'.[471] Moréas' Tidogolain reappeared in Retté's *Thulé des brumes* (1891); his Esmérée, in Klingsor's *Filles-Fleurs* (1895).

The first act of defection from the Symbolist Middle Ages was the founding of Moréas's École Romane in 1891. Already in his conversation with Byvanck earlier that year, Moréas, while boasting of his acquaintanceship with 'les richesses cachées de notre langue', was showing decreasing enthusiasm for medieval literature. Reciting an unspecified 'poème du moyen âge', he asked 'Qu'en pensez-vous? Cela n'est-il pas magnifique et sonore?', but went on to say 'Je vous accorde qu'à la longue c'est un peu monotone et que la syntaxe est plus que naïve. Aussi ce ne sont là que nos matériaux, et c'est seulement à un certain point de vue que je regarde cette langue comme notre modèle.'[472] He revealed to Byvanck that he had invented the term 'poésie Romane', which was to replace Symbolism, and that the aim of the *poètes romans* would be to remove the 'ligne de démarcation' existing between the Middle Ages and the Renaissance (he repeated this in his Preface to *Le Pèlerin passionné*). But then he proclaimed: 'Ce que j'ai fait auparavant n'a été qu'un balbutiement.'[473] He was leaving the Middle Ages behind. Even while he was boldly attempting to solder them to the classical tradition, he came to regard them as irremediably tainted with the Symbolist stigma, and repudiated his medieval poems as a mere 'balbutiement'. He told Huret that he had quite emancipated himself from the 'pessimisterie' and 'vague à l'âme germanique'[474] of his former master Verlaine, 'pris du pied droit dans le sépulcre romantique'.[475] In 1893 he excised the medieval poems from *Le Pèlerin passionné,* and published them apart as *Autant en emporte le vent.* His next volume of verse, *Ériphyle* (1893), was completely pagan in inspiration.

In the following year (1892) a critic spoke out in the *Revue indépendante* against the Symbolist imagery of Régnier and his fellows, 'son nauséeux ressassement d'ennui, de doute, de soir, de passé, toute la montre des ferrailleries et des casseroles de la poétique conventionnelle'. 'L'Au-delà n'existe pas', he declared, 'C'est un mot, un adverbe.'[476] From then on murmurs of protest against the Symbolist Middle Ages grew increasingly frequent. Vielé-Griffin took exception to Hérold's

---

[471] *Revue indépendante,* xxiii (June 1892), p. 382.
[472] Byvanck, op. cit. p. 74. [473] Ibid. pp. 86-8.
[474] Huret, op. cit. p. 81. [475] Ibid. p. 428.
[476] *Revue indépendante* (Sept. 1892), pp. 355-8 ('G.M.').

Chevaleries sentimentales in 1893: 'Toute cette mascarade romantique est trop noble d'allure . . . nous aimerions . . . un haut de forme ou une franche casquette parmi ces morions et ces cimiers, – un cheval de labour au milieu de ces palefrois et le vent E. -S. -E., sur tous ces parfums.'[477] Hugues Rebell spoke in the same year of 'une poésie qui, loin de nous émouvoir, nous rappellerait plutôt les froides abstractions de Guillaume de Lorris'.[478] Mauclair gave full rein to his indignation in 1894: 'Je souhaiterais qu'on nous laissât enfin tranquilles avec le Graal, le cygne, l'oiseau de Siegfried, les casques, les palefrois, les glaives, les cités de rêve et autres lieux communs . . . Est-ce que cette ferblanterie est de la vie? . . .!'[479] In 1901 he went once more into the attack against the Symbolists' 'décor de moyen âge insupportable'.[480] Bernard Lazare in 1895 upbraided his contemporaries in the stern accents of Michelet:

Entre ces jeunes gens qui tous ont méprisé l'heure présente et s'en sont allés chercher la lumière dans le passé, ceux-ci ont été séduits par le catholicisme esthétique, ceux-là par la philosophie et la mystagogie alexandrines, ces derniers par la thaumaturgie et la goëtie moyen-nageuses. . . . Ils ont tort, car l'autrefois est couché sous une lourde pierre et il entraîne dans la nuit ceux qui veulent soulever le bloc rude sous lequel il est scellé.[481]

In the same year Retté (who, as we have seen, had himself contributed to the creation of the Symbolist Middle Ages) told a collection of poets whose work he was reviewing in *La Plume:* 'Je dirais volontiers à tous ces poètes: Trop de vitrailleries, trop de machicoulis, de fenêtres gothiques, de heaumes d'or, de pennons fussent-ils de Lancastre, trop de princesses hiératiques, de Lénor châtelaines, de Suzeraines au pouvoir sûr, trop d'idéal en longueur – et, à la fin, trop de lys.'[482] In 1898 he heaped further abuse in *La Plume* upon the Symbolists' 'moyen âge poussiéreux . . . rance à faire vomir'.[483] 1896 saw the emergence of the *naturiste* movement, with Le Blond's *Essai sur le naturisme,* condemning 'cette fade littérature de songe et de langueurs'[484] in the name of 'un panthéisme gigantesque et radieux'.[485] 'Si nous comprenions leur emblème social, leur symbolisme supérieur, tant d'outils discrédités, les

---

[477] *Entretiens politiques et littéraires*, vi. 25 June 1893, p. 387.

[478] *L'Ermitage*, iv (Sept. 1893), 154.

[479] *Éleusis*, 1894, p. 167.

[480] *L'Art en silence,* 1901, p. 203.

[481] *Figures contemporaines*, 1895, pp. 223-4.

[482] *La Plume,* 1 June 1895, p. 260.

[483] Ibid. 15 Jan. 1898, p. 34.

[484] *Essai sur le naturisme,* Mercure de France, 1896, p. 70.   [487] Ibid. p. 13.

sonnantes truelles, et les fourches sournoises, et les râteaux bruissants nous paraîtraient d'une beauté aussi haute que les riches et claquants étendards des chevaleries évanouies.'[486]

Saint-Pol-Roux illustrates this universal defection from the Symbolist Middle Ages in his prose poem 'Le Poëte au vitrail' (addressed to Marinetti, the founder of *futurisme,* and dated 1895):

Je naquis en cette Tour', says the poet, 'qu'aujourd'hui seulement, à l'âge d'homme, j'ai quittée.

La salle . . . ne recevait l'impression du dehors qu'au moyen d'un vitrail scellé au sud-est et figurant une Dame bariolée dont le verre épousait les lignes de plomb.

Then came a day when,

L'encrier saisi, rageusement je le jetai contre le vitrail qui vole en éclats, l'Image s'éparpillant en vaines lamelles, à mes pieds sa banderole disloquée.

In that instant he recognizes the tower as 'la Tour de Servitude':

. . . le monde entier m'envahit dans un jet de brise, et directement je perçois la divine Beauté délivrée de ses prêtres et de leurs mensonges.[487]

We have seen that not all Symbolist poets emerged from their ideal Middle Ages. Some remained captivated by it for ever — Saint-Pol-Roux himself, for instance, in spite of the foregoing —, and one (Vielé-Griffin) converted its imagery to the service of 'la Vie'.

But most deserted it in the end; either for the Hellenic world which returned to favour in the mid nineties (Régnier changed 'Élaine', the heroine of his poem 'Le Salut à l'Étrangère', to 'Hélène' as early as 1890); or for the modern world celebrated by the *naturistes.*

So the Symbolist Middle Ages perished (although it bequeathed some of its substance to the twentieth century — to Péguy and Claudel, for instance; to Proust; and to some post-Symbolist poets); but this is not the end of the story. After the Dreyfus case the Middle Ages were once again — as in 1851 and 1870 — enlisted in the cause of the nation's moral regeneration: the various political groups which came into being at this time (Péguy's *Cahiers de la quinzaine* group, Mithouard's *Occident* group, Maurras's *Action française*) all took a fervent interest in them, each setting them in its individual version of the true French tradition. They continued on their never-ending journey; but consideration of the post-Dreyfus phase would be outside the limits of this study.

[486] Ibid. p. 73.
[487] Saint-Pol-Roux, *Les Reposoirs de la procession* (III). 1907, pp. 15-19.

CONCLUSION

The main conclusion to be drawn from this study is that it has little to do with the Middle Ages themselves, and everything to do with the preoccupations of the nineteenth century. For the men of this century each fashioned, out of their hopes and fears for the modern world, a private vision of the medieval past — did not Fustel de Coulanges go as far as to say in 1871 that on these 'moyens âges imaginaires' the very fate of the nation depended? —, and their favourite question, before they approached any present problem, was 'Que trouvons-nous au moyen âge?'

What *did* they find in the Middle Ages? Everything and anything that they wished to find. Some, dismayed by rapid change and a sense of irrecoverable loss, sought reassurance and consolation in the vision of a stable order of things, steeped in Gothic tranquillity; while others, dissatisfied with a mundane, monotonous present, sought fresh stimulus for their jaded sensibilities in dreams of bygone ferocity, 'un passé hanté de mystères mauvais'. After the Romantics' universal delight in pictures-que disorder, we have seen a new generation seek order and authority in the Middle Ages (Veuillot), or sanguinary passion (Barbey d'Aurevilly), or the triumph of rationality (Viollet-le-Duc), or 'les charmes de l'horreur' (Baudelaire) — and a still later generation seek in them 'haute théologie et solide morale' (Verlaine), or 'des mystères révoltants' (Rimbaud), or 'des tristesses transies' (Maeterlinck), or '[des] trépidations folles et rouges' (Verhaeren). We have seen the Romantic Middle Ages, 'l'âge de la féerie et des enchantements' (Chateaubriand), 'bourdonnement dans les oreilles, éblouissement dans les yeux' (Hugo), 'monde de poésie en ce monde de prose' (Gautier), give way to its Second Empire successor, 'temps dur, temps maudit, et gros de désespoir' (Michelet), 'un monde qui se meurt' (Quinet), 'hideux siècles de foi, de lèpre et de famine' (Leconte de Lisle) — which in turn is replaced by 'le beau moyen âge qui vous prend aux entrailles' of the 1880s and 90s, 'l'époque où nous vécûmes le plus près de Dieu' (Huysmans), 'ces âges si péremptoirement défunts' (Aurier), 'l'unique été des coeurs' (Maeterlinck). We have seen the countless metamorphoses undergone by 'nos pères' in the course of the century: the pre-Romantic faithful troubadours who kept their word in love, the 'héros chrétiens' and *preux sans peur et sans reproche* of Chateaubriand and the early Hugo (converted by the government of 1851 into 'les preux nouveaux' of the Crimea), Michelet's anguished serfs shedding bitter tears into the field of toil, Renan's 'lourds badauds, laids de costume et de figure', Taine's 'bêtes féroces' and 'brutes féodales', the later Hugo's 'chevaliers errants' confronting 'les rois vautours et les princes de proie', Montalembert's valiant monks, 'champions du droit et de la vérité', Leconte de Lisle's demented ones, 'bouchers tondus' and 'loups sanglants', his crusading 'horde carnassière' (converted in 1870 into the Prussian armies advancing upon Paris) – and, lastly, the creatures of the *fin de siècle* imagination, smouldering with perverse passion – Huysmans's Gilles de Rais, Mikhaël's 'étrange Évêque', Schwob's cruel children – and the passionless, crepuscular beings thronging the pages of Symbolist verse: palely loitering knights who have let fall both sword and shield, 'bannerets lassés que nul espoir ne tente', 'princesses de songe et de sagesse', 'Dames des lys languissants et fanés'.

What Flaubert called 'le frisson historique' was experienced with equal force by each succeeding generation of the nineteenth century; but its effect was different upon each: the Romantics wandered among the ruined edifices of their forefathers, and were visited by visions of the 'magnificence of yore', while the age of positivism, whose watchword was 'rendons-nous le passé présent', set about restoring ruins, measuring twelfth-century crania to gauge its ancestors' cerebral development, and scrutinizing the faces of medieval statues in order to find concrete evidence of suffering caused by feudal oppression – and the idealistic generation of the century's last two decades worshipped the past *'en tant que passé'*, returned to the enraptured contemplation of ruins, and set up in their theatres 'un décor de jadis et de songe' to suggest their evanescent vision of 'ce qui fut peut-être'. When the men of the fifties and sixties recreated the Middle Ages in their writing, it was more often than not the state of the Second Empire which they were in fact describing; for the men of the eighties and nineties, it was the state of their own soul which took on a medieval guise. The former consoled themselves with visions of a future *débâcle,* borrowed from the past: Michelet's cathedral melting in the sea of tears shed by the oppressed, Quinet's tomb walls of Merlin's prison collapsing, Taine's 'moyen âge sombrant sous ses vices', Hugo's dissolution of the tyrant Othon's hideous kingdom. The latter, 'une génération de vaincus' who had grown up 'sous le signe de la Défaite', were haunted by visions of feudal desolation, defeated armies, and defaced escutcheons, seeing themselves as 'doux vassaux du Destin qui les broie', and their state of mind as 'une peine immense et féodale'.

Visions of the Middle Ages, then, abound in writing of the French nineteenth century; and in their extraordinary diversity they reflect the richness and vitality of the age which produced them. The most memorable are the most subjective ones — that is when the subject is a great writer: Michelet's above-mentioned melting cathedral, Hugo's vision of the orgy in the citadel captured by Ratbert —

> Le drapeau de l'empire, arboré sur ce bruit,
> Gonfle son aigle immense au souffle de la nuit —,

Baudelaire's vision of his contemporaries swept along in 'le branle universel de la danse macabre', Flaubert's Saint Julien in a world at first radiant and then invaded by total desolation, Verlaine's 'chevalier Malheur' emerging from a mysterious Arthurian landscape. It was when they were inspired by the Middle Ages, in fact, — a theme whose roots went down so deep into the nineteenth-century consciousness, and which brought forth their secret reserves of tenderness and ferocity — that many of these writers were most fully themselves.

SELECT BIBLIOGRAPHY

Place of publication Paris, except where otherwise stated.

Primary Sources

Adam, Paul, *Les Volontés merveilleuses: Être,* Librairie illustrée (1891).
Ampère, J-J., *Littérature, voyages et poésies,* 2 vols., ii, Didier, 1850.
Ampère, J-J., *Mélanges d'histoire littéraire et de littérature,* 2 vols., i, Lévy, 1867.
Aroux, E., *Les Mystères de la chevalerie et de l'amour platonique au moyen âge,* Renouard, 1858.
Aurier, G.-Albert, 'Le Livret de l'imagier: Frontispice', *MF* iv (Feb. 1892), pp. 168-9.
Aurier, G.-Albert, *Oeuvres posthumes,* Mercure de France, 1893.
Autran, J., *La Légende des paladins* (1875), in *Oeuvres complètes,* v, Lévy, 1877.
Banville, T. de, *Les Stalactites* (1846), Lemerre, 1873.
Banville, T. de, *Le Sang de la coupe. Trente-six Ballades joyeuses,* Lemerre, n.d.
Banville, T. de, 'Le Salon de 1861', *Revue fantaisiste,* ii, 15 May 1861, pp. 38-51.
Banville, T. de, *Gringoire,* Lévy, 1866.
Banville, T. de, *Idylles prussiennes (1870-1871),* Lemerre, 1872.
Banville, T. de, *Mes Souvenirs,* Charpentier, 1882.
Banville, T. de, *Les Exilés. Les Princesses,* Lemerre, 1890.
Banville, T. de, *Critiques,* ed. V. Barrucand, Fasquelle, 1917.
Barbey d'Aurevilly, J., *Les Prophètes du passé* (1851), 3rd edn., Palmé, 1880.
Barbey d'Aurevilly, J., *L'Ensorcelée* (1852), Garnier-Flammarion, 1966.
Barbey d'Aurevilly, J., *Les Philosophes et les écrivains religieux,* Amyot, 1860.
Barbey d'Aurevilly, J., *Les Historiens politiques et littéraires,* Amyot, 1861.
Barbey d'Aurevilly, J., *Les Poètes,* Amyot, 1862.
Barbey d'Aurevilly, J., *Les Ridicules du temps,* Rouveyre & Blond, 1883.
Barbey d'Aurevilly, J., *Les Critiques, ou les juges jugés,* Frinzine, 1885.
Barbey d'Aurevilly, J., *Sensations d'histoire,* Frinzine, 1887.
Barbey d'Aurevilly, J., *Les Historiens,* Quantin, 1888.

Barbey d'Aurevilly, J., *Les Poètes*, Lemerre, 1889.

Barbey d'Aurevilly, J., *Littérature étrangère*, Lemerre, 1890.

Barbey d'Aurevilly, J., *De l'histoire*, Lemerre, 1905.

Barbey d'Aurevilly, J., *Disjecta membra*, 2 vols., La Connaissance, 1925.

Barbey d'Aurevilly, J., *Lettres à Trébutien*, 4 vols., Bernouard, 1927.

Barbier, Jules, *Jeanne d'Arc*, Lévy, 1874.

Barbier, Jules, *La Gerbe: Poésies, 1842-1883*, Lemerre, 1884.

Bard, Joseph, *Les Mélancoliques*, Renduel, 1832.

Bataille, Henry, *La Chambre blanche*, Mercure de France, 1895.

Bataille, Henry, *Théâtre complet*, i, Flammarion, 1922.

Baudelaire, Ch., *Oeuvres complètes*, Pléiade, 1961.

Beauvoir, Roger de, *L'Écolier de Cluny*, 2nd edn., 2 vols., Fournier, 1832.

Belmontet, L., *Poésies guerrières*, Imprimerie Impériale, 1858.

Bernard, Thalès, *Adorations*, Krabbe, 1855.

Bernard, Thalès, *Lettres sur la poésie*, Vanier (1857).

Bernard, Thalès, *Poésies mystiques*, Vanier, 1858.

Bernard, Thalès, *Mélodies pastorales*, Taride, 3me livraison, 1860; 5me livraison, 1868; 7me livraison, 1869.

Bernard, Thalès, Preface to A. Millien, *La Moisson*, Vanier, 1860.

Bernard, Thalès, Preface to A. Millien, *Chants agrestes*, Dentu, 1862.

Bernard, Thalès, *Histoire de la poésie*, Dentu, 1864.

Bernard, Thalès, *Lettre sur la poésie*, privately printed, 1868.

Blémont, Émile, *Esthétique de la tradition*, Maisonneuve, 1890.

Bloy, Léon, *Le Désespéré* (1886), *Oeuvres*, edd. Bollery & Petit, iii, Mercure de France, 1964.

Bloy, Léon, *La Femme pauvre* (1897), Mercure de France, 1962.

Bloy, Léon, *Belluaires et porchers* (1905), *Oeuvres*, edd. Bollery & Petit, ii, 1964.

Bonaparte, Prince N-L., *Études sur le passé et l'avenir de l'artillerie*, ii, Dumaine, 1851.

Bonnemère, E., *Histoire des paysans*, 2 vols., i, Chamerot, 1856.

Bornier, H. de, *La Fille de Roland* (1875), London, Dent, 1930.

Bornier, H. de, 'L'Héroïsme au théâtre', *Le Correspondant*, cxcviii, 10 Feb. 1900, pp. 527-46.

Boulmier, Joseph, *Rimes chevaleresques*, privately printed, 1868.

Bourges, E., *Élémir Bourges, ou l'éloge de la grandeur: Correspondance inédite avec Armand Point*, ed. G. Marie, Mercure de France, 1962.

Broglie, A. de, 'Le Moyen Âge et l'Église catholique', *RDM* 1 Nov. 1852, pp. 409-45.

Brunetière, F., *Études critiques sur l'histoire de la littérature française*, première série, Hachette, 1880.

Calliat, V., *La Sainte-Chapelle de Paris, après les restaurations commencées par M. Duban . . . terminées par M. Lassus*, Bance, 1857.

Campaux, A., *François Villon, sa vie et ses oeuvres*, Durand, 1859.

Caumont, A. de, *Mes Souvenirs*, Caen, n.d.

Chassin, Ch.-L., 'Le Moyen Âge satirique', *Revue française*, xvi (1859), pp. 528-38.

Comte, Auguste, *Cours de philosophie positive*, v, Rouen frères, 1841.

Coppée F., *Poésies, 1864-1869*, Lemerre, 1873.

Coppée F., *Poésies, 1874-1878*, Lemerre, 1879.

Coppée F., *Poésies 1886-1890*, Lemerre, 1891.

Coppée F., *Dans la prière et dans la lutte*, Lemerre, 1901.

Coppée F., *Des vers français*, Lemerre, 1906.

Coppée F., *Souvenirs d'un parisien*, Lemerre, 1910.

Coppée, F., & d'Artois, A., *La Guerre de cent ans*, Lemerre, 1878.

Corblet, J., 'L'Architecture du moyen-âge jugée par les écrivains des deux derniers siècles', *Revue de l'art chrétien*, iii (1859), pp. 68-74, 97-103, 198-208, 201-6, 398-405, 540-4.

Crépet, E. (ed.), *Les Poëtes français*, 4 vols., i, Gide, 1861.

Cros, Charles, *Oeuvres complètes*, Pauvert, 1964.

Declareuil, J., *Prestiges*, Girard (1893).

Delécluze, E-J., *Roland, ou la Chevalerie*, 2 vols., Labitte, 1845.

Delécluze, E-J., *Souvenirs de soixante années*, Lévy, 1862.

Delvau, A. (ed.), *Bibliothèque bleue*, Lécrivain & Toubon, 1859-60.

Denis, Maurice, *Journal*, i, La Colombe, 1957.

Deschamps, Émile, *Oeuvres complètes*, 6 vols., i, Lemerre, 1872.

Des Essarts, E., 'François Villon', *L'Artiste*, 00, 1 Nov. 1859, pp. 106-8.

Des Gachons, A. & J. (edd.), *L'Album des légendes*, 2 vols., 1894-5.

Didron, A-N., *Paganisme dans l'art chrétien*, V. Didron, 1853.

Didron, A-N., 'Le Moyen Âge en Italie: les artistes', *Annales archéologiques*, xv (1855), pp. 112-21.

Dierx, L., *Aspirations*, Dentu, 1858.

Dierx, L., *Oeuvres complètes*, i, Lemerre, 1894.

Du Camp, Maxime, *Les Beaux-Arts à l'Exposition Universelle de 1855*, Librairie nouvelle, 1855.

Du Camp, Maxime, *Les Chants modernes*, Lévy, 1855.

Du Camp, Maxime, *Les Convictions*, Librairie nouvelle, 1858.

Du Camp, Maxime, *Souvenirs littéraires*, 2 vols., Hachette, 1882-3.

Du Camp, Maxime, *Souvenirs d'un demi-siècle*, 2 vols., Hachette, 1949.

Elskamp, Max, *Oeuvres complètes*, Édns. Seghers, 1967.

Erdan, A. (A-A. Jacob), *La France mystique* (1855), 2nd edn., 2 vols., Amsterdam, 1858.

Fellens, Ch., *La Féodalité, ou les droits du seigneur, événements mystérieux, lugubres, scandaleux . . .*, 2 vols., privately printed, 1850.

Flaubert, G., *Madame Bovary* (1856), Garnier, 1955.

Flaubert, G., *Trois Contes* (1877), Garmier, 1961.

Flaubert, G., *Bouvard et Pécuchet* (1881), Garnier, 1965.

Flaubert, G., *Correspondance*, 9 vols., Conard, 1926-33.

Flaubert, G., *Correspondance: Supplément*, 4 vols., Conard, 1954.

Flaubert, G., *Oeuvres complètes*, 2 vols., Édns. du Seuil, 1964.

Fontainas, A., *Crépuscules. Les Vergers illusoires. Nuit d'épiphanies. Les Estuaires d'ombre. Idylles et élégies. L'Eau du fleuve*, Mercure de France, 1897.

Fontanes, L-J-P., *Oeuvres*, 2 vols., i, Hachette, 1839.

Franay, Gabriel (Mme L. Quioc), *Mon Chevalier*, A. Colin, 1893.

France, Anatole, *Poésies*, Lemerre, n.d.

France, Anatole, *Oeuvres complètes illustrées*, 26 vols., Calmann-Lévy, 1925-37.

Fustel de Coulanges, 'La justice royale au moyen âge', *RDM* 1 Aug. 1871, pp. 536-56.

Fustel de Coulanges, 'L'invasion germanique au Ve siècle', *RDM* 15 May 1872, pp. 241-68.

Fustel de Coulanges, 'De la manière d'écrire l'histoire en France et en Allemagne', *RDM* 1 Sept. 1872, pp. 241-51.

Fustel de Coulanges, *Histoire des institutions politiques de l'ancienne France*, i, Hachette, 1875.

Gagneur, Louise, *La Croisade noire*, A. Faure, 1865.

Garcin, E., 'Les Païens à travers les siècles', *Revue moderne,* liv (Sept.-Oct. 1869), pp. 5-38, 221-67, 498-523, 722-51.

Gasparin, A. de, *Le Christianisme au moyen âge: Innocent III*, Geneva, Cherbuliez, 1859.

Gaume, J-J., *Le Ver rongeur des sociétés modernes, ou le Paganisme dans l'éducation*, Gaume frères, 1851.

Gaume, J-J., *Lettre à M. le Rédacteur en chef de 'l'Univers'*, Autun (1851).

Gautier, Léon, *Comment faut-il juger le moyen âge?*, Palmé (1858).

Gautier, Léon, *Études historiques pour la défense de l'Église*, Blériot, 1864.

Gautier, Léon, *Études littéraires pour la défense de l'Église*, Poussielgue, 1865.

Gautier, Léon, *Les Épopées françaises*, 3 vols., Palmé, 1865-8.

Gautier, Léon, *Les Épopées françaises*, 2nd edn., 4 vols., Palmé, 1878-92.

Gautier, Léon, 'L'idée religieuse dans la poésie épique du Moyen Âge', *Revue du monde catholique*, xx, 10 Jan. 1868, pp. 224-65.

Gautier, Léon (ed.), *La Chanson de Roland*, 2 vols., i, Tours, Mame, 1872.

Gautier, Léon, *Vingt Nouveaux Portraits*, Palmé, 1878.

Gautier, Léon, *La Chevalerie*, Palmé, 1884.

Gautier, Léon, *Portraits du XIXe siècle*, 4 vols., Sanard & Derangeon, 1894-5.

Gautier, Théophile, *Les Jeunes-France* (1833), Charpentier, 1881.

Gautier, Théophile, *La Préface de 'Mademoiselle de Maupin'* (1835), ed. G. Matoré, Droz, 1946.

Gautier, Théophile, *Tra los montes,* 2 vols., i, V. Magen, 1843.

Gautier, Théophile, *Les Grotesques,* 2 vols., ii, Desessart, 1844.

Gautier, Théophile, *Les Beaux-Arts en Europe,* 2 vols., i, Lévy, 1855.

Gautier, Théophile, *L'Art moderne,* Lévy, 1856.

Gautier, Théophile, *Histoire de l'art dramatique en France depuis vingt-cinq ans,* 6 vols., Magnin & Blanchard, 1858-9.

Gautier, Théophile, *Loin de Paris,* Lévy, 1865.

Gautier, Théophile, *Histoire du romantisme* (1874), Charpentier, 1905.

Gautier, Théophile, *Portraits contemporains,* Charpentier, 1874.

Gautier, Théophile, *Souvenirs de théâtre, d'art et de critique,* Charpentier 1883.

Gautier, Théophile, *Poésies complètes,* ed. Jasinski, 2nd edn., 3 vols., Nizet, 1970.

Gebhart, E., 'La Vie réelle et la poésie chez les peuples d'Occident au moyen âge', *Revue des cours littéraires,* vii, 25 Dec. 1869, pp. 55-62.

Génin, F. (ed.), *La Chanson de Roland,* Imprimerie Nationale, 1850.

Gérardy, Paul, *Roseaux. Les Chansons naïves. Les Croix. Les Ballades naïves. Les Chansons du prince Lirelaire. A tous ceux de la ronde,* Mercure de France, 1898.

Ghil, René, *Oeuvres complètes,* 3 vols., Messein, 1938.

Glatigny, A., *Poésies,* Lemerre, 1870.

Glatigny, A., *Le Testament de l'illustre Brizacier,* Édns. de la Revue théâtrale, 1906.

Gobineau, A. de, *La Cour d'amour,* ed. R. Béziau, *MF* (Feb. 1963), pp. 260-99.

Goncourt, E. & J. de, *Journal,* 4 vols., ed. R. Ricatte, Fasquelle & Flammarion, 1956.

Gourmont, Remy de, 'La Béatrice de Dante et l'idéal feminin en Italie à la fin du XIIIe siècle', *Revue du monde latin,* vi (June-July-Aug. 1885), pp. 174-90, 286-96, 442-51.

Gourmont, Remy de, *Sixtine, roman de la vie cérébrale,* Savine, 1890.

Gourmont, Remy de, 'Notes sur Huysmans: *Là-bas* et ailleurs', *MF* ii (June 1891), pp. 321-5.

Gourmont, Remy de, *Le Latin mystique,* 2nd edn., Mercure de France, 1892.

Gourmont, Remy de, *Théodat,* Mercure de France, 1893.

Gourmont, Remy de, *Le Pèlerin du silence,* Mercure de France, 1896.

Gourmont, Remy de, *Le Livre des masques,* Mercure de France, 1896.

Gourmont, Remy de, *Le Deuxième Livre des masques,* Mercure de France, 1898.

Gourmont, Remy de, *Le Vieux Roi,* Mercure de France, 1897.

Gourmont, Remy de, *Promenades littéraires,* 7 vols., Mercure de France, 1904-27.

Gourmont, Remy de, *Divertissements,* Crès, 1912.

Guerne, Vicomte de, *Les Siècles morts,* iii, *L'Orient chrétien,* Lemerre, 1897.

Guizot, F-P-G., *Histoire de la civilisation en France,* 5 vols., Pichon & Didier, 1829-32.

Heine, H., *De l'Allemagne,* 2 vols., Renduel, 1835.

Heine, H., 'Les Dieux en exil', *RDM* 1 Apr. 1853, pp. 5-38.

Heine, H., *Lutèce,* Lévy, 1855.

Heine, H., *Poëmes et légendes,* Lévy, 1855.

Hennique, L., *Amour,* Tresse & Stock, 1890.

d'Héricault, Ch., *Souvenirs et portraits,* Téqui, 1902.

d'Héricault, Ch., & Montaiglon, A. de (edd.), *Oeuvres complètes de Gringoire,* 2 vols., i, Jannet, 1858.

Hérold, A-F., *Chevaleries sentimentales,* Librairie de l'art indépendant, 1893.

Hérold, A-F., *Images tendres et merveilleuses,* Mercure de France, 1897.

Hérold, A-F., *Au hasard des chemins,* Mercure de France, 1900.

Hirsch, Ch.-H., *Légendes naïves,* Girard, 1894.

Hugo, Victor, *La Préface de 'Cromwell'* (1827), ed. M. Souriau, 1897.

Hugo, Victor, *Notre-Dame de Paris* (1831), Garnier, 1959.

Hugo, Victor, *Napoléon le Petit* (1852), Pauvert, 1964.

Hugo, Victor, *La Légende des siècles. La Fin de Satan. Dieu,* Pléiade, 1950.

Hugo, Victor, *Promontorium somnii,* edd. Journet & Robert, Les Belles Lettres, 1961.

Hugo, Victor, *William Shakespeare* (1864), Édn. de l'Imprimerie Nationale, 1937.

Hugo, Victor, *Dieu* (*Le Seuil du gouffre*), edd. Journet & Robert, Nizet, 1961.

Hugo, Victor, *L'Âne,* ed. P. Albouy, Flammarion, 1966.

Hugo, Victor, *Oeuvres poétiques,* 2 vols., Pléiade, 1964-7.

Hugo, Victor, *Oeuvres complètes,* édition chronologique, ed. J. Massin, 18 vols., Club Français du Livre, 1967-70.

Huysmans, J-K., *À Rebours* (1884), Fasquelle, 1965.

Huysmans, J-K., *Là-bas,* Tresse & Stock, 1891.

Huysmans, J-K., *En route,* Tresse & Stock, 1895.

Huysmans, J-K., *La Cathédrale,* Tresse & Stock, 1898.

Huysmans, J-K., *De tout,* Stock, 1902.

Huysmans, J-K., *Certains* (1889), 4th edn., Stock, 1904.

Huysmans, J-K., *En marge: Études et préfaces,* ed. L. Descaves, Lesage, 1927.

Huysmans, J-K., *'Là-haut', suivi du journal d"En route'*, edd. Cogny & Lambert, Casterman, 1965.

Huysmans, J-K., *Lettres inédites à Jules Destrée*, Droz & Minard, 1967.

Kahn, Gustave, *La Pluie et le beau temps*, Vanier, 1896.

Kahn, Gustave, *Premiers Poèmes*, Mercure de France, 1897.

Kahn, Gustave, *Limbes de lumières*, Brussels, Deman, 1897.

Kahn, Gustave, *Le Livre d'images*, Mercure de France, 1897.

Kahn, Gustave, *Le Conte de l'or et du silence*, Mercure de France, 1898.

Kahn, Gustave, *Symbolistes et décadents*, Vanier, 1902.

Klingsor, Tristan (Léon Leclère), *Triptyque des châtelaines*, Thulé (Annonay), 1892.

Klingsor, Tristan, *Triptyque à la Marguerite*, Thulé (Annonay), 1894.

Klingsor, Tristan, *Filles-fleurs*, Mercure de France, 1895.

Klingsor, Tristan, *Squelettes fleuris*, Mercure de France, 1897.

Klingsor, Tristan, *L'Escarpolette*, Mercure de France, 1899.

Kotzebue, A., *Souvenirs de Paris en 1804*, traduits de l'allemand, sur la deuxième édn., 2 vols., an XIII (1805).

Lacaussade, A., *Poésies*, i, Lemerre, 1896.

Lacroix, P., & Seré, F. (edd.), *Le Moyen-âge et la Renaissance*, 5 vols., 1848-51.

Lafagette, R., *Mélodies païennes*, A. Le Chevalier, 1873.

Laforgue, Jules, *Oeuvres complètes*, ii, *Poésies*, Mercure de France, 1922.

Laforgue, Jules, *Oeuvres complètes*, iii, *Moralités légendaires*, Mercure de France, 1924.

Lahor, J. (Henri Cazalis), *L'Illusion*, Lemerre, 1875.

Langlois, Ch.-V., 'À propos de l'enseignement de l'archéologie nationale', *Revue bleue*, xlviii, 7 Nov. 1891, pp. 596-9.

Langlois, E-H., *Essai historique, philosophie et pittoresque sur les danses des morts*, 2 vols., Rouen, 1851.

Laprade, V. de, *Le Sentiment de la nature chez les modernes*, Didier, 1868.

Laprade, V. de, *Oeuvres poétiques*, iii, *Poèmes civiques. Tribuns et courtisans*, Lemerre, n.d.

Laprade, V. de, *Oeuvres poétiques*, vi, *Les Voix du silence*, Lemerre, 1889.

Laprade, V. de, *Lettres inédites à Charles Alexandre, 1852-1871*, ed. P. Séchaud, Lyon, 1934.

La Sizeranne, R. de, *La Peinture anglaise contemporaine* (1895), Hachette, 1922.

Laurent-Pichat, L., *Chroniques rimées*, Librairie nouvelle, 1856.

Laurent-Pichat, L., *L'Art et les artistes en France*, Dubuisson (1859).

Laurent-Pichat, L., *Les Poètes du combat*, Jung-Treuttel, 1862.

Laurent-Pichat, L., 'Victor Hugo', *La Réforme littéraire*, 20 July 1862, pp. 2-3.

Laurent-Pichat, L., *Les Réveils*, Lemerre, 1880.

Lazare, Bernard, *Le Miroir des légendes*, Lemerre, 1892.

Lazare, Bernard, *Figures contemporaines*, Perrin, 1895.

Le Cardonnel, L., *Poèmes* (1904), 6th edn., Mercure de France, n.d.

Le Cardonnel, L., *Carmina sacra*, Mercure de France, 1912.

Leconte de Lisle, *Poèmes antiques*, Lemerre, n.d.

Leconte de Lisle, *Poèmes barbares*, Lemerre, n.d.

Leconte de Lisle, *Poèmes tragiques*, Lemerre, n.d.

Leconte de Lisle, *Derniers Poèmes*, Lemerre, n.d.

Leconte de Lisle, *Histoire populaire du Christianisme*, Lemerre, 1871.

Leconte de Lisle, *Histoire du moyen âge*, Lemerre, 1876.

Leconte de Lisle, *La Dernière Illusion de Leconte de Lisle: Lettres inédites à Émilie Leforestier*, ed. I. Putter, Droz, 1968.

Leconte de Lisle, *Articles, préfaces, discours*, ed. E. Pich, Soc. d'Édn. Les Belles Lettres, 1971.

Lecoy de la Marche, A., *Histoire de l'histoire*, Annecy, 1862.

Lefèvre, Andre, *La Flûte de Pan*, Dentu, 1861.

Lefèvre, Andre, *La Lyre intime*, Hetzel, 1864.

Lefèvre, Andre, *L'Épopée terrestre*, Marpon, 1868.

Lefèvre, Andre, *Religions et mythologies comparées*, Leroux, 1877.

Lefèvre, Andre, *L'Homme à travers les âges*, C. Reinwald, 1880.

Lemaître, Jules, *Les Contemporains*, i-vii, Lecène & Oudin, 1886-99.

Lenient, Ch., 'La Poésie patriotique en France', *Revue des cours littéraires*, vii, 15 Oct. 1870, pp. 721-8.

Lenient, Ch., *La Poésie patriotique en France au moyen âge*, Hachette, 1891.

Lenient, Ch., *La Poésie patriotique en France dans les temps modernes*, 2 vols., ii, Hachette, 1894.

Le Pas, A. & L., *Légendes des litanies de la Sainte Vierge*, Dentu, 1860.

Le Roy, Grégoire, *La Chanson du pauvre*, Mercure de France, 1907.

Littré, E., *Histoire de la langue française*, 2 vols., Didier, 1863.

Littré, E., *Études sur les barbares et le moyen âge*, Didier, 1867.

Littré, E., *Littérature et histoire*, Didier, 1875.

Lorrain (Jean) (P-A-M. Duval), *Le Sang des dieux* (1882), E. Joseph, 1920.

Lorrain (Jean), *La Forêt bleue*, Lemerre, 1883.

Lorrain (Jean), *Modernités*, Giraud, 1885.

Lorrain (Jean), *Théâtre*, Ollendorff, 1906.

(Lusse, de), *Recueil de romances historiques, tendres et burlesques*, 1767.

Maeterlinck, M., *'L'Ornement des noces spirituelles', de Ruysbroeck l'Admirable, traduit du flamand, et accompagné d'une introduction par Maurice Maeterlinck*, 2nd edn., Brussels, Lacomblez, 1891.

Maeterlinck, M., *Les Sept Princesses*, Brussels, Lacomblez, 1891.

Maeterlinck, M., *Le Trésor des humbles,* Mercure de France, 1896.

Maeterlinck, M., *Théâtre,* 3 vols., Brussels, Lacomblez, 1901-2.

Maeterlinck, M., *Bulles bleues, souvenirs heureux,* Monaco, Édns. du Rocher, 1948.

Maeterlinck, M., *Poésies complètes,* ed. J. Hanse, Brussels, La Renaissance du Livre, 1965.

Maillard, Léon, *Notes pour demain:* (1) *L'Imagier Andhré des Gachons,* La Plume, 1892.

Mallarmé, S., 'Variations sur un sujet: (III) Catholicisme', *Revue Blanche,* viii, 1 Apr, 1895, pp. 319-23.

Mallarmé, S., *Correspondance,* 3 vols., Gallimard, 1959-69.

Mallarmé, S., *Oeuvres complètes,* Pléiade, 1961.

Marchangy, L-A-F. de, *La Gaule poétique,* 8 vols., Chaumerot, 1813-17.

Martin, Henri, *Jeanne Darc,* Furne, 1857.

Martin, Henri, *Histoire de France,* 4th edn., iii, Furne, 1858.

Martin, Henri, *Études d'archéologie celtique,* Didier, 1872.

Mary-Lafon, J-B., *Fierabras, légende nationale,* Librairie nouvelle, 1857.

Mauclair, C., 'Notes sur un essai de dramaturgie symbolique', *Revue indépendante,* xxii (Mar. 1892), pp. 305-17.

Mauclair, C., *Éleusis, causeries sur la cité intérieure,* Perrin, 1894.

Mauclair, C., *Sonatines d'automne,* Perrin, 1895.

Mauclair, C., *L'Art en silence,* Ollendorff, 1901.

Mazel, H., 'Tendances religieuses de l'art contemporain', *L'Art,* li, 1 Aug. 1891, pp. 45-56.

Ménard, Louis, *Poëmes* (1855), 2nd edn., Charpentier, 1863.

Ménard, Louis, *Rêveries d'un païen mystique* (1876), A. Durel, 1909.

Ménard, Louis, *Lettres d'un mort: Opinions d'un païen sur la société moderne,* Librairie de l'Art Indépendant, 1895.

Ménard, L. & R., *Tableau historique des beaux-arts,* Didier, 1866.

Mendès, C., *Contes épiques,* Librairie des Bibliophiles, 1872.

Mendès, C., *La Légende du Parnasse contemporain,* Brussels, 1884.

Mendès, C., *Rapport à M. le Ministre de l'Instruction publique sur le mouvement poétique français de 1867 à 1900,* Imprimerie Nationale, 1902.

Mendès, C., *Théâtre en vers,* Fasquelle, 1908.

Méray, A., *Les Libres Prêcheurs, devanciers de Luther et de Rabelais,* A. Claudin, 1860.

Mérimée, P., *La Jaquerie* (1828), ed. P. Jourda, Champion, 1931.

Mérimée, P., *Histoire de Don Pèdre 1er* (1848), ed. G. Laplane, Didier, 1861.

Mérimée, P., *Portraits historiques et littéraires* (1874), ed. P. Jourda, Champion, 1928.

Mérimée, P., *Études sur les arts au moyen âge,* Lévy, 1875.

Mérimée, P., *Lettres à Viollet-le-Duc,* ed. P. Trahard, Champion, 1927.

Mérimée, P., *Correspondance générale,* ed. M. Parturier, 17 vols., première série (6 vols.), Le Divan, 1941-7; deuxième série (11 vols.), Toulouse, Privat, 1953-64.

Merrill, Stuart, 'Le Christ de Frère Sérapion', *La Basoche* (Aug. 1885), pp. 357-61.

Merrill, Stuart, *Poèmes, 1887-1897,* Mercure de France, 1897.

Merrill, Stuart, *Prose et vers,* Messein, 1925.

Michelet, Jules, *Introduction à l'histoire universelle* (1831), A. Colin, Bibiothèque de Cluny, 1962.

Michelet, Jules, *Histoire de France,* i-iii (1833-7), 2nd edn., Hachette, 1835-45; iv-vi, Hachette, 1840-4.

Michelet, Jules, *Cours professé au Collège de France, 1839,* ed. O. A. Haac, *RHLF,* liv (1954).

Michelet, Jules, *Le Peuple* (1846), ed. L. Refort, Didier, 1946.

Michelet, Jules, *Histoire de la Révolution française* (1847), 2 vols., Pléiade, 1961-2.

Michelet, Jules, *La Renaissance* (1855), 2nd edn., Chamerot, 1857.

Michelet, Jules, *La Sorcière* (1862), 2 vols., ed. L. Refort, Didier, 1952-6.

Michelet, Jules, *La Régence,* Chamerot, 1863.

Michelet, Jules, *Bible de l'humanité,* Chamerot, 1864.

Michelet, Jules, Preface to 1869 edn. of *Histoire de France,* in *Histoire de France,* i, Marpon & Flammarion, 1879.

Michelet, Jules, *Nos Fils,* Lacroix, Verbeockhoven, 1870.

Michelet, Jules, *La France devant l'Europe,* 2nd edn., Florence, Feb. 1871.

Michelet, Jules, *Histoire du XIXe siècle,* 3 vols., i, Germer-Baillière, 1872.

Michelet, Jules, *L'Étudiant* (Cours de 1847-8), Lévy, 1877.

Michelet, Jules, *Le Banquet, papiers intimes,* Lévy, 1879.

Michelet, Jules, *Ma Jeunesse,* ed. Mme Michelet, Lévy, 1884.

Michelet, Jules, *Lettres inédites à Alfred Dumesnil et à Eugène Noël,* ed. P. Sirven, P.U.F., 1924.

Michelet, Jules, *Journal,* ed. P. Viallaneix, 2 vols., Gallimard, 1959-62.

Michiels, A., *Histoire des idées littéraires en France au dix-neuvième siècle,* 2 vols., Renouard, 1842.

Mikhaël, Ephraïm, *Oeuvres,* Lemerre, 1890.

Mockel, A., *Chantefable un peu naïve,* Liège, 1891.

Mockel, A., *Propos de littérature,* Librairie de l'Art Indépendant, 1894.

Mockel, A., *Esthétique du symbolisme,* ed. M. Otten, Brussels, 1962.

Moland, Louis, 'Sur un projet d'anthologie classique du moyen-âge', *Revue de l'enseignement chrétien,* i (Nov. 1852), pp. 581-91.

Moland, Louis, *Origines littéraires de la France,* Didier, 1862.

Moland, L., & d'Héricault, Ch., *Nouvelles françoises en prose du XIIIe siècle,* Jannet, 1856.

Montalembert, Ch. de, *Histoire de sainte Élisabeth de Hongrie* (1836), 6th edn., Sagnier & Bray, 1854.

Montalembert, Ch. de, *Des intérêts catholiques au dix-neuvième siècle* (Nov. 1852), 3rd edn., Lecoffre, Dec. 1852.

Montalembert, Ch. de, *Les Moines d'Occident, depuis saint Benoît jusqu'à saint Bernard,* 7 vols., i, Lecoffre, 1860.

Montalembert, Ch. de, *Oeuvres,* i, *Discours, 1837-1844,* Lecoffre, 1860.

Montalembert, Ch. de, *Oeuvres,* vi, *Mélanges d'art et de littérature,* Lecoffre, 1861.

Montalembert, Ch. de, *Correspondance de Montalembert et de l'abbé Texier,* Firmin-Didot (1899).

Moréas, Jean, *Oeuvres,* i, Mercure de France, 1923.

Moréas, Jean, *Esquisses et souvenirs,* Mercure de France, 1908.

Moréas, Jean, *Cent soixante-treize lettres de Jean Moréas,* ed. R. Jouanny, Minard, 1968.

Morice, Ch., *La Littérature de tout à l'heure,* Perrin, 1889.

Mourey, G., *Passé le détroit,* Ollendorff, 1895.

Murger, Henry, *Scènes de la Bohême,* 2nd edn., Lévy, 1851.

Musset, A. de, *Poésies complètes,* Pléiade, 1962.

Nerval, Gérard de, *Oeuvres,* 2 vols., Pléiade, 1960.

Nerval, Gérard de, *Oeuvres complémentaires,* i, *La Vie des lettres,* ed. J. Richer, Minard, 1959.

Nisard, D., *Histoire de la littérature française,* 4 vols., i, Firmin-Didot, 1844.

Nodier, Charles, *Mélanges de littérature et de critique,* 2 vols., Raymond, 1820.

Nodier, Charles, *Poésies diverses,* Delangle, 1827.

Nodier, Charles, 'Du fantastique en littérature' (1830), *Oeuvres,* v, Renduel, 1832, pp. 69-112.

Noussanne, H. de, *Jasmin Robba,* Hetzel, 1894.

O'Neddy, Philothée (Théophile Dondey), *Feu et flamme* (1833), ed. M. Hervier, Soc. d'Édn. Les Belles-Lettres, 1926.

Paris, Gaston, *Histoire poétique de Charlemagne,* A. Franck, 1865.

Paris, Gaston, *La Poesie du moyen âge,* première série, Hachette, 1885.

(Paris, Paulin), *Apologie de l'école romantique,* Dentu, 1824.

Paris, Paulin, *Collège de France: Cours de langue et de littérature françaises du moyen âge, discours d'ouverture, 1er mars 1853,* Dupont, n.d.

Paris, Paulin, 'Variétés: la Chanson et le Mystère de Roland', *Polybiblion littéraire,* deuxième série, i (1875), pp. 526-31.

Péladan, J., *La Décadence latine, éthopée,* i, *Le Vice suprême* (1884), 13th edn., Chamuel, 1896.

Péladan, J., *La Décadence esthétique,* i, *L'Art ochlocratique, salons de 1882 et 1883,* C. Dalou, 1888.

Péladan, J., *Salon de la Rose+Croix: Règle et monitoire*, Dentu, 1891.

Péladan, J., *Amphithéâtre des sciences mortes, i, Comment on devient mage*, Chamuel, 1892.

Péladan, J., *La Queste du Graal, proses lyriques de l'éthopée*, au Salon de la Rose+Croix (1892).

Péladan, J., *Constitutions de la Rose+Croix: Le Temple et le Graal*, Tours, 1893.

Péladan, J., *L'Art idéaliste et mystique*, Chamuel, 1894.

Poictevin, F., *Presque*, Lemerre, 1891.

Poictevin, F., *Heures*, Lemerre, 1892.

Point, Armand, 'Primitifs et symbolistes', *L'Ermitage*, vi (July 1895), pp. 11-16.

Popelin, C., *Poésies complètes*, Charpentier, 1889.

Quatremère de Quincy, *Encyclopédie méthodique: Architecture*, i-ii, Panckouke, 1788-1820.

Quatremère de Quincy, *Dictionnaire historique d'architecture*, 2 vols., i, Le Clère, 1832.

Quicherat, J., *Aperçus nouveaux sur l'histoire de Jeanne d'Arc*, Renouard, 1850.

Quicherat, J., 'Cours d'archéologie française du moyen âge', *Journal général de l'instruction publique*, xxii, 21 May 1853, pp. 320-2.

Quillard, P., *La Lyre héroïque et dolente*, Mercure de France, 1897.

Quinet, E., *Ahasvérus* (1833), nouvelle édn., Au Comptoir des Imprimeurs Unis, 1843.

Quinet, E., *Oeuvres complètes*, ii, *Les Jésuites. L'Ultramontanisme*, Germer-Baillière, n.d.

Quinet, E., *Oeuvres complètes*, ix, *La Grèce moderne, Histoire de la poésie*, 4th edn., Hachette, n.d.

Quinet, E., *Oeuvres complètes*, xvi-xvii, *Merlin l'Enchanteur*, i-ii (1860), 4th edn., Hachette, n.d.

Quinet, E., *Oeuvres complètes*, xxiv, *Le Livre de l'exilé*, Hachette, 1882.

Quinet, E., *Oeuvres complètes*, xxvi, *L'Esprit nouveau* (1874), 5th edn., Hachette, n.d.

Quinet, E., *Histoire de mes idées*, Germer-Baillière, n.d.

Quinet, E., *Oeuvres complètes*, xxix-xxx, *Lettres à sa mère*, Hachette, n.d.

Quinet, E., *Lettres d'exil à Michelet et à divers amis*, 4 vols., Lévy, 1885-6.

Radcliffe, Anne, *La Forêt, ou l'Abbaye de Saint-Clair* (*The Romance of the Forest*, 1791), 3 vols., Lecointe & Pougin, 1830-1.

Rambosson, Y., *Le Verger doré*, Mercure de France, 1895.

Recueil de rapports sur l'état des lettres et les progrès des sciences en France: Progrès des études classiques et du moyen âge, Imprimerie Impériale, 1868.

Réforme de l'enseignement: Recueil des lois, décrets, arrêtés, instructions, circulaires, et notes ministérielles concernant les modifications apportées à l'instruction publique pendant le ministère de M. H. Fortoul, 2 vols., Delalain, 1856.

Régnier, H. de, *Poèmes, 1887-1892,* 3rd edn., Mercure de France, 1897.

Régnier, H. de, *Premiers Poèmes. Les Lendemains. Apaisement. Sites. Épisodes. Poésies diverses,* Mercure de France, 1899.

Régnier, H., *La Canne de jaspe,* 3rd edn., Mercure de France, 1897.

Régnier, H., *Figures et caractères,* Mercure de France, 1901.

Renan, E., *Oeuvres complètes,* 10 vols., ed. H. Psichari, Calmann-Lévy, 1947-61.

Renaud, Armand, *Les Poèmes de l'amour,* Librairie nouvelle, 1860.

Retté, A., *Cloches en la nuit,* Vanier, 1889.

Retté, A., *Thulé des brumes,* Bibliothèque artistique et littéraire, 1891.

Retté, A., *Une Belle Dame passa,* Vanier, 1893.

Retté, A., *Aspects,* Bibliothèque artistique et littéraire, 1897.

Reybaud, L., *Jérôme Paturot à la recherche d'une position sociale et politique,* ii-iii, Paulin, 1843.

Ricard, L-X. de, *Ciel, rue et foyer,* Lemerre, 1866.

Ricard, L-X. de, 'Le Parnasse et les parnassiens', *Revue indépendante,* xxiii (June 1892), pp. 324-35.

Ricard, L-X. de, *Petits Mémoires d'un parnassien,* ed. M. Pakenham, Minard, 1967.

Rimbaud, A., *Oeuvres,* ed. S. Bernard, Garnier, 1960.

Rodenbach, G., *L'Art en exil,* Librairie moderne, 1889.

Rodenbach, G., *Bruges-la-Morte,* Flammarion (1892).

Rodenbach, G., *La Vocation,* Ollendorff, 1895.

Rodenbach, G., *Le Carillonneur,* Fasquelle, 1897.

Rodenbach, G., *L'Élite,* Fasquelle, 1899.

Rodenbach, G., *Oeuvres,* 2 vols. Mercure de France, 1923-5.

Rodenbach, G., *Évocations,* Brussels, La Renaissance du Livre, 1924.

Romieu, A., *Le Spectre rouge de 1852,* Ledoyen, 1851.

Rostand, E., *La Princesse lointaine* (1895), Fasquelle, 1901.

Sainte-Beuve, C-A., 'Espoir et voeu du mouvement littéraire et poétique après la Révolution de 1830' (1830), *Oeuvres,* i, Pléiade, 1949, pp. 369-77.

Sainte-Beuve, C-A., *Ancienne Littérature (Partie médiévale): Cours professé à l'Université de Liège, 1848-9,* Soc. d'Édn. Les Belles Lettres, 1971.

Sainte-Beuve, C-A., *Causeries du lundi,* 3rd edn., 15 vols., Garnier, 1857-70.

Sainte-Beuve, C-A., *Nouveaux lundis,* 13 vols., Levy, 1863-70.

Sainte-Palaye, La Curne de, *Mémoires sur l'ancienne chevalerie,* ed. Ch. Nodier, 2 vols., Girard, 1826.

Saint-Pol-Roux, *L'Âme noire du prieur blanc, naïve légende*, Mercure de France, 1893.

Saint-Pol-Roux, *Épilogue des saisons humaines*, Mercure de France, 1893.

Saint-Pol-Roux, *La Dame à la faulx*, Mercure de France, 1899.

Saint-Pol-Roux, *Les Reposoirs de la procession*, iii, *Les Féeries intérieures, 1885-1906*, Mercure de France, 1907.

Saint-Valry, A-S., *La Chapelle de Notre-Dame-du-Chêne. Les Ruines de Montfort-l'Amaury*, Ladvocat, 1826.

Samain, A., *Au jardin de l'infante* (1893), 117th edn., Mercure de France, 1922.

Samain, A., *Des lettres, 1887-1900*, Mercure de France, 1933.

Schuré, E., *Histoire du lied* (1868), 2nd edn., Sandoz & Fischbacher, 1876.

Schuré, E., *Les Grandes Légendes de France*, Perrin, 1892.

Schwob, M., *Coeur double*, Ollendorff, 1891.

Schwob, M., *Le Roi au masque d'or*, Ollendorff, 1893.

Schwob, M., *Spicilège*, Mercure de France, 1896.

Schwob, M., *Vies imaginaires* (1896), 6th edn., Gallimard, 1957.

Schwob, M., *La Lampe de Psyché*, Mercure de France, 1903.

Silvestre, A., *Rimes neuves et vieilles*, Dentu, 1866.

Silvestre, A., *Au pays des souvenirs*, Librairie illustrée (1892).

Silvestre, A., *Tristan de Léonois*, Fasquelle, 1897.

Silvestre, A. & E. Morand, *Grisélidis, mystère*, E. Kolb, 1891.

Sismondi, J-C-L. Simonde de, *Histoire des républiques italiennes du moyen âge*, i (1807), Nicolle, 1809.

Sismondi, J-C-L. Simonde de, *De la littérature du midi de l'Europe*, 4 vols., Treuttel & Würtz, 1813.

Souza, R. de, *La Poésie populaire et le lyrisme sentimental*, Mercure de France, 1899.

Staël, Mme de, *De la littérature considérée dans ses rapports avec les institutions sociales* (1800), 2 vols., 1812.

Staël, Mme de, *De l'Allemagne* (1810), 4th edn., 4 vols., Nicolle, 1818.

Stern, Daniel (Comtesse d'Agoult), *Florence et Turin*, Lévy, 1862.

Tailhade, L., *Imbéciles et gredins*, Édn. de la Maison d'Art, 1900.

Tailhade, L., *Poèmes aristophanesques*, Mercure de France, 1904.

Tailhade, L., *Poèmes élégiaques*, Mercure de France, 1907.

Tailhade, L., *Plâtres et marbres*, Figuière, 1913.

Tailhade, L., *Lettres à sa mère*, Van den Berg & Enlart, 1926.

Taine, H., 'De l'esprit francais importé en Angleterre: Littérature des Normands', *Revue de l'instruction publique*, xv, 28 Feb. 1856, pp. 655-8.

Taine, H., *Essais de critique et d'histoire* (1858), 2nd edn., Hachette, 1866.

Taine, H., *Histoire de la littérature anglaise* (1864), i; iv, 2nd edn., Hachette, 1866.

Taine, H., *Nouveaux Essais de critique et d'histoire* (1865), 2nd edn., Hachette, 1866.

Taine, H., *Philosophie de l'art*, Germer-Baillière, 1865.

Taine, H., *Voyage en Italie* (1866), 2 vols., Julliard, 1965.

Taine, H., *De l'idéal dans l'art*, Germer-Baillière, 1867.

Taine, H., *Notes sur Paris: Vie et opinions de M. Frédéric-Thomas Graindorge*, Hachette, 1867.

Taine, H., *Philosophie de l'art en Grèce* (1869), 2nd edn., Germer-Baillière, 1882.

Taine, H., *Les Origines de la France contemporaine*, i, *L'Ancien Régime*, Hachette, 1876.

Taine, H., *Derniers Essais de critique et d'histoire*, Hachette, 1894.

Taine, H., *Carnets de voyage: Notes sur la province, 1863-1865*, Hachette, 1897.

Taine, H., *H. Taine, sa vie et sa correspondance*, 4 vols., Hachette, 1902-7.

Valéry, Paul, *Lettres à quelques-uns*, Gallimard, 1952.

Valéry, Paul, *André Gide – Paul Valéry: Correspondance, 1890-1942*, Gallimard, 1955.

Valéry, Paul, *Paul Valéry – Gustave Fourment: Correspondance, 1887-1933*, Gallimard, 1957.

Verhaeren, E., *Poèmes*, 3 vols., Mercure de France, 1895-8.

Verhaeren, E., *Impressions*, i, Mercure de France, 1926.

Verlaine, P., *Sagesse*, ed. V. P. Underwood, London, Zwemmer, 1944.

Verlaine, P., *Oeuvres poétiques complètes*, Pléiade, 1962.

Verlaine, P., *Correspondance*, ed. Van Bever, 3 vols., Messein, 1922-9.

Veuillot, L., *Oeuvres diverses*, vi, *Le Droit du seigneur* (1854), Lethielleux, 1925.

Veuillot, L., *Oeuvres diverses*, viii, *Çà et là* (1860), Lethielleux, 1926.

Veuillot, L., *Oeuvres diverses*, xi, *Les Odeurs de Paris* (1867), Lethielleux, 1926.

Veuillot, L., *Mélanges*, v, *1851-1853*, Lethielleux, 1934.

Veuillot, L., *Mélanges*, vi, *1854-1856*, Lethielleux, 1935.

Veuillot, L., *Correspondance*, ed. F. Veuillot, 12 vols., Lethielleux, 1931-2.

Vielé-Griffin, F., *Oeuvres*, i-ii, Mercure de France, 1924-6.

Vigny, A., *Oeuvres complètes*, i, Pléiade, 1948.

Villemain, A-F., *Tableau de la littérature du moyen âge*, rev. edn., ii, Didier, 1855.

Villiers de l'Isle-Adam, *Contes cruels. Nouveaux Contes cruels*, ed. P-G. Castex, Garnier, 1968.

Villiers de l'Isle-Adam, *Axël,* La Colombe, 1960.

Viollet-le-Duc, E-E., *Dictionnaire raisonné de l'architecture française du XIe au XVIe siècle,* 10 vols., Bance & Morel, 1854-68.

Viollet-le-Duc, E-E., *Dictionnaire raisonné du mobilier français, de l'époque carlovingienne à la Renaissance,* 6 vols., Bance, 1858.

Viollet-le-Duc, E-E., *Description du château de Pierrefonds,* Bance, 1857.

Viollet-le-Duc, E-E., *Entretiens sur l'architecture,* 2 vols., Morel, 1863-72.

Viollet-le-Duc, E-E., *Lettres inédites,* Librairies-Imprimeries réunies, 1902.

Vitet, Ludovic, *Essais historiques et littéraires,* Lévy, 1862.

Wyzewa, T. de, *Nos Maîtres,* Perrin, 1895.

Zola, E., *Le Rêve* (1888), *Oeuvres complètes,* ed. H. Mitterand, v, Cercle du Livre précieux, 1967.

Secondary Sources

Ahlstrom, A., *Le Moyen Âge dans l'oeuvre d'Anatole France,* Soc. d'Édn. Les Belles Lettres, 1930.

Albert, Maurice (ed.), *Un Homme de lettres sous l'Empire et la Restauration* (*Edmond Géraud*), Flammarion (1893).

Albouy, P., *La Création mythologique chez Victor Hugo,* Corti, 1963.

Aquarone, S., *The Life and Works of Émile Littré,* Leyden, 1958.

Arnould, E-J., 'Taine et le moyen âge anglais', *RLC* xvi (1936), pp. 494-520.

Aubert, Marcel, 'Le Romantisme et le moyen âge', in *Le Romantisme et l'art,* H. Laurens, 1928.

Bac, F., *Mérimée inconnu,* Hachette (1939).

Baldensperger, F., 'Le "Genre Troubadour"', and 'La "Lénore" de Bürger dans la littérature française', in *Études d'histoire littéraire,* première série, Hachette, 1907.

Baldensperger, F., *La Littérature,* Flammarion, 1913.

Baldensperger, F., 'La Grande Communion romantique de 1827: Sous le signe de Walter Scott', *RLC* vii (1927), pp.47-86.

Baldick, R., *The Life of J-K. Huysmans,* Oxford, Clarendon Press, 1955.

Barrington, M., *Blaye, Roland, Rudel, and the Lady of Tripoli,* Salisbury, Bennett Bros., 1953.

Barthes, R., *Michelet par lui-même,* Édns. du Seuil, 1965.

Barzun, J., 'Romantic Historiography as a Political Force in France', *Journal of the History of Ideas,* ii (June 1941), pp. 318-29.

Baschet, R., *E-J. Delécluze, témoin de son temps,* Boivin, 1942.

Bauer, H. F., *Les 'Ballades' de Victor Hugo: Leurs origines françaises et étrangères,* Champion, 1936.

Baussan, C., *Léon Gautier,* Lethielleux, 1944.

Bedner, J., *Le Rhin de Victor Hugo: Commentaires sur un récit de voyage,* Groningen, 1965.

Bénichou, P., *Nerval et la chanson folklorique,* Corti, 1970.

Bergerat, E., *Théophile Gautier: Entretiens, souvenirs, et correspondance,* Charpentier, 1879.

Berret, Paul, *Le Moyen Âge dans la 'Légende des siècles' de Victor Hugo,* Paulin, n.d.

Berret, Paul, *'La Légende des siècles' de Victor Hugo,* Mellottée, 1945.

Béziau, R., *'La Cour d'amour,* dernière nouvelle de Gobineau', *RHLF* lxiii (Oct. -Dec. 1963), pp. 652-63.

Béziau, R., 'Une Opinion inédite sur les cours d'amour: *La Cour d'amour* de Gobineau', *Revue des sciences humaines,* xxix (Jan.-Mar. 1964), pp. 67-78.

Biré, E., *Victor de Laprade, sa vie et ses oeuvres,* Perrin (1886).

Block, H. M., *Mallarmé and the Symbolist Drama,* Detroit, 1963.

Bornecque, J-H., *Les 'Poèmes saturniens' de Paul Verlaine,* Nizet, 1967.

Bowden, M. M., *Tennyson in France,* Manchester, 1930.

Butler, J. D., *Jean Moréas: A critique of his poetry and philosophy,* The Hague, Mouton, 1967.

Byvanck, W. G. C., *Un Hollandais à Paris en 1891: Sensations de littérature et d'art,* Perrin, 1892.

Camus-Clavier, M-L., *Le Poète Léon Dierx,* P.U.F., 1942.

Carré, J-M., *Michelet et son temps,* Perrin, 1926.

Carter, A. E., *The Idea of Decadence in French Literature, 1830-1900,* Toronto, University of Toronto Press, 1958.

Cassagne, A., *La Théorie de l'art pour l'art en France, chez les derniers romantiques et les premiers réalistes,* Hachette, 1906.

Castex, P., & J. Bollery, *Contes cruels: Étude historique et littéraire,* Corti, 1956.

Champagne, P., *Essai sur Albert Mockel,* Champion, 1922.

Champion, P., *Marcel Schwob et son temps,* Grasset, 1927.

Chevrillon, A., *Taine, formation de sa pensée,* Plon, 1932.

Clarac, P., 'Un Chapitre des *Frères Karamazov* et les "Raisons du Saint-Père" de Leconte de Lisle', *RLC* vi, 1926, pp. 512-17.

Cohen, G., *Auguste Comte et sa conception du moyen âge,* Brussels, 1934.

Commémoration de Stuart Merrill à Versailles, 23 juin 1929, Mercure de France, 1930.

Cons, L., *État présent des études sur Villon,* Soc. d'Édn. Les Belles Lettres, 1936.

Cornell, W. K., *Adolphe Retté,* New Haven, Conn., Yale University Press, & London, O.U.P., 1942.

Coulon, M., 'Le Symbolisme d'Ephraïm Mikhaël', *MF* ci, 1 Feb. 1913, pp. 476-500.

Cuénot, C., *Le Style de Paul Verlaine,* Centre de documentation universitaire, 1963.

Davignon, H., *L'Amitié de Max Elskamp et d'Albert Mockel: Lettres inédites*, Brussels, 1955.

Décaudin, M., *La Crise des valeurs symbolistes, 1895-1914*, Toulouse, Privat, 1960.

Delord, Taxile, *Histoire du Second Empire, 1848-1869*, 6 vols., Germer-Baillière, 1869-75.

Doneux, Guy, *Maurice Maeterlinck*, Brussels, 1961.

Doolittle, Dorothy, *The Relations between Literature and Medieval Studies in France from 1820 to 1860*, Bryn Mawr, 1933.

Ducros, Jean, *Le Retour de la poésie française à l'antiquité grecque au milieu du XIXe siècle*, Champion, 1918.

Duméril, E., *Le Lied allemand et ses traductions poétiques en France*, Champion, 1933.

Durry, M-J., *Gérard de Nerval et le mythe*, Flammarion, 1956.

Edelman, N., *Attitudes of Seventeenth-century France toward the Middle Ages*, New York, 1946.

Edelman, N., 'La Vogue de François Villon en France de 1828 à 1873', *RHLF* xliii (1936), pp. 211-23, 321-39.

Estève, E., 'Le Moyen Âge dans la littérature du XVIIIe siècle', *Revue de l'Université de Bruxelles*, xxix (1923-4), pp. 353-82.

Fairlie, A., *Leconte de Lisle's Poems on the Barbarian Races*, Cambridge, Cambridge University Press, 1947.

Flottes, P., *Leconte de Lisle, l'homme et l'oeuvre*, Hatier-Boivin, 1954.

Frankl, Paul, *The Gothic: Literary Sources and Interpretations through Eight Centuries*, Princeton, N.J., 1960.

Fuchs, M., *Théodore de Banville*, Moulins (1912).

Galand, René, *L'Âme celtique de Renan*, P.U.F., 1959.

Gaudon, J., *Le Temps de la contemplation: L'Oeuvre poétique de Victor Hugo des 'Misères' au 'Seuil du gouffre'*, Flammarion, 1969.

Gautier, J-M., 'Le "Génie du Christianisme" est-il un de nos premiers "digests"?', *RHLF* xlviii (1948), pp. 211-22.

Gautier, J-M., 'Quelques aspects de l'archaïsme dans l'oeuvre de Chateaubriand', *FS* ii (1948), pp. 315-23.

Gengoux, J., *La Pensée poétique de Rimbaud*, Nizet, 1950.

Geninasca, J., Une Lecture de 'El Desdichado', *Archives des Lettres Modernes*, no. 59, 1965.

Girard, H., *Un Bourgeois Dilettante à l'époque romantique: Émile Deschamps, 1791-1871*, Champion, 1921.

Giraud, V., *Essai sur Taine, son oeuvre et son influence*, 4th edn., Hachette, 1909.

Gossman, L., *Medievalism and the Ideologies of the Enlightenment: The World and Work of La Curne de Sainte-Palaye*, Baltimore, Md., 1968.

Gout, Paul, *Viollet-le-Duc, sa vie, son oeuvre, sa doctrine*, Champion, 1914.

Griffiths, R., *The Reactionary Revolution: The Catholic Revival in French Literature, 1870-1914*, London, Constable, 1966.

Grodecki, L., *Le Château de Pierrefonds*, Caisse Nationale des Monuments Historiques, n.d.

Guichard, L., *La Musique et les lettres en France au temps du wagnérisme*, P.U.F., 1963.

Guiette, R., *Max Elskamp*, Poètes d'Aujourd'hui, Seghers, 1953.

Halbwachs, P., 'Le Poète de l'histoire: (1) Avant l'exil', in V. Hugo, *Oeuvres complètes*, ed. J. Massin, vii, Club Français du Livre, 1968, pp. i-xxxiii.

Halls, W. D., 'Some Aspects of the Relationship between Maeterlinck and Anglo-American Literature', *Annales de la Fondation Maurice Maeterlinck*, i (1955), pp. 9-25.

Halphen, L., *L'Histoire en France depuis cent ans*, A. Colin, 1914.

Hanse, J., 'De Ruysbroeck aux *Serres chaudes* de Maurice Maeterlinck', in *Le Centenaire de Maurice Maeterlinck (1862-1962)*, Brussels, Palais des Académies, 1964, pp. 75-129.

Hanse, J., & Vivier, R. (edd.), *Maurice Maeterlinck, 1862-1962*, Brussels, La Renaissance du Livre, 1962.

Hatfield, H., *Aesthetic Paganism in German Literature from Winckelmann to the Death of Goethe*, Cambridge, Mass., Harvard University Press, 1964.

Hautecoeur, L., *Littérature et peinture en France du XVIIe au XXe siècle*, A. Colin, 1942.

Henry, M-L., *La Contribution d'un Américain au symbolisme français: Stuart Merrill*, Champion, 1927.

Herlihy, J. F., *Catulle Mendès, critique dramatique et musical*, Lipschutz, 1936.

Hunt, H. J., *The Epic in Nineteenth-century France*, Oxford, Blackwell, 1941.

Huret, Jules, *Enquête sur l'évolution littéraire*, Charpentier, 1891.

Ibrovac, M., *José-Maria de Heredia: Sa Vie, son oeuvre*, Les Presses Universitaires, 1923.

Ibrovac, M., *José-Maria de Heredia: Les Sources des 'Trophées'*, Les Presses Universitaires, 1923.

Ireson, J. C., *L'Oeuvre poétique de Gustave Kahn*, Nizet, 1962.

Jacoubet, H., *Le Comte de Tressan et les origines du genre troubadour*, P.U.F., 1923.

Jacoubet, H., *Le Genre troubadour et les origines françaises du romantisme*, Soc. d'Édn. Les Belles-Lettres, 1929.

Jacoubet, H., 'Moyen Âge et romantisme', *Annales de l'Université de Grenoble*, xvi (1939), pp. 83-103.

Jasinski, R., *Les Années romantiques de Théophile Gautier*, Vuibert, 1929.

Jeanné, E., *L'Image de la Pucelle d'Orléans dans la littérature historique française depuis Voltaire*, Liège, 1935.

Jeanroy, A., 'Les Études sur la littérature française du moyen âge: (1) Du XVIe siècle à 1914', in *La Science Française*, ii, Larousse, 1933.

Job-Lazare (E. Kuhn), *Albert Glatigny, sa vie, son oeuvre*, 1878.

Jones, P. Mansell, *Verhaeren*, London, Bowes & Bowes, 1957.

Jouanny, R-A., *Jean Moréas, écrivain français*, Minard, 1969.

Jourda, P., 'L'Évolution de Moréas', *Revue des cours et conférences*, xxxvi, 30 Apr. & 15 May 1935, pp. 97-113, 215-26.

Jullian, C., *Extraits des historiens français du XIXe siècle*, 6th edn., Hachette, 1922.

Kerdyk, R., *André Fontainas*, Librairie de France, 1924.

Killen, A. M., *Le Roman terrifiant ou roman noir, de Walpole à Anne Radcliffe, et son influence sur la littérature française jusqu'en 1840*, 2nd edn., Champion, 1923.

Knowles, Dorothy, *La Réaction idéaliste au théâtre depuis 1890*, Droz, 1934.

Kolney, F., *Laurent Tailhade*, Édns. du Carnet Critique, 1922.

Kuhn, R., *The Return to Reality: a Study of Francis Vielé-Griffin*, Droz & Minard, 1962.

Kukenheim, L., & Roussel, H., *Guide de la littérature française du moyen âge*, 2nd edn., Leiden, 1959.

Lafenestre, G., *Les Primitifs à Bruges et à Paris, 1900-1902-1904*, Librairie de l'art ancien et moderne, 1904.

Lanson, René, *Le Goût du moyen âge en France au XVIIIe siècle*, Van Oest, 1926.

Larat, J., *La Tradition et l'exotisme dans l'oeuvre de Charles Nodier*, Champion, 1923.

Leblond, M-A., *Leconte de Lisle d'après des documents nouveaux*, Mercure de France, 1906.

Lecanuet, E., *Montalembert*, 3 vols., Poussielgue, 1895-1902.

Le Meur, L., *La Vie et l'oeuvre de François Coppée*, Spes, 1932.

Léon, Paul, *La Vie des monuments français*, Picard, 1951.

Léon, Paul, *Mérimée et son temps*, P.U.F., 1962.

Lescure, A-M. de, *François Coppée, l'homme, la vie et l'oeuvre*, Lemerre, 1889.

Lind, Melva, *Un Parnassien universitaire: Emmanuel des Essarts*, P.U.F., 1928.

Maigron, L., *Le Roman historique à l'époque romantique*, Hachette, 1898.

Maigron, L., *Le Romantisme et les moeurs*, Champion, 1910.

Maigron, L., *Le Romantisme et la mode*, Champion, 1911.

Mallion, J., *Victor Hugo et l'art architectural*, Grenoble, 1962.

Martino, P., *Parnasse et symbolisme,* 10th edn., A. Colin, 1958.

Maurras, Ch., & R. de la Tailhède, *Un Débat sur le romantisme,* Flammarion, 1928.

Michaud, G., *Message poétique du symbolisme,* 4 vols., Nizet, 1947.

Mondor, H., *Vie de Mallarmé,* 2 vols., Gallimard (1941-2).

Monod, G., *La Vie et la pensée de Jules Michelet,* 2 vols., Champion, 1923.

Montal, R., *René Ghil, du symbolisme à la poésie cosmique,* Brussels, Édns. Labor, 1962.

Moreau, Pierre, *L'Histoire en France au XIX siècle,* Soc. d'Édn. Les Belles Lettres (1935).

Noulet, E., *Léon Dierx,* P.U.F., 1925.

Otten, M., 'Un Aspect de la pensée religieuse de Max Elskamp', *Bulletin de l'Académie Royale de Langue et de Littérature Françaises* (Brussels), xxxvi (1958), pp. 37-48.

Pasquier, A., *Maurice Maeterlinck,* Brussels, La Renaissance du Livre, 1963.

Pauphilet, A., *Le Legs du moyen âge,* Melun, 1950.

Peyre, Henri, *Louis Ménard,* New Haven, Conn., Yale University Press, 1932.

Pommier, J., *Renan, d'après des documents inédits,* Perrin, 1923.

Pommier, J., 'Michelet et l'architecture gothique', *Études de lettres,* xxvi (Lausanne, Dec. 1954), pp. 17-35.

Pougin, A., *'Partant pour la Syrie:* Histoire d'un pseudo-chant national', *La Chronique musicale,* iv, 1 June 1874, pp. 193-203.

Pouillart, R., 'Maurice Maeterlinck de 1889 à 1891', *Annales de la Fondation Maurice Maeterlinck,* viii (1962), pp. 11-37.

Praz, Mario, *The Romantic Agony,* London, O.U.P., 1933.

Pronger, L. J., *La Poésie de Tristan Klingsor, 1890-1960,* Minard, 1965.

Psichari, H., *Renan et la Guerre de 70,* A. Michel, 1947.

Psichari, H., *La 'Prière sur l'Acropole' et ses mystères,* Centre National de la Recherche Scientifique, 1956.

Putter, I., *The Pessimism of Leconte de Lisle: Sources and Evolution,* Berkeley, University of California Publications in Modern Philology, 1954.

Quinet, Mme E., *Cinquante Ans d'amitié: Michelet-Quinet (1825-1875),* A. Colin, 1899.

Raitt, A. W., *Villiers de l'Isle-Adam et le mouvement symboliste,* Corti, 1965.

Raitt, A. W., *Prosper Mérimée,* London, Eyre & Spottiswoode, 1970.

Raynaud, Ernest, 'L'École romane française', *MF* xiv (May 1895), pp. 131-45.

Rees, G., *Remy de Gourmont,* Boivin, 1940.

Réizov, B., *L'Historiographie romantique française, 1815-1830,* Moscow, Édns. en langues étrangères, n.d.

Reymond, J., *Albert Glatigny,* Droz, 1936.

Richard, N., *Louis le Cardonnel,* Didier, 1946.

Richer, J., *Nerval, expérience et création,* Hachette, 1963.

Robichez, J., *Le Symbolisme au théâtre: Lugné-Poe et les débuts de l'Oeuvre,* L'Arche, 1957.

Rogier, L., *Les Poètes contemporains: Thalès Bernard et l'école allemande,* Vanier, 1859.

Saint-Paul, A., *Viollet-le-Duc et son système archéologique,* Tours, 1881.

Schärer, K., *Thématique de Nerval, ou le monde recomposé,* Minard, 1968.

Schenck, E. M., *La Part de Charles Nodier dans la formation des idées romantiques de Victor Hugo jusqu'à la Préface de 'Cromwell',* Champion, 1914.

Schneider, M., *La Littérature fantastique en France,* Fayard, 1946.

Séchaud, P., *Victor de Laprade, l'homme, son oeuvre poétique,* Picard, 1934

Souriau, M., *Histoire du Parnasse,* Spes, 1929.

Spencer, Philip, *Politics of Belief in Nineteenth-century France,* London, Faber & Faber, 1954.

Spoelberch de Lovenjoul, Ch. de, *Histoire des oeuvres de Théophile Gautier,* 2 vols., Charpentier, 1887.

Starkie, E., *Arthur Rimbaud,* 3rd edn., London, Faber & Faber, 1961.

Stewart, Nancy, *La Vie et l'oeuvre d'Henri de Bornier,* Droz, 1935.

Summerson, John, *Heavenly Mansions, and Other Essays on Architecture,* London, Cresset Press, 1949.

Swart, K. W., *The Sense of Decadence in Nineteenth-century France,* The Hague, Nijhoff, 1964.

Thérive, A., *Le Parnasse,* Oeuvres représentatives, 1929.

Underwood, V. P., *Verlaine et l'Angleterre,* Nizet, 1956.

Van Bever, A., & Léautaud, P., *Poètes d'aujourd'hui,* 3 vols., Mercure de France, 1947.

Veuillot, E., *Louis Veuillot,* 4 vols., Retaux, 1899-1913.

Viallaneix, P., *La Voie royale: Essai sur l'idée du peuple dans l'oeuvre de Michelet,* Delagrave, 1959.

Vier, J., *La Comtesse d'Agoult et son temps,* iv, A. Colin, 1961.

Viollet-le-Duc, 1814-1879, Caisse Nationale des Monuments Historiques, 1965.

Warmoes, J., 'Le Climat esthétique à l'époque de Maeterlinck', *Synthèses* (Brussels), xvii (Aug. 1962), pp. 24-35.

Zayed, G., *La Formation littéraire de Verlaine,* Droz & Minard, 1962.

Zumthor, P., 'Le Moyen Âge de Victor Hugo', in V. Hugo, *Oeuvres complètes,* ed. J. Massin, iv, Club Français du Livre, 1967, pp. i-xxxi.

GENERAL INDEX

Important references are in italic

Abelard, 1–2, 52, 170
About, Edmond, 94
Académie des Inscriptions et Belles-
   Lettres, 1 n.
Académie des Sciences Morales et
   Politiques, 78
Action Française, 290
Adam, Paul, *211*, 271 n, *279*
Adenet le Roi, 274
Agoult, Marie, comtesse d', *170*
Albigensians, 57, *78*, 94, *101*, 148,
   149 n., *152–3*, *157*, *159*, *160*
Albouy, P., 129 n.
Alembert, J. Le R. d', 1
Amaury, Arnaud, 158
Ampère, Jean-Jacques, *13–14*, 20, *22*,
   35 n., 82, 104
Antoine, A.-L., 246
Arbois de Jubainville, H. d', 105–6,
   209
Ariosto, 188, 198
Aroux, Eugène, *100–1*
Artaud, Antonin, 222
Arthurian legend, 33, 39, 53 n, 59,
   104–7, 168, *176–8*, 212 n., 223,
   235, 264, 293
Artois, Armand d', 201
Aubanel, T., 229
Aubertin, C., 209
Aubineau, Léon, 76
Aude, 108, 169, *205*
Aurier, Albert, *216*, *281–2*, 291
Autran, Joseph, *203–4*

Bac, F., 38 n., 39 n.
Baldensperger, F., xiii n., 2, 4, 200 n.
Ballu, T., 37
Balzac, H. de, 173, 237
Banville, T. de, xiii, 98, 110–11, *116*,
   118, *119*, 125, *169–70*, *172–5*,
   195, *200*, 202, 204–5, 224 n.,
   235 n.
Barbey d'Aurevilly, Jules, xiv, *43–4*,
   59, *83–5*, 115, *127*, 138 n., 144,
   147, 156, *166–7*, 189, 208, 214,
   215, 218–19, 227 n., 279, 291
Barbier, Jules, *202–3*
Bard, Joseph, 11

Barre, A., 274
Barrès, Maurice, 117, 185 n., 235 n.,
   273
Barrès, Mme., 238
Bartsch, K., 274
Baschet, R., 21 n.
Bataille, Henry, 248, *280*
Bathory, Countess, 161
Baudelaire, Charles, xiv, *26*, 114, 124,
   128, *166–8*, *179*, *181–3*, 186,
   223, 232, 244 n., 250, 266–7, 269,
   291. 293
Bayard, 4
Bazaine, Marshal, 205
Beauvoir, Roger de, 20 n., *27*
Bédier, Joseph, 209
Béliard, M., 212
Belmontet, Louis, *32*
Bénichou, P., 34 n., 35 n., 97 n., 275 n.
Béranger, P.-J. de, 114–15
Bergerat, E., 111 n., 114 n.
Berlioz, H., 94
Bernard, Émile, 213, 216 n.
Bernard, Suzanne, 225
Bernard, Thalès, *96–9*, 109, 111, 115,
   161
Bernhardt, Sarah, 204
Béroul, 176
Berret, P., 31 n., 124, 131, 144 n.,
   171 n.
Berthe *au grand pied*, 247
Bertrand, Aloysius, 9, 12, 14, 15,
   23–4, 124, *229*, 278
Beulé, C.-E., 39
Béziau, R., 211
Bignan, A., 21
Biré, E., 203 n.
Bladé, J.-F., 98, 209
Blaze de Bury, H., 169
Blémont, Émile, 97, 188, 275
Block, H. M., 240 n.
Blondel de Nesles, 4, 32
Bloy, Léon, xiv, *217–19*, 224, *233*,
   238, 265
Bodart, R., 222 n.
Boès, Karl, 261
Boileau-Despréaux, Nicolas, 171, 271
Bonnefoy, Marc, 206 n.

167–8, 170, 172, 186, 189 *n.*, *203*,
217 *n.*, 218, 225–6, 248–9, 252,
289, 291, 292, 293
Michiels, Alfred, 104–5, 129
Mikhaël, Ephraïm, 241, 242, *258*,
263–4, 266, 292
Millais, J. E., 212 *n.*, 263
Millien, Achille, 97, 275
Millot, Abbé C.-F.-X., 1
Mistral, F., 203
Mithouard, Adrien, 290
Mockel, Albert, *240–41*, *242*, 244,
246, 248, 251, 265, *270–71*, 275,
284
Moland, Louis, 95, 103, 174
monasteries, medieval, and Romantics,
11; and Chateaubriand, 11, 159 *n.*;
and A. France, 183; and Leconte
de Lisle, 147–8, 152–3, 156–9;
and Michelet, 52; and
Montalembert, 82–3; and Renan,
59–60, 64; and Verhaeren, 269
Moncrif, F.-A.-P. de, 6–7, 17
Monod, G., 199
Montalembert, C.-R.-F., comte de, xiv,
37, 43, 49, 59, *80–3*, 87, 144, 156,
292
Montégut, Émile, 42, 53–4, 130
Montfaucon (gibbet), *20*, 22, *132*,
171 *n.*, 172, 221
Morand, E., 286
Moréas, Jean, 224, *235*, 240 *n*, 241,
242, 250, 251, 259, 261, 262, 265,
267, *270–75*, *288*
Moreau, Gustave, 232, *259–60*, 280
Moreau, Pierre, xiii *n*, 184–5
Morice, Charles, 239, 244, 246
Mortimer, J. H., 182
Mounet-Sully, 204–5
Mourey, Gabriel, 238, 260
Murger, Henry, 172, 174
Musée des Monuments Français, 2,
86 *n.*
Musset, Alfred de, 5, *11*, 17, 59, 122,
156

Napoleon I, Emperor, 39 *n.*, 177
Napoleon III, Emperor, *31–40*, 41,
43, 55, 61, 64, 70, 75, 77, 82, 88,
91, 117, 135, 139 *n.*, 175, 176
naturalism, 243, 252, 285
naturisme, 238, 289–90
Nerval, Gérard de, 22, 24, *25–6*, *92*,

97, 171, 223, 237, 270, 275 *n.*
Nettement, Alfred, 127
Neveux, Pol, 242
Nieuwerkerke, comte de, 39
Nisard, Désiré, 99, 104, *171*
Nodier, Charles, 2, 5, *6*, 7, 10, *12*, 16,
22, 23, 24, 25, 91, *150*, 210 *n.*
Notre-Dame (cathedral), 15, *19–20*,
37, *38*, *39*, *46*, *57*, *69 n*, 199, 214,
231
Noulet, E., 229
Noussanne, H. de, 239

Ocagne, Maurice d', 237
O'Neddy, Philothée (Théophile
Donday), *13*
Orfer, Léo d', 272
Orléans, Louis, duc d', *39*, *64*, *70*,
231
Orléans, Princess Marie d', 39 *n.*
Ottin, L., 238
Ozanam, A.-F., 58, 213

painting, medieval, and Taine, 156; and
writers of the 1880s and 90s,
209–10, 212–17, 246, 265, 280
Paris, Gaston, 35, 37, *88–9*, 90, 104,
127–8, *197–8*, 203, *207–8*, 209,
270, 276
Paris, Paulin, *6*, 9, *35*, 88, 100 *n.*, *104*,
205
Parthenon, 65, 66, 110, 114
Pascal, F., 213 *n.*, 278 *n.*
Pasquier, A., 286 *n.*
Paulmy, marquis de, 1
Pauphilet, A., 16
Pedro the Cruel, 91, *160*
Péguy, Charles, 290
Péladan, Joséphin, xiv, *211*, *214–17*,
230, *233*, 241, 244, 253 *n.*, 266, 273
Pelletan, Eugène, xiv, *43*, 123, *126–7*,
142 *n.*
Penguilly-L'Haridon, O., 182
Persigny, duc de, 36
Petit de Julleville, L., 67 *n.*, 209
philosophes, 1, 12, 21, 146, 147
Pierrefonds (castle), *39–40*, 64, 88,
231, 239, 286
Piétri, F., 160 *n.*
Pilon, E., 241
plain-song, 94, 217, 233
Planche, Gustave, *94*
Plessis, Frédéric, 185

Poe, Edgar Allan, 156 *n.*, 229, 232, 244, 259, *264*
Poictevin, Francis, *214*, 277 *n.*
Point, Armand, *213*
Pommier, J., 45 *n.*, 47 *n.*
Pontmartin, Armand de, 83—4
Popelin, Claudius, 162, 190 *n.*
positivism, *85—91*, 210, 212, 252, 292
Praz, Mario, 213 *n.*
Pre-Raphaelitism, xiii, *212*, 222, 237, 259, *260—65*, 271, 280
Procter, Adelaide Anne, 223 *n.*
Prompsault, J.-H.-R., 171
Proust, Marcel, 290
Psichari, H., 61 *n.*, 65 *n.*
Pugin, A. W., 67 *n.*
Putter, I., 145 *n.*, 146 *n.*, 153 *n.*
Puymaigre, T. J., comte de, 268

Quatremère de Quincy, 52, *62*, 87 *n.*
Quicherat, Jules, 63
Quillard, Pierre, 240, 241, 242, 246, *267—9*, 270, *283—4*
Quinet, Edgar, xiii, 16 *n.*, 27, 45, 48—9, *52—3*, *54*, 62, *74 n.*, 88, *92*, 95, 101, 118, 119, 120, 130, 176—8, 291, 292

Radcliffe, Anne, *17*, 18, *21*
Raguenel, Tiphaine, 214
Raitt, A. W., 37 *n.*, 93 *n.*, 179 *n.*
Rambosson, Yvanhoé, 251, 263
Réau, L., 38
Rebell, Hugues, 289
Régnier, Henri de, 235, 240, 245, *249*, *256*, 258, *259—60*, *262—3*, 265, 267, *270*, 288, 290
Reims (cathedral), 45, 56
Rémusat, Charles de, 94
Renaissance, attitudes towards the: writers in opposition to Second Empire, 75; Parnassians, 119; Symbolists, 212—13, 216; École Romane, 288; Banville, 119; Gaume, 76; T. Gautier, 118—19; Huysmans, 218, 224; Leconte de Lisle, 118—19; A. Lefèvre, 118; Ménard, 118—20; Michelet, 47, 52; Renan, 63, 66; Ricard, 119—21; Taine, 68, 70, 71
Renan, Ernest, xiv, 35, 52, *57—66*, 67—71, 75, 79, 84, 85—6, 90, *92—3*, 94, 99, 100, 101, *103*, 104,

106—7, 110, 117, 132, 137, 190, *195—6*, 252, 291—2
Renaud, Armand, *162—3*
Renaud de Beaujeu, 274
Renouvier, Charles, 79
Retté, A., 241, 243, 247, 262—3, 266—267, 288, *289*
Reybaud, Louis, *27—8*
Reymond, J., 125 *n.*
Reymond, Marcel, 212
Reynaud, Jean, 102
Reynaud, Louis, 277
Ribot, Théodule, 74
Ricard, L.-X. de, *119—21*, 125, 145, 163
Richard, N., 263 *n.*
Richer, J., 26 *n.*
Rimbaud, A., *185*, 221, *224—6*, 252, 275, 291
Rivière, J., 252
Robichez, J., 247 *n.*, 287
Rochet, Louis, 40, 199
Rodenbach, G., *219—20*, *231*, 243, 245, *249—50*, 265, *266*, *270*
Roland, 9, 40, *107—9*, *133*, *140*, *141*, *142*, 144, *168—70*, *195*, *197—9*, *202—5*, 210, 221, 237, 247, 271
Rolland, E., 209
Romieu, Auguste, *41—2*
Rosières, Raoul, 206 *n.*
Rosny, J.-H., 217
Rossetti, D. G., 212, 253, 254, *260*, 263—4
Rostand, E., xiv, 236, 246, *286—7*
Rouen (cathedral), 42 *n.*
Rouland, G., 36
Rudel, Jaufré, 286—7
ruins, and Anne Radcliffe, 17, 21; and Romantics, 2—3, 7—8; and Parnassians, 121—2; and Symbolists, 231, 292
Ruskin, J., 67 *n.*, 213
Rutebeuf, 6, 209, 216 *n.*, 271—2
Ruysbroeck, J., *219*, 224 *n.*, 241

Sabatier, P., 212, 241
Sacy, Silvestre de, 61, 76, 77
Saint-Antoine (*Ermitage* critic), 241, 243, 244
Saint-Ouen (church in Rouen), 47, 48
Saint-Pol-Roux, 240, 242, 246, 285, *290*
Saint-René Taillandier, 94, 96, 178

INDEX OF NINETEENTH-CENTURY AND EARLIER WORKS, NEWSPAPERS AND PERIODICALS